Past and Present Publications

Church Courts, Sex and Marriage in England, 1570–1640

Past and Present Publications

General Editor: PAUL SLACK, *Exeter College, Oxford*

Past and Present Publications comprise books similar in character to the articles in the journal *Past and Present*. Whether the volumes in the series are collections of essays – some previously published, others new studies – or monographs, they encompass a wide variety of scholarly and original works primarily concerned with social, economic and cultural changes, and their causes and consequences. They will appeal to both specialists and non-specialists and will endeavour to communicate the results of historical and allied research in readable and lively form. This series continues and expands in its aims the volumes previously published elsewhere.

For a list of titles in Past and Present Publications, see end of book.

Church Courts, Sex and Marriage in England, 1570–1640

MARTIN INGRAM

Lecturer in Modern History,
The Queen's University of Belfast

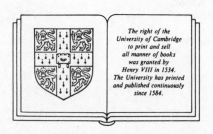

CAMBRIDGE UNIVERSITY PRESS

Cambridge
New York Port Chester Melbourne Sydney

Published by the Press Syndicate of the University of Cambridge
The Pitt Building, Trumpington Street, Cambridge CB2 1RP
40 West 20th Street, New York, NY 10011, USA
10 Stamford Road, Oakleigh, Melbourne 3166, Australia

First published 1987
Reprinted 1988
First paperback edition 1990

Printed in Great Britain by the University Press, Cambridge

British Library catáloguing in publication data

Ingram, Martin
Church courts, sex and marriage in England, 1570–1640. –
(Past and present publications).
1. Ecclesiastical courts – England – History – 16th century
2. Ecclesiastical courts – England – History – 17th century
I. Title II. Series
262.9 KD8680

Library of Congress cataloguing in publication data

Ingram, Martin
Church courts, sex and marriage in England, 1570–1640. –
(Past and present publications).
Bibliography.
Includes index.
1. Ecclesiastical courts – Great Britain – History
2. Marriage law – Great Britain – History
3. Sex crimes – Great Britain – History
I. Title
KD8680.I54 1987 347.42′04 87-11708
344.2074

ISBN 0 521 23285 6 hard covers
ISBN 0 521 38655 1 paperback

UP

To my Father and
the memory of my Mother

Contents

Tables

Maps

Preface

This book is concerned primarily with the church courts; secondarily it deals with various aspects of sexual behaviour and marriage; more generally it tries to convey something about the nature of early modern English society, and what it was like to live in small-scale communities where many forms of personal behaviour were subject to legal sanction. My immense debt to the numerous scholars who have worked or are currently working in these fields will, I trust, be apparent from the notes and references. But during the long period of the book's gestation I have incurred many personal obligations which I should like to acknowledge here. Cliff Davies, who tutored me in early modern history at Wadham, originally suggested that I might study the church courts. The doctoral thesis on which parts of this work are based was supervised by Keith Thomas; I am deeply grateful to him for the stimulus he offered, for the vigilance with which he guided my work, and for his constant encouragement and kindness. My thanks are also due to Joan Thirsk, who acted as joint supervisor for a while and opened my eyes to many possibilities which I would otherwise have missed. I am grateful, too, to Patrick Collinson, who gave me much needed encouragement at a critical time. In addition I should like to register my appreciation of the assistance offered by the staffs of the various libraries and record offices which I have used; I owe a particular debt of thanks to Mrs Dorothy Owen of Cambridge University Library; to Mr K. H. Rogers, the Wiltshire County Archivist; and to Miss Pamela Stewart, formerly Assistant Archivist for the diocese of Salisbury. For many stimulating discussions, for valuable criticisms and suggestions and for other forms of assistance I should like to thank Ian Green, David Hempton, John Morrill, Jim Sharpe, John Walter and Keith Wrightson. My greatest debt of all is to my wife, Gill.

Conventions and abbreviations

Dates are given Old Style, but the year is taken as beginning on 1 January. With the exception of a few well-known locations, all places mentioned in the text are or were in Wiltshire unless otherwise indicated. Reference to this and other counties, and to ecclesiastical jurisdictions, etc., is on the basis of boundaries as they existed in the period 1570–1640. In quotations from contemporary sources the spelling and punctuation have generally been modernised. The place of publication of books cited is London unless otherwise stated; some titles are abbreviated. For call numbers, means of reference, etc., to manuscript sources, see the appropriate section of the Bibliography. It should be noted here, however, that many items of the Salisbury diocesan records were unfoliated when I used them. Detailed reference to these volumes is generally by date of court day (e.g., 12/7/1623) and name of case, whether office (disciplinary) prosecution (e.g., *Office v. Bankes*) or instance (party and party) suit (e.g., *Kettle v. Cowdrey*). In addition the following abbreviations have been used in the notes:

Agric. hist. rev.	*Agricultural history review*
Archaeol.	Archaeological
B.L.	British Library
Bull. Inst. Hist. Res.	*Bulletin of the Institute of Historical Research*
C.U.L.	Cambridge University Library
East.	Easter session
Econ. hist. rev.	*Economic history review*
Ely D.R.	Ely Diocesan Records
Eng. hist. rev.	*English historical review*
Hil.	Hilary session
Hist.	Historical
H.M.C.	*Historical Manuscripts Commission*

Jl	*Journal*
L.M.	Leicester Museums and Art Gallery, Department of Archives
Mich.	Michaelmas session
Proc. Brit. Acad.	*Proceedings of the British Academy*
P.R.O.	Public Record Office, London
Rev.	*Review*
R.O.	Record Office
ser.	series
Soc.	Society
S.T.C.	A. W. Pollard and G. R. Redgrave, *A short-title catalogue of books printed in England, Scotland and Ireland and of English books printed abroad, 1475–1640*, 2nd edn revised and enlarged by W. A. Jackson, F. S. Ferguson and Katharine F. Pantzer, 2 vols. (1976–86).
Trans.	*Transactions*
Trans. Roy. Hist. Soc.	*Transactions of the Royal Historical Society*
Trin.	Trinity session
V.C.H.	*Victoria County History*
W.R.O.	Wiltshire Record Office, Trowbridge
W.S.R.O.	West Sussex Record Office, Chichester

Introduction

On 28 July 1639, Katherine Atkins of Sutton in the Isle of Ely was absent from her parish church both morning and afternoon. To make matters worse, she spent the time she should have been at prayers in 'railing and scolding with her neighbours'. Her son-in-law warned her 'to hold her tongue and to be silent else she would be put into the bawd court, for there was none but rogues and whores went thither', while his wife added 'that there was never none of them there yet and says let us now keep out of the bawdy court'. It was a vain hope. In the event all three were reported to the court of the bishop of Ely: Katherine for absence from church and for scolding, the others for abusing the name of the ecclesiastical courts.[1]

Today the church courts eke out a shadowy existence, their jurisdiction limited to a few ecclesiastical matters and their activities all but unknown to the mass of the laity. In early modern England the situation was very different. The ecclesiastical courts formed an elaborate, omnipresent complex of institutions organised at the levels of province, diocese and archdeaconry. Their jurisdiction naturally included much of a purely ecclesiastical nature, but it also extended to some of the most intimate aspects of the personal life of the population as a whole. The apparitors or messengers of the courts were a familiar sight as they strode or rode about the countryside serving citations and transmitting orders, and the courts which they served existed in every cathedral in the land. One fully fitted out courtroom still survives at Chester, formal yet curiously intimate, with a raised throne for the judge, a table where the registrar sat and inscribed the record and before which the culprit stood, the whole being enclosed for protection against draughts in a panelled, pew-

[1] W. M. Palmer (ed.), *Episcopal visitation returns for Cambridgeshire: Matthew Wren, bishop of Ely, 1638–1665* (Cambridge, 1930), p. 54.

like structure.[2] But the courts sometimes left such hallowed precincts to go on circuit, and sessions were held in improvised surroundings in parish churches or in inn parlours. It was not strictly true that only rogues and whores went thither. To be sure, there were plenty such among the accused, and some said – with what degree of justice will appear in the following pages – that the judges and court officials were themselves rogues. But a sizeable proportion of the population must at some time in their lives have experienced the atmosphere of an ecclesiastical court as suitor, accuser, witness or defendant.

The scope of ecclesiastical justice in Elizabethan and early Stuart England was very wide. Though the courts had long ago abandoned their claim to jurisdiction over advowsons (rights of presentation to church livings), they still dealt with many matters concerning ecclesiastical benefices, such as simony, spoliation and dilapidation. The courts also enforced the maintenance of ecclesiastical buildings, took action to ensure that the internal arrangements, fittings and liturgical equipment of parish churches and chapels conformed to official requirements, and adjudicated disputes over the possession of pews. Many forms of misconduct by the clergy, including neglect of duty, offences against conformity in doctrine and ritual, and scandalous behaviour, were dealt with under church law; and the courts supervised such matters as the licensing of curates and preachers. The laity were subject to ecclesiastical justice in a variety of ways. Despite encroachments by the royal courts, the church in early modern England still had an extensive jurisdiction in disputes over the payment of tithes and of various fees due to the clergy. They also enjoyed a wide jurisdiction over wills and the administration of intestate estates. Even more striking to modern eyes, the courts punished a wide range of sins of commission and omission on the part of the laity, especially religious offences and personal immorality. Within limits imposed by statute, they could bring prosecutions for apostasy, idolatry and heresy; catholic recusancy, sectarianism and related offences; the abuse of ministers or ecclesiastical officers and misbehaviour in church or churchyard; wilful absence from church, failure to receive the communion, and neglect of baptism, churching or catechism; the profanation of Sundays and holy days by working, playing games or drinking in service time; practising witchcraft and sorcery; scolding, talebearing and defa-

[2] Illustrated in E. R. C. Brinkworth, *Shakespeare and the bawdy court of Stratford* (London and Chichester, 1972), p. 9.

mation; usury; drunkenness; and a wide variety of sexual offences. Finally, the courts had an extensive jurisdiction in matrimonial matters. They adjudicated disputes over marriage contracts, issued marriage licences, heard petitions for separation and annulment, and brought prosecutions for irregular marriage, unlawful separation and similar offences.

Some of these matters were dealt with as suits between parties – rather like civil actions in the secular courts. Many, including most matters involving a strong moral element, were handled as 'office' or disciplinary cases: the courts themselves initiated prosecutions in a fashion roughly analogous to criminal proceedings. But such prosecutions were not, at least in theory, primarily designed to exact retribution for offences. They were intended to *reform* the culprit, and were ostensibly undertaken 'for the soul's health' (*pro salute animae*), to restore offenders to a healthy relationship with God and their neighbours. Yet proceedings were by no means secret. On the contrary, the rehabilitation of the sinner was conducted in a blaze of publicity as a system of communal discipline. The characteristic penalty imposed by the courts was public penance, a ritual of repentance and reconciliation, but equally a deeply humiliating experience designed to deter others and give satisfaction to the congregation for the affront of public sin. The ultimate sanction of the courts, whether in suits between parties or in disciplinary cases, was excommunication. The essence of this penalty was the exclusion of the offender from the communion of the faithful; but, symbolic of the fact that the church was supposed to be coterminous with the whole society, excommunication could also involve civil disabilities. In fine, the church courts reflected the fact that in early modern England the notions of 'sin' and 'crime' were not clearly differentiated.[3]

The range and nature of their activities gave the ecclesiastical courts, at least in theory, a place of the utmost importance in the social fabric. Yet until quite recently these institutions had a poor reputation among historians and their work was little studied. In

[3] Ronald A. Marchant, *The church under the law: justice, administration and discipline in the diocese of York, 1560–1640* (Cambridge, 1969), p. 4. On notions of 'sin' and 'crime', see J. A. Sharpe, *Crime in early modern England, 1550–1750* (1984), pp. 5–6. The English church courts are set in wider context in Bruce Lenman, 'The limits of godly discipline in the early modern period with particular reference to England and Scotland', in Kaspar von Greyerz (ed.), *Religion and society in early modern Europe, 1500–1800* (1984), pp. 124–45.

part this combination of neglect and contempt sprang from a distaste for records apparently packed mainly with sordid details of fornication, adultery, bigamy and other unsavoury peccadilloes of obscure individuals; a distaste which was itself a reflection of the general lack of interest displayed by the majority of historians before about 1970 in the study of marriage, illicit sexuality and other aspects of social history which are now regarded as of major importance. But there were other, more profound, reasons.

One was the fact that the Elizabethan and early Stuart church courts had suffered criticism and indeed flagrant abuse from certain groups of contemporaries. There were currents of internal criticism, springing from a desire to improve governmental and pastoral efficiency, voiced even by such fully committed exponents of the established church as archbishop Whitgift.[4] But a much more thoroughgoing critique was mounted by puritan advocates of further reformation and alteration in church government, and by common law rivals of the church courts. Puritan critics were in general not averse to moral discipline exercised by public institutions, but they regarded the church courts in their existing form as unsuitable instruments for godly reformation. They saw them as relics of the popish past, palpable signs of a church 'but halfly reformed'. They argued that the professional bureaucrats who ran the courts – mostly laymen in the period after the Reformation – were suspect in their commitment to protestantism and generally more interested in court business as a source of income than as a means of spiritualising and moralising the people. Some argued that in dealing with the immoral the strictures of the courts were too mild: public penance, it was said, was too light a punishment for such heinous sins as adultery. Above all there was fierce criticism of the church courts' extensive and indeed routine use of excommunication (at variance with the practice of the early church) and its pronouncement by lay officials. In fine, many puritan critics wished for a radical reform of the ecclesiastical courts, or even for their replacement as agents of religious and moral discipline by locally organised consistories on the Genevan model or by godly lay magistrates working in harmony with parish ministers.[5]

[4] John Strype, *The life and acts of John Whitgift*, 3 vols. (Oxford, 1822 edn), vol. 1, pp. 231–2, 364–6, 396, vol. 2, pp. 446–52.

[5] Patrick Collinson, *The Elizabethan puritan movement* (1967), pp. 38–41, 187–9, 457; Ralph Houlbrooke, 'The decline of ecclesiastical jurisdiction under the

In the later reign of Elizabeth, the use of the church courts under the aegis of archbishop Whitgift to prosecute puritan critics of ecclesiastical government stimulated additional opposition to them. Certain procedures of the courts, notably the *ex officio* oath (which was administered to all defendants in serious disciplinary cases and could, it was objected, force individuals of tender conscience to incriminate themselves) were bitterly attacked. Such grievances continued to be voiced in the reign of James I; and they flared up with renewed vigour in the 1630s, when the church courts were employed to impose supposedly Arminian doctrine and practices in the face of opposition from staunchly Calvinist elements in the church.[6]

Further criticism, combined with specific action tending to diminish the role of the church courts, came from another quarter – from the common law rivals of the ecclesiastical tribunals and from other interests which were concerned to strengthen the secular power relative to the jurisdiction of the church. All through the middle ages there had been sporadic conflict between church and state, above all in the later fourteenth century. The upshot was that effective royal control over many aspects of the church was already a reality long before 1500. But it was not until the Henrician Reformation that the church was finally and decisively subjected to the crown. At this juncture the role of the spiritual jurisdiction in the English polity was a major issue; and for a while it seemed possible, amid the tumultuous changes of the 1530s, that the church courts would be all but destroyed and that the bulk of their business would pass under secular control.[7] In the event the courts survived largely intact, subject to the supreme headship of the monarch; and whereas Henry VIII had purported to discover that the clergy were but half his subjects, by the early seventeenth century the church courts and the lawyers who staffed them were regarded as among the major bulwarks of monarchical government. But this situation aroused

Tudors', in Rosemary O'Day and Felicity Heal (eds.), *Continuity and change: personnel and administration of the church in England, 1500–1642* (Leicester, 1976), p. 251.

6 Collinson, *Elizabethan puritan movement*, pp. 266–7, 270–1, 409–12; Mary H. Maguire, 'Attack of the common lawyers on the oath *ex officio* as administered in the ecclesiastical courts in England', in *Essays in history and political theory in honour of Charles Howard McIlwain* (Cambridge, Mass., 1936), pp. 199–229.

7 Houlbrooke, 'Decline of ecclesiastical jurisdiction', pp. 239–44; G. R. Elton, *Reform and renewal: Thomas Cromwell and the common weal* (Cambridge, 1973), pp. 129–35.

criticisms that the ecclesiastical lawyers were infected with absolutist notions, while some critics persisted in regarding the spiritual jurisdiction as essentially foreign, a hateful fifth column which might eventually provide a road for the reintroduction of catholicism.[8] As one Elizabethan put it, the operation of the church courts meant that 'the pope hath his horse ready saddled and bridled, watching but the time to get up again'.[9]

Another threat to ecclesiastical jurisdiction came from piecemeal encroachment by common lawyers. Their rivalry with the church courts was proverbial, and medieval England had seen major jurisdictional conflicts in matters of tithe, testaments and debts (the last being dealt with by the church courts as 'breach of faith'). In their battles with the spiritual courts – to some extent stimulated, it must be said, by the demands of suitors – the common lawyers availed themselves of the statutes of *praemunire* (fourteenth-century laws designed to limit ecclesiastical power relative to the crown) and, increasingly after the Reformation, of writs of prohibition (a device to stay proceedings in particular cases in the spiritual courts and transfer them to the common law on the grounds that the former had exceeded their jurisdiction). To justify these encroachments, common lawyers voiced criticisms of some of the procedures and principles of law which their rivals employed. Common law attacks eventually coalesced with those of puritan detractors, especially when the controversy over the use of the *ex officio* oath in the 1590s provided a common focus for complaint. The result was an extensive contemporary literature of denigration in which the church courts were characterised as oppressive, unjust, corrupt and inefficient. The effect of such trenchant criticisms could not be fully dispelled by the numerous essays published in defence of the church courts, notably Richard Cosin's *Apologie of and for sundrie proceedings by iurisdiction ecclesiastical* (1591).[10] The battery of critical arguments remained current under the early Stuarts and helped to justify the suspension of most of the church's judicial apparatus amid the breakdown of Charles I's government in the early 1640s.[11]

Indeed this contemporary propaganda lived on to exercise a strong influence on later historians' views of ecclesiastical justice:

[8] Brian P. Levack, *The civil lawyers in England, 1603–1641* (Oxford, 1973), ch. 3.
[9] Quoted in Levack, *Civil lawyers*, p. 159.
[10] Houlbrooke, 'Decline of ecclesiastical jurisdiction', pp. 253–6.
[11] 17 Car. I c. 11.

the puritan/common law myth of the corrupt, unpopular church courts became the myth of historical textbooks in the nineteenth and early twentieth centuries. This adverse historical view was strengthened by another factor, the notion that the post-Reformation courts were by their very nature at odds with major social and political developments, and hence bound to be both unpopular and ineffectual. Certainly to modern eyes much of their work appears archaic, even bizarre. Though today we accept, grudgingly or otherwise, the intrusion of the state into our lives on a scale which early modern Englishmen would have regarded as grossly tyrannical, we do assume that moral behaviour and religious observance are largely matters not for the public forum but for private conscience. And in a state which, despite the continued existence of an established church, is essentially secular in its organisation, there can be no place for religious authorities to exercise jurisdiction over the population at large and to attempt to control its behaviour by judicial means grounded on spiritual sanctions. In retrospect the church courts were obviously doomed to decline. But when was the crucial period in which this decline set in? In the past many historians assumed that it was in the sixteenth and early seventeenth centuries that the burgeoning of new attitudes and changing circumstances rapidly rendered the church courts anachronistic. The temporary abolition of the courts in the 1640s seemed a palpable confirmation of this assumption. The fact that the structure of ecclesiastical justice was revived after 1660, and that the courts continued to play a significant social role in the later seventeenth and even into the eighteenth century, could be written off as a mere detail – a coda to the movement of historical change.

The two themes of obsolescence and contemporary criticism were skilfully blended by Christopher Hill, who in the 1960s argued that the Elizabethan and early Stuart church courts were not only lax, inefficient and corrupt, but also hated because many aspects of their work were repugnant to what he termed the 'industrious sort of people'. In particular, he asserted that the courts' attacks on puritan activities were widely resented; that their testamentary and tithe jurisdiction was disliked by the property-owning classes; and that their power to bring prosecutions for such offences as usury and labouring on saints' days was anathema to the 'industrious sort', whom he saw as representatives of a nascent capitalism. His attitude to the church courts' jurisdiction over sexual delinquency and other forms of immorality was less clear. On the one hand, he stressed that some contemporary writers criticised the courts for not punishing sexual offenders with sufficient rigour; on the other hand, he suggested that changing social and religious ideas were tending to produce a shift in emphasis from public control over morality to the operation of the private conscience. In any event, Hill argued, the church courts were rapidly becoming socially anachronistic in the early seventeenth century. Their collapse in the early 1640s was thus readily comprehensible.[12]

Hill's brilliantly argued thesis depended heavily on contemporary puritan and common law critical literature. When he wrote, in fact, comparatively little was still known about the day to day operations of the church courts. For a long time the actual records of ecclesiastical justice were largely inaccessible. Some fragments of material were published in the nineteenth century and the early years of the twentieth, but the bulk of diocesan archives was at that time lying, unsorted and virtually unusable, in neglected cathedral repositories. Some were rescued from this obscurity in the inter-war years; but many only became available to scholars in the 1950s or later.[13] Research on these archives, coupled with a growing appreciation of the nature of the society in which they were generated, has led in some respects to a much more sympathetic view of ecclesiastical justice and a more realistic assessment of its strengths, weaknesses and social significance.

In the first place, the reputation of the legal system which governed the church courts' work has been largely rehabilitated. Clearly it was not perfect – no system of law ever is. But Ronald Marchant showed that the traditional view of ecclesiastical justice as oppressive was a travesty of the truth. The criticisms of contemporary common lawyers were, he pointed out, motivated essentially by self interest and largely unjustified. By any standard the system of law practised

[12] Christopher Hill, *Society and puritanism in pre-revolutionary England* (1964), chs. 8–10.

[13] For a survey of the conditions of storage of diocesan archives in the early 1950s, and of how far they were accessible to scholars, see the *Pilgrim Trust survey of diocesan archives*, 4 vols. (1952). Extracts from the judicial records of the diocese of London were published by W. H. Hale, *A series of precedents and proceedings in criminal causes from 1475 to 1640* (1847); and see also J. Raine (ed.), *Depositions and other ecclesiastical proceedings from the courts of Durham, extending from 1311 to the reign of Elizabeth*, Surtees Soc., 21 (1845); C. Jenkins (ed.), *The act book of the archdeacon of Taunton*, Somerset Record Soc., 43 (1928); E. R. C. Brinkworth (ed.), *The archdeacon's court: liber actorum, 1584*, Oxfordshire Record Soc., 23–4 (Oxford, 1942–6).

in the church courts was worthy of respect, and in terms of fairness to plaintiffs and defendants it was in some ways superior to common law procedures. Ralph Houlbrooke came to similar conclusions. He stressed in particular the extent to which canon law encouraged the peaceful settlement of lawsuits by compromise and arbitration, and concluded that 'ecclesiastical court procedure was a good deal more speedy, flexible, inexpensive, and readily understandable than has been commonly allowed'.[14]

But how was this law administered in practice? Were the church courts guilty of corruption and lax administration, as their detractors claimed? Detailed studies indicate that the courts were certainly not entirely free from slackness and venality, which varied in degree from place to place and time to time, but to regard them as exceptionally corrupt and inefficient is wrong. Marchant found that the church courts in the diocese of York in the period 1560–1640 were, in general, remarkable for their probity and vigour, though there were periods of administrative torpor and some instances of venality. E. R. C. Brinkworth found that 'fair and considerate dealing' governed the disciplinary activities of the court of the archdeacon of Oxford in 1584–5. There was no evidence of corruption; the supervision of clergy, church officials, and ordinary laity was thoroughgoing; and the business of the court was 'pursued with diligence and in detail'. He was even more impressed by the records of the archdeaconry of Buckingham for the period 1634–6, concluding that in those years the supervision of the religious and moral life of Buckinghamshire was to all appearances minute and thorough.[15] J. P. Anglin, in a study of the court of the archdeacon of Essex in the period 1571–1609, was satisfied of its probity and general efficiency; while Jean Potter came to a similar assessment of ecclesiastical court administration in the diocese of Canterbury under the early Stuarts.[16] Houlbrooke's study of the church courts in the dioceses of Norwich and Winchester in the period 1520–70 was only slightly less

[14] Marchant, *Church under the law*, pp. 1–11, 243–5 and *passim*; Ralph Houlbrooke, *Church courts and the people during the English Reformation, 1520–1570* (Oxford, 1979), p. 271 and *passim*.

[15] Marchant, *Church under the law*, pp. 243–5 and *passim*; Brinkworth (ed.), *Archdeacon's court*, vol. 1, p. xv, vol. 2, pp. v-vi; E. R. C. Brinkworth, 'The Laudian church in Buckinghamshire', *Univ. of Birmingham hist. jl*, 5 (1955–6), pp. 31–59.

[16] J. P. Anglin, 'The court of the archdeacon of Essex, 1571–1609' (University of California Ph.D. thesis, 1965), p. 306 and *passim*; J. M. Potter, 'The ecclesiastical courts in the diocese of Canterbury, 1603–1665' (London University M. Phil. thesis, 1973), pp. 207–13 and *passim*.

favourable. He recognised that there was probably much petty corruption and inefficiency among court personnel, but doubted whether it was worse than in other courts of law at this time.[17] The most striking evidence of corruption so far discovered relates to the diocese of Gloucester in the early part of Elizabeth's reign. F. D. Price, though favourably impressed by the vigour of the church courts under the personal supervision of bishop John Hooper (1551–3), found that a marked decline set in during the weak episcopate of Richard Cheyney (1562–79). Under the aegis of Thomas Powell, chancellor of the diocese from 1576 till his dismissal in 1579, the courts became inefficient and venal. In the light of the other findings, however, the experience of Gloucester at this time appears atypical.[18]

The idea that the church courts represented outmoded values at odds with social and economic developments has also been shown to be wrong, or at least a seriously misleading oversimplification. In particular, Hill's argument that the ecclesiastical courts were engaged in a futile resistance to the development of a capitalist society does not bear close scrutiny. Marchant has shown, for example, that the idea that church court prosecutions for usury aroused the wrath of commercially minded men is misguided: the numbers of such prosecutions were in practice negligible. He has also argued convincingly that the church courts' testamentary jurisdiction provided a largely satisfactory service, remarking acidly that 'the imagination flinches before the thought of a state-run system of probate offices managed by the courtiers of James I, which must have been the only alternative to a church probate system'. Further, there is no immediate reason to suppose that the kind of discipline which the church courts exercised over sexual offenders was anomalous. Marchant stressed that immorality was punished not only by the ecclesiastical courts but also by the justices of the peace and borough

[17] Houlbrooke, *Church courts and the people*, p. 271.

[18] F. D. Price, 'Gloucester diocese under bishop Hooper, 1551–3', *Trans. Bristol and Gloucestershire Archaeol. Soc.*, 60 (1938), pp. 51–151; F. D. Price, 'An Elizabethan church official – Thomas Powell, chancellor of Gloucester diocese', *Church quarterly rev.*, 128 (1939), pp. 94–112; F. D. Price, 'The abuses of excommunication and the decline of ecclesiastical discipline under Queen Elizabeth', *Eng. hist. rev.*, 57 (1942), pp. 106–15. For continuing difficulties at Gloucester later in Elizabeth's reign, see F. D. Price, 'Elizabethan apparitors in the diocese of Gloucester', *Church quarterly rev.*, 134 (1942), pp. 37–55; F. D. Price, 'Bishop Bullingham and chancellor Blackleech: a diocese divided', *Trans. Bristol and Gloucestershire Archaeol. Soc.*, 91 (1972), pp. 175–98.

authorities, and the motives and attitudes of these secular agents do not seem much dissimilar to those of ecclesiastical judges. There might be complaints about the effectiveness of such discipline and debate about the right mode of punishment, but the numbers of people who actually wanted to see the abolition of moral discipline by public authorities were very small. Houlbrooke concurs, arguing that the correction of fornicators, adulterers and other moral offenders by the church courts probably received a large measure of popular support.[19] As will be seen later, the idea that the ecclesiastical courts were undermined by changing circumstances and attitudes can be restated in a form which is more in accord with the facts. But the processes were subtle, the time-scale of change was a long one, and at least up to 1640 it is realistic to regard most aspects of the church courts' work as in reasonable accord with the values of the wider society.

Thus in a number of important respects earlier adverse assessments of the late Tudor and early Stuart church courts have been either overthrown or substantially modified. It is nonetheless accepted that there were weaknesses in the structure of ecclesiastical justice; though the precise extent, nature and seriousness of these problems remains a matter of opinion. Houlbrooke has argued that the changes associated with the Reformation, especially the repudiation of papal supremacy, attacks on clerical privileges and sacerdotal powers, and the 'hardening reality' of religious division, struck at the roots of the authority of the church courts in England; and the violent changes in official policy in the turnabout years of the mid-sixteenth century created a corrosive atmosphere of uncertainty. Certain aspects of the church courts' work were especially affected. A large increase in tithe suits in the period 1520–70 reflected difficulties caused by a decline in popular respect for the clergy, economic changes, and alterations in the law of tithe. The courts' work concerning the maintenance, furnishing and ornamenting of parish churches was also made more difficult through repeated and inconsistent changes in government policy. More importantly, the ecclesiastical courts faced intractable problems in trying to enforce doctrinal conformity and uniformity of worship in the context of the acute religious divisions and uncertainties of the Reformation period. Meanwhile the structure of the spiritual jurisdiction was further

[19] Marchant, *Church under the law*, pp. ix, 218, 235, 242; Houlbrooke, *Church courts and the people*, p. 263.

weakened by piecemeal encroachments from the common law. All these problems were reflected in a significant decline in the effectiveness of the church courts' spiritual sanctions by the early part of Elizabeth's reign – a decline observable not only at Winchester and Norwich (the focus of Houlbrooke's detailed study) but also at Gloucester and no doubt elsewhere, to an extent which probably cannot be explained merely in terms of lax administration.[20]

Houlbrooke concludes that the church courts emerged from the Reformation years gravely weakened by religious and political changes, like 'a house shifted from its foundations by heavy bombing'.[21] And this explosive image underlies his assessment of the later history of the spiritual jurisdiction. In the period 1570–1640, he argues, the church courts' condition was that of progressive deterioration or, at best, of stasis. Henceforth they had to operate within limits imposed by common and statute law: there was no possibility of extending the scope of ecclesiastical jurisdiction into any major new sphere. Moreover, even the existing areas of jurisdiction suffered continued encroachment from the common law. Further, the problem of contumacy (non-appearance or other forms of disobedience on the part of defendants) was never solved: indeed the percentage of culprits amenable to discipline seems to have declined. More basically, religious debate and division persisted, perpetuating the problems of enforcing uniformity, and fuelling puritan attacks on the courts in the reign of Elizabeth and in the 1630s. Episcopal attempts at internal reform were inadequate and largely ineffectual, and for a long time the crown failed to give the courts adequate support. James I and, even more, Charles I tried to uphold ecclesiastical justice. But their efforts came too late to restore the church courts' moral authority, while their association with the personal rule and the policies of archbishop Laud led to the débâcle of the 1640s.[22]

In one sense this analysis is incontrovertible. In another it is misleading. To view the courts from the perspective of the more favourable conditions of the pre-Reformation period tends to obscure their achievements within the new context after about 1570. So also does undue emphasis on what happened after 1640. Recent

[20] Houlbrooke, *Church courts and the people*, pp. 261–71 and *passim*; Houlbrooke, 'Decline of ecclesiastical jurisdiction'.
[21] Houlbrooke, 'Decline of ecclesiastical jurisdiction', p. 257.
[22] Houlbrooke, *Church courts and the people*, p. 269.

studies of the early Stuart monarchy and its relations with parliament and the political nation generally have stressed the dangers of hindsight. The events of the 1640s could not have been foreseen a few years earlier and were by no means inevitable. Arguably a slightly different configuration of political circumstances and personalities in the 1630s could have significantly affected the fortunes of the English monarchy – and of the church courts.[23]

Other studies offer (or provide evidence to support) a somewhat less pessimistic interpretation of the activities of the church courts in the period from about 1570 to 1640. As the events of the Reformation years receded into the mists of time, and as the Elizabethan religious settlement became better established and – especially after the defeat of the presbyterian movement in the 1590s – in larger measure accepted,[24] the ecclesiastical courts were in important respects reinvigorated. Marchant has shown that, in the diocese of York, the disciplinary machinery for the supervision of religious and moral behaviour was overhauled and the numbers of disciplinary cases vastly increased. Whereas archbishop Grindal's visitation of 1575 produced some 1200 defendants, archbishop Neile's in 1636 brought over 5000 culprits to the attention of the courts – a scale of increase which cannot possibly be explained simply in terms of increased population.[25] There are indications of similar developments elsewhere. Brinkworth noted that the fullness of the disciplinary act book of the archdeacon of Oxford in 1584–5 reflected a recent tightening up of the system, probably instigated by archbishop Whitgift.[26] More generally, it is no accident that, in many diocesan archives, the records of the disciplinary work of the church courts survive in bulk from around 1570: new brooms were at work in

[23] Major contributions to the 'revisionist' school of early Stuart history include Conrad Russell, 'Parliamentary history in perspective, 1604–29', *History*, 61 (1976), pp. 1–27; Conrad Russell, *Parliaments and English politics, 1621–1629* (Oxford, 1979); Kevin Sharpe (ed.), *Faction and parliament: essays on early Stuart history* (Oxford, 1978). For some dissentient views, see Theodore K. Rabb and Derek Hirst, 'Revisionism revised: two perspectives on early Stuart parliamentary history', *Past and present*, no. 92 (Aug. 1981), pp. 55–99.

[24] Nicholas Tyacke, 'Puritanism, Arminianism and counter-revolution', in Conrad Russell (ed.), *The origins of the English civil war* (1973), pp. 119–27; Patrick Collinson, *The religion of protestants: the church in English society, 1559–1625* (Oxford, 1982), pp. viii–ix and *passim*.

[25] Marchant, *Church under the law*, pp. 230–1; W. J. Sheils (ed.), *Archbishop Grindal's visitation, 1575: comperta and detecta book*, Borthwick texts and calendars: records of the northern province, 4 (York, 1977), p. ix.

[26] Brinkworth (ed.), *Archdeacon's court*, vol. 2, pp. v–vi.

archidiaconal and diocesan registries around the middle years of Elizabeth's reign.

To be sure, this expansion of disciplinary activity was not without its problems, of which the most important was contumacy. Marchant has stressed that, in the diocese of York in the early seventeenth century, a large proportion of offenders failed to attend court even after excommunication. In the diocesan visitation of 1623, only 33 per cent of defendants satisfied the court; in 1575 over 68 per cent had done so.[27] This apparent decline in the effectiveness of discipline was, in part, probably a function of the expanding number of prosecutions: the intensification of discipline could as a side effect 'create' more reprobates. Yet the numbers of the contumacious have to be balanced against the very large numbers of people – perhaps more than ever before – who did appear before the church courts.[28] Moreover it is clear that the figures for the diocese of York in 1623 were exceptionally dire. Much better results were achieved in the same area by archbishop Neile in 1636; while in the archdeaconry of Buckingham in the same year, according to Brinkworth, excommunication was 'a censure to be respected' and 'in the great majority of cases' led eventually to the submission of the culprit.[29]

It was not only the disciplinary work of the courts that expanded after 1570. Most kinds of party and party business also flourished, with especially large increases in numbers of tithe and defamation suits in many areas.[30] Houlbrooke regards this expansion of business as a symptom of the courts' weakness, on the grounds that before the Reformation matters of tithe and defamation had often been handled as disciplinary cases and that their transfer to the contentious sphere symbolised the degradation of the courts' moral authority.[31] But this is a questionable judgement. The change may be just as plausibly explained in terms of administrative convenience, a reasonable desire to increase the profits of justice by boosting the more lucrative instance side of the courts' work, the preferences of

27 Marchant, *Church under the law*, p. 205; Sheils (ed.), *Archbishop Grindal's visitation*, pp. ix-x.

28 In the diocese of York, a larger number of defendants appeared to answer charges in 1623 than in 1575, even though in percentage terms the attendance rate was lower.

29 Marchant, *Church under the law*, p. 230 (see also pp. 208, 226); Brinkworth, 'Laudian church in Buckinghamshire', pp. 33–4.

30 Marchant, *Church under the law*, pp. 15–20, 61–3, 66–80, 110–11, 192–5; Houlbrooke, *Church courts and the people*, pp. 87–8, 108, 146.

31 Houlbrooke, 'Decline of ecclesiastical jurisdiction', pp. 246–7.

plaintiffs, or other adaptations to changed social, economic and legal circumstances which did not necessarily imply any diminution in the church courts' moral stature. The significance of common law encroachments should also not be exaggerated. Although the late Elizabethan and early Stuart church courts certainly had to operate within limits set by the common law, their existing jurisdiction was nibbled at rather than gobbled up wholesale, and much of their work was not challenged. The numbers of prohibitions received by any one court were quite small and became fewer after about 1620.[32] As Brian Levack has shown, by the early seventeenth century common lawyers were in many respects working harmoniously with their ecclesiastical counterparts. Even Sir Edward Coke, often regarded as the arch-enemy of the church courts, recognised that 'the temporal law and the ecclesiastical law have been so coupled together that they cannot exist the one without the other'.[33]

It will be plain from this discussion that the last word has not yet been pronounced on the viability and social significance of the church courts in late Elizabethan and early Stuart England. This book explores the issues further, not merely by examining the court records of dioceses and archdeaconries hitherto unstudied, but also by approaching these materials in new ways and viewing them in a different perspective. This fresh approach is based on the conviction that the role of ecclesiastical justice can be properly understood only through deeper study of the court records, closer reference to the social context, and a more realistic appreciation of what the courts could hope to achieve.

The pioneering modern works on the church courts, notably Marchant's study of ecclesiastical justice in the diocese of York, largely confined themselves to the investigation of personnel, procedure and, to a limited extent, the incidence of different kinds of case and the proportion of offenders amenable to discipline. This approach was dictated by the fact that at the outset so little was known about the courts and the most urgent need was simply to discover how they operated.[34] On the basis of such findings Ralph

[32] Levack, *Civil lawyers*, pp. 74–6, 80–1; Houlbrooke, 'Decline of ecclesiastical jurisdiction', p. 256.

[33] Levack, *Civil lawyers*, pp. 126–8. For the quotation from Coke, see *ibid.*, p. 145.

[34] Such pioneering studies of ecclesiastical courts (apart from those already cited) include F. S. Hockaday, 'The consistory court of the diocese of Gloucester', *Trans. Bristol and Gloucestershire Archaeol. Soc.*, 46 (1924), pp. 195–287; Irene

Houlbrooke was able to probe more deeply in his study of the church courts in the period of the Reformation, giving more attention to the actual substance of cases, to the way the judges handled them and to changes in the pattern of litigation over time. Even so, his analysis of many types of church court business remained quite cursory, while many aspects of the social context were left unexplored.[35] This book attempts, for the period *c.* 1570–1640, to penetrate even more deeply and to relate the work of the courts more closely to the society which they served. It investigates the social characteristics, attitudes and motives of the people involved with the courts as plaintiffs, informants or defendants, and explores in greater detail than has hitherto been attempted the nature of the symbiosis between the structures of ecclesiastical justice and those of the wider society. The problem of excommunication illustrates the shallowness of existing knowledge and the need for the approach adopted here. Large numbers of people suffered this penalty in early modern England. Who were these people? What was their social background? Were they hardened reprobates, indifferent to religion and morality, or was the reality more complex? How were they regarded in local society, and how far did their contumacy undermine the church courts? Answers to these questions are at present either wholly lacking or very imperfect.

A more detailed, contextual approach inevitably leads to a more realistic assessment of the church courts' achievements and failures. Previous studies of ecclesiastical justice have often been marred by a tendency to judge the courts by impossible standards. Houlbrooke,

J. Churchill, *Canterbury administration*, 2 vols. (1933), vol.1, chs. 9–11; E. R. C. Brinkworth, 'The study and use of archdeacons' court records, illustrated from the Oxford records, 1566–1759', *Trans. Roy. Hist. Soc.*, 4th ser., 25 (1943), pp. 93–119; Brian L. Woodcock, *Medieval ecclesiastical courts in the diocese of Canterbury* (1952); J. S. Purvis, *An introduction to ecclesiastical records* (1953), chs. 2–3; Carson I. A. Ritchie, *The ecclesiastical courts of York* (Arbroath, 1956); Robert Peters, *Oculus episcopi: administration in the archdeaconry of St Albans, 1580–1625* (Manchester, 1963).

35 For example, Houlbrooke's 1979 study did not try to relate prosecutions for sexual immorality to the actual incidence of offences. More sociological in approach is Ralph Houlbrooke, 'The making of marriage in mid-Tudor England: evidence from the records of matrimonial contract litigation', *Jl family history*, 10 (1985), pp. 339–52. Socially orientated studies of ecclesiastical justice in the period before 1500 include Michael M. Sheehan, 'The formation and stability of marriage in fourteenth-century England: evidence of an Ely register', *Mediaeval studies*, 33 (1971), pp. 228–63; R. H. Helmholz, *Marriage litigation in medieval England* (Cambridge, 1974).

for example, asserts that the leading question to ask in assessing the effectiveness of ecclesiastical justice is how close they came to achieving the purposes for which they were designed.[36] But in the functioning of legal institutions in this period the gap between ideals and reality was characteristically wide, and the approach suggested by Houlbrooke almost inevitably leads to pessimistic judgements. It must be recognised that there existed a variety of social, political and administrative constraints which the courts themselves could not possibly hope to alter; hence it is in many ways more satisfactory to ask how well the institutions of ecclesiastical justice performed within the circumstances in which they found themselves. Moreover contemporaries habitually used courts of law (including the church courts) in pragmatic ways which may in retrospect appear to have vitiated the ends of justice but which at the time were perfectly acceptable, if not to stern-minded and idealistic puritan critics then at least to the bulk of 'honest householders' with whom the ecclesiastical courts had most to deal. The mechanisms of spiritual justice must be viewed in their contemporary context if they are to be satisfactorily assessed.

An in-depth, contextual approach makes it impossible, however, to study all aspects of ecclesiastical justice in equal detail within the confines of one short work. In the following chapters no major element of church court business is totally ignored, and the book includes a detailed analysis of the coercive apparatus which was fundamental to the courts' existence; but the study focuses primarily on those aspects of ecclesiastical justice which were directly concerned with sexual immorality and with the formation and breakdown of marriage. These include disciplinary prosecutions for fornication, adultery, incest and related offences; matrimonial causes; and defamation suits, most of which involved slanders of a sexual nature. This selection is not meant to imply that other aspects of church court business were of little importance, but it does rest on the assumption that prosecutions relating to sex and marriage were themselves of major legal and social significance. Such business occupied a large proportion of the courts' time and included matters which contemporary social theory and the ecclesiastical law regarded as of the utmost gravity and fundamental to the maintenance of social order; and it coloured popular attitudes to the extent that the

[36] Houlbrooke, *Church courts and the people*, p. 262.

tribunals of the church were often colloquially known as the 'bawdy court' or the 'bum court'.[37] Close study of the sex and marriage business of the church courts is crucial to assessing the social significance and viability of these institutions.

In wider perspective, the importance of this area of ecclesiastical jurisdiction lies in its relationship to demographic, familial and social structures. An accumulating body of demographic evidence indicates that pre-industrial Europe (including England) was characterised, from at least the sixteenth century and probably earlier, by a unique marriage pattern whose salient features were a relatively high mean age of first marriage for both men and women and a substantial proportion of people who never married.[38] The existence of this pattern was of profound significance: it was a major factor affecting population levels, and it helps to explain the economic divergence between industrialising western Europe and the rest of the world in the nineteenth century.[39] Early modern England was also characterised by other demographic and social structural features of great interest. Household structures were generally nuclear in form, consisting simply of one married couple and their unmarried children. Moreover, kinship ties beyond the simple family were (the topmost echelons of society possibly excepted) generally weak and highly circumscribed. Neighbourhood bonds were usually more important than ties with kinsfolk and affines. Yet communal bonds were not particularly strong either. There was, in fact, a good deal of geographical mobility, especially on the part of adolescents and young adults. Many of these were hired on an annual basis as household or living-in farm servants – the widespread importance of such service was yet another of the most salient features of the social structure at this period – and periodically moved to new engagements in different parishes. They were for the most part unmarried; indeed the institution of service may be seen as a means whereby many young people filled out the long gap between puberty and the assumption of the status and responsi-

[37] Brinkworth, *Shakespeare and the bawdy court*, pp. 3, 30. For use of the term 'bum court', see W.R.O., B/DB 8, fol. 101; B/DB 12, fols. 66–8.

[38] The classic discussion of the European marriage pattern is John Hajnal, 'European marriage patterns in perspective', in D. V. Glass and D. E. C. Eversley (eds.), *Population in history* (1965), pp. 101–43.

[39] Alan Macfarlane, 'Modes of reproduction', *Jl development studies*, 14, no. 4 (July 1978), pp. 100–20. For fuller treatment, see Alan Macfarlane, *Marriage and love in England: modes of reproduction, 1300–1840* (Oxford, 1986).

bilities of householder or housewife. Thus the young in early modern England experienced a lengthy period of adolescence and, at a time when they were sexually mature, enjoyed a high degree of personal mobility and relatively little supervision from their families – a far cry from the 'lock up your daughters' policy pursued in some societies. Yet it is known from demographic evidence that the incidence of illegitimacy in the late sixteenth and the seventeenth centuries was, though not negligible, low relative to modern times or even to the eighteenth century.[40]

These demographic facts raise intriguing problems. How did people view marriage, and did ideas about what constituted entry into the married state – a more complex matter than appears at first sight – alter in this period? What criteria affected the decision to marry and the choice of marriage partner, and how far was the selection of a spouse controlled by family or other interests rather than by the intending couple themselves? What was the nature of marital relationships, how was power distributed within families, and how vulnerable were marriages to breakdown? What were the social characteristics and motives of the minority who produced children outside wedlock? Numerous historians, using a wide range of sources, are currently engaged in answering these and related questions (their conclusions are critically reviewed and supplemented in Chapter 4). This book is not intended as a study of sex and marriage as such, though inevitably the records of ecclesiastical justice do shed a good deal of incidental light on many aspects of popular attitudes to matrimony and illicit sexuality. The main focus of interest is the activities of the courts themselves. But since these courts constituted (at least in theory) the most important external agency for the enforcement of sexual discipline and the exercise of public control over marriage, their role is of crucial importance to an understanding of the social mechanisms by which the patterns of late age of marriage, relatively low incidence of bastardy and other features of marital and sexual behaviour were maintained and reinforced. Thus the study of the church courts' work in these fields not only provides the opportunity to assess the significance of ecclesiastical justice in relation to patterns of major importance to the nature and development of English society; it also contributes directly to our understanding of those patterns.

40 For a brief introduction to these and related features of early modern English society, see Peter Laslett, *The world we have lost further explored* (1983).

This book attempts, then, to understand and assess the work of the ecclesiastical courts in late Elizabethan and early Stuart England, especially those aspects which directly concerned sexual behaviour and marriage, in relation to the wider social context. Inevitably this involves major methodological problems. Despite the extensive research undertaken in recent years on the nature of early modern English society, many issues still remain obscure or contentious. In so far as our knowledge of the wider society is imperfect, there will *a fortiori* be gaps and deficiencies in our understanding of the church courts' work. For this reason alone the following study cannot claim anything approaching completeness or final certainty. There are, moreover, further problems involved in the handling of the available evidence. The records of the ecclesiastical courts, generated for purposes far removed from those of modern social historians, conceal more than they reveal. More seriously, false impressions about the nature of the work the courts were performing and the social milieu in which they operated can easily be created by the use of common form expressions and by the tendency of plaintiffs, defendants and witnesses to couch their statements to correspond with the legal principles which governed the church courts' conduct of business. But, with due regard to the law and procedures of the courts, it is possible with reasonable confidence to tease out fact from legal fiction, to distinguish between information and behaviour shaped by specific legal needs and those which were unaffected by such constraints, and hence to come to a closer understanding of the actual social significance of the courts' activities. The nature of the symbiosis between the institutions of ecclesiastical justice and the wider society may be further clarified by supplementing the legal archives themselves with other sources of information. Simple uses of this procedure are the augmentation of the information about plaintiffs and defendants supplied by the court records with material drawn from local archives (wills, manorial records, tax lists, and so on), and gauging the intensity of prosecutions for offences such as bridal pregnancy and bastard-bearing by comparing the judicial record with information derived from parish register analysis. At a higher level of complexity, changes in the courts' activities and social role may be illuminated by reference to demographic movements, economic fluctuations and developments, social structural shifts, and intellectual and cultural changes.

Another methodological issue is sampling. The bulk of the surviving records of the late Elizabethan and early Stuart church courts is vast, and any single individual can study in detail only a small portion. In this book the main unit of analysis is the western portion of the diocese of Salisbury, coterminous with the county of Wiltshire. The apparently drastic excision of the eastern third of the see, which covered the county of Berkshire, does little violence to the integrity of diocesan administration. The archdeaconry of Berkshire was a relatively independent jurisdiction, which was mainly administered from the archidiaconal registry at Oxford. Its personnel and administrative traditions were distinct from those of the Wiltshire courts, which formed a closely related group centred on Salisbury.[41]

Wiltshire represents an appropriate unit of study for several reasons. A fairly populous, medium-sized county, it provides a sample of reasonable extent. Moreover, it is located in an area of England (the borders of the south and south-west) which has received little attention in recent studies of the church courts. The county has the additional advantage of including within its borders a number of topographically, economically and socially distinct regions, including not only agricultural areas but also many parishes in which industry was of major importance. It thus provides the opportunity of gauging the impact of the church courts in different social contexts.

Some questions, such as the precise social status and relationships of individuals before the courts, cannot be adequately dealt with at the county level. It is necessary to descend to an even smaller unit of analysis, the parish. It must of course be recognised that, even within economically or topographically distinct regions, there was considerable diversity of economic and social development at the parochial level.[42] In employing the technique of parish sampling, the ideal would be to draw on the experience of perhaps a dozen different communities to capture the main elements of local variation. Sadly, the immense labour involved in such local studies makes this impracticable. In this book two parishes are put under the microscope: Keevil, a medium-sized agricultural and clothmaking village located in west central Wiltshire; and Wylye, a smaller, mainly agricultural

41 The surviving records of the archdeaconry of Berkshire are located in the Berkshire R. O., Shire Hall, Reading.

42 Martin Ingram, 'Religion, communities and moral discipline in late sixteenth- and early seventeenth-century England: case studies', in Kaspar von Greyerz (ed.), *Religion and society in early modern Europe, 1500–1800* (1984), pp. 177–93.

parish situated in the south of the county. Their experience should be regarded as illustrative rather than strictly speaking representative of the impact of the church courts in rural communities.

Questions of representativeness arise even when the main unit of analysis is a moderately large area like the county of Wiltshire. Moreover, certain features of the records of the Salisbury church courts make it desirable to check conclusions based on these materials by reference to other areas. The administration of ecclesiastical justice in Wiltshire in the period *c*. 1570–1640 is represented by a large accumulation of surviving archives. Their particular strengths are an exceptionally rich series of depositions in party and party suits and the fact that, at least for some periods and for certain of the jurisdictions which operated within the county, the examinations of defendants in disciplinary cases were recorded in exceptional detail. On the other hand, the various series of court records are not entirely complete, while certain kinds of information which are sometimes or normally found in the records of ecclesiastical courts are absent or deficient in the case of the Wiltshire archives. Like the Norwich diocesan records studied by Houlbrooke,[43] the registers of party and party actions at Salisbury do not invariably specify the nature of the suits or even the abode of the litigants – indeed such information was omitted from the act books more and more often as the period progressed and by the early seventeenth century was only rarely entered. To some extent the lacunae can be filled by cross-referencing to the complementary files of cause papers and to the volumes of depositions. But the former are (as is commonly the case in diocesan archives) very incomplete, while the latter provide no information about cases in which no witnesses were called.[44] The records of disciplinary prosecutions at Salisbury also have important limitations. In some of the Wiltshire courts in the late sixteenth century, the nature of the charge against the defendant was not normally specified in the act books if the culprit failed to appear. In all the Wiltshire courts from the early years of the seventeenth century it became the practice to omit the names of contumacious non-attenders entirely from the formal registers of

[43] Houlbrooke, *Church courts and the people*, pp. 273–4.

[44] The records of the Salisbury courts are listed and described in Pamela Stewart, *Diocese of Salisbury: guide to the records of the bishop, the archdeacons of Salisbury and Wiltshire, and other archidiaconal and peculiar jurisdictions*, Wiltshire County Council, Guide to the Record Offices, pt 4 ([Trowbridge], 1973).

proceedings, which hence assumed the nature of 'appearance books' recording only those cases in which a defendant made at least one appearance to answer a charge. The names of those who did not appear at all (and who were usually excommunicated) were recorded in supplementary series of court papers, while the charges against them were to be found in the files of presentments and informations – but the survival of these classes of record is, except for the jurisdiction of the dean of Salisbury,[45] very imperfect.

It would be wrong to overemphasise these deficiencies of the Wiltshire records. On close examination all church court archives prove to be more or less problematic, and some are far less informative and pose greater problems of interpretation than the Salisbury diocesan materials.[46] The particular strengths of these archives abundantly justify their use; the deficiencies can to a considerable extent be minimised by careful analysis of what survives and by rigorous cross-checking. It is none the less valuable to extend the scope of the inquiry beyond the confines of Wiltshire, not merely to allay possible doubts arising from imperfect source materials, but also, more generally, to gauge how far the experience of this county was typical. To some extent material from existing studies of the church courts, such as Marchant's study of the diocese of York, may be used for this purpose. In addition, the archives of a further three ecclesiastical jurisdictions have been extensively sampled. These are the archdeaconry of Leicester (more or less coterminous with the county of Leicester), the diocese of Ely (covering the Isle of Ely and most of Cambridgeshire), and the archdeaconry of Chichester (covering most of West Sussex). These areas were chosen both because the strengths of their surviving church court records complement those of the Salisbury courts and in order to provide samples representative of midland, eastern and southern England respectively.[47] Comparison between these areas and the pattern of develop-

[45] For the jurisdiction of the dean of Salisbury, see below, p. 37.

[46] For example, see J. A. Vage, 'Ecclesiastical discipline in the early seventeenth century: some findings and some problems from the archdeaconry of Cornwall', *Jl Soc. Archivists*, 7 (1982), pp. 85–105.

[47] The records of the church courts in these areas are listed and described in A. M. Woodcock, *Handlist of records of Leicester archdeaconry* (Leicester, 1954); Dorothy M. Owen, *Ely records: a handlist of the records of the bishop and archdeacon of Ely* (Cambridge, 1971); Francis W. Steer and Isabel M. Kirby, *Diocese of Chichester: a catalogue of the records of the bishop, archdeacons and former exempt jurisdictions* (Chichester, 1966), pp. 1–99.

ments in Wiltshire naturally reveals some differences, but the similarities are far more striking. This impressive convergence suggests that the conclusions presented in succeeding chapters may, at least in their main outlines, stand proxy for much if not all of late Elizabethan and early Stuart England.

Part 1

The legal and social background

1. *The structure of ecclesiastical justice*

In the past the church courts have often been viewed in isolation, and hence misjudged. They can, in fact, only be properly understood as part of a much larger system of legal institutions operating in early modern England. To an extent the jurisdiction of the church courts overlapped or was actually in direct competition with other tribunals, while more broadly many of the activities of the spiritual courts invite comparison with those of secular justice. In many ways all legal institutions in this period, whether temporal or spiritual, faced similar difficulties and similar opportunities; and all had to work within a climate of popular opinion which, though largely accepting the rule of law, did not regard the courts and legal practitioners as an unmitigated blessing. It is therefore instructive, before looking specifically at the institutions of ecclesiastical justice, to survey the wider legal context.

The importance of law and legal institutions in the society of Elizabethan and early Stuart England is hard to exaggerate. Government, whether royal, ecclesiastical or seigneurial, was largely channelled through legal forms, and as a result the boundaries between judicial and administrative action were far less clearly drawn than is the case today. To a greater extent than at present, moreover, contemporaries looked to the law not only for the maintenance of order – broadly conceived to include many economic matters, religious observance and personal morality – but also the resolution of conflict within the society. Not only the church courts but also a wide range of secular tribunals existed to meet these needs, including the great common law and equity courts at Westminster, the courts of assize, county quarter sessions, and a variety of local manorial and borough courts.[1]

[1] G. R. Elton (ed.), *The Tudor constitution*, 2nd edn (Cambridge, 1982), chs. 5–7, 10; Sharpe, *Crime in early modern England*, pp. 21–7; Martin Ingram, 'Communities and courts: law and disorder in early seventeenth-century Wiltshire', in J. S. Cockburn (ed.), *Crime in England, 1550–1800* (1977), pp. 110–15.

Although the picture is complicated by shifts in patterns of business between courts, it is plain that there was overall a considerable expansion of legal activity in the late sixteenth and early seventeenth centuries. This was a great age of litigation, and the growth of party and party business in the church courts must be seen as part of a trend which embraced the secular courts too. In the courts of king's bench and common pleas, for example, the volume of cases reaching an advanced stage of process (a minority of the total actually commenced, since many causes were discontinued) increased from over 13,000 in 1580 to over 29,000 in 1640. Detailed information to document the growth in secular litigation from the perspective of any particular county is at present lacking, but figures available for Wiltshire at certain dates in the early seventeenth century are sufficient to highlight the immense volume of litigation which was being undertaken in that period. In the common pleas alone, for example, over 700 Wiltshire suits were depending at various stages of process in Michaelmas term 1618. In this county and elsewhere the litigants were by no means confined to the aristocracy and gentry. People from a very broad social spectrum, including some of the middling and lower middling ranks and excluding only the very poor, had recourse to the law.[2]

While party and party litigation flourished, the courts were also extensively and in some respects increasingly used to try to control crime and disorder and to regulate many aspects of social life. If the work of the church courts in policing the moral and religious behaviour of the population is at first sight apt to appear intrusive, it must be recalled that they worked within a wider context in which a good deal of legal supervision was a normal part of life. Manor courts, where they still existed, were sometimes highly active. In 1602, for example, the courts of the manor of Keevil cum Bulkington (comprising a court baron for the manorial tenants and a court leet or 'view of frankpledge' with jurisdiction over all the inhabitants of the tithing of Keevil) handled over 130 prosecutions for a variety of offences ranging from the playing of unlawful games to failure to scour watercourses.[3] County justices could not match the minuteness

[2] C. W. Brooks, 'Litigants and attorneys in the king's bench and common pleas, 1560–1640', in J. H. Baker (ed.), *Legal records and the historian* (1978), pp. 41–59; Ingram, 'Communities and courts', pp. 114–16.

[3] W.R.O., 288/1, Keevil cum Bulkington Court Bk, 1602–26 (unfoliated). See also Walter J. King, 'Leet jurors and the search for law and order in seventeenth-century England: "galling persecution" or reasonable justice?', *Histoire sociale: social history*, 13 (1980), pp. 305–23.

of such local regulation, but their powers were greater, the scope of their activities was increasing in this period, and overall there was a marked growth in the volume of many of the kinds of business which they handled. The trend may be illustrated by the records of presentments made at the Wiltshire quarter sessions by hundred jurors (representatives of the major administrative divisions of the county), high constables and other agents. Setting aside an unusual spate of special presentments made by the 'searchers of woollen cloth' in 1602, there were over three times as many presentments in 1615, and over four times as many in 1628, as there had been in the last year of Elizabeth's reign.[4] The work of the justices in petty sessions also expanded in the early seventeenth century, especially during the period of Charles I's personal rule (1629–40).[5]

Attitudes to this burgeoning legal activity were complex. The prime movers in maintaining and even expanding the regulatory or disciplinary activities of both the spiritual and the temporal courts were the secular and religious authorities. Royal officials and the ecclesiastical hierarchy regarded legal sanctions as essential to the well-being of the commonwealth and vital to the maintenance of political and social order, especially in the context of the economic and religious changes and tensions of the sixteenth and seventeenth centuries.[6] But the courts were highly dependent for the detection and prosecution of offenders on hundred jurors, constables, churchwardens and other non-professional local officers, who were supposed to represent the communities from which they were elected or otherwise appointed. Established habits of deference, and coercion exercised by the authorities, could only go so far in ensuring the co-operation of these people. In the last resort the precise contours of regulatory and disciplinary activity depended on

[4] W.R.O., QS/GR 1615, 1628; QS/Minute Bk 2, 1598–1604; QS/Minute Bk 7, 1626–31. See also Joel Hurstfield, 'County government, c. 1530–c. 1660', in *V.C.H. Wilts.*, vol. 5, pp. 80–110.

[5] On the emergence of petty sessions, see Frederic A. Youngs, Jr, 'Towards petty sessions: Tudor JPs and divisions of counties', in DeLloyd J. Guth and John W. McKenna (eds.), *Tudor rule and revolution* (Cambridge, 1982), pp. 201–16. On Wiltshire, see Hurstfield, 'County government', pp. 93, 98–103.

[6] Keith Wrightson, 'Two concepts of order: justices, constables and jurymen in seventeenth-century England', in John Brewer and John Styles (eds.), *An ungovernable people: the English and their law in the seventeenth and eighteenth centuries* (1980), pp. 21–46; Paul Slack, 'Books of orders: the making of English social policy, 1577–1631', *Trans. Roy. Hist. Soc.*, 5th ser., 30 (1980), pp. 1–22. The economic and religious developments of the period are surveyed below, Chapters 2–3.

how far local agents were willing to assist the courts in an active and positive fashion. This in turn depended on more general attitudes to law-breaking and other forms of deviance at the parish level, and on the nature of local neighbourhood relations.

There is at present incomplete agreement among historians on these matters. Lawrence Stone argues that contemporary society was harshly intolerant, riven with conflict, lacking any unifying bond save for occasional outbursts of mass hysteria. He thus depicts the late sixteenth- and early seventeenth-century village as a place 'filled with malice and hatred', teeming with an 'extraordinary amount of back-biting, malicious slander...and petty spying' which was only too easily channelled into disciplinary prosecutions in the secular and ecclesiastical courts. This view is, however, insecurely based on a superficial reading of lurid instances of disharmony without consideration of how far they were normal or representative. No doubt there were quarrels and disagreements a-plenty in village life, but Stone's interpretation undoubtedly exaggerates the degree of tension and insecurity.[7]

Keith Thomas has likewise argued that the villages and small towns of Tudor and Stuart England lacked much of the modern concepts of privacy and self-determination, and that social relations were ruled by the 'tyranny of local opinion' and intolerance towards deviant behaviour. In contrast to Stone's picture of an atomised society, however, Thomas stresses that these features of social life were rooted in a powerful ideal of communal harmony and consensus.[8] As will be seen, this interpretation overestimates the limitations on privacy and personal freedom.[9] But Thomas is surely right to stress the high value placed on an ideal of communal harmony, however difficult this might be to achieve in practice. The demand for 'peace', 'love', 'charity' and 'quietness' among neighbours is a constant refrain in contemporary records.[10]

In some ways this desire for local harmony and for a consensus of values encouraged co-operation with the secular and ecclesiastical

[7] Lawrence Stone, *The family, sex and marriage in England, 1500–1800* (1977), pp. 98–9.

[8] Keith Thomas, *Religion and the decline of magic: studies in popular beliefs in sixteenth- and seventeenth-century England* (1971), pp. 526–30.

[9] See below, Chapter 8.

[10] For example, see W.R.O., QS/GR Hil. 1610/142; B/DB 20, fol. 10; AS/ABO 11, fol. 21; D/Pres. 1614–15 (unnumbered file), Gt Durnford, 2/5/1615. See also Thomas, *Religion and the decline of magic*, p. 529.

authorities. Certainly parishioners had little compunction in taking legal or other action against blatant disturbers of the peace or egregious non-conformists. In extreme cases they might be run out of town: thus the inhabitants of Kington St Michael reported of a newcomer in 1619 that he had lately lived in Bathway in Somerset but had been 'by the inhabitants excluded, by reason of his troublesome and lewd course of life and behaviour'.[11] More often recalcitrants were reported for disciplinary action by the church or secular courts, and the form in which the complaints were made was strongly redolent of communal values. Thus John Temple of Highworth was presented to the court of the dean of Salisbury in 1598 for being a 'common quarreller, a brawler, fighter and a disturbator of his honest neighbours in so much that he is utterly unworthy to live in a commonwealth'; while in 1624 the parishioners of Fittleton petitioned the justices to apprehend and bind over a certain Susan Browne on the grounds that she was a 'woman of very evil life and conversation, raising of false rumours and fames of the parishioners...to their great disturbance'.[12] It is notable, moreover, that such charges of disturbing the peace often embraced not only the stirring up of strife as such but also a variety of other offences such as irreligion, drunkenness and sexual immorality. It is plain that such forms of misbehaviour, many of which are today regarded merely as matters of personal morality, could in this period be viewed by the populace at large as breaches of public order and worthy of prosecution; indeed, personal moral lapses were often referred to specifically as 'crimes'. In other words, the authorities' view that the legal regulation of personal behaviour was fundamental to the maintenance of social order was at least to some extent shared by the mass of the governed. Herein lay the basis for active co-operation between the representatives of local communities and the church courts and other institutions of social discipline.

This degree of consensus was not, however, sufficient to ensure slavish compliance with the demands of the authorities. On the contrary, it was a commonplace of the period that when local officers were called upon to name offenders they had a strong tendency to under-present or even to report that 'all is well' (*omnia bene*) when, according to the strict letter of the law, this was certainly not the

11 W.R.O., QS/GR Trin. 1619/189.
12 W.R.O., D/Pres. 1597–9 (unnumbered file), Highworth, 24/5/1598; QS/GR Mich. 1624/195.

case. Among other reasons for such laxity were sheer negligence, inability to comprehend the multitude of regulatory laws, and fear of reprisals from people who were prosecuted. But deeper and more positive factors were also involved. Not all forms of behaviour which the law proscribed were regarded as reprehensible in the local community, while the zeal of presenting officers was also restrained by neighbourly tolerance and a desire not to stir up trouble in the community by taking people to court. Hence some matters were liable to be passed over either because they were regarded as too trivial for (or even undeserving of) legal action, or because it was felt that recourse to the law would stir up additional tensions and bitterness, threaten local harmony, and hence make the cure worse than the disease. In these respects the ideal of neighbourly 'peace' and 'quiet' could limit how far people were prepared to use the disciplinary and regulatory apparatus of the courts.[13]

Local communities thus tended to use the institutions of legal regulation selectively. This did not necessarily imply conflict with the courts, since judges and lawyers were often well aware of the pressures acting on local officers and did not, in any case, seriously expect total compliance with the letter of the law. All things being equal, a balance could be achieved whereby the demands of the authorities were met on important issues while the precise pattern of prosecutions was allowed to reflect what local communities were themselves most concerned about. But the balance was a delicate one. Problems could arise if the courts, whether secular or ecclesiastical, tried to enforce new values and standards of behaviour far in advance of popular acceptance or to insist too rigorously on the prosecution of matters which were not regarded very seriously in the parishes. Another potentially disturbing factor was disagreement at the local level. Unresolved tensions between individuals or factions within communities could generate malicious or dubiously justified prosecutions, which the courts had to handle delicately if they were not to aggravate existing conflicts. More fundamentally, the nature of the symbiosis between courts and communities could be affected by divergences of opinion between different social groups about what constituted acceptable behaviour. As Keith Wrightson has

[13] Ingram, 'Communities and courts', pp. 127–34; J. A. Sharpe, 'Enforcing the law in the seventeenth-century English village', in V. A. C. Gatrell, Bruce Lenman and Geoffrey Parker (eds.), *Crime and the law: the social history of crime in western Europe since 1500* (1980), pp. 97–119; Wrightson, 'Two concepts of order'.

emphasised in a series of perceptive studies of the role of the courts in local society, the economic, social and religious changes and tensions of the late sixteenth and early seventeenth centuries were particularly likely to generate such disagreements; in this sense the period was an especially sensitive one for the disciplinary tribunals.[14]

Ambiguities of attitude also affected litigation between parties. The figures relating to such litigation suggest to the modern eye that while conflict and disagreement over a variety of issues were common they were to an impressive extent contained within the rule of law;[15] and the increasing numbers of lawsuits can to a large extent be explained in terms of an expanding population, an increasingly active land market, the growing volume and complexity of economic transactions (including the greater use of bills, bonds and other credit instruments), and numerous other social and economic factors.[16] Yet some contemporaries viewed the matter differently, regarding the multiplicity of lawsuits with disquiet as a symptom of disease within the body politic and, more specifically, blaming the rapacity of lawyers, the malice of suitors and wilful litigiousness.[17] Individuals who were much given to vexatious or dubiously justified litigation, like Richard Griffin of Malmesbury who was accused in 1606 of procuring 'process of subpoena out of his majesty's court of star chamber against...fourteen or fifteen' people, tended to attract the odium of their neighbours.[18] Even when lawsuits were more justifiable, members of the community who were not directly involved were inclined to regard them as regrettable. They deplored the expense and feared the bitterness and disruption of neighbourhood

[14] Keith Wrightson and David Levine, *Poverty and piety in an English village: Terling, 1525–1700* (New York, 1979), ch. 5; Keith Wrightson, 'Alehouses, order and reformation in rural England, 1590–1660', in Eileen Yeo and Stephen Yeo (eds.), *Popular culture and class conflict, 1590–1914* (Brighton, 1981), pp. 1–27.

[15] Lawrence Stone, *The crisis of the aristocracy, 1558–1641* (Oxford, 1965), pp. 240–2; Ingram, 'Communities and courts', p. 116; Alan Macfarlane and Sarah Harrison, *The justice and the mare's ale: law and disorder in seventeenth-century England* (Oxford, 1981); J. A. Sharpe, '"Such disagreement betwyx neighbours": litigation and human relations in early modern England', in John Bossy (ed.), *Disputes and settlements: law and human relations in the west* (Cambridge, 1983), pp. 167–87.

[16] Brooks, 'Litigants and attorneys', pp. 46, 48–52.

[17] See the views cited in Ingram, 'Communities and courts', p. 110; Brooks, 'Litigants and attorneys', pp. 45–6; Sharpe, '"Such disagreement betwyx neighbours"', pp. 169–70.

[18] W.R.O., QS/GR Trin. 1606/106.

relations which could result from a protracted legal battle: yet again recourse to the law was perceived to be in partial conflict with the ideal of communal harmony. Hence attempts were often made to persuade litigants to bring their suits to a speedy out-of-court settlement; and there were well-established procedures for the mediation and arbitration of disputes by parish ministers, justices of the peace acting informally, local gentlemen or other substantial inhabitants, or simply the neighbours and friends of the parties.[19] In default of such friendly settlement, contemporaries naturally accepted litigation as preferable to violent self-help. The onus was then on the courts to provide effective, cheap, easily available and swift justice, and to limit the possibilities for the vexatious manipulation of legal procedures by unscrupulous litigants.

None of the legal institutions of this period could wholly satisfy these exacting demands; how far the church courts in particular were able to do so, and how well they fared amid the complexities of attitude towards disciplinary prosecutions, are major themes of the following study. As a necessary first step in the analysis, the remainder of this chapter provides a brief preliminary description, interspersed with some initial assessments and comparisons with other courts, of the institutions of ecclesiastical justice and the manner in which they were administered. In essentials the structures of the spiritual jurisdiction were much the same everywhere in England, but inevitably there was some degree of local variation in organisation and procedure. The following survey pays particular attention to the administrative situation in the Wiltshire portion of the diocese of Salisbury and in the other jurisdictions – the diocese of Ely, the archdeaconry of Leicester and the archdeaconry of Chichester – which will be repeatedly referred to in subsequent chapters.

It must be recognised at the outset that all early modern legal institutions were by today's standards irrational and inefficient. The bodies of law which guided them, and the procedures by which this law was administered, were shot through with anomalies created by the accretions of time and maintained by vested interests and by administrative and intellectual inertia. The course of justice was inevitably hampered by rudimentary and cumbersome filing systems,

[19] Ingram, 'Communities and courts', pp. 125–7; Sharpe, '"Such disagreement betwyx neighbours"', pp. 173–8.

by the need for every instrument and record to be laboriously written out by hand, by the slowness with which the messengers of the courts travelled on foot or horseback through miry lanes to remote parishes and farmsteads. The church courts inescapably shared in these characteristics of early modern legal administration. Yet by contemporary standards the ecclesiastical courts formed a well-organised and on the whole coherent system of justice; and, in so far as there were remediable weaknesses, some efforts were made to deal with them in the course of this period. Certain features of the system may seem strange to modern eyes, but for the most part this is the strangeness of unfamiliarity rather than of inherent absurdity.

The church courts in Elizabethan and early Stuart England formed a hierarchy of overlapping jurisdictions centring on the key unit of ecclesiastical administration, the diocese. At Salisbury, as in every other see, the most important forum was the bishop's consistory court. Organised into a number of different branches to deal with the various kinds of ecclesiastical court business, it formed the hub of diocesan administration and justice. In some other dioceses there was in addition an episcopal court of audience, which dealt with particularly important matters under the bishop's personal supervision; while in certain large or populous dioceses, such as Lincoln, some of the functions of episcopal jurisdiction were delegated to commissaries empowered to hold courts in designated areas.[20]

The unit of ecclesiastical administration immediately below the level of the diocese was the archdeaconry. Some small dioceses, such as Ely, comprised only one archdeaconry. More commonly there were two or more, while the exceptionally large diocese of Lincoln had six – including the archdeaconry of Leicester. Salisbury diocese consisted of the three archdeaconries of Berkshire (coterminous with the county), North Wiltshire and Salisbury. Traditionally the archdeacon was regarded as the 'bishop's eye' (*oculus episcopi*), an essential coadjutor who was in theory capable, by virtue of bearing fewer responsibilities and usually administering a smaller area, of a

[20] For the emergence of these and other key features of diocesan administration, see Dorothy Owen, 'Ecclesiastical jurisdiction in England, 1300–1550: the records and their interpretation' in Derek Baker (ed.), *The materials, sources and methods of ecclesiastical history*, Studies in church history, 11 (1975), pp. 199–221; Dorothy Owen, 'An episcopal audience court', in Baker (ed.), *Legal records and the historian*, pp. 140–9; Colin Morris, 'The commissary of the bishop in the diocese of Lincoln', *Jl ecclesiastical history*, 10 (1959), pp. 50–65.

more continuous and detailed oversight of clerical and lay discipline. Thus the archdeacons in most dioceses shared in the administration of ecclesiastical justice. An exception was the diocese of Chichester. There the judicial authority of the archdeacons had been all but eliminated by the mid-sixteenth century, and ecclesiastical justice was administered almost entirely through the episcopal courts, organised in two branches based respectively at Chichester and Lewes.[21]

Elsewhere the exact nature of the relationship between the archidiaconal and episcopal courts varied considerably. Some archdeaconry courts, like Berkshire, were relatively independent, dealing with more or less the full range of church court business and subject to only limited supervision by or competition from the bishop's courts.[22] In the archdeaconry of Leicester, as in other parts of the diocese of Lincoln, the archidiaconal court was inextricably intertwined with the court of the episcopal commissary.[23] Other archdeaconry courts remained jurisdictionally separate from but firmly subordinate to the episcopal tribunals, with restrictions on the kinds of business they could handle. Thus the archdeacon of Ely was (among other restrictions) excluded from jurisdiction in the Isle of Ely and in certain parishes in Cambridgeshire and barred from hearing matrimonial causes.[24] In the diocese of Salisbury, the two Wiltshire archdeaconry courts were clearly subordinate to the bishop's consistory and dealt with only a limited range of business, mainly disciplinary prosecutions, the routine grant of probates and administrations and some contentious testamentary cases.

Diocesan administration and justice were complicated by the existence of 'peculiar' jurisdictions, areas which for a variety of historical reasons were more or less independent of the authority of the bishop, the archdeacon or both.[25] Such peculiars were particularly numerous in the diocese of Salisbury. In the Wiltshire portion alone, about fifty parishes and chapelries were independent of the bishop

[21] Stephen Lander, 'Church courts and the Reformation in the diocese of Chichester, 1500–58', in O'Day and Heal (eds.), *Continuity and change*, pp. 215–37. See also Roger B. Manning, *Religion and society in Elizabethan Sussex* (Leicester, 1969), ch. 2.

[22] Based on sampling of Berkshire archdeaconry act books in the Berkshire R.O.

[23] Woodcock, *Handlist of records of Leicester archdeaconry*, p. 4.

[24] Owen, *Ely records*, pp. vii, 71.

[25] Owen, 'Ecclesiastical jurisdiction', pp. 203–4; Houlbrooke, *Church courts and the people*, pp. 34–5.

and archdeacons. Most of these were either part of the peculiar jurisdiction of the dean of Salisbury (which also included numerous parishes in Berkshire, Dorset and Devon) or prebendal peculiars held by members of the cathedral chapter. (The latter were not entirely independent but were subject to the quasi-episcopal authority of the dean.) A further nine Wiltshire parishes were bishop's peculiars, exempt from the jurisdiction of the archdeacons (Map 1).

Overarching the diocesan courts were the institutions of the two English provinces of Canterbury and York. The courts of the southern province were based in London. They comprised the prerogative court of Canterbury, which dealt with probate in cases where the deceased had substantial amounts of property in more than one diocese,[26] and the courts of arches and of audience, which by this period functioned primarily as courts of appeal for cases heard in the diocesan courts of the province.[27] A rather different pattern prevailed in the northern province, where there was no clear differentiation between the provincial courts and those of the diocese of York.[28]

There had never been an English ecclesiastical court to deal with appeals arising from the two provinces. Before the Reformation such causes had gone to Rome; by the later sixteenth century they were dealt with by the court of delegates, which was not in fact an ecclesiastical court but a royal tribunal, staffed by civil lawyers, which also heard appeals from the court of admiralty, the court of chivalry and the courts of the chancellors of the universities of Oxford and Cambridge.[29]

The sixteenth century saw the development of other institutions which could handle spiritual causes but which were not, strictly speaking, church courts. These were the courts of the 'commissioners for causes ecclesiastical', commonly known as the courts of high commission. They exercised by royal commission – on a statutory basis after 1559 – the authority of the crown as supreme governor of the church in England. A key feature of these tribunals was their

[26] Christopher Kitching, 'The prerogative court of Canterbury from Warham to Whitgift', in O'Day and Heal (eds.), *Continuity and change*, pp. 191 – 214.

[27] Churchill, *Canterbury administration*, vol. 1, chs. 10–11; M. Doreen Slatter, 'The records of the court of arches', *Jl ecclesiastical history*, 4 (1953), pp. 139–53.

[28] Marchant, *Church under the law*, pp. 64, 79, 103–7.

[29] G. I. O. Duncan, *The high court of delegates* (Cambridge, 1971), pp. 1–32 and *passim*.

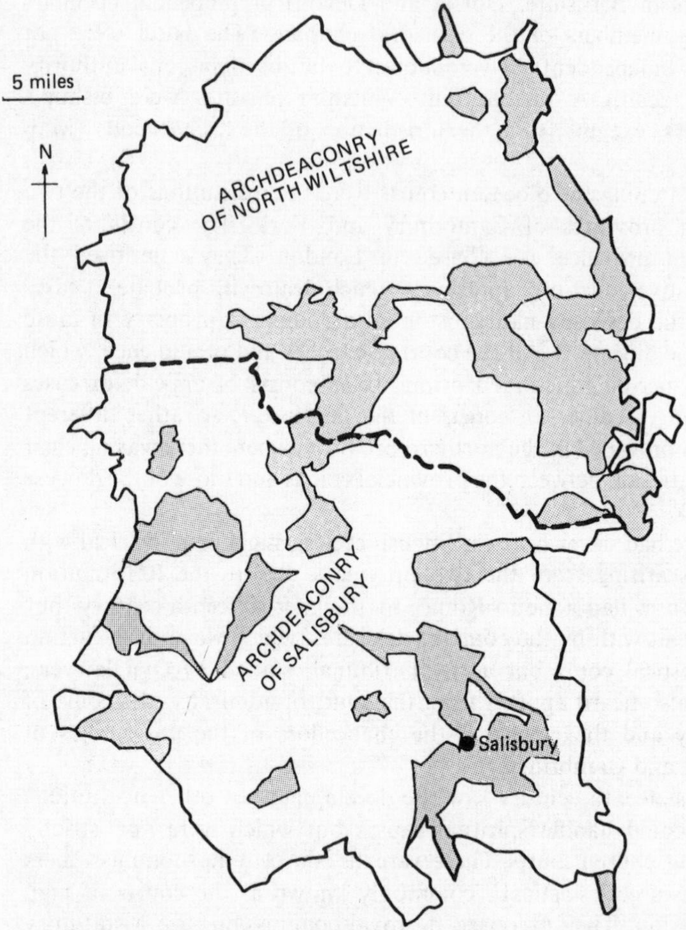

Areas under peculiar jurisdiction or otherwise exempt from the jurisdiction of the bishop and/or archdeacons

Boundary between the archdeaconries of Salisbury and North Wiltshire

Map 1 Ecclesiastical jurisdictions in Elizabethan and early Stuart Wiltshire.

power of coercion: unlike the ordinary church courts they were able to fine, imprison, and take bonds to enforce appearance or the performance of court orders. From 1559 the high commission constituted a regular court sitting in London, while similar bodies to deal with the north of England were established at York and Durham. The commissioners' primary task was to enforce royal policy in matters of religion, but they also dealt with cases involving immorality and matrimony, including what were in effect suits between parties.[30] Unfortunately, little is known in detail of the local impact of the London court of high commission, because most of its records have perished. Stray surviving act books for the period April 1634–May 1636 reveal only twelve causes relating to Wiltshire, involving a total of twenty-five defendants; but it is possible that the court had played a somewhat more active role in the county at an earlier date.[31]

In many dioceses of the province of Canterbury other commissions with local or special authority were in existence from time to time. They were often established at the request, and designed to augment the authority, of bishops and ecclesiastical court officers, who were normally included among the commissioners. Increased powers were particularly welcome in the reign of Elizabeth, when diocesan authorities were seeking to re-establish their influence after the shocks of the Reformation years; and this was the peak period for the issue of local commissions. Later they became less common. Conflicts between clerical and lay commissioners, and attacks by common lawyers, have been adduced as reasons to explain this change.[32] But perhaps the basic reason was that such special courts became less necessary, partly because the main responsibility for punishing recusancy was from the 1580s shifted to the secular courts, and partly because the traditional institutions of ecclesiastical justice

[30] Assessments of the nature and function of the courts of high commission have been considerably modified in recent years: see Roland G. Usher, *The rise and fall of the high commission*, 2nd edn, with introduction by Philip Tyler (Oxford, 1968), esp. pp. i–xxxiv; Philip Tyler, 'The significance of the ecclesiastical commission at York', *Northern history*, 2 (1967), pp. 27–44; Elton (ed.), *Tudor constitution*, pp. 221–6.

[31] P.R.O., SP 16/261, 324. Another act book survives for the period November 1639–December 1640: SP 16/434.

[32] Usher, *High commission*, introd. Tyler, pp. vi–xii, xxxi–xxxiv; Roger B. Manning, 'The crisis of episcopal authority during the reign of Elizabeth I', *Jl British studies*, 11 (1971–2), pp. 1–25; Houlbrooke, 'Decline of ecclesiastical jurisdiction', pp. 250–1, 256.

regained some of their confidence as the church of England became better established.[33] Yet the importance of these local commissions, even in their heyday, should not be exaggerated. In the diocese of Salisbury such commissions appear to have operated, probably sporadically, from about 1580 to the early years of the seventeenth century. Between late July and late September 1584 – a particularly active period to judge from the fragmentary surviving records – the commissioners handled about twenty cases. This was a significant, but in numerical terms modest, supplement to the ordinary business of the church courts.[34]

A few words of assessment are called for at this stage. The overall pattern of ecclesiastical jurisdictions is apt to look alarmingly complex. In fact the main structures were clear and were probably no more baffling to contemporaries than the patchwork of secular jurisdictions.[35] Of course the system did have weaknesses. Some dioceses were so large as to pose formidable administrative problems, and even the larger archdeaconries could be difficult to oversee effectively. With a view to overcoming these problems, some Elizabethan commentators advocated the restructuring of ecclesiastical discipline on the basis of rural deaneries, more manageable units of perhaps a dozen or twenty parishes. But such schemes would have entailed a considerable administrative upheaval, while the proliferation of jurisdictions might have created its own problems. Whether for good or ill, nothing was done.[36] At the other extreme, the lesser peculiars were often too small to be really viable. Some were certainly maladministered, and to an extent this undermined other jurisdictions – instances of this will crop up in later chapters.[37] But it is unlikely that the existence of exempt jurisdictions seriously harmed the administration of ecclesiastical justice as a whole. Jurisdictional conflicts between different ecclesiastical courts sometimes

[33] See below, Chapter 3.

[34] W.R.O., B/ABO 1, fols. 1–12. Cf. F. D. Price, 'The commission for ecclesiastical causes for the dioceses of Bristol and Gloucester, 1574', *Trans. Bristol and Gloucestershire Archaeol. Soc.*, 59 (1937), pp. 180–4; Peter Clark, 'The ecclesiastical commission at Canterbury, 1572–1603', *Archaeologia cantiana*, 89 (1974), pp. 183–97.

[35] Ingram, 'Communities and courts', pp. 111–15; Louis A. Knafla, '"Sin of all sorts swarmeth": criminal litigation in an English county in the early seventeenth century', in E. W. Ives and A. H. Manchester (eds.), *Law, litigants and the legal profession* (1983), pp. 50–67.

[36] Collinson, *Elizabethan puritan movement*, pp. 180–3.

[37] See below, Chapters 6, 11.

constituted another disturbing factor, but the impression is that at least by about 1600 such wrangles were less common and less damaging than they had been in earlier centuries.[38]

Much the same can be said about the actual law which the post-Reformation church courts administered as about the pattern of their jurisdictions: at first sight it is apt to look more complicated than, in practice, it often was. Certainly there were many technicalities, and complex tithe cases and the like required an expert to unravel them. But most of the disciplinary work of the courts, and even some of the simpler kinds of suits between parties, were readily comprehensible to anyone with a smattering of legal knowledge or even a sound commonsense, while the common run of fornicators or sabbath-breakers could hardly complain that they were faced with arcane legal principles.[39]

The church law of the Elizabethan and early Stuart periods was compounded of many ingredients. Its basis was the pre-Reformation ecclesiastical law, which derived from three sources. The first, and most important, was the *Corpus juris canonici*, the common body of canon law of the western church, modified by local custom and supplemented by the legislation of English provincial synods and councils. The second was the *Corpus juris civilis*, the code of Roman law, parts of which formed the basis of the law administered in testamentary matters and supplemented the canon law of marriage. The third element was what has been called ecclesiastical common law, supposedly older than the law contained in the papal codes and deriving from immemorial usage.[40]

The legislation of Henry VIII left this traditional body of law in operation so far as it was not contrary to the royal prerogative and to the law and customs of the realm,[41] but plans were repeatedly mooted to draw up a substantially new corpus. Indeed such a new code, informed by protestant principles, was actually drafted in the reign of Edward VI and published with minor changes in 1571 as the *Reformatio legum ecclesiasticarum* (Reform of church laws). But it never received official confirmation, partly because of Elizabeth's

[38] Marchant, *Church under the law*, p. 12; Owen, 'Ecclesiastical jurisdiction', p. 204; Houlbrooke, *Church courts and the people*, pp. 31–2, 34–5.
[39] Brinkworth, *Shakespeare and the bawdy court*, p. 19.
[40] *The canon law of the church of England, being the report of the archbishops' commission on canon law* (1947), chs. 3–4. [41] 25 Hen. VIII c. 19.

(and earlier Northumberland's) reluctance to grasp the nettle of a major reform of ecclesiastical jurisdiction, but more basically because the code was in some respects provocative of lay interests and unrealistically harsh.[42]

Despite the failure of schemes for major recodification, the law by which the ecclesiastical courts operated was in time considerably modified. Substantial changes were made through a string of parliamentary statutes. In addition, many new regulations about the fittings and furniture of churches, liturgical arrangements, the conduct of the clergy, and numerous other matters, were prescribed in successive royal and episcopal injunctions and orders. A collection of twelve new canons became law in 1597; while these, along with many of the miscellaneous regulations of Elizabeth's reign and new measures designed to tighten the structure of ecclesiastical justice in the light of puritan and other criticisms, were digested into a collection of 141 canons which became law in the southern province in 1604 and in the province of York in 1606.[43] As will be seen, judicial decisions also tended to modify the practical effect of certain aspects of ecclesiastical law, especially with regard to the formation of marriage, even though the letter of the law remained unchanged.[44]

Meanwhile ecclesiastical jurists were working to assimilate the old and new elements in church law. In the absence of canon law studies at the universities (proscribed in 1535), such activities were focused in the institution of Doctors' Commons, an association of civil lawyers which built up a magnificent canon and civil law library and served to train ecclesiastical lawyers in the traditional jurisprudence of the church.[45] In the closing years of Elizabeth's reign the efforts of the assimilators bore fruit in a number of major works of ecclesiastical jurisprudence, notably Henry Swinburne's studies of the law of testaments and of marriage and Francis Clarke's treatise on procedure.[46]

[42] Edward Cardwell (ed.), *The reformation of the ecclesiastical laws* (Oxford, 1850). See also W. K. Jordan, *Edward VI: the threshold of power* (1970), pp. 357–61; Houlbrooke, *Church courts and the people*, pp. 17–18.

[43] *Canon law of the church of England*, pp. 71–3; Houlbrooke, *Church courts and the people*, pp. 18–19. The canons of 1597 and 1604 are printed in Edward Cardwell (ed.), *Synodalia: a collection of articles of religion, canons, and proceedings of convocations*, 2 vols. (Oxford, 1842), vol. 1, pp. 147–329.

[44] See below, Chapter 5.

[45] Levack, *Civil lawyers*, pp. 16–20.

[46] Henry Swinburne, *A briefe treatise of testaments and last willes* (1590–1); Henry

How was ecclesiastical law administered? The jurisdiction of the church courts fell into three main divisions: 'instance', 'office' and 'record' or 'non-contentious' business. The last, comprising the routine granting of marriage licences, probates and administrations, and the like, was really administrative business in quasi-judicial guise: it requires little explanatory comment, though it formed an extremely important part of the church courts' work. 'Instance' and 'office' jurisdiction were very roughly equivalent to what we now call civil and criminal justice. Instance causes were disputes between parties, initiated 'at the instance' of individuals who thought they had been wronged. Office (or 'correction') causes were disciplinary prosecutions 'for the reformation of morals and the soul's health'. However, in terms of the matters at issue this apparently simple distinction was sometimes a little blurred. For example, defamation and matrimonial causes usually came before the courts as instance suits in which one party sought redress against another. But since these matters involved a strong moral or even criminal element they could also be dealt with as disciplinary cases under office jurisdiction. On the other hand, not all office cases were equally concerned with religion and morality. Many related to semi-administrative matters such as the repair of churches and the routine provision of liturgical books and vestments, and to testamentary matters, which, depending on the circumstances, might or might not involve a genuinely criminal or fraudulent element.

Procedurally there was a further distinction between disciplinary prosecutions initiated by the judge alone 'of his mere office' (*ex officio mero*) and cases in which the office of the judge was 'promoted' by a third party. The latter, involving more complex procedures which enabled the issues to be thrashed out in detail, were far less common; characteristically they concerned probate and a variety of matters concerning the upkeep and provision of churches, but sexual transgressions, and offences relating to religious observance and practice, were sometimes dealt with in this way.

The great bulk of disciplinary prosecutions were 'mere office' cases initiated by the judge alone. Sometimes the latter was

Swinburne, *A treatise of spousals or matrimonial contracts* (1686); Francis Clarke, *Praxis in curiis ecclesiasticis* (Dublin, 1666). On Swinburne, see J. Duncan M. Derrett, *Henry Swinburne (?1551–1624): civil lawyer of York*, Borthwick papers, 44 (York, 1973).

'informed' or 'notified' of suspicious circumstances by court officers, parish ministers or other informants. He could thereupon summon the suspect for examination and if necessary would order an inquiry (called an 'inquisition') in the accused person's home parish to ascertain the truth.[47] How far these methods were used varied considerably from diocese to diocese and at different times, but in general they were merely subsidiary to regular reports from the parishes.

The main source of such reports were churchwardens and their deputies (variously called 'sidesmen', 'questmen', etc.), who were elected annually in each parish by a variety of customary methods. As well as performing other administrative duties, they were specifically required under oath to furnish 'presentments' on the physical state of ecclesiastical buildings and on the religious and moral behaviour of the incumbent and the parishioners. Presentments could be made voluntarily at any time, and in this way small numbers of cases trickled into the courts throughout the year. But full reports were obligatory at regular intervals, and churchwardens who failed to exhibit 'bills of presentment' when they were demanded, or to do so satisfactorily, were themselves subject to prosecution.

The supervision of churchwardens was achieved by means of visitations – tours of inspection made by or on behalf of bishops, archdeacons and others who exercised ecclesiastical jurisdiction. The pattern and frequency of such visitations varied according to local custom. The bishop of Salisbury conformed to the theoretical norm in carrying out a visitation shortly after his accession to the see (the 'primary' visitation) and every third year thereafter; but in some dioceses episcopal visitations were conducted at longer or shorter intervals than this.[48] Archdeacons generally visited twice a year, around Easter and Michaelmas. The archdeacon of Salisbury conformed to this pattern throughout the late sixteenth and early seventeenth centuries. The archdeacon of North Wiltshire, however, conducted visitations thrice yearly in Elizabeth's reign; probably to conform with the spirit of new regulations embodied in the canons of 1604,[49] the pattern was later changed to the normal biannual one. Peculiar jurisdictions often had their own idiosyncratic arrange-

[47] Clarke, *Praxis*, p. 406. For examples of the use of this procedure, see W.R.O., B/ABI 3, fol. 38v; B/DB 8, fol. 108; B/ABI 53, fols. 5v–6.
[48] Houlbrooke, *Church courts and the people*, p. 29.
[49] Canon 116.

ments: the dean of Salisbury, for example, visited annually. Individual dioceses were also subject to metropolitical visitations conducted as soon as practicable after the installation of a new archbishop.[50]

The business of the visitation was conducted at special courts convened in strategically placed towns and villages on the visitation itinerary. Churchwardens and sidesmen were summoned to appear and were furnished with articles of inquiry (usually taking the form of printed booklets) which specified the matters on which information was required. They were then examined and required to make a full and true presentment according to the tenor of their oaths.[51] Churchwardens who could write sometimes drew up their own presentment bills; otherwise the information was taken orally and recorded by court officers.[52] The canons of 1604 specified that ministers might, if they wished, join in the churchwardens' presentments or exhibit bills of their own, but they were actually obliged only to provide a separate list of recusants.[53] Once received, the presentment bills were scrutinised by the officers of the court and weeded of irrelevances. The specific accusations which remained, technically called 'detections', formed the basis for office prosecutions. Some of these matters could be dealt with immediately at the visitation courts, but the majority were held over to be heard subsequently.

In some dioceses the church authorities demanded additional presentments, called quarter bills, *between* visitations. Certain Elizabethan critics regarded this practice as excessive, and the canons of 1604 ruled that churchwardens were not bound to present oftener than twice a year 'unless it be at the bishop's visitation'.[54] This regulation was apparently ignored in the dioceses of Chichester and Ely, where quarterly presentments continued to be the norm

[50] Dorothy M. Owen, *The records of the established church in England excluding parochial records*, British Records Association, archives and the user, 1 (1970), p. 45.

[51] Articles of inquiry for Salisbury diocese are listed in the Bibliography under 'England, church of'.

[52] Based on examination of W.R.O., D/Pres., 1583–1641.

[53] Canons 113–14. For examples of ministers joining in presentments, see W.R.O., D/Pres., 1622/1, 1631/41, 1638/78; and of ministers presenting on their own account, see W.R.O., D/Pres., 1631/34. The requirement for ministers to exhibit separate lists of recusants was apparently more honoured in the breach than in the observance.

[54] Strype, *Life of Whitgift*, vol. 2, p. 447; canon 116.

throughout the early seventeenth century. In the archdeaconries of Salisbury and North Wiltshire, however, practice was immediately adjusted to conform with the new canon: after 1604 presentments were never demanded more than twice a year (in years of episcopal visitation the archdeacons visited only once and received only a single set of presentments).

Some historians have criticised the superficiality of the presentment system. During visitations the officers of the courts did not have time to examine each pair of churchwardens thoroughly or to check rigorously the fullness of their reports. Underpresentment was the inevitable result.[55] But, as we have seen, this situation was by no means peculiar to the church courts. The issue of just how effective the church's detection system actually was will crop up repeatedly in later chapters; but it may be stated now that, by contemporary standards, ecclesiastical visitations represented an impressive and reasonably thorough fact-finding operation, and the degree of penetration they achieved compared well with the analogous system of quarter sessions presentments.

The organisation of the courts to deal with the volume of cases which came before them enhances the impression of diligence and thoroughness. By the later sixteenth century, on account of the pressure of business, there were generally separate sessions for the handling of instance and disciplinary causes respectively. Courts for the transaction of suits between parties met in plenary session during the law terms either weekly (as at Ely and Chichester), fortnightly (as at Salisbury in the early seventeenth century), or at somewhat more irregular but still frequent intervals (as in the archdeaconry of Leicester). Supplementary sessions were convened when necessary. These courts were normally static, meeting in an accustomed place which was often within cathedral precincts; if witnesses or others were unable to attend, commissions were appointed to examine them locally.

Courts to deal with correction business generally met with similar or greater frequency, often with additional sessions in the wake of visitations, when the pressure of disciplinary business was particularly great. Sometimes, as in the archdeaconry of Salisbury and the diocese of Chichester, these correction courts were immobile, but more remote areas were often served by taking the court on circuit.

[55] Anthony Fletcher, *A county community in peace and war: Sussex, 1600–1660* (1975), pp. 82–5.

Thus the bishop of Salisbury's correction court customarily went on tour in northern Wiltshire and in Berkshire to hear disciplinary causes arising from visitations, while the courts of the archdeacons of North Wiltshire and Leicester were constantly peripatetic.

Inevitably these efforts to make the church courts accessible did not please everyone. In the parliament of 1597 some interests complained that sessions were *too* frequent and that the circuit system was troublesome and inconvenient. The churchwardens of Cricklade in 1585 took a different view: they presented the archdeacon of Wiltshire at the bishop's visitation for what proved to be a temporary lapse in 'not keeping courts at Cricklade according to the old order', alleging that 'for the want thereof the whole deanery is like to be undone'.[56] On the whole it seems likely that the frequency and ubiquity of the courts were an advantage which, all other things being equal, facilitated the expedition of justice.

What form did court proceedings take? The old idea that the church courts conducted all their business in Latin has been exposed as a myth. As in other courts of law in this period, the formal instruments and records were at least in part *written* in Latin, but the actual conduct of cases in the presence of defendants was in English.[57] Moreover the complexity of procedure was no greater than in other contemporary tribunals: the overwhelming majority of defendants in disciplinary cases, and even the parties in the simpler kinds of instance suit, can have found no difficulty whatsoever in understanding what was going on even if they did not command the services of a lawyer.

The ordinary church courts had no power to make arrests, and all defendants had to be summoned to appear by means of citations. The primary citation had to be served personally. If this proved impossible because the defendant could not be located, it was followed up by means of a citation 'by ways and means' (*viis et modis*), which could be served simply by affixing it to the door of the defendant's dwelling-house or to the doors of the parish church. As will be seen, securing attendance in these ways often posed problems, especially in disciplinary cases.[58] Defendants who failed to present themselves after citation were ultimately subject to the penalty of excommunication for contumacy; but it was common for the judge

[56] Strype, *Life of Whitgift*, vol. 3, pp. 374–6; W.R.O., B/*Detecta* Bk 6, fol. 41v.
[57] Cf. Hill, *Society and puritanism*, p. 310.
[58] See below, Chapter 11.

to 'reserve' the penalty for several sessions to allow time for compliance.

According to legal theorists, proceedings following the appearance of defendants were in either 'plenary' or 'summary' form. In practice the judges, usually with the parties' best interests in mind, allowed some degree of procedural flexibility; but the distinction did hold to a considerable extent.[59] Most types of instance suit and all promoted office causes were prosecuted by the more elaborate procedure, which involved a series of set stages, normally handled by ecclesiastical lawyers called proctors on behalf of their clients. The first stage was 'contestation of suit'. The plaintiff or promoter presented a statement of the case, technically known as a 'libel' in instance actions and 'articles' in promoted office causes. The defendant had to reply, point by point, generally on oath. Usually the defendant denied some or all of the facts alleged, sometimes presenting a counter-case in the form of an 'allegation' which the plaintiff had to answer.[60]

The next stage of the proceedings was 'probation': the judge 'assigned terms' (i.e. allotted a specified period) for the production and examination of witnesses. If necessary the latter could be compelled to appear on pain of excommunication. Once in court the witnesses were put on oath and examined, theoretically in private, as to their knowledge of the facts alleged in libel, articles or allegation. Their written depositions were subsequently published in court and were then available for scrutiny by both parties. Either side could administer 'interrogatories' to hostile witnesses, to expose weaknesses or bias in the evidence, or enter 'exceptions' (the substance of which had to be proved) to call in question the character or competence of the deponents. At any time during the probatory terms, moreover, the parties could enter 'additional positions' to strengthen their case or produce 'exhibits' in the form of documentary evidence. If necessary the probatory terms were extended to

[59] Cf. Woodcock, *Medieval ecclesiastical courts*, pp. 53–4; Helmholz, *Marriage litigation*, pp. 112–13; Houlbrooke, *Church courts and the people*, pp. 41–2.

[60] The account of plenary procedure in this and the following paragraphs owes much to the miracle of compression achieved by Owen, *Records of the established church*, pp. 40–1. The most convenient contemporary account is Henry Conset, *The practice of the spiritual or ecclesiastical courts* (1685), which is essentially a translation and rearrangement of Clarke's *Praxis*.

ensure that both sides got a fair hearing and that all material facts were brought to light.

Eventually the judge assigned terms to 'propound all acts' and to 'conclude', after which no further evidence could be accepted. A date for giving sentence was then assigned. In the interim, 'informations' were held in chambers: the lawyers handling the case reviewed the evidence on both sides and argued out points of law to aid the judge in coming to a decision. Finally, on the day appointed, judgement was given in the form either of a definitive sentence or, in simpler cases, of an informal decree. The unsuccessful party was normally allowed time to appeal. If an appeal was lodged the higher court sent an 'inhibition' to stay the proceedings and the lower court sent up a copy of all the relevant acts and papers. Otherwise a citation was issued for the appearance of the defeated party; punishment was inflicted if appropriate; the costs were taxed and an order made about payment. Defendants who had lost their case usually had to certify to the court that they had performed the terms of the sentence, and were liable to excommunication for contumacy if they failed to do so.

It used to be assumed that plenary proceedings in the church courts (of which the foregoing is a highly simplified account) were scandalously slow and vexatious.[61] Certainly the level of efficiency varied somewhat from court to court and from time to time, and no doubt standards sometimes slipped badly. Moreover there seems to have been a secular tendency for proceedings to grow more elaborate. In the Salisbury courts, for example, interrogatories and exceptions were used more frequently in the seventeenth century than earlier. This may have been the result of lawyers' efforts to maximise their profits, the growing legal sophistication of the church courts' clientele (associated with the general litigiousness of the period), or a combination of both factors.[62] Such procedural drift was by no means confined to the church courts, and its effects on the administration of ecclesiastical justice should in any case not be exaggerated.[63]

[61] Hill, *Society and puritanism*, p. 325.

[62] Cf. Houlbrooke, 'Decline of ecclesiastical jurisdiction', p. 248.

[63] W. J. Jones, *The Elizabethan court of chancery* (Oxford, 1967), pp. 9–17, 335–6; Thomas G. Barnes, 'Star chamber litigants and their counsel, 1596–1641', in Baker (ed.), *Legal records and the historian*, pp. 7–28; Stephen D. White, *Sir Edward Coke and the grievances of the commonwealth* (Manchester, 1979), ch. 3.

Canon law provided safeguards against dilatory proceedings, and litigants and their proctors were not slow to invoke them. If plaintiffs failed to exhibit libels within a reasonable time their causes were dismissed, while parties who wilfully retarded suits were condemned to pay the expenses of their opponents.[64]

In normal circumstances proceedings were reasonably expeditious. The actual duration of causes from commencement to final sentence naturally varied considerably according to the complexity of each individual case and how hard it was fought, which in turn depended partly on the type of suit in hand. Defamation causes and many matrimonial suits were often straightforward and therefore speedy, while tithe actions frequently dragged on because the issues were apt to be complex and the evidence extensive. A simple cause of whatever type could be over in a matter of weeks, while a difficult one could take two or three years. In the consistory court of Salisbury in the early seventeenth century the average duration of causes pursued to final sentence was about nine to twelve months. This level of performance seems to have been fairly typical of the Elizabethan and early Stuart church courts in general, and it probably compared well with that of secular tribunals.[65]

In practice, moreover, only a minority of cases passed through all the procedural stages and were prosecuted to a finish. Many causes were in fact dropped almost as soon as they were begun, either because the initial citation was sufficient to bring the defendant to heel or because the plaintiff had second thoughts about proceeding. Numerous other suits were discontinued at a later stage, sometimes at the very point of sentence, often by means of mediation or arbitration by court officers or other agents acting informally. It has already been stressed that such arrangements were by no means peculiar to the church courts; but they were certainly facilitated by the canon law principle that, unless the suit raised issues which could not be compromised (like whether or not the parties were man and wife), the litigants should be positively encouraged to reach an out of court settlement to restore harmony between them as soon as possible.[66]

[64] For examples, see W.R.O., B/ABI 49, fol. 173; B/ABI 50, fols. 62, 159, 170v; B/ABI 51, fol. 22.

[65] Cf. Marchant, *Church under the law*, p. 65; Potter, 'Ecclesiastical courts in the diocese of Canterbury', pp. 20, 72–3.

[66] Houlbrooke, *Church courts and the people*, pp. 43–4, 271.

Summary procedure was another means whereby the trouble of litigation could be minimised. It differed from plenary form principally in that the formalities of presenting the plaintiff's case were minimised and some of the other procedural stages were omitted or compressed. The method was not admissible in all kinds of instance suit,[67] but it was occasionally used in simple defamation and tithe cases and, more frequently, in straightforward matrimonial causes. The parties in marriage suits may sometimes have been in a fragile emotional state and were often young and fairly poor: by using simplified procedures the courts could despatch their cases with a minimum of fuss.

Specialised versions of summary procedure were used for all disciplinary cases save for promoted office suits. The precise mode of proceeding varied, depending on the gravity of the charge and how the case had come before the courts. In some serious cases, where the presentment raised wider issues which required investigation, or where the matter had not actually been detected by the churchwardens, the formalities were really not much less than in plenary cases. The judge administered a formal list of articles or charges, and the defendant was required to answer them on oath – the notorious oath *ex officio*. In the event of a denial the judge could proceed to proof by witnesses and might appoint a 'necessary promoter' or 'coadjutor' – normally a court officer – to prosecute the cause through its various procedural stages. This relatively elaborate and thorough mode of investigation was frequently used against nonconforming ministers and hence aroused puritan criticisms; but it was sometimes employed against notorious sexual offenders, bigamists, and the like.

However, the great majority of disciplinary cases were dealt with much less formally. The articles administered to the defendant were abbreviated, often consisting merely of a copy of the presentment, and normally witnesses were not used. The defendant could be put on oath, but even this formality was omitted in simple cases concerning failure to pay church rates, sabbath-breaking, and the like, or if a voluntary confession was forthcoming. A defendant who denied a relatively grave charge, such as immorality, was usually ordered to undergo 'compurgation': that is, to produce a specified number of honest neighbours, usually of the same sex and standing, who were prepared to swear in court that they believed the charge

[67] Conset, *Practice*, pp. 22–3, 177–81.

to be unfounded. A proclamation was read out beforehand in the suspect's parish church, calling on anyone who had material grounds to object against the purgation to appear in court. If convincing objections were made – objectors were examined on oath, much like witnesses, and their statements recorded in writing – or if compurgators were not forthcoming, the defendant was judged to have failed the purgation and was pronounced guilty. But if the compurgators were duly produced and swore in the suspect's favour, and if there were no objectors, the defendant was restored to good name and fame and dismissed, usually with an admonition to avoid cause of suspicion in the future.

Just how well compurgation worked is of particular significance in assessing the effectiveness of ecclesiastical discipline; for this reason, and because the procedure is so different from modern methods of ascertaining guilt, it will be discussed in more detail later. The same applies to the penalties employed by the church courts; but it is necessary at this stage to provide a brief preliminary outline of punitive procedure. In many simple cases of absence from church, failure to receive the communion and similar venial sins, the culprit was merely ordered to make good the omission by a specified date and certify that this had been done. Sins of commission were normally visited with some form of punishment. Clergymen could, in grave cases, be suspended from office or even permanently deprived of their benefices. In pre-Reformation times, laymen had sometimes been punished by whipping, especially in cases of immorality, but by this period it was generally accepted that the penalties of the church courts could touch neither life, limb nor property. In practice there were three major sanctions open to them: excommunication (or its milder version, suspension), admonition and penance.

Theoretically the most drastic weapon in the ecclesiastical armoury was excommunication. This was the ultimate penalty for contumacy (failure to appear before the courts when summoned or to obey their orders) and was also a canonical or statutory penalty for certain offences such as clandestine marriage and violence committed in church or churchyard.[68] The essence of this sanction was exclusion from the communion of the faithful, but legal theory distinguished between two degrees of excommunication, the lesser

[68] Edmund Gibson, *Codex juris ecclesiastici anglicani*, 2nd edn, 2 vols. (Oxford, 1761), vol. 1, pp. 192, 430.

and the greater. The major penalty involved total exclusion from the church and from the society of Christian people, and those who consorted with excommunicates, bought and sold with them, or gave them succour or harbour were themselves subject to excommunication. It also entailed serious legal disabilities: for example, the excommunicate could not act as plaintiff or witness in a lawsuit and could not serve as executor, administrator or guardian. The solemnity of greater excommunication could be further increased by a sentence of 'aggravation' if the culprit incurred the penalty afresh or remained obstinate for forty days. After this interval, in any case, the name of the excommunicate could be 'signified' to the crown in chancery: on receipt of a royal writ *de excommunicato capiendo* it was the sheriff's duty to arrest the offender and confine him in prison until he submitted.[69] Absolution from excommunication could, however, be secured with relative ease. The culprit had first to take an oath to obey the judge and the mandates of the church. The sentence was then lifted, either absolutely or subject to certain conditions such as the performance of penance.

Lesser excommunication, usually called suspension, was milder in its effects. It deprived the offender of the services of the church but did not involve total ostracism or legal disabilities. It had been widely used in the church courts on the eve of the Reformation as the usual penalty for contumacy, but it largely went out of use around the middle of the sixteenth century because amid the religious disruptions of that time it was proving ineffective. But it was still the normal penalty for non-appearance in the diocese of Ely in the late sixteenth and early seventeenth centuries.[70]

The mildest of the penalties used in the church courts was admonition, a simple reproof from the judge. Court records indicate that admonitions could vary in severity from the 'charitable' to the 'strict', but regrettably they do not reveal what was actually said. Their tone no doubt varied according to the character and interests of individual judges. They could be the opportunity for genuine pastoral guidance or they might be just a dry and formal reprimand.

The third available penalty was penance, which was in theory supposed to work for the health of the culprit's soul, to deter others and to give satisfaction to the congregation for the affront of public sin. Malefactors generally had to confess their fault openly in church

[69] John Ayliffe, *Parergon juris canonici anglicani* (1726), pp. 257, 260–1.

[70] Houlbrooke, *Church courts and the people*, p. 49. See also below, Chapter 11.

and to ask God for forgiveness.[71] The precise details of the penances awarded by the courts varied greatly from case to case, as did their severity. The standard kind of penance was a very formal and public affair. Dressed in a white sheet and carrying a white rod, the offender had to confess before the whole congregation during service time on a Sunday or major holiday; and often the moral of the occasion was reinforced by the reading of an appropriate sermon or homily. More severe penances involved making such a confession on more than one occasion, sometimes in the market-place of the nearest town, or further personal humiliations such as appearing bare-legged. On the other hand, the severity of penance could be lessened by allowing the culprit to wear ordinary clothes; while the mildest penances merely involved confessing the offence before the minister and selected representatives of the congregation (usually the churchwardens) at a time when large numbers of people were unlikely to be present in church.

The more elaborate kinds of penance were plainly an experience which most people wished to avoid. For some offenders there was a legally permissible escape route: penances could, at the discretion of the judge, be wholly or partly commuted into money payments to be applied to 'pious uses' such as the provision of sermons, church repairs and, above all, the relief of the poor. (In the archdeaconry of North Wiltshire in the late 1590s culprits were often ordered to bestow a quantity of grain for the use of poor households.)[72] Such concrete acts of contrition, similar to the pious bequests often made by testators on their death-beds, continued a long medieval tradition and had obvious social utility; many Elizabethan critics, however, denounced the commutation of penance as a travesty of godly discipline. To meet such objections the church passed legislation to regulate the practice, but it never wholly abandoned it.[73]

Apart from the possible payment of commutation money, people involved with the church courts usually found themselves out of pocket. Court fees were payable both by defendants in disciplinary cases and by the parties in instance actions – though judges did have

[71] William Lyndwood, *Provinciale* (*seu constitutiones angliae*) (Oxford, 1679), p. 326. For examples of penances, see Hubert Hall, 'Some Elizabethan penances in the diocese of Ely', *Trans. Roy. Hist. Soc.*, 3rd ser., 1 (1907), pp. 263–77.

[72] For example, W.R.O., AW/*Detecta* Bk, 1586–99, fols. 159v–160v.

[73] Cardwell (ed.), *Synodalia*, vol. 1, pp. 142–3, 156–7; Strype, *Life of Whitgift*, vol. 1, pp. 231–2, 238, 365, vol. 2, p. 452, vol. 3, pp. 57, 131–2. See also below, Chapter 11.

discretion to waive or reduce fees when there were mitigating circumstances or when the people involved were very poor. The primary purpose of these fees was simply to pay for the running of the courts, but costs also had a part to play in the actual course of justice. In instance suits, defeated defendants normally had to pay the bulk of the plaintiffs' expenses, while even successful ones were sometimes 'condemned in charges' if the judge believed that they were in some measure culpable. In disciplinary cases, fee charges were to all intents and purposes part of the punitive apparatus of the courts. The fact that they were incurred by innocent and guilty alike probably did not, in itself, worry contemporaries overmuch. It was the same in other courts, and the conventional wisdom was that anyone who had given cause for suspicion had to be prepared to pay the costs of vindicating his reputation.[74]

Nevertheless the financial exactions of the church courts were the subject of much contemporary complaint. Some of the attacks came from common lawyers with vested interests to pursue – though the secular courts were also criticised for excessive fee-taking. Other criticisms came from puritans, who urged extremely rigorous standards of personal and public morality and desired above all to raise the standard of the church's pastoral activities. For many such men, the very notion of courts of morality run by lay bureaucrats for professional profit was at best suspect, at worst anathema.[75]

Archbishop Whitgift went some way towards meeting criticisms by requiring the officers of the various ecclesiastical jurisdictions to submit schedules of the fees they charged for official approval, and by issuing a standard table of fees which was to prevail in cases of dispute. These provisions were confirmed by the canons of 1604.[76] Ronald Marchant's survey of a number of different jurisdictions in northern and southern England indicates that the fees actually charged in the church courts were mostly in rough accord with the official regulations.[77] It was the same in Salisbury diocese. A single scale of fees was apparently administered in all the Wiltshire jurisdictions throughout the late sixteenth and early seventeenth

[74] Thomas, *Religion and the decline of magic*, p. 528 and the references there cited.

[75] Hill, *Society and puritanism*, pp. 307–9, 324–9; cf. Marchant, *Church under the law*, pp. 19, 243–4; Houlbrooke, 'Decline of ecclesiastical jurisdiction', p. 251.

[76] Canon 135; cf. Strype, *Life of Whitgift*, vol. 2, pp. 377–8. The table is printed in Ayliffe, *Parergon*, pp. 551–2.

[77] Marchant, *Church under the law*, pp. 141–6.

Table 1 *Fees charged in the Salisbury church courts (1570–1640), compared with Whitgift's standard (1597)*

	Salisbury	Whitgift
*(a) Fees due to judge and registrar**		
Act	4d.	4d.
Citation	8d.	10d.
Decree	9d.	1s. 8d.
Examination of plaintiff or defendant	1s. 6d.	1s. 6d.
Examination of first witness	1s. 8d.	1s. 6d.
Examination of other witnesses	10d.	9d.
Copy of libel or allegation	1s. 8d.	By length
Copy of answer	1s. 0d.	By length
Copy of deposition	8d.	By length
Sentence	12s. 0d.	12s. 0d.
Oath *ex officio*	4d.	?
Articles	3s. 4d.	?
Order of penance	1s. 4d.	?
Proclamation for compurgation	3s. 0d.	2s. 0d.
Compurgation fee: defendant	1s. 6d.	1s. 6d.
Compurgation fee: first compurgator	1s. 6d.	1s. 6d.
Compurgation fee: other compurgators	9d.	8d.
Letters testimonial	11s. 4d.	11s. 8d.
Excommunication and schedule thereof	1s. 1d.	1s. 10d.
Absolution and certificate thereof	2s. 3d.	2s. 10d.
Dismissal (office or instance causes)	10d.	10d.
(b) Fees due to proctor		
Advice	3s. 4d.	2s. 0d.
Drawing up libel	5s. 0d.	5s. 0d.
Drawing up personal answer	3s. 4d.	2s. 6d.
Drawing up allegation, etc.	3s. 4d.	3s. 4d.
Attendance (each court day)	1s. 4d.	1s. 0d.
Attendance (on day of final sentence)	2s. 0d.	?1s. 0d.
Information of judge	3s. 4d.	—**

* Shared in varying proportions between judge and registrar.
** Whitgift's table probably assumed that an advocate would be retained for this purpose.

centuries. It differed in many details from Whitgift's standard; but, save that the proctorial fees charged at Salisbury were appreciably higher, there was overall little to choose between the two scales (see Table 1).

Just how expensive was ecclesiastical justice? Many of the charges for particular items were in themselves modest, but the nature of plenary proceedings inevitably involved the accumulation of costs. To secure a final sentence could be a very expensive business; on the other hand, a plaintiff who chose to discontinue a suit thereby incurred no serious penalty but could obtain a dismissal for a small sum, a fact which doubtless encouraged compromise. The cost of pursuing a cause to the finish naturally varied according to the complexity of the case, as a few Wiltshire examples will illustrate. In *Abbot v. Blandford* (1615), an unusually simple defamation cause, the plaintiff's costs were taxed at £2 10s. 0d. In a slightly more complex slander suit, *Briant v. Lavington* (1615), costs were assessed at £4 13s. 4d. But in *Hussy v. Flower* (1616), a bitterly fought matrimonial cause, the defendant eventually had to pay costs of £11 0s. 0d.[78]

The charges incurred in summary disciplinary cases likewise varied greatly. In simple cases of no great gravity, a Wiltshire culprit who appeared promptly and confessed freely could secure a dismissal for 22d. But in more serious cases, notably prosecutions for sexual immorality, the defendant usually had to pay for the *ex officio* oath, articles, and a detailed examination, and the charges became much steeper. Thus fornicators and adulterers normally faced a total bill of at least 8s. 4d. To establish innocence by means of compurgation was very expensive, usually costing well over a pound. Moreover, defendants who failed to appear promptly faced further costs: in Wiltshire the various charges involved in securing absolution after excommunication amounted to 4s.

How far the church courts insisted in actual practice on the full payment of such fees did vary somewhat from time to time and area to area. But most were probably fairly assiduous, and this was certainly true in Wiltshire. Excommunications were sometimes decreed solely for failure to discharge costs, even when the defendant had performed penance or otherwise fulfilled all the orders of the court. As the early seventeenth century wore on, the Salisbury courts showed an increasing tendency to adjourn cases before sentence when fees were outstanding, apparently as a means both of giving culprits more time to scrape together the necessary cash and of exerting pressure on them to do so. Only a small proportion of very poor defendants were excused fees altogether. However, the courts

[78] W.R.O., B/ABI 42, 23/1/1616; B/ABI 43, 22/10/1616; B/ABI 44, 23/9/1617.

were not totally inflexible and were often prepared to settle for part payment.[79]

In a period when the daily wages of a labourer were less than a shilling, the sums involved in court fees were clearly not negligible. Reluctance to see poor neighbours put to financial expense was clearly one reason why churchwardens sometimes turned a blind eye to presentable offences, and why excessive or unnecessary litigation was frowned upon. Equally it is not surprising that grumbles about the church courts' financial exactions continued even after Whitgift had taken action to peg the price of ecclesiastical justice. On the other hand, it is doubtful whether adulterers or other notorious offenders received much sympathy from their fellow-parishioners when they had to dig deep into their purses. In any case it is plain that the fees charged by the church courts were not particularly high by contemporary standards. The costs of criminal justice at quarter sessions and assizes were comparable, and litigation in the diocesan courts was probably cheaper than suing in the common law courts at Westminster. Moreover the fixing of fees around 1600, at a time of continuing inflation, and often at levels similar to those which had prevailed since the mid-sixteenth century, meant that in real terms the church courts were offering a cheaper and cheaper service as time progressed.[80] Overall it would be a mistake to attach too much importance to contemporary complaints about fees. In so far as the question was important at all, it was subsidiary to the wider issue of how far the courts were perceived to be socially useful.

The subject of fees leads us to consider the personnel who ran the courts and depended on them for an income. Their role was crucial. Whatever the intrinsic strengths and weaknesses of the machinery of ecclesiastical justice, its operation in practice was heavily influenced by the quality of its administrators and by the spirit in which they approached their task. It is possible to make some generalisations about the degree of ability, probity and diligence displayed by the people who ran the church courts in Elizabethan and early Stuart times; but the precise pattern naturally varied from court to court

[79] For fuller details, see Martin Ingram, 'Ecclesiastical justice in Wiltshire, 1600–1640, with special reference to cases concerning sex and marriage' (University of Oxford D. Phil. thesis, 1976), pp. 312–13; and cf. Marchant, *Church under the law*, pp. 141–4.

[80] Marchant, *Church under the law*, p. 145.

and from time to time, and it would be a mistake to attach too much importance to temporary periods of torpor or corruption.

The bishops and other ecclesiastical dignitaries in whom jurisdiction was vested were not, in general, primarily responsible for the day to day administration of justice. Bishops normally sat in court on an irregular basis at best; and, though such appearances were not uncommon in Elizabeth's reign, when the church was trying hard to re-establish discipline and raise religious standards after the dislocations of the Reformation, they tended to diminish in the somewhat easier conditions of the early seventeenth century. Thus in Salisbury diocese, it was not unusual to find bishops like John Jewel (1560–71) and John Piers (1577–89) dealing personally with cases involving scandalous clergy, serious nonconformity and notorious sexual offences;[81] but their Jacobean and Caroline successors were much less in evidence. The fact was that bishops were generally too busy, and often lacked the specialised legal knowledge, to administer justice on a regular basis. Archdeacons and lesser dignitaries were more likely to be found in court, at least to deal with straightforward disciplinary cases; but they, too, often delegated most of their judicial functions. They and their episcopal superiors might none the less exercise a supervisory control over the courts and influence the nature of judicial policy. How far they did so naturally varied according to the character of individual bishops and the extent to which such intervention was perceived to be necessary; and these activities are now often difficult to trace unless they resulted in a major shake-up of administration or a significant shift in religious policy.[82]

The offices of official principal, vicar general and chancellor had been developed in the middle ages to bear the main burden of episcopal justice and administration. By the later sixteenth century these offices were commonly held by a single person, normally a layman, who was generally referred to as the chancellor of the diocese. The corresponding post at the archdeaconry level was that of official.[83] Legal expertise and administrative ability were the prime qualifications demanded of these men; and, despite some

[81] For examples, see W.R.O., B/ABI 13, fols. 79, 167; B/ABI 17, fol. 76v. See also Anne Whiteman, 'The church of England, 1542–1837', in *V.C.H. Wilts.*, vol. 3, p. 34.

[82] Cf. Houlbrooke, *Church courts and the people*, pp. 21–4.

[83] For the development of these offices, see R. L. Storey, *Diocesan administration in fifteenth-century England*, 2nd edn, Borthwick papers, 16 (York, 1972).

contemporary complaints that bishops appointed unqualified friends and relatives, it is plain that these requirements were generally met.[84] Most diocesan chancellors were experienced lawyers with a doctorate in civil law: in Salisbury diocese, for example, this was true of Thomas White (1572–90), William Wilkinson (1590–1613), Bartholomew Jessop (1615–20) and Marmaduke Lynne (1620–40).[85] The learning and responsibilities of such men gave them considerable status in local society, and they were frequently active in administrative and judicial work beyond the confines of the church courts. Thus White, Wilkinson and Lynne all served as active justices of the peace for the county of Wiltshire. Formal legal qualifications and administrative abilities did not, of course, necessarily guarantee a satisfied public and were in themselves unlikely to please idealistic puritan critics, who attached greater value to pastoral and spiritual qualities.[86] But many diocesan chancellors do emerge from the records as men of sound commonsense and humane wisdom, familiar with and sensitive to the life of the local communities with which they had to deal. It would be gravely misleading to imagine them as remote and inflexible lawyers and bureaucrats.

The office of archdeacon's official was less prestigious and normally less lucrative than that of diocesan chancellor, and it was hence more difficult to attract highly qualified candidates. Thus two of the officials of the archdeaconry of North Wiltshire in this period – William Watkins, rector of Little Hinton (*c.* 1580–1601), and Henry Hungerford (1613–23) – could boast only the status of master of arts (Hungerford also briefly served as diocesan chancellor from 1613–15, probably as a stopgap measure).[87] However, such men were probably perfectly capable of dealing with the straightforward disciplinary cases and routine administrative matters which formed the bulk of their duties. In any case, in the two Wiltshire archdeaconries over much of the period the issue of the abilities of the official as such did not arise, since the posts were combined with

84 Levack, *Civil lawyers*, pp. 22–4, 63–5, 205–82 *passim*.

85 For the careers of these men, see Levack, *Civil lawyers*, pp. 244, 251, 279; G. D. Squibb, *Doctors' Commons: a history of the College of Advocates and Doctors of Law* (Oxford, 1977), p. 153.

86 See the arguments and counter-arguments marshalled in John Bridges, *A defence of the government established in the church of Englande for ecclesiasticall matters* (1587), p. 1298.

87 Between August 1614 and his resignation in April 1615, Hungerford was joint chancellor with Bartholomew Jessop: see W.R.O., B/ABI 40, fol. 112v; B/ABI 41, fols. 228v–9.

that of diocesan chancellor. This arrangement was to the personal advantage of successive chancellors and in some ways facilitated the administration of justice by minimising conflicts and overlaps between the work of different jurisdictions. As will be seen later, chancellor Wilkinson's acquisition of the post of official to the archdeacon of North Wiltshire in 1601 (he was already official of the Salisbury archdeaconry) made possible a much needed reform of marriage licence administration.[88]

The quality of the legal advice available in the church courts, especially to suitors in party and party actions, was almost as vital to the due administration of justice as the capacity of judges. Such expertise was mainly the responsibility of proctors. (Ecclesiastical advocates, roughly equivalent to barristers and of higher legal status than proctors, were sometimes consulted in writing but rarely practised in person in the local church courts.)[89] The numbers of proctors increased in the sixteenth century, and this has sometimes been seen as a symptom of malaise in the ecclesiastical courts; but in fact the growth was largely dictated by the expansion of court business. In late Elizabethan and early Stuart Salisbury there were usually about three steady practitioners plus a few others who acted more rarely, hardly an excessive number by any standard.[90] At Salisbury, as elsewhere, it was not necessary for proctors to possess a degree; indeed many, including some of the most successful, were simply public notaries who acquired their legal knowledge through apprenticeship to an existing proctor or in the registrar's office.[91] How adequate was the training they received? The canons of 1604 asserted that proctors frequently brought their clients' actions to grief through negligence and ignorance, and tried to establish procedures to remedy the situation. But the background to these complaints was complex, and the allegations of proctorial incapacity certainly cannot be taken at face value.[92] In reality, the great majority of proctors seem to have been skilled, able and assiduous men; the lazy and incompetent simply failed in their profession. Successful

[88] *H.M.C., Calendar of the manuscripts of the Most Hon. the Marquis of Salisbury*, 24 vols. (1883–1976), vol. 11, p. 437. See also below, Chapter 6.
[89] Marchant, *Church under the law*, p. 54. No indications have been found that advocates attended personally in the Salisbury courts.
[90] Cf. Houlbrooke, 'Decline of ecclesiastical jurisdiction', p. 248.
[91] For further details, see Ingram, 'Ecclesiastical justice in Wiltshire', pp. 48–51; Marchant, *Church under the law*, pp. 17–18, 54–5.
[92] Canons 130–1; cf. Marchant, *Church under the law*, pp. 54–7.

and long-established practitioners, like Thomas Shuter at Salisbury (practised 1610–41), could eventually become highly respected men of considerable local reputation. An affectionate letter written shortly after Shuter's death bears witness to his great skill, knowledge and experience, and serves as a further reminder that many of the people who worked in the church courts were neither faceless bureaucrats nor the monsters of puritan propaganda, but dedicated individuals who did their best according to their lights.[93]

Another vital position in the structure of ecclesiastical justice was the office of registrar; indeed, as Rosemary O'Day has emphasised, the post was coming to be of increasing importance in post-Reformation diocesan administration. Registrars were public notaries responsible for registering the court acts, maintaining a variety of other records, producing the multitude of processes and other documents required for the expedition of justice and performing various functions vital to the judicial process, such as the examination of witnesses and the preparation of office prosecutions on the basis of churchwardens' presentments. They were thus in a position to set the courts' administrative tone. Since they invariably employed scribes and deputies, they furthermore exercised a degree of patronage and enjoyed the prestige which went with it. The office was also one of considerable financial responsibility and potential profit. Last but not least, registrars enjoyed opportunities to influence the course of justice, and their favour was often solicited by litigants and by individuals threatened with disciplinary prosecutions.[94]

Registrars normally held life patents, and some were able to strengthen their grip further by securing the reversion of their office to members of their own family. A good example is provided by the situation in Wiltshire, where Thomas Sadler senior and junior dominated the offices of registrar to the bishop of Salisbury and the archdeacon of North Wiltshire from the later part of Elizabeth's reign to the eve of the civil war. Thomas Sadler senior sprang from an armigerous family, was an active justice of the peace, and was knighted in 1623. The position of registrar was thus only one among a number of sources of personal dignity; but it was probably the most important, and at the heralds' visitation in 1623 he recorded

[93] W.R.O., D/AB 41, fol. 126; cf. Marchant, *Church under the law*, p. 50.

[94] Rosemary O'Day, 'The role of the registrar in diocesan administration', in O'Day and Heal (eds.), *Continuity and change*, pp. 77–94. For examples of the registrar's influence on justice, see W.R.O., D/Pres. 1628/11, 26, 50–1.

proudly that he was 'principal registrar of the diocese of Sarum under six bishops'.[95] The registrars of archdeaconries and lesser jurisdictions were naturally of less importance than their diocesan counterparts, but even these held positions of considerable responsibility. The office of registrar thus demanded, and was usually filled by, men of proven administrative ability.

Although the professional qualifications of the personnel associated with the church courts were generally satisfactory, their character and behaviour in other respects sometimes proved an obstacle to the due administration of ecclesiastical justice. Some tactless bishops or their diocesan officials, wading in the murky waters of local faction and power politics (which almost invariably had religious dimensions), fell foul of county gentry interests and urban magistrates. The classic case was that of bishop Richard Curteys of Chichester (1570–82), whose ill-advised attempt to outface religious conservatives among the Sussex gentry discredited him not only locally but also in the eyes of the privy council.[96] But mishaps of this nature were in part symptomatic of the difficult religious and political adjustments which were occurring locally and nationally in the early and middle years of Elizabeth's reign;[97] they were much less in evidence in the more settled conditions of the Jacobean church.[98] And, of course, they did not afflict every diocese. Successive bishops of Salisbury were involved in factional disputes with the city authorities and other interests, but the resulting enmities were hardly sufficient to affect the normal running of diocesan administration and justice.[99]

Another potential problem was strife between bishops and archdeacons and the professional administrators who ran their courts. Chancellors, officials and registrars were hard to dislodge or even to influence, and their tendency to act independently and to resist

[95] G. W. Marshall (ed.), *The visitation of Wiltshire, 1623* (1882), p. 14.

[96] Manning, *Religion and society*, chs. 5–6.

[97] For other more or less serious examples of episcopal embroilment with local interests around this time, see A. Hassell Smith, *County and court: government and politics in Norfolk, 1558–1603* (Oxford, 1974), pp. 210–25; Manning, *Religion and society*, p. 111n.

[98] Collinson, *Religion of protestants*, pp. 78–9; but cf. William J. Sheils, 'Some problems of government in a new diocese: the bishop and the puritans in the diocese of Peterborough, 1560–1630', in O'Day and Heal (eds.), *Continuity and change*, pp. 171–2, 176.

[99] Alison Wall, 'Faction in local politics, 1580–1620: struggles for supremacy in Wiltshire', *Wilts. archaeol. magazine*, 72/3 (1980), pp. 129–30.

episcopal supervision sometimes caused serious conflicts. Again such difficulties seem to have been most in evidence in the first half of Elizabeth's reign, partly because of the administrative incapacity of some of the bishops involved (notably Richard Cheyney of Gloucester and John Parkhurst of Norwich), partly because of religious conservatism among diocesan administrators, which hardly disposed them to embark vigorously on the enforcement of the protestant settlement.[100] Slowly but surely the situation improved as the Elizabethan church became better established. But as late as the 1590s the structure of diocesan justice at Gloucester was seriously disrupted by conflicts between bishop John Bullingham and his chancellor,[101] while even in more peaceful sees there were occasional rumbles of discontent. At Salisbury in 1600, bishop Henry Cotton was in dispute with William Wilkinson over the extent of the chancellor's jurisdiction: the former wanted to retain personal control over institutions to benefices and the licensing of curates in order to oversee the quality of the ministry in the diocese, and had no desire to levy fees for these pastoral functions; but Wilkinson wanted the cash.[102] A more serious conflict occurred in the archdeaconry of Berkshire in 1639, when John Ryves appeared personally in court and refused henceforth to recognise the acts of his official. It is interesting to note, however, that in spite of this disruption the pattern of litigation in the court was unaffected.[103] Accounts of internecine strife between church dignitaries and court administrators make for dramatic and unedifying reading; but the impact on the common run of suitors and defendants should not be exaggerated.

The archdeacon of Berkshire's attempt to dislodge his official centred on the allegation that the latter had failed to arrange for satisfactory substitutes in his absence; and other, similar conflicts were sometimes occasioned, at least partly, by charges of malpractice on the part of episcopal or archidiaconal administrators.[104] Just how serious were problems of venality and other abuses in the ecclesi-

[100] Houlbrooke, *Church courts and the people*, pp. 22–7; Ralph Houlbrooke, 'The protestant episcopate, 1547–1603: the pastoral contribution', in Felicity Heal and Rosemary O'Day (eds.), *Church and society in England: Henry VIII to James I* (1977), pp. 93–4.

[101] Price, 'Bishop Bullingham and chancellor Blackleech', *passim*.

[102] *H.M.C.*, *Salisbury MSS*, vol. 10, pp. 160–2.

[103] Marchant, *Church under the law*, p. 113.

[104] Price, 'Bishop Bullingham and chancellor Blackleech', *passim*; Collinson, *Elizabethan puritan movement*, pp. 450–1.

astical courts? As was emphasised in the introduction, the notorious corruption which existed at Gloucester in the 1570s and to some extent later was certainly atypical. However, any detailed investigation of diocesan archives over an extended period will almost invariably reveal some traces of venality. The contrary would indeed be surprising, for all contemporary courts were venal by modern standards. Some secular judges were involved in major scandals,[105] while the corrupt face of the common law was unpleasantly familiar in the day to day life of local communities. In Wiltshire – and it was much the same in other counties – numerous people were harassed by common informers who extorted cash under threat of commencing prosecutions in the court of exchequer. The sheriff's officers were also a major nuisance: gangs of armed bailiffs operated protection rackets and sometimes terrorised whole villages.[106] This general context of graft and extortion must be constantly borne in mind in assessing evidence of venality in the church courts.

Corruption was (as far as senior personnel are concerned) most likely to be found in the office of the registrar, whose independence and extensive financial transactions provided ample opportunity for venal practices. The conduct of the registrar of the small prebendal court of Highworth, who in 1622 was accused not only of corruption but also of indecent exposure and of appearing drunk in court, was happily not typical;[107] but less spectacular cases of venality did undoubtedly occur. That Thomas Sadler senior, registrar of the bishop of Salisbury and archdeacon of North Wiltshire, was not immune from the attractions of illegal income is known from other sources. In 1626, in his capacity as J.P., he was convicted of corrupt dealings concerning the militia and thereupon censured by the privy council, fined and dismissed from the commission of the peace.[108] Close scrutiny of the court records maintained by Sadler and his son reveals a number of accounting discrepancies and anomalous financial entries which probably represent *douceurs* tendered by offenders to secure freedom from disciplinary prosecutions, unauthorised dismissals or illegal commutations of penance. It must be said, however, that such traces of corruption are faint and the scale of operation was probably not large.[109]

105 White, *Sir Edward Coke*, pp. 53–4; Marchant, *Church under the law*, p. 245.
106 Ingram, 'Communities and courts', pp. 122–5 and the references there cited.
107 W.R.O., D/Pres. 1622/26.
108 Hurstfield, 'County government', p. 86.
109 For fuller details, see Ingram, 'Ecclesiastical justice in Wiltshire', pp. 313–15.

It is highly doubtful whether many judges or proctors indulged in anything which contemporaries would have regarded as serious corruption,[110] though some certainly did and a few were involved in major scandals. Sir John Lambe, chancellor of Peterborough diocese and official and bishop's commissary in the archdeaconry of Leicester, was accused of corrupt practices in the parliament of 1621; but the inhabitants of Northampton who brought these charges were motivated by puritan zeal, and it is by no means certain that he was guilty.[111] William Watkins, official of the archdeaconry of North Wiltshire in the later part of Elizabeth's reign, was undoubtedly venal; the discovery of some of his misdeeds was probably one of the reasons which impelled William Wilkinson, the diocesan chancellor, to secure control of the archdeaconry.[112]

The apparitors or messengers of the courts must have been sorely tempted to take bribes or practise extortion. They were normally men of humble status, some of whom professed trades and perhaps actually combined them with court work to eke out a meagre living.[113] Certainly their official rewards were modest. Yet their work, which involved constant footslogging and sometimes exposed them to odium and abuse, was very arduous.[114] Indeed it tended to become more so as the work of the church courts expanded, since in some areas (including Wiltshire) the numbers of apparitors failed to increase in proportion. It is hence not surprising to find occasional references to corrupt dealings, usually involving small sums of money or such payments in kind as 'a quart of wine'.[115] But it is unlikely that the problem was a really serious one. Apparitors accused of grave irregularities were liable to be dismissed from office, not least because such venality was likely to diminish the legitimate fee income of judges and registrars.[116]

Potentially more serious for the church courts than low-level venality was administrative slackness. The general contention of this

[110] Levack, *Civil lawyers*, pp. 48–9, 71–2; Marchant, *Church under the law*, pp. 59, 245.

[111] Levack, *Civil lawyers*, pp. 48–9; Sheils, 'Problems of government in a new diocese', pp. 176, 185–6.

[112] W.R.O., B/ABO 2, fols. 30v–31, 33.

[113] W.R.O., B/DB 9, fols. 154–5; B/Misc. Ct Papers 29/47 (unfoliated), deposition of Lewis Leonard.

[114] In 1615 several men of Castle Donington (Leicestershire) threatened that they 'would throw Holeborne the apparitor into the Trent' if he came to serve process on them: L.M., 1 D 41/13/40, fols. 27v–28.

[115] W.R.O., B/DB 35, fol. 28.

[116] W.S.R.O., Ep. I/17/21, fol. 77.

chapter has been that by and large the institutions of ecclesiastical justice were well organised and that their senior personnel maintained high professional standards – taking, as Thomas Wilson insisted, 'great pains for small gains'.[117] But the quality of the administrative tradition did vary from diocese to diocese, while at some time or other most courts experienced periods of administrative torpor.[118] The Wiltshire jurisdictions were probably never among the most dynamic or best-organised church courts in England: some of the peculiarities of the Wiltshire records which were commented upon earlier are perhaps a symptom of this.[119] But for much of the period the overall standard was perfectly reasonable and there are only occasional signs of administrative lapses.[120]

In the 1620s and 1630s, however, the administrative tone of the Wiltshire courts does seem to have deteriorated. What was going wrong? It will be shown later that these decades witnessed a marked decline in some important types of business, and this may have contributed to demoralisation among the officers of the courts.[121] But comparison with other dioceses suggests that this was probably not the most important factor: in some areas, perhaps especially those under direct Laudian influence, the 1630s were an administratively dynamic period for the church courts.[122] The malaise at Salisbury seems to have been due primarily to personal factors. Chancellor Lynne appears to have been less assiduous than his Elizabethan and Jacobean predecessors. He employed surrogates far more frequently than had White and Wilkinson, the most frequent substitute being the subdean, Giles Thornborough, who lacked formal legal or other academic qualifications. This probably did not harm the interests of individual suitors, since Lynne was invariably in court to bring causes to final sentence and to deal with other

117 Quoted in Marchant, *Church under the law*, p. 31

118 Marchant, *Church under the law*, *passim*; Houlbrooke, *Church courts and the people*, pp. 265–6 and *passim*.

119 See above, pp. 22–3.

120 For example, W.R.O., B/DB 9, fols. 157v–8 (irregularities in taking depositions); B/ABI 35, fol. 125 (order forbidding proctors to examine clients judicially).

121 See below, Chapter 12.

122 Marchant, *Church under the law*, pp. 195–203, 230–4; Brinkworth, 'Laudian church in Buckinghamshire'; Martin D. W. Jones, 'The ecclesiastical courts before and after the civil war: the office jurisdiction in the dioceses of Oxford and Peterborough, 1630–1675' (University of Oxford B. Litt. thesis, 1977), pp. 27–8, 235. My sampling of the records of the archdeaconry of Leicester indicates a marked expansion of business in the 1630s.

Table 2 *Scope of ecclesiastical justice in Elizabethan Wiltshire*

(*a*) *Instance and promoted office causes in the Salisbury consistory court, 1566*

Tithe	20	Testamentary	18
Clerical dues	1	Promoted office	8
Defamation	23	Miscellaneous	2
Matrimonial	5	Unidentified	10
		Total	*87*

(*b*) *Presentments arising from the episcopal visitation, 1585*

Church repairs/supplies: responsibility of churchwardens	51	
Church repairs/supplies: responsibility of clergy	32	
Church repairs/supplies: responsibility of specified laymen	41	
Faults of clergy (other than sexual immorality)	54	
Faults of parish clerks	1	
Faults of schoolmasters	2	
Unlicensed midwives/physicians	0	
Churchwardens failing to account	4	
Withholding church dues/stock	42	
Abuse of ministers	2	
Misbehaviour in church/churchyard	9	
Catholic recusancy (specified or implied)	17	
Neglect of church attendance	46	
Not receiving holy communion	101	
Working on Sundays/holidays	6	
Playing unlawful games	0	
Drinking, etc., in service time	3	
Drunkenness/cursing	1	
Scolding/defamation	6	
Witchcraft/sorcery	7	
Usury	1	
Matters concerning probate and administration	8	
Standing excommunicate	22	
Miscellaneous	16	
Prenuptial fornication	9	(5)
Bastardy/illicit pregnancy	113	(71)
Other sexual immorality	62	(39)
Harbouring pregnant woman, etc.	7	(7)
Bigamy	5	(2)
Clandestine marriage/matters concerning contract	12	(7)
Unlawful separation	6	(5)
Total	*686*	

Note: The main series of figures under (*b*) refers to accused *persons* (except that churchwardens are counted as one). Bracketed figures refer to the number of separate *cases* (characteristically but not invariably involving two specified persons) in matters concerning marriage and sexual immorality.

important matters; but his frequent absences probably encouraged administrative slackness. The registrars in this period also seem to have been more easy-going than was the case earlier, while the proctorial body badly needed an injection of new blood. Bishop Davenant, out of favour at court and frustrated by the growing influence of the Laudians in the English church, apparently did little to stop the rot.[123] Unmindful of the disaster which was shortly to overtake the ecclesiastical jurisdiction, the Salisbury church court establishment slid into somnolence. There were signs of an impending shake-up in 1640, when Thomas Hyde replaced Marmaduke Lynne as chancellor of the diocese, but it came too late to have much noticeable effect.[124]

Yet it would be a mistake to exaggerate these difficulties, or to let them obscure the fact that for most of the period church court business, at Salisbury as elsewhere, was expanding or buoyant. In the Salisbury consistory court in 1566 there were fewer than 90 instance and promoted office causes. By 1615 there were over 150, and even in the year from April 1640, on the very eve of the courts' temporary abolition, over 130 suits were commenced.[125] Disciplinary prosecutions increased too. In 1573 some 220 office cases came before the court of the archdeaconry of Salisbury; in 1603 there were over 450.[126]

Table 2 illustrates the range of court business around the middle years of Elizabeth's reign. Matters concerning tithe, testaments and defamation predominated among party and party suits, but marriage cases occupied a significant place too. As regards disciplinary work, much of the courts' time was occupied with matters concerning the upkeep of churches and the enforcement of religious conformity among clergy and lay people; but the large numbers of prosecutions for sexual immorality and offences connected with matrimony fully explain why these tribunals were colloquially known as the 'bawdy courts'. Though the pattern of prosecutions was to change somewhat over the period 1570–1640, this overall configuration largely persisted. It is plain that potentially the ecclesiastical courts could play a highly important social role. Just how well did they perform in practice?

123 For further details, see Ingram, 'Ecclesiastical justice in Wiltshire', pp. 42–5.

124 W.R.O., B/ABI 54, fols. 63v–4. On Hyde's career, see Levack, *Civil lawyers*, p. 242.

125 Based on analysis of W.R.O., B/ABI 3, 41–2, 54; B/Citations 5.

126 Based on analysis of W.R.O., AS/ABO 1a, 8.

2. *Economic and social structures*

The institutions of ecclesiastical justice described in the previous chapter were perhaps best suited to serve a society made up of small-scale, static communities unified by strong bonds of moral and religious sentiment. But English society had of course never been quite like that, and it was made less so by the multifarious economic and religious changes of the sixteenth and early seventeenth centuries.[1] Yet if social and mental structures set firm boundaries on what the church courts could hope to achieve, there none the less remained ample areas in which they could perform a valuable function; and it is arguable that some of the changes of the period 1570–1640 actually worked in the church courts' favour or, at least, offered them new opportunities. This and the succeeding chapter explore the social background with particular reference to economic and social structures and to religious beliefs and observances, and, since the nature of the church courts' work gave them some chance of influencing the latter, offer some preliminary insights into how the courts performed in practice. The survey outlines the situation in England as a whole but focuses more especially on conditions in the county of Wiltshire and illustrates the variety of experience at the very local level by reference to the sample parishes of Wylye and Keevil.

The church courts worked in a complex social and economic environment. In mid-Elizabethan England commercial agriculture was already highly developed, there was a relatively sophisticated

[1] The literature on the economic and social changes of the period is vast, and the references which follow are necessarily highly selective. Valuable introductions are provided by L. A. Clarkson, *The pre-industrial economy in England, 1500–1750* (1971); D. C. Coleman, *The economy of England, 1450–1750* (Oxford, 1977); Keith Wrightson, *English society, 1580–1680* (1982). For a stimulating though controversial view of the nature of medieval English society, see Alan Macfarlane, *The origins of English individualism: the family, property and social transition* (Oxford, 1978).

marketing system, and the metropolis and other, smaller urban centres exerted considerable influence on the economy. Although the majority of the population were engaged in agriculture, industrial activities were also an important generator of wealth, especially the woollen cloth industry which in the middle ages had spread from the confines of the towns to many rural areas in many parts of England. There was in addition a lively internal trade in foodstuffs, industrial raw materials and other products, and an active overseas trade based on the export of woollen cloth.[2]

Both in town and country social differentiation and economic inequalities were very marked. The aristocracy and gentry, forming a tiny proportion of the total population, played a dominant social role, though in the main urban centres small groups of rich merchants and financiers rivalled them in wealth if not in status. Below them in the social hierarchy came a broader group of substantial yeomen, husbandmen, craftsmen and traders. These solid householders formed the backbone of society and, especially in rural areas, dominated the social life of many communities. The less fortunate among them merged imperceptibly into the ranks which formed the bottom half of the social pyramid: poor cottagers, day-labourers, and the really indigent.[3]

Although contemporaries conceived society in terms of a stratified hierarchy, there was in fact a significant amount of social mobility. The most prosperous yeoman and trading families might eventually aspire to at least minor gentry status, and most villages experienced the phenomenon of thrusting families struggling towards titles of honour – if only the respectful courtesy of 'master' or 'mistress' in place of the homely appellations of 'goodman' and 'neighbour' – and jostling with their peers for prestige and precedence. On the other hand, unsuccessful or cadet scions of gentry families often sank into the ranks beneath them, while a similar process of downward drift was repeated with infinite variations in the middling and lower echelons of society.[4]

Geographical mobility was another marked social feature. The

[2] For a conspectus (with extensive bibliography), see D. M. Palliser, *The age of Elizabeth: England under the later Tudors, 1547–1603* (1983). For further information, see especially Joan Thirsk (ed.), *The agrarian history of England and Wales, IV: 1500–1640* (Cambridge, 1967).

[3] Wrightson, *English society*, ch. 1; Palliser, *Age of Elizabeth*, ch. 3; Laslett, *World we have lost further explored*, ch. 2.

[4] Wrightson, *English society*, pp. 26–38; Palliser, *Age of Elizabeth*, pp. 83–94.

old idea that people in Tudor and Stuart England lived their lives from birth to death within the confines of one small village or town has been exposed as a myth. Even the wealthier groups often migrated, often to acquire better farms or businesses elsewhere, and there was even greater movement among the poorer ranks of landless labourers and artisans.[5] Moreover, for virtually all ranks of society there was a particular period in the life-cycle when migration was especially likely. This was the time of adolescence and early adulthood, from the early teens to the mid-twenties, when many young people left their families to become apprentices or living-in farm-workers or domestic servants. Such servants were customarily hired by the year, and at the end of their term of contract often migrated to another parish: the existence of this sizeable and shifting group formed one of the most prominent features of the social structure.[6] Only vagrants, including gypsies, minstrels, professional beggars, and numerous labourers and artisans forced out of a settled existence by economic adversity, were as a group even more mobile. Defined by their itinerancy, which deprived them of such vestiges of status as even the poorest householders could claim, they tramped the major routeways between London and other urban centres, often covering large distances in their search for an honest or dishonest living.[7]

Economic changes in the late sixteenth and early seventeenth centuries modified and in some respects accentuated these patterns. The basic engine of change was demographic. Over the period 1500–1700 the population of England roughly doubled (albeit from the low base of about 2.5 millions), the most intense phase of expansion occurring in the years *c*. 1560–*c*. 1630.[8] Associated with this demographic increase was a marked rise in prices. Between about 1500 and 1640 the price of foodstuffs increased nearly sevenfold; industrial prices were more sluggish, but even they increased threefold.[9] This inflation was largely the result of the failure of

[5] Wrightson, *English society*, pp. 41–4.

[6] Ann Kussmaul, *Servants in husbandry in early modern England* (Cambridge, 1981).

[7] Peter Clark, 'The migrant in Kentish towns, 1580–1640', in Peter Clark and Paul Slack (eds.), *Crisis and order in English towns, 1500–1700* (1972), pp. 117–63; A. L. Beier, 'Vagrants and the social order in Elizabethan England', *Past and present*, no. 64 (Aug. 1974), pp. 3–29; Paul Slack, 'Vagrants and vagrancy in England, 1598–1664', *Econ. hist. rev.*, 2nd ser., 27 (1974), pp. 360–79.

[8] E. A. Wrigley and R. S. Schofield, *The population history of England, 1541–1871: a reconstruction* (1981), p. 528.

[9] R. B. Outhwaite, *Inflation in Tudor and early Stuart England*, 2nd edn (1982), pp. 11–17.

production to keep pace with rising demand. Yet the productive response was by no means negligible. High food prices stimulated improvements in agricultural output and in the marketing system.[10] There was also some industrial development, though the pattern of change was complex and some new growths, such as the 'new draperies', were counterbalanced by dislocation and decline in the old-established broadcloth industry.[11]

The costs and benefits of these economic shifts were not shared equally among the population and entailed a degree of social structural change. In general, the rich became richer while the plight of the poor worsened and their numbers increased. Farmers who owned or rented substantial amounts of land could increase production and benefit from high prices. The wealthier yeomen and husbandmen thus tended to do well, and in some areas their standard of living improved markedly.[12] The increasing prosperity of these groups also produced some spin-off effects. The land market, already very active since the massive disposals of church lands at the Reformation, was further quickened, a development which probably increased spatial mobility and facilitated movement up the social scale. The material improvements experienced by the wealthiest village families also tended to sharpen their social aspirations, and rivalry between parish notables probably increased.[13]

Meanwhile the poorer sections of society were struggling to make ends meet. Small farmers often became vulnerable, and some were eventually forced to sell out.[14] People who were largely or wholly dependent on wages, including both agricultural labourers and industrial artisans, became worse off as wage-rates declined in real terms; moreover, unemployment and underemployment increased as population expansion outran economic growth.[15] The result was

[10] Thirsk (ed.), *Agrarian history IV*, *passim*.

[11] D. C. Coleman, *Industry in Tudor and Stuart England* (1975); B. E. Supple, *Commercial crisis and change in England, 1600–1642* (Cambridge, 1959).

[12] Thirsk (ed.), *Agrarian history IV*, pp. 301–6; Joan Thirsk, 'Seventeenth-century agriculture and social change', *Agric. hist. rev.*, 18, supplement (1970), pp. 148–77.

[13] Sir John Habakkuk, 'The rise and fall of English landed families, 1600–1800, III: Did the gentry rise?', *Trans. Roy. Hist. Soc.*, 5th ser., 31 (1981), pp. 195–217; Wrightson and Levine, *Poverty and piety*, pp. 103–9, 122–5.

[14] Thirsk, 'Seventeenth-century agriculture and social change', pp. 156–7; Margaret Spufford, *Contrasting communities: English villagers in the sixteenth and seventeenth centuries* (Cambridge, 1974), chs. 3–4.

[15] E. H. Phelps Brown and S. V. Hopkins, 'Seven centuries of the prices of consumables, compared with builders' wage-rates', *Economica*, new ser., 23 (1956), pp. 299–302, 305–6; but cf. Donald Woodward, 'Wages rates and living standards

an alarming increase in the problems of poverty and vagrancy, especially in densely settled regions, in areas affected by industrial decline and in many towns.[16] Harvest failures and commercial dislocations periodically magnified the scale of misery and pushed large numbers of poor people from the brink of bare subsistence into the chasm of real want. The worst of these episodes of distress were the late 1590s, when a run of disastrous harvests led to an upsurge of mortality in many areas, and the crisis of the early to mid-1620s, when the miseries of adverse harvest conditions, industrial contraction and trade slump were capped by a visitation of plague in 1625.[17]

Regionally, the impact of these general trends varied according to local differences of economic and social structure. The Wiltshire portion of the diocese of Salisbury provides a particularly good case study, both because the area included regions of diverse economic structure, and because in some parts of the county the social stresses induced by economic change were particularly marked. In broad terms Wiltshire may be divided into two contrasting regions, the 'chalk' and the 'cheese'. The chalklands, covering much of the southern and eastern parts of the county, together with the Cotswold strip in the far north-west and a narrow Corallian limestone ridge between them, supported a sheep and corn husbandry which favoured large farms and capitalist farming systems. In these areas, most of the land still lay in open fields, and manorial organisation generally remained strong. In contrast, in the claylands, which covered much of the north-western parts of the county, dairy farming predominated. In this region much land had been enclosed, numerous manors had been broken up or had declined into insignificance, and the majority of farms were family concerns (Map 2).[18]

Wiltshire was also noted for its industrial activities, especially the

in pre-industrial England', *Past and present*, no. 91 (May 1981), pp. 28–46. See also D. C. Coleman, 'Labour in the English economy of the seventeenth century', *Econ. hist. rev.*, 2nd ser., 8 (1955–6), pp. 280–95.

16 John F. Pound, *Poverty and vagrancy in Tudor England* (1971); A. L. Beier, *The problem of the poor in Tudor and early Stuart England* (1983); and the references cited above, n. 7.

17 Andrew B. Appleby, *Famine in Tudor and Stuart England* (Liverpool, 1978), ch. 9 and *passim*; Thirsk (ed.), *Agrarian history IV*, pp. 631–3; Supple, *Commercial crisis and change*, chs. 3–5.

18 Eric Kerridge, 'Agriculture, c. 1500–c. 1793', in *V.C.H. Wilts.*, vol. 4, pp. 43–64.

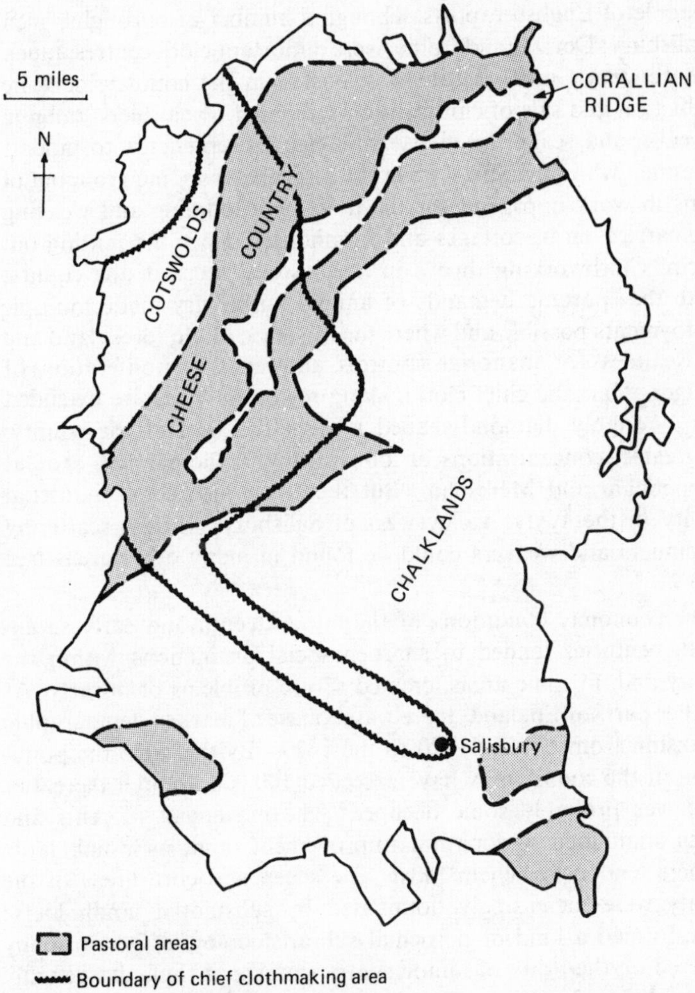

Map 2 Economic regions in Elizabethan and early Stuart Wiltshire. (This map combines information from two published maps: G. D. Ramsay, *The Wiltshire woollen industry in the sixteenth and seventeenth centuries* (1943), frontispiece, and E. Kerridge, 'Agriculture c. 1500–c. 1793', in *The Victoria County History: Wiltshire*, vol. 4 (1959), p. 43.)

production of the heavy 'white' (undyed) broadcloths which formed the staple of English exports. Though a number of boroughs, such as Salisbury, Devizes and Calne, were important cloth centres, much of the county's manufacture was located in the countryside. The production and sale of cloth was co-ordinated by clothiers, ranging in wealth and scale of activity from rich entrepreneurs to modest tradesmen who themselves wove cloth. There was some grouping of looms in workshops, but for the most part spinning and weaving were carried on in cottages and farmhouses under the putting-out system. Clothworking throve in the pastoral areas of the county, where the sporadic demands of animal husbandry made multiple employments possible and where the existence of old forest land and the weakness of manorial controls allowed the proliferation of cottages. Thus the chief clothmaking region of Wiltshire extended over a roughly diamond-shaped area in the west of the county, the greatest concentrations of looms being in the parishes around Chippenham and Melksham. But there was also some industrial activity in the Wylye valley west of Salisbury, while a scattering of spinners and weavers could be found in many other areas (see Map 2).[19]

The economic conditions of the late sixteenth and early seventeenth centuries tended to sharpen social distinctions within the county and, in some areas, created severe problems of poverty. As in other parts of England, there was a phase of marked demographic expansion from around 1570 to the 1620s. By this time the population of the county may have exceeded 100,000, though thereafter there was probably some decline.[20] The movement of rents and prices stimulated agricultural improvement, and, as usual, large farmers tended to benefit most. The sheep and corn areas of the county were increasingly dominated by substantial landholders; these formed a kind of parochial sub-aristocracy, of whom many hovered on the brink of minor gentry status and some did actually assume titles of courtesy. Family and part-time farmers, who had up to the early sixteenth century formed a numerous class occupying perhaps half the farmland, tended gradually to get squeezed out. By the mid-seventeenth century they probably made up less than 50 per

19 G. D. Ramsay, *The Wiltshire woollen industry in the sixteenth and seventeenth centuries*, 2nd edn (1965), chs. 1–2.

20 David Underdown, 'The problem of popular allegiance in the English civil war', *Trans. Roy. Hist. Soc.*, 5th ser., 31 (1981), pp. 78, 93–4; C. C. Taylor, 'Population studies in seventeenth- and eighteenth-century Wiltshire', *Wilts. archaeol. magazine*, 60 (1965), pp. 100–8.

cent of the farming population in these areas and worked only a third of the land. On the other hand, landless or virtually landless wage-labourers increased in numbers and comprised up to half the working population in the sheep and corn lands by 1640. With the value of wages cut by inflation, the economic condition of these farm labourers was hardly affluent, but except in times of severe dearth they could probably subsist adequately. In many parishes, moreover, the wealthier inhabitants took active steps to minimise the numbers of poor people by imposing restrictions on immigration and settlement, while the plight of native paupers was mitigated by poor relief schemes and charitable bequests. Thus the sheep and corn areas of Wiltshire remained relatively stable during the economic vicissitudes of this period. Social and economic differentiation increased gradually within a conservative ethos.[21]

In the pastoral regions of the county and in the clothing towns the process of social structural change was rather different and more unstable. Although there was some engrossment and consolidation of holdings in the cheese country (accompanied, as usual, by the increasing prominence of wealthy sub-gentry families in parish society), small farms continued to be economically viable and indeed proliferated, especially in the clothing areas, where agriculture could be combined with industrial work. Clothmaking also attracted the landless and near-landless, and thus the clothing regions became densely populated in the later sixteenth century, as also did towns like Chippenham, Calne and Salisbury. Although industrial wages did not keep pace with inflation – it was asserted in 1613 that wage-rates had not increased in the previous forty years though prices had doubled – the small farmers, cottagers and urban artisans who depended heavily on spinning and weaving could make an adequate living so long as harvests were reasonable and the cloth trade remained healthy.[22] However, the period 1580–1640 witnessed a long-term decline in demand for broadcloths, punctuated by a series of short-term dislocations which alternated or coincided with harvest failures and other natural disasters.

The export trade in woollen cloth had already been much disrupted during the third quarter of the sixteenth century. Conditions improved in the period 1575–1600, though the benefits were offset by

[21] Kerridge, 'Agriculture', pp. 55–61, 64.

[22] *Ibid.*, pp. 45–6, 49, 55, 58–9, 64; Ramsay, *Wiltshire woollen industry*, pp. 2–5, 15–17, 63; Paul Slack, 'Poverty and politics in Salisbury, 1597–1666', in Clark and Slack (eds.), *Crisis and order*, pp. 164–203.

the poor harvest of 1586 and the great dearth of 1595–7. But there are indications that the Wiltshire cloth industry was again under pressure at the beginning of the new century, and distress was increased by plague in 1603–4. The ravages of this disease, coming on top of the mortality of the late 1590s, probably reduced the numbers of the poor; and the survivors were able to benefit from the prosperity which the cloth industry enjoyed for much of the ensuing decade. But the cycle of industrial dislocation and bad harvests began again after 1614, and serious distress ensued in the early 1620s. With export markets disrupted by the Thirty Years War, there was widespread unemployment in the clothing areas, while a poor harvest in 1622 aggravated its effects. Chronic industrial depression followed, punctuated by years of particular difficulty in 1625, 1631 and 1635.[23]

Meanwhile some of the poorer inhabitants of the clothing regions had suffered another form of economic disaster as a result of the disafforestation and enclosure of the old royal forests of Blackmore, Pewsham, Selwood and Braydon. The process had begun in 1612 and gathered momentum in the 1620s and 1630s. The upshot was extensive rioting, which won the commoners slight concessions but failed to halt the disafforestation programme as a whole. Earlier there had been food riots in the clothing areas in 1595, 1614 and 1622.[24] Less spectacular forms of crime were another symptom of social distress. The dearth year of 1623 was marked by a striking upsurge of theft prosecutions in the county quarter sessions; and indeed the annual average of theft cases in the remaining four years of the quinquennium 1620–4 was significantly higher than in preceding years.[25] All these disorders reflected the chronic and worsening poverty which characterised much of north-west Wiltshire in this period.

The parishes of Wylye and Keevil illustrate some of the local variations in these patterns. Wylye, a small parish with between 200 and 250 inhabitants by 1640, was situated in south Wiltshire about ten miles north-west of Salisbury.[26] Its economy was based mainly

23 Ramsay, *Wiltshire woollen industry*, chs. 5–6; Supple, *Commercial crisis and change*, *passim*; Slack, 'Poverty and politics', *passim*.

24 Buchanan Sharp, *In contempt of all authority: rural artisans and riot in the west of England, 1586–1660* (Berkeley, Calif., 1980), pp. 18, 23–4, 82–174 *passim*.

25 Ingram, 'Communities and courts', p. 112.

26 The history of Wylye has been reconstructed by collating all readily available records (listed in the Bibliography) for the period 1570–1640.

on sheep and corn husbandry. But there was some clothmaking in the parish, and its location on the confluence of the highways to Salisbury from Taunton and Exeter (via Mere) and from Bristol and Bath (via Warminster) gave the village some importance as a victualling centre: the community boasted an inn, several licensed and unlicensed alehouses, and a number of butchers. Hence the social structure of this village was somewhat different from the purely agricultural communities characteristic of the chalklands of south and east Wiltshire, primarily in that householders of middling rank were more prominent and the occupational pattern more diverse.

These and other features emerge from an analysis of information contained in the exceptionally detailed parish registers.[27] About 10 per cent of the male inhabitants were of gentle or yeoman status. There was in fact no established gentry family regularly resident in the parish; but John Potticarie, who was both a clothier and proprietor of the village inn, was eventually wealthy enough to style himself 'gentleman'.[28] Some of the Wylye yeomen rivalled him in wealth. They farmed substantial holdings, and were sufficiently interested in agricultural improvement to participate in a scheme to float the watermeadows in 1632.[29] A further 30 per cent of Wylye householders were medium to small farmers, designated 'husbandman' (*agricola*) in the registers; while nearly as numerous were a variety of craftsmen and tradesmen of modest wealth. The poorer inhabitants, mostly described as 'labourer' (*operarius*), made up the remaining 30 per cent: a broad band of 'poor folks', 'poor householder[s]...that soweth no corn', whose bare living from wage labour was occasionally supplemented by pious bequests of corn or cash from the wealthier inhabitants and by parochial relief.[30]

The population experienced distress and high mortality during the exceptionally acute dearths of 1595–7 and suffered even more severely as a result of plague in 1603–4.[31] But these disasters were succeeded by two decades of greater stability, which probably muted

[27] G. R. Hadow (ed.), *The registers of the parish of Wylye in the county of Wilts.* (Devizes, 1913).

[28] Hadow (ed.), *Wylye registers*, p. 28.

[29] Eric Kerridge (ed.), *Surveys of the manors of Philip, first earl of Pembroke and Montgomery, 1631–2*, Wilts. Archaeol. and Natural History Soc.: Records Branch, 9 (Devizes, 1953), pp. 138–40.

[30] W.R.O., Archdeaconry court of Salisbury probate records, wills of Katherine Crouche, 24/11/1581, Richard Barnes, 15/11/1595.

[31] The heavy mortality of 1603–4 is specifically ascribed to 'pestilence': Hadow (ed.), *Wylye registers*, p. 39.

tensions between rich and poor and perhaps limited conflicts within the middling to upper ranks: at any rate serious interpersonal disputes springing primarily from economic factors were apparently few.[32] By the 1620s and 1630s, however, the population was again expanding quite rapidly; and even a small, predominantly agricultural village like this felt the strains of increasing poverty.

Economic and demographic changes had even more impact on Keevil, a larger village with over 700 inhabitants by the early seventeenth century.[33] The parish lay in west central Wiltshire, a few miles from the market towns of Westbury, Bradford and Melksham but slightly off the beaten track,[34] and apart from Keevil village itself contained a number of lesser settlements, notably the hamlet of Bulkington, which was the centre of a separate tithing.[35] Located partly on the clay and partly on the Corallian limestone ridge, the parish supported a form of mixed husbandry in which dairying played a significant role; and the agriculture of the community was still supervised by a number of manorial jurisdictions, of which the manor of Keevil cum Bulkington was the largest and most active. But the situation of the parish in the broadcloth-producing area of Wiltshire provided opportunities for industrial employments and by-employments. Though clothing was not as prominent as in some highly industrialised villages like the neighbouring parish of Seend, in Elizabethan Keevil the spinning, weaving and marketing of woollen cloth were probably as important as agriculture as generators of wealth.

A newly established gentry family, the Lamberts, maintained a manor house in Keevil but usually resided elsewhere, while a minor gentleman (owner of one of the lesser manors) lived in Bulkington during much of the period. But the day to day life of the parish was largely dominated by a small group of wealthy yeoman and clothier families (the latter tending over time to reduce their involvement in industry and concentrate on farming). These people did well in the economic conditions of the later sixteenth and the seventeenth

[32] For other types of tension, see below, pp. 120–3.

[33] On the history of Keevil and the sources available for its reconstruction, see K. H. Rogers, 'Keevil', in *V.C.H. Wilts.*, vol. 8, pp. 250–63; Ingram, 'Religion, communities and moral discipline', pp. 184–93.

[34] The major road from Trowbridge to Devizes ran for a short distance through the north of the parish but not through the village itself.

[35] A 'tithing' was an administrative subdivision of a parish in which public order was primarily the responsibility of an elected 'tithingman'.

centuries, consolidating and extending their wealth and aspiring, in some cases, to gentry status. Below them in rank were constellations of substantial and less substantial husbandman and craftsman families. Together these middling to upper echelons comprised perhaps half the population of the village. The remainder had little or no land, but while the cloth trade remained buoyant they could rely on spinning and weaving as a source of income. Families at this level were of variable wealth, but many were clearly close to the margins of subsistence. Their situation was particularly precarious because the family farm system of the region limited opportunities for agricultural wagework: until the very end of this period few people in the village were specifically designated 'day-labourer'.

Rapid population expansion in the reign of Elizabeth was checked by a violent upsurge of mortality after the bad harvests of 1595–7. However the population increased again in the buoyant industrial circumstances and more favourable harvest conditions of the decade after 1604. In these years there was an influx of immigrants, and cottages and subtenancies were allowed to proliferate. The decline of the cloth industry after 1614 – chronic, irreparable, and aggravated by bad harvests in the 1620s – changed the social structure more decisively. The economy of the parish came to rely increasingly on agriculture, and a more pronounced divide developed between a group of relatively solid (though unequally wealthy) families with sufficient land to weather economic vicissitudes and the impoverished ranks of the landless or near-landless. In the difficult years of the 1620s the problem of poverty was evidently acute: in 1625 it was said that 'a great company of poor impotent people' were living in barns and outhouses in the parish.[36]

Socio-economic conditions in Keevil generated more conflict than in Wylye. The tensions were of two main types, springing respectively from vertical and horizontal social divisions. In the first place there was fierce rivalry among some of the major sub-gentry families, leading to protracted disputes and tensions over land, status and prestige. Such quarrels, especially those between the families of Jones and Blagden, were particularly intense in the first three decades of the seventeenth century and amounted almost to sporadic feuding; inevitably they came to involve individuals from lower down the social scale who were bound to the main protagonists by ties of kinship or economic interest. The second form of conflict was grow-

[36] W.R.O., QS/GR East. 1625/139.

ing tension between the wealthier inhabitants and the mass of the poor. In some ways the more substantial parishioners responded positively to the problem of poverty, providing relief through charitable bequests and the operation of the poor laws. In 1625 the parish even mooted a scheme to erect an almshouse (as was actually done in the clothing village of Bromham and other places).[37] The harder face of charity was revealed – sporadically in the first two decades of the seventeenth century, and more forcefully and consistently in the 1620s – in efforts to prevent the building of cottages without adequate land, to restrict subtenancies, to close the parish to immigrants and to encourage the poor to seek work elsewhere. Moreover, there are signs of diminishing tolerance towards the customary rights of the poor, such as gleaning, and of a harsher attitude to petty theft.[38] Less favourable economic circumstances encouraged a harsher regime of social control.

The socio-economic developments of the period 1570–1640, as they played themselves out at the national, regional and local levels, are important in understanding the problems faced by and the opportunities open to the ecclesiastical courts. Their implications will be teased out in detail in later chapters, but some preliminary comments are possible here. In so far as England was becoming economically and socially more complex, the problems of administering ecclesiastical justice may have increased. More basically, the church courts were faced with the challenge of policing a considerably enlarged population; while the fact that it was the poorer and more mobile sectors of society that expanded most in all probability made the task of enforcing discipline yet more formidable. On the other hand, social changes created opportunities for the church courts, as they did also for other legal institutions. The quarrels and disputes which were so notable a feature of parishes like Keevil helped to nourish the expansion of litigation in this period. One of the ways in which the church courts were affected was in the growing numbers of defamation suits, which were often intimately bound up with quarrels between neighbours and

[37] *Ibid.* See also Rogers, 'Keevil', p. 263; W. R. Powell and Elizabeth Crittall, 'Bromham', in *V.C.H. Wilts.*, vol. 7, p. 186.

[38] W.R.O., 288/1, view of frankpledge, 29 Sept. 21 Jac. (1623) (orders against keeping subtenants and inmates, survey of undertenancies and cottages, order against the gathering of bean stubs on pain of stocking, etc.); QS/GR Hil. 1639/12, 128, 188, 208 (theft prosecution indicating a conflict between customary rights and strict property rights).

parochial rivalries.[39] Further, the disciplinary work of the courts was given an enhanced social significance by the economic dislocations and growing problems of poverty which afflicted so many parishes in this period. The secular and ecclesiastical authorities were extremely sensitive to the potential threat to social order entailed in these developments, and they saw the closer regulation of society by legal institutions as an important means of combating the danger. Such ideas undoubtedly struck a chord among at least some sections of the society at large. The middling groups in the parishes, who mainly bore the burden of poor relief, and who viewed with concern for themselves and for society in general the untoward effects of increasing poverty, were characteristically the people who filled local offices such as that of constable, tithingman, leet juror, overseer of the poor – and churchwarden; and in these roles it was natural that they should look to the secular and ecclesiastical courts for aid in combating the problems of poverty and the crimes and vices which they associated with it.[40] They thus resorted to local manor courts and the county quarter sessions to regulate cottage building and immigration into parishes, and to punish crimes like petty theft. As will be seen, economic concerns likewise sharpened moral sentiments and encouraged churchwardens – especially in areas where economic pressures were greatest – to co-operate with the ecclesiastical courts in the punishment of sexual immorality and the regulation of marriage entry.

[39] See below, Chapter 10.
[40] See above, pp. 29–31.

3. *Religion and the people*

Much of the discussion so far has stressed similarities of role between the church courts and other contemporary legal institutions. In contrast to other courts, however, the ecclesiastical tribunals were uniquely dependent on spiritual sanctions, and hence on the state of religious feeling within the country and the degree of religious uniformity. It hardly needs emphasising that in the long term the religious changes of the sixteenth and seventeenth centuries did seriously undermine the structures of ecclesiastical justice. The process of the Reformation, interrupted by the Marian reversion to catholicism, shattered religious unity and burdened the church courts with the exceedingly difficult task of trying to maintain conformity amid the drastic and inconsistent shifts of government policy. In the reign of Charles I, Laudian policies and Calvinist reactions to them created fresh disunity; while the temporary abolition of the institutions of ecclesiastical justice in the period 1641–60, the emergence of protestant nonconformity on a substantial scale in the mid- to late seventeenth century, and ultimately the passage of the toleration act in 1689, in the long run crippled many aspects of the church courts' work. However, from the perspective of the period from the 1570s to the 1630s the picture appears very different. In these years the church of England proved remarkably successful in containing both catholicism and protestant sectarianism and in firmly establishing the protestant state church. The main problem facing churchmen was lax religious observance, or even religious indifference, among some sections of the population; but even on this front some progress was made in raising standards, and in any case the problem was probably not as great as some historians have suggested. The ecclesiastical courts played a major role in these processes and benefited from them to the extent that, at least from the last years of Elizabeth to the early years of Charles I's reign, they were operating within a much more stable religious environment.

The ecclesiastical courts worked on the assumption that the English church embraced the whole of the population, but adherents of the catholic faith implicitly rejected this notion. Catholic survivalism was stiffened from the 1570s by the activities of missionary priests from the continent; correspondingly, the government took more active steps to combat recusancy by means of a legal campaign waged by both the secular and the ecclesiastical courts.[1] It is often said that the latter were ineffective in dealing with recusancy. This is true in the sense that committed catholics consistently refused to obey the summons of the church courts, which could therefore do no more than keep them in a permanent state of excommunication. Yet this in itself may have served a valuable function in keeping the recusant population under pressure and discouraging expansion. Moreover the church courts, by means of parochial presentments, were often more efficient in detecting and identifying recusants than were county quarter sessions and other secular tribunals, which generally relied on presentments made on a hundredal basis; and information gathered by the ecclesiastical courts was used as the basis for action by the secular authorities.[2] Even the latter, however, could not totally eradicate recusancy; and indeed the catholic community experienced modest growth in the early seventeenth century. But as a proportion of the total population the numbers of converts were insignificant: the government was successful in containing catholicism to a tiny and embattled minority.[3]

Geographically, catholic recusancy was a patchy phenomenon. The areas of greatest recusant strength were in the north of England, but there were sizeable catholic populations in some regions of the south, including parts of West Sussex. Wiltshire (and the same could be said of Leicestershire and the diocese of Ely) was more typical of the situation in Canterbury province. Legal records are not a wholly satisfactory guide to catholic strength in the area, but they are

[1] For a brief survey of government policy, see Penry Williams, *The Tudor regime* (Oxford, 1979), pp. 264–92. On the development of the catholic community, see John Bossy, *The English catholic community, 1570–1850* (1975), pts 1–2; but cf. Christopher Haigh, 'The continuity of catholicism in the English Reformation', *Past and present*, no. 93 (Nov. 1981), pp. 37–69; Christopher Haigh, 'From monopoly to minority: catholicism in early modern England', *Trans. Roy. Hist. Soc.*, 5th ser., 31 (1981), pp. 129–47; Patrick McGrath, 'Elizabethan catholicism: a reconsideration', *Jl ecclesiastical history*, 35 (1984), pp. 414–28.

[2] For example, see Anthony G. Petti (ed.), *Recusant documents from the Ellesmere manuscripts*, Catholic Record Soc., 60 (1968), pp. 102–44.

[3] Bossy, *English catholic community*, pp. 182–94, 278–82.

sufficient to indicate roughly the dimensions of the phenomenon; they also illustrate how the detection of recusancy was gradually intensified as a result of government pressure. A list of catholic recusants in Wiltshire in 1601, based on significations of excommunication from the church courts, contained a mere 41 names; while a return of 1610, drawn up by the bishop's registrar for use by the justices of the peace, still mentioned only 54 individuals. By the 1620s, however, the detection of recusants had been considerably tightened up, and in 1626 another return from the bishop's registry formed the basis for the indictment of 141 recusants at the county quarter sessions. Even this more substantial total suggests that in numerical terms catholic recusancy in Wiltshire was a minor problem. Such recusant strength as existed was mainly confined to a few parishes in the southernmost quarter of the shire, particularly Stourton (the seat of the recusant Edward, Lord Stourton). Over most of the county the influence of catholic recusancy was minimal.[4]

Even more vital to the success of the church of England than the drive against catholicism was the nourishing of protestantism among the conforming majority. At the beginning of Elizabeth's reign the church was undoubtedly ill equipped for this task: it was suffering from a general shortage of clergy and an even more acute shortage of really committed, able protestant ministers. Conditions were most dire in the north of England, but even in the southern dioceses the situation was often very grave. However, by the early seventeenth century a remarkable improvement had occurred in the numbers and quality of the clergy, the result partly of direct episcopal and government action and partly of educational trends and other social developments affecting aspiring clerics.[5]

Wiltshire provides an apt illustration both of the problems of the early Elizabethan church and of subsequent improvements. Bishop Jewel's report to archbishop Parker in 1561 indicated that to serve more than 300 Wiltshire parishes and chapelries there were only 220 clerics (including unbeneficed curates). At least 54 of them were pluralists and only 173 resided. Of the 220 men named, 25 were described as 'learned in Latin', 8 as 'studious in Latin', and 48 as

[4] Petti (ed.), *Recusant documents*, pp. 124–6; *H.M.C.*, *Report on manuscripts in various collections*, 8 vols. (1901–14), vol. 1, p. 83; W.R.O., QS/GR Trin. 1626/124–6 and corresponding indictments.

[5] Rosemary O'Day, *The English clergy: the emergence and consolidation of a profession, 1558–1642* (Leicester, 1979), ch. 10; Collinson, *Religion of protestants*, ch. 3.

simply 'learned'; 80 counted as 'moderately learned', 19 as 'in some way learned', 14 as 'unlearned', and 5 as 'utterly unlearned'. There were only 37 graduates in all, and excluding the cathedral clergy there were only 20 preachers in the whole county, several of whom were unlicensed.[6]

Jewel and his successors laboured to improve this situation, both by efforts to weed out or reform negligent and scandalous ministers and by ordaining and promoting able men, who were coming forward in increasing numbers as candidates for the ministry.[7] By the early years of James I's reign considerable progress had been made. In 1584 there were already 121 preachers in the diocese (including the archdeaconry of Berkshire); in 1603 there were 200.[8] Neglect of duty through non-residence was gradually eliminated. Thus the very full presentments from the archdeaconry of North Wiltshire in 1599, arising from three visitations held in that year, revealed only four cases of dereliction. And in 1604, when the bishop's consistory court mounted a mopping-up campaign against non-residence, only eleven Wiltshire ministers had to be prosecuted. In only one of these cases, moreover, was it actually necessary to proceed to deprivation.[9]

The results of these developments are more fully revealed in a clergy exhibit book made up for archbishop Abbot's metropolitical visitation in 1613.[10] This volume listed the names of 308 Wiltshire clerics (including 65 subordinate curates), indicating a much more favourable manpower situation than in the early years of Elizabeth's reign. Pluralism still existed – no early modern diocese could be wholly free of it – but on a much reduced scale: in 1613 some twenty Wiltshire churches were held in plurality with others in the county, while a further nine are known to have been held by ministers who also possessed benefices outside the diocese. (Most of the pluralists

[6] Whiteman, 'Church of England', pp. 33–4; Corpus Christi College, Cambridge, MS 97, fols. 184–93 (the actual terms used in the MS were *latine doctus*, *latine studiosus*, *doctus*, *mediocriter doctus*, *utcunque doctus*, *indoctus* and *omnino indoctus*).

[7] Whiteman, 'Church of England', pp. 34–5.

[8] Strype, *Life of Whitgift*, vol. 1, pp. 307–8, vol. 3, p. 102 (7 of the preachers listed in 1584 were described as 'recusants', i.e. they refused the three articles of 1583); B.L., Harley MS 280, fol. 159.

[9] W.R.O., AW/*Detecta* Bk, 1586–99, fols. 138v (cf. fol. 156), 139, 139v, 140 (the *comperta* in which these presentments occur are not dated but can be confidently ascribed to 1599 from internal evidence); B/ABI 33a, fol. 146v.

[10] W.R.O., B/Exhibit Bk, 1613.

Table 3 *Educational attainments of the Wiltshire clergy revealed by the exhibit book prepared for archbishop Abbot's metropolitical visitation, 1613*

	Rectors/vicars/perpetual curates	Curates serving annexed/ subordinate chapelries, etc.	Curates deputising for pluralists	Other subordinate curates	*Total*	%
Cathedral clergy	23	—	—	—	*23*	
Subtotal	*23*	—	—	—	*23*	
Parish clergy						
Contumacious	18	5	2	0	*25*	
No entry save name	15	3	0	2	*20*	
Appeared, no other information	64	7	3	1	*75*	
Subtotals	*97*	*15*	*5*	*3*	*120*	
Graduate licensed preachers	52	2	2	0	*56*	33.9
Graduate unlicensed preachers	9	0	0	2	*11*	6.7
Graduates (no information re preaching)	5	4	1	3	*13*	7.9
Graduate non-preachers	1	2	2	1	*6*	3.6
Non-graduate licensed preachers	23	1	2	1	*27*	16.4
Non-graduate unlicensed preachers	4	0	1	0	*5*	3.0
Non-graduate non-preachers	29	5	3	10	*47*	28.5
Subtotals	*123*	*14*	*11*	*17*	*165*	100.0
Totals	*243*	*29*	*16*	*20*	*308*	

were cathedral clergy and particularly well-qualified ministers.) Non-residence no longer posed a serious problem, and total dereliction of duty was evidently very uncommon.[11]

The 1613 returns also testify to the improved educational attainments and preaching strength of the clergy (see Table 3). Of the 23 cathedral clergy, all but 3 were graduates, some of them of considerable intellectual eminence. The exhibit book unfortunately provides no information about the qualifications of 120 of the parochial clergy; but of the remaining 165, some 52 per cent were

[11] For a more detailed analysis, see Ingram, 'Ecclesiastical justice in Wiltshire', pp. 73–7.

graduates, 60 per cent were preachers, and 41 per cent were both. Men lacking both a university degree and the ability to preach comprised less than 30 per cent of those for whom information is available. The exact number of preachers in the county at this date cannot be known for certain; but a total of about 130 seems a reasonable estimate, indicating a moderately favourable situation in comparison with other dioceses in southern England.[12] Moreover improvement continued apace during the reigns of James I and Charles I, in Wiltshire as in other areas. The bishop of Salisbury's subscription book (recording among other things the qualifications of ordinands) reveals that by the 1620s and 1630s it was rare for candidates for the ministry to lack a degree, and the number of preachers gradually increased.[13]

But paper qualifications do not necessarily guarantee that ministers exercised their pastoral functions effectively. The Salisbury cathedral clergy confessed in 1634 that the 'good ordinance' which bound prebendaries to preach by turns in the cathedral had been 'broken by many', while the canons admitted that they had been 'defective...in preaching at those churches whence we receive rents and profits'.[14] But complaints about the neglect of preaching by the parochial clergy were rare, whilst incidental references to sermons in the early seventeenth century suggest that the growing numbers of licensed preachers were indeed fulfilling their duties conscientiously. Nor should it be assumed that all non-preaching ministers were worthless 'dumb dogs', as puritan propagandists implied. They could also be, as one contemporary pointed out, 'honest ministers, well able to catechise and privately to exhort, though they have not the gift of utterance and audacity to preach in the pulpit'.[15] Non-preachers were supposed to arrange for others to preach monthly sermons (quarterly before 1604) and themselves to read the homilies regularly. While it cannot be certainly established that they conscientiously fulfilled these requirements, it is notable that presentments for neglect had decreased sharply by the early seventeenth century, suggesting that a reasonable level of performance had been achieved.

[12] In comparison, there were said to be 211 preachers in the diocese of Chichester in 1603, and 123 in the diocese of Ely: B.L., Harley MS 280, fols. 158, 159v. (The figure for Chichester may, however, be an exaggeration: see K.C. Fincham, 'Ramifications of the Hampton Court conference in the dioceses, 1603–1609', *Jl ecclesiastical history*, 36 (1985), pp. 215–16.)

[13] Barrie Williams (ed.), *The subscription book of bishops Tounson and Davenant, 1620–40*, Wilts. Record Soc., 32 (Devizes, 1977), pp. 9–10 and *passim*.

[14] *H.M.C., Fourth report* (1874), appendix, p. 128.

[15] B.L., Harley MS 280, fol. 169v.

By the end of James I's reign there were also few complaints that ministers neglected the catechising of the young and ignorant, though they did sometimes face difficulties from recalcitrant parishioners.[16]

Throughout this period there always remained room for further clerical improvement; nor were the church's resources necessarily deployed to maximum effect. Thus the parliamentary ejectors of the 1640s and 1650s were able to uncover a number of seriously negligent or scandalous clergy;[17] while analysis of the returns of 1613 suggests that there was some concentration of the least able ministers in the southernmost portions of the shire, where the persistence of catholic recusancy really demanded a major pastoral effort on the part of the established church. But the significance of such defects should not be overemphasised; and overall the detailed evidence bears out Anne Whiteman's suggestion that early seventeenth-century Wiltshire, like other parts of England, was characterised by a growing body of well-educated, diligent ministers.[18]

But how loyal were ministers of whatever level of attainment, in Wiltshire and elsewhere, to the ecclesiastical hierarchy and the church court establishment which represented it? It will be recalled that puritan critics of the existing structure of church government bitterly denounced the supposed abuses of the ecclesiastical courts. But movements for a serious alteration in the structure of the church were largely crushed in the 1590s and the early years of James I's reign.[19] Recent studies have emphasised that by the second and third decades of the seventeenth century the great majority of clergy had settled into acceptance of the established church; puritan aspirations were to a large extent absorbed into the mainstream of church life and expressed themselves mainly in pastoral endeavours which often utilised the existing machinery of ecclesiastical discipline.[20] This was true even in areas of greatest puritan strength, such as parts of East Anglia. In Wiltshire, where puritanism had never been a really major

[16] The appearance books of the three main Wiltshire jurisdictions for the period 1615–29 reveal an average of less than one case per annum of either the neglect of preaching by qualified ministers or not providing monthly sermons, while prosecutions for failing to catechise were even fewer. For examples of parishioners' reluctance to receive instruction, see W.R.O., B/DB 9, fol. 24v; AW/ABO 5, 27/3/1618, *Office v. Lovedaie*; AW/ABO 6, 7/12/1626, *Office v. Web*.

[17] Whiteman, 'Church of England', pp. 40–2.

[18] *Ibid.*, p. 35. [19] Collinson, *Elizabethan puritan movement*, pp. 385–467.

[20] Tyacke, 'Puritanism, Arminianism and counter-revolution', pp. 119–27; Collinson, *Religion of protestants*, pp. viii–ix and *passim*.

force, this process of assimilation was speedily effected and there were remarkably few signs of serious clerical nonconformity throughout most of the early seventeenth century.[21]

By the end of Elizabeth's reign a few Wiltshire clergy had, it is true, despaired of the established church and become separatists or near-separatists; but in the early years of James's reign they were eliminated by flight or deprivation.[22] Separatist congregations were largely eradicated also. There were Brownists or Barrowists in Bradford, Hilperton, Chippenham and Salisbury in the late sixteenth century, but there are no signs of their existence after 1600.[23] However, a group of Brownists was undoubtedly still active in and around the remote cloth weaving parish of Slaughterford in the opening years of the new century, with connections with exiled congregations in Amsterdam. It included Thomas White, a former curate of Slaughterford, and Thomas Powell, who had recently been a licensed preacher, and apparently met in the houses of a certain Mr William Hore and one Thomas Cullimer. The evidence of prosecutions in the church courts and quarter sessions indicates that the group was small, consisted predominantly of clothworkers and – save for members of the Cullimer family, who were still being prosecuted for non-attendance at church in the 1620s – did not long survive as a coherent entity.[24] An isolated reference points to the existence of a conventicle of unknown character at Broughton Gifford in 1605, and there were baptists in Salisbury in the 1620s and early 1630s; but, as far as is known, it was not until the period of the civil war and its aftermath that sectarian congregations developed in any numbers.[25]

21 Whiteman, 'Church of England', pp. 34–5, 37–8.

22 For example, Mr John Jessop, rector of Manningford Bruce, who was repeatedly in trouble for nonconformity at the end of Elizabeth's reign, was deprived in 1605: see W.R.O., AW/ABO 1, 15/5/1601, 15/2/1603, 11/12/1604; Sir Thomas Phillipps, *Institutiones clericorum in comitatu Wiltoniae*, 2 vols. (Salisbury and Middle Hill, 1821–5), p. 4. Jessop is probably identifiable with the 'Mr Ies.' or 'Mr Io. Ie.' referred to in Francis Johnson, *An inquirie and answer of Thomas White his discoverie of Brownisme* ([Amsterdam], 1606), Epistle and p. 12.

23 Marjorie E. Reeves, 'Protestant nonconformity', in *V.C.H. Wilts.*, vol. 3, p. 100.

24 W.R.O., AW/ABO 2, 1/10/1605, *Office v. Margaret Browne*; AW/ABO 3, 19/4/1607, *Office v. Thomas Taylor*; AW/ABO 6, 17/4/1624, 10/12/1624, *Office v. Anne Cullimore*; AW/ABO 6, 27/5/1624, 10/12/1624, 21/2/1627, *Office v. Catherine Cullimore*; QS/GR East. 1604/148. See also Reeves, 'Protestant nonconformity', p. 100.

25 W.R.O., B/ABO 5, 26/6/1605, *Office v. John Blanchard et al.*; Reeves, 'Protestant nonconformity', pp. 101–4.

The vast majority of people in this period were at least nominally conforming members of the established church. But what was the nature of their religious beliefs and practices? Were they in reasonable accord with the Christian principles which underlay the structure of ecclesiastical justice; or were such principles an alien system remote from ordinary people's real interests? Some recent historians have stressed that the church and official religion had probably never achieved anything like a complete hold over the population. Moreover, the abolition during the Reformation years of many of the visual, dramatic and participatory elements of religious ritual seriously disrupted the pattern of popular devotion, while the post-Reformation church faced enormous difficulties in inculcating the new, Bible-centred protestant version of the Christian message in the hearts and minds of a largely illiterate laity.[26] Admittedly there is evidence, from Wiltshire as elsewhere in England, that literacy was on the increase in the late sixteenth and early seventeenth centuries, and to this extent the barriers to the reception of protestantism may have diminished somewhat over time.[27] Thus of male deponents in defamation causes in the Salisbury consistory court around 1590, rather less than 25 per cent could sign their names; the corresponding figure around 1620 was a little over 40 per cent. But it is plain that, as in other parts of England, the educational advances which such figures represent were very socially specific, affecting the topmost ranks of society, the yeomanry and certain tradesman groups much more than other sectors. Book learning was much less in evidence among husbandmen and many artisan groups; while poor cottagers and labourers (who rarely appeared as witnesses), and the female population generally, remained overwhelmingly illiterate.[28]

In the light of such information, and influenced by the categories

[26] Thomas, *Religion and the decline of magic*, chs. 3, 6; Christopher Haigh, 'Puritan evangelism in the reign of Elizabeth I', *Eng. hist. rev.*, 92 (1977), pp. 30–58; Imogen Luxton, 'The Reformation and popular culture', in Heal and O'Day (eds.), *Church and society*, pp. 57–77; Wrightson and Levine, *Poverty and piety*, pp. 12–13.

[27] For England generally, see David Cressy, *Literacy and the social order: reading and writing in Tudor and Stuart England* (Cambridge, 1980); Margaret Spufford, *Small books and pleasant histories: popular fiction and its readership in seventeenth-century England* (1981). Spufford surmises that reading skills were much more widely diffused than evidence based on the ability to sign one's name (the chief touchstone of 'functional literacy' employed by Cressy) would suggest.

[28] Based on analysis of W.R.O., B/DB 10–12, 30–40. (Berkshire deponents were excluded from the calculations.)

used by contemporary moralists and clerical commentators, some historians have tended to present a polarised view of religious belief and behaviour in this period based on the notions of the 'godly' and the 'multitude'. The former are portrayed as small in numbers but deeply pious, often literate and characteristically drawn from the upper echelons of the social order – gentlemen, merchants, yeomen and substantial husbandmen and craftsmen. Often in alliance with puritan ministers, they sometimes succeeded in dominating the government of particular parishes in town or country, forming a spiritual and social elite self-characterised as the 'better sort'. The 'multitude' comprised the mass of the population, consisting largely of ignorant folk whose religious knowledge and commitment were tenuous at best. They were more drawn to alehouses and festivities than to church and sermon and, especially in parishes dominated by 'godly' groups, were liable to prosecution for neglect of religious duties, drunkenness and similar offences.[29] From a rather different perspective, Keith Thomas has likewise argued that commitment to the church and official religion was minimal among large sections of the common people in sixteenth- and seventeenth-century England. Not only were religious ignorance and indifference widespread, but there also existed strong undercurrents of thought which, if not wholly atheistic, were strongly sceptical of basic Christian doctrines and could lead to a virtual rejection of all religion. Hence the orthodoxies of the national church were seriously challenged by magic, astrology and other non-religious systems of belief.[30] These lines of interpretation, if they are accepted, might suggest that for much of the population the disciplinary work of the church courts was inimical or irrelevant.

Margaret Spufford and Patrick Collinson, however, have questioned whether religious commitment was as class-determined as some historians have implied. Moreover, on the basis of the study of the dedicatory clauses of wills from a number of Cambridgeshire villages, the former has argued for 'the reality of religion' for a broad spectrum of the population in the sixteenth and seventeenth centuries. She concludes that the 'close study of the wills of orthodox villagers bears out the general impression...of a society in

[29] Wrightson and Levine, *Poverty and piety, passim*; Wrightson, *English society*, pp. 206–20; Peter Clark, *English provincial society from the Reformation to the revolution: religion, politics and society in Kent, 1500–1640* (Hassocks, 1977), esp. pp. 149–62.

[30] Thomas, *Religion and the decline of magic*, ch. 6.

which even the humblest members, the very poor, and the women, and those living in physical isolation, thought deeply on religious matters and were often profoundly influenced by them'.[31] The evidence she adduces hardly supports such an extreme case; but the emphasis on a broad spectrum of unspectacular orthodoxy (if not remarkable piety) is salutary. The evidence from Wiltshire and elsewhere suggests that it is a mistake to overemphasise either the presence of 'godly' groups or the existence of people largely indifferent to religion. Most people were located somewhere between these poles.

To be sure, there did exist in Wiltshire, as in other parts of England, numbers of especially pious lay people with a diligent interest in the word of God. Their numbers may have been increasing in this period, aided among other things by advancements in literacy among the middling to upper strata of society; though it is unfortunately impossible to gauge these numbers on a county-wide basis. In the records of the church courts, such people sometimes stand out from chance references, such as that to John Ansty of Maiden Bradley who was said to have 'Mr Smith's sermons' in his house in 1623;[32] or when their desire to hear sermons, frustrated by the absence or negligence of their own parish minister, led them to defy the strict letter of the law and 'gad' to hear preachers in neighbouring parishes. Presentments for this offence, originating from places scattered widely over the county, appeared regularly but in very small numbers in the records of the Wiltshire church courts in the early seventeenth century – though it is of course uncertain how many 'gadders' escaped delation.[33] A rather different kind of case from Calne in 1634 provides an interesting vignette of other activities of the 'godly' laity. Thomas Tyler, prosecuted for repeating sermons to the parishioners in the church after evening prayer, alleged that the minister had given him permission to read over his notes of the Tuesday lectures and Sunday sermons, adding that many in the congregation had requested him to do so 'for their memories' sake'.[34] Other references indicate that the small clothmaking and market town of Calne had developed a sizeable 'godly' congregation by the reign of Charles I, as had Salisbury and some

[31] Collinson, *Religion of protestants*, ch. 5; Spufford, *Contrasting communities*, pp. 319–44.

[32] W.R.O., AS/ABO 13, 19/7/1623, *Office v. Ansty*; the sermons were presumably those of Henry Smith.

[33] For further discussion of such cases, with examples, see Whiteman, 'Church of England', p. 37.

[34] W.R.O., D/AB 39, 24/9/1634, *Office v. Tyler*.

other urban centres.[35] Coherent 'godly' groups – as opposed merely to particularly pious individuals or families – may also have existed in some of the rural parishes of Wiltshire;[36] though no instance has so far come to light where the 'godly' actually succeeded in dominating the parish for an extended period, as seems to have happened in the Essex village of Terling studied by Keith Wrightson and David Levine.[37]

At the other extreme, there were individuals in Wiltshire who virtually rejected Christian beliefs or at least expressed contempt for them. Alexander Champion of Downton, who in his cups in 1612 compared heaven and hell to a table and form and claimed that he could step from one to the other, provides an example of tavern blasphemy; while John Derpier, a gentleman of Buttermere who in 1607 'did affirm and maintain this most heretical and damnable opinion that there was no god and no resurrection and that men died a death like beasts', perhaps represents a more carefully considered scepticism.[38] Even more striking is the case of two Lacock weavers who in 1656 expressed views which combined antinomian ideas with star worship, a denial that heaven and hell existed save in a man's own conscience, and a willingness to sell all religions for a jug of beer; the pair may have been influenced by the Ranter Thomas Webbe, who was rector of the neighbouring parish of Langley Burrell.[39] But in Wiltshire, as in other parts of the country, such cases came to light with the utmost rarity.[40] While they prove that

[35] On Calne, see W.R.O., D/Pres. 1616–17/16; D/Pres. 1634/26; D/AB 37, fol. 29. On Salisbury, see Slack, 'Poverty and politics', pp. 183–9.

[36] Presentment patterns and other indications suggest that this was true of, for example, the clothworking parish of Seend in west central Wiltshire. On the general history of this parish, see Edward Bradby, *Seend: a Wiltshire village past and present* (Gloucester, 1981).

[37] Wrightson and Levine, *Poverty and piety*, ch. 6 and *passim*.

[38] W.R.O., AS/ABO 11, 23/5/1612, *Office v. Champion*; D/Pres. 1607–9, Gt Bedwyn, 13/10/1607. See also QS/GR East. 1635, examinations, contemp. no. 4. On irreligion in England generally, see Christopher Hill, 'Irreligion in the "puritan" revolution', in J. F. McGregor and B. Reay (eds.), *Radical religion in the English revolution* (Oxford, 1984), pp. 191–211. See also Michael Hunter, 'The problem of "atheism" in early modern England', *Trans. Roy. Hist. Soc.*, 5th ser., 35 (1985), pp. 135–57.

[39] *H.M.C., Various collections*, vol. 1, pp. 132–3. See also Christopher Hill, *The world turned upside down: radical ideas during the English revolution* (1972), pp. 182–3. This unusual case has been repeatedly quoted: see, for example, Thomas, *Religion and the decline of magic*, p. 171; McGregor and Reay (eds.), *Radical religion*, pp. 133–4, 199, 205.

[40] For an isolated allegation of atheism in Sussex, see W.S.R.O., Ep.I/17/12, fol. 66.

atheistic or near-atheistic ideas were not unknown, they hardly suggest that they were common.

There is no reason to challenge Thomas's assertion that the Christianity of the mass of the population was compatible with magical beliefs and recourse to magical practices of which the church disapproved; yet the evidence, on the whole, does not suggest that magical systems were a really serious rival to official religion. Studies of witchcraft and magic in England have given too much attention to apparently exceptional areas, especially the county of Essex, where for reasons which have not yet been fully explained the numbers of witchcraft prosecutions were unusually high. An area like Sussex, where as far as is known only one witch was executed throughout the sixteenth and seventeenth centuries, provides a striking contrast.[41] It is unknown how many secular witch trials and executions occurred in Wiltshire, since the main series of Elizabethan and early seventeenth-century criminal assize records for the western circuit does not survive.[42] The western assize gaol books indicate that seven Wiltshire individuals were indicted for witchcraft in the years 1670–1700, compared with five from Essex in the same period; but it would be unsafe to infer from this that in earlier periods the two areas had experienced prosecutions on a similar scale.[43] Witchcraft prosecutions in the Wiltshire church courts were fairly rare during most of the period 1570–1640. In 1559 John Jewel expressed concern about the number of 'witches and sorceresses' in the west country (though it is plain from the context that he made no clear distinction between diabolical magic and popular catholic devotions), and during his episcopate and those of his immediate successors the Salisbury consistory court did prosecute a few cases of alleged sorcery each year; predictably, in view of Jewel's attitude, many of them originated in the areas of relatively strong catholic survival in south Wiltshire.[44] But the numbers of prosecutions diminished

41 Alan Macfarlane, *Witchcraft in Tudor and Stuart England* (1970); cf. Sharpe, *Crime in early modern England*, pp. 54–6.

42 Most of the cases which occurred in the Wiltshire quarter sessions have been abstracted or printed verbatim: see Macfarlane, *Witchcraft*, pp. 62–3 and the references cited on p. 320.

43 C. L'Estrange Ewen, *Witchcraft and demonianism* (1933), pp. 441–6; Macfarlane, *Witchcraft*, p. 271.

44 Hastings Robinson (ed.), *The Zurich letters*, Parker Soc. (Cambridge, 1842), pp. 44–5. For examples of presentments for sorcery/witchcraft in Elizabethan Wiltshire, see W.R.O., B/*Detecta* Bk 6, fols. 6v, 7, 9, 14v, 18 (all from south Wiltshire parishes), 25 (Devizes).

rapidly after about 1585, and, though conventional inquiries about witches and sorcerers continued to be made in visitation articles, only a handful of cases is known to have occurred in the early seventeenth century.[45] The impression is that in late Elizabethan and early Stuart times witchcraft and magical practices were not of major concern either to the ecclesiastical authorities or to the majority of the people of Wiltshire; and the same appears true of many other areas of England.[46]

It is plausible to suppose, as did the judicious Hooker, that the minds of the majority of people in a country which had been officially Christian for centuries were to some extent influenced by orthodox thought and belief; but it is largely a matter for conjecture precisely what degree of religious knowledge the lower strata of society commonly possessed.[47] The highly pessimistic comments of such men as Peter Ince, who as rector of the Wiltshire parish of Donhead St Mary during the interregnum lamented the utter religious ignorance of the local inhabitants, have to be interpreted in the light of the very high standards of doctrinal sophistication which he and others like him demanded of lay people.[48] Arthur Dent's *Plaine mans path-way to heaven* (1601), which credited its stereotyped rustic characters with at least a jumbled and misty half-knowledge, may be closer to the truth. In the church courts, the depths of popular ignorance were occasionally plumbed when objections were entered against witnesses' capacity to give reliable testimony. Edward Somerode, a 24-year-old cobbler from Broughton Gifford who was called as a witness in 1617, confessed that 'he received the communion at Easter last but was never taught the catechism...[and]

[45] For example, W.R.O., AS/ABO 7, fols. 174v, 182; AS/ABO 11, 25/2/1614, *Office v. Elizabeth Smith* (cf. QS/GR East. 1612/157a); B/ABO 8, 13/9/1616, *Office v. Alice Hey*; AW/ABO 6, 17/3/1630, *Office v. John and William Denby*.

[46] Sharpe, *Crime in early modern England*, pp. 54–6; Philip Tyler, 'The church courts at York and witchcraft prosecutions, 1567–1640', *Northern history*, 4 (1969), pp. 84–109; Peter Rushton, 'Women, witchcraft and slander in early modern England: cases from the church courts of Durham, 1560–1675', *Northern history*, 18 (1982), p. 124. But cf. Michael MacDonald, *Mystical bedlam: madness, anxiety and healing in seventeenth-century England* (Cambridge, 1981), pp. 107–10, 199, 208–11, suggesting persistent undercurrents of witchcraft beliefs which did not necessarily lead to court action.

[47] Richard Hooker, *Of the laws of ecclesiastical polity*, Everyman edn, 2 vols. (1954), vol. 2, p. 17.

[48] Geoffrey F. Nuttall, *Visible saints: the congregational way, 1640–1660* (Oxford, 1957), p. 136; cf. Thomas, *Religion and the decline of magic*, p. 166.

knoweth not what an oath is or what punishment is appointed for those that swear falsely'. But it should be emphasised that such lamentable ignorance was very rarely shown to exist among deponents. Admittedly the poorest and most ignorant folk were least likely to be called as witnesses, but some of those that did testify were able to acquit themselves moderately well. Philip Smith, a self-confessed pauper from Marlborough in 1618, was able to tell how many groats made a shilling but did not know how many were in three shillings; yet even he was able to give a fair account of the spiritual consequences of taking a false oath, and could repeat the Lord's Prayer.[49]

The manner in which Sundays and holidays were observed offers another approach to popular religious attitudes and practices, and one which reveals the church courts directly attempting, with some co-operation from parochial interests, to raise standards by means of prosecutions. The officially prescribed standards of observance were moderately high, and it is hardly surprising to find that in some respects practice fell far short of the ideal. This was especially so with regard to working on Sundays and, more particularly, the lesser holidays. In theory, throughout this period the courts upheld the canon law ban on manual labour on saints' days and the sabbath; but in Elizabeth's reign in most areas little attempt was made to enforce the regulations. In the archdeaconry of Wiltshire in 1593, for example, only three people were presented for Sunday work and the same number for labouring on saints' days; in 1599, only one person was detected for each offence.[50] A similarly lax situation prevailed in the archdeaconries of Leicester and Chichester and, no doubt, in many other areas.[51] Prosecutions in the diocese of Ely in the late sixteenth century appear to have been unusually intense: there were 33 cases from the county of Cambridgeshire in the period November 1590 to March 1591 alone.[52] This degree of attention to Sunday and holiday work remained uncommon even in the early seventeenth century, but in most jurisdictions the number of prosecutions did increase somewhat after 1600. Thus in Wiltshire, in the period 1615–29, an annual average of about 25 people appeared before the

49 W.R.O., B/DB 32, fol. 147; B/Libels 2/10; B/DB 34, fols. 164–5.
50 W.R.O., AW/*Detecta* Bk, 1586–99, fols. 93v, 95v, 103, 104v, 144, 157 (dating inferred from internal evidence).
51 Based on analysis of L.M., 1 D 41/13/12; W.S.R.O., Ep.I/17/8.
52 Based on analysis of C.U.L., Ely D.R., B/2/11, fols. 42–110v.

courts of the three major jurisdictions to face charges of unlawful work.

It is, however, impossible to believe that even these more substantial totals represented more than a small fraction of actual offenders. Even the canon law conceded that *necessary* works were permissible and that bakers and millers might lawfully serve the needs of the poor.[53] Such excuses were frequently urged by offenders in court, and it is probable that many evaded presentment by claiming a necessity.[54] In any case it is plain that attitudes to unlawful work – especially labouring on lesser feast-days – were generally tolerant, and the consensus necessary for strict regulation was often lacking. Thus Wolfstan Swetnam of Bishop's Lavington confessed to mowing on St Bartholomew's day and alleged that 'because he saw others...were a-mowing likewise...he thought he might do it without offence'; while Leonard Bonnis of Fisherton Anger admitted that he had worked on holidays 'as others do'. In 1628 the churchwardens of Ogbourne St Andrew confessed that the whole parish was guilty of failing to observe holidays; while at Mere in 1622 it was presented that 'we have three fairs in our town on holy days in the year by means whereof we are all guilty in this article'.[55] To an extent the church courts were prepared to collude with these attitudes. The presentments of churchwardens were sometimes supplemented by apparitors' informations, but generally the courts showed no great urgency in prosecuting cases of unlawful work. Even those offenders who were brought to court often met lenient treatment: in Wiltshire they were usually let off with an admonition.[56]

A more obviously reprehensible divergence from the religious observance of Sundays and holidays was drunkenness and alehouse haunting. Contemporary moralists and puritan-minded preachers inveighed against the sin of inebriety, striking a chord not only with the godly but also with many practical-minded men who saw tippling as an encouragement to poverty and vice and as a threat to public order. Hence, from the mid-sixteenth century onwards, a series of

[53] Wilfred B. Whitaker, *Sunday in Tudor and Stuart times* (1933), p. 25.

[54] For example, W.R.O., AS/ABO 12, 15/12/1617, *Office v. Clarck*, 20/6/1618, *Office v. Cooper*; AS/ABO 13, 12/7/1623, *Office v. Bankes*.

[55] W.R.O., B/ABO 10, 7/3/1621 (second court held on that day); AS/ABO 15, 24/3/1637; D/Pres. 1628/33; D/Pres. 1622/35.

[56] Sometimes, however, offenders were punished with one of the milder forms of penance; this seems to have been common practice in some other areas, such as the diocese of Ely.

parliamentary statutes was passed to regulate aleselling and suppress immoderate drinking, and in most counties (including Wiltshire) increasing efforts were made to enforce these measures in the quarter sessions and in local manorial and borough courts.[57] The ecclesiastical courts, for their part, were able to bring prosecutions for drunkenness, while people who allowed drinking or card-playing in their houses during service time, and those who took part in the merrymaking, were guilty of the offence of 'ill rule'. But it is plain that the church courts were not considered to be a major forum for the attack on the evils of drink; and while there was some increase in presentments for these delicts in the late sixteenth and early seventeenth centuries, the overall numbers remained small in most areas. In Wiltshire, action was taken only against the most egregious and notorious drunkards, while detections for ill rule were largely confined to a few centres such as the borough of Wilton and mostly concerned licensed or unlicensed alesellers. However, taking into account the evidence from both the ecclesiastical and the secular courts, it is plain that tippling and drunkenness were major social problems in this period, and that alehouses were a powerful rival attraction to church and sermon. Pressure from the authorities could, at best, do no more than contain the problem.

Some presentments for ill rule related to activities more complex than simple tippling and gaming and less obviously reprehensible in the eyes of the authorities. In 1605, for example, Henry Harris of Yatton Keynell denied disorder on the Sabbath but admitted that 'having lost a cow being all the goods he had was advised by a friend of his to provide a stand of ale and he would bring him company to help him towards his losses'; and he added that, when a complaint was made to the justices about the matter, they discharged him and rebuked the churchwardens for informing against him.[58] The fact was that although such 'help-ales' might lead to absence from church and to drinking and dancing during service time, they could be justified as an expression of neighbourly charity. Similar ambi-

[57] The literature on this subject is now extensive. For the general background, see Peter Clark, *The English alehouse: a social history, 1200–1830* (1983), chs. 3–8. On legislative action, see Joan Kent, 'Attitudes of members of the house of commons to the regulation of "personal conduct" in late Elizabethan and early Stuart England', *Bull. Inst. Hist. Res.*, 46 (1973), pp. 41–71. On the local impact of regulation, see Wrightson, 'Alehouses, order and reformation'. For the activities of the Wiltshire justices, see Hurstfield, 'County government', pp. 99–101.

[58] W.R.O., AW/ABO 2, 11/11/1605; and for similar examples, see AW/ABO 4, 27/11/1610, *Office v. Leach*; AS/ABO 14, 23/6/1626, *Office v. Miles et al.*

guities arose with other types of ales, feasts and revels, and with 'dancing matches', 'summer sports', and various other games and pastimes; indeed attitudes to these observances were so diverse that the matter became an issue of national politics in the early seventeenth century.

Generalisations about the nature and incidence of recreations and festivities in late Elizabethan and early Stuart England are, in the present state of research, extremely hazardous. Undoubtedly many forms of ritual and drama were destroyed during the Reformation years, or so seriously undermined that they rapidly declined during Elizabeth's reign.[59] Just how much survived into the seventeenth century, and the local pattern of such persistence, are issues which historians have only just begun to explore systematically. David Underdown has suggested that, in Wiltshire, games and revels survived best in the more socially stratified and conservative chalkland parishes of the south and south-east of the county. In contrast, in the pastoral zone of north-west Wiltshire (especially the clothing areas), the hostility of puritan clergy and the middling sort led to the suppression or disappearance of church ales and other festivities by the early seventeenth century.[60] But analysis of hundreds of references to games and sports, culled from the records of church courts and quarter sessions, and from a variety of local sources, suggests that this idea of a chalk/cheese cultural contrast should not be pressed too far. It is plain that church ales as such (that is, festivities designed to raise funds for the parish church) were in this period gradually going out of use, not only in clothmaking communities like Calne and Steeple Ashton but also in downland parishes like Damerham and Martin. The church rates which replaced them reflected the growing bureaucratisation of parochial finances and generally owed little or nothing to puritan ideology. Within this broad pattern of decline, church ales survived best in *small* villages – such as Hannington in the north, Etchilhampton in central Wiltshire, and Hatch in the south – where the small number of

59 Luxton, 'Reformation and popular culture'; Charles Phythian-Adams, 'Ceremony and the citizen: the communal year at Coventry, 1450–1550', in Clark and Slack (eds.), *Crisis and order*, pp. 57–85.

60 Underdown, 'Problem of popular allegiance', pp. 86–8; David Underdown, 'The chalk and the cheese: contrasts among the English clubmen', *Past and present*, no. 85 (Nov. 1979), p. 35. For fuller treatment, see David Underdown, *Revel, riot and rebellion: popular politics and culture in England, 1603–1660* (Oxford, 1985), ch. 4 and *passim*.

households made festive fund-raising still practicable. However they were still held (albeit sporadically) in some larger villages in the early seventeenth century, not only in the downlands but also in the clothing region.[61] Festivities other than church ales were kept up in numerous parishes throughout the county. Some south Wiltshire villages, such as Donhead St Mary and Donhead St Andrew, Mere, Steeple Langford, Winterslow and Enford, do seem to have had an especially vigorous festive tradition. But by no means all of these communities were of the classic downland type, while there were some notable festive centres in north and north-west Wiltshire too. Thus elaborate feasts or revels, organised 'dancings', 'Whitsun sports', and so forth, are found in clothmaking communities like Trowle (in Bradford parish), Box, Castle Combe, Long Newnton, Christian Malford, Tockenham, Poulshot, Seend and Potterne, and also in some of the non-clothmaking communities of north Wiltshire like Wroughton.[62] Moreover, all over Wiltshire a variety of competitive games was played – football, bowls, stoolball, archery, skittles and throwing the sledge. The local popularity of these pastimes undoubtedly varied, but hardly in ways which accord readily with a chalk/cheese contrast.[63]

The sociology of these games and festivities is even more obscure than their topographical distribution, but certain generalisations are possible. Dancing evidently appealed most (though not exclusively) to the young and unmarried; but these youngsters included individuals from middling and substantial families as well as poorer folk.

[61] For evidence of the process of decline in some parishes, see W. Symonds, 'Winterslow church reckonings, 1542–1661', *Wilts. archaeol. magazine*, 36 (1909–10), p. 33; A. E. W. Marsh, *A history of the borough and town of Calne* (Calne, 1903), pp. 372–3; W.R.O., B/DB 51a, fols. 88, 100v. For some survivals, see W.R.O., AW/ABO 5, 6/7/1621, *Office v. Batson*, 27/10/1621, *Office v. Becket*; B/ABO 8, 28/9/1618, *Office v. Tarrant*; AS/ABO 11, 24/6/1615, *Office v. Gray and Scammell*; B/DB 28, fols. 62v–5; B/DB 41, fols. 70v–1; W.R.O., 173/1 (Lacock churchwardens' book), fols. 17v, 19v. I hope to discuss ales and festivities more fully on another occasion.

[62] For the south Wiltshire parishes, see Underdown, 'Problem of popular allegiance', p. 87 and the references there cited; W.R.O., B/ABO 1, fol. 7v; AS/ABO 12, 4/7/1618, *Office v. Robert and Thomas Birte*; B/ABO 11, fol. 38v; AS/ABO 14, 28/10/1626, *Office v. Cardy*. For the north Wiltshire parishes, see W.R.O., QS/GR Hil. 1617/101; QS/GR Mich. 1633/119, 178; QS/GR Mich. 1617/141; QS/GR Trin. 1641/183–5; QS/GR Trin. 1612/179; QS/GR Trin. 1617/147; QS/GR Mich. 1620/197; AS/ABO 12, 9/3/1616, *Office v. Curtis*, 2/8/1617, *Office v. Richard and Thomas Hulbert*, 16/10/1617, *Office v. Sumner, Cox and Foot*; QS/GR Trin. 1635/201; B/DB 34, fols. 92v–3.

[63] For examples, see Whiteman, 'Church of England', p. 38.

Other games attracted a wide following in some parishes: for example, bowling – presumably less decorous than its modern equivalent and often played in inn or alehouse yards – was often indulged in by middle-aged and elderly men of substance. Whether downland or clothmaking parishes are considered, the idea of a simple contrast between a sober 'middling sort' and the festive life of the poor is certainly misleading.

The fact is that, in Wiltshire as elsewhere in England, there was considerable *variety* of opinion among the middling and upper ranks of society about the beneficence or otherwise of sports and games. Some puritan clergy saw them as scandalous relics of a pagan past: thus in 1618 a Marlborough minister informed midsummer merry-makers 'that they served the devil by it and not God, and that it was an idol which they served, meaning thereby one that played the part of a morris dancer'.[64] Probably more common were strictures that games and dances encouraged drunkenness, immorality, theft and violence. But, although holiday activities were no doubt often undecorous, and while scattered references do indicate that they occasionally led to serious crimes and misdemeanours, the stock puritan accusation of utter licentiousness was probably a gross exaggeration.[65] More weighty was the charge that games and frolics drew people away from church services: this was a common complaint in presentments against minstrels, fiddlers, 'crowders' and festive leaders like 'Thomas Stafford, lord of our summer house, and Edward Sartaine, termed lord prince of that company' who enticed the young people of Westbury to dance during morning prayers on midsummer day in 1637.[66]

The royal declarations of sports of 1618 and 1633, and people who approved of them, chose rather to emphasise the social and political utility of popular festivities. So long as they took place after evening prayers and (from 1625) did not involve recourse to other parishes, most Sunday and holiday games were declared to be not only lawful but also beneficial in that they provided both needful recreation and

64 W.R.O., B/ABO 8, 6/10/1618, *Office v. Fowler*; cf. Hill, *Society and puritanism*, p. 187.

65 For examples of licentiousness/criminality, see B/ABO 8, 28/9/1618, *Office v. Tarrant*; AS/ABO 14, 15/11/1627, *Office v. John Cholsey, junior*; B/DB 42, fol. 123v; QS/GR Mich. 1617/142. Cf. Hill, *Society and puritanism*, pp. 183–92.

66 W.R.O., AS/ABO 11, 27/3/1617, *Office v. Thomas and Robert Birte*; D/Pres. 1606–8 (unnumbered), Bishopstone; Precentor/Pres. 1614–40 (unnumbered), Westbury, 27/6/1637.

opportunities for the reconciliation of neighbours at enmity.[67] This effort to accommodate popular festivities has been castigated as a romantic attempt to recreate a mythical harmonious past, a denial of the realities of social change, or even a wilful disregard of the social problems of poverty and drunkenness which afflicted so many parishes in the early seventeenth century.[68] Certainly the idea that games served as reconciliatory mechanisms is hard to substantiate. But in other respects the arguments in favour of allowing customary recreations were by no means absurd, while the other side of the government's case – that to ban sports wholesale would increase parochial tensions, alienate the lower orders and make loyalty to the national church harder to inculcate – did have a certain cogency.

The pattern of prosecutions in the secular and ecclesiastical courts, in Wiltshire and elsewhere, not only reflects the lack of consensus on the issue of Sunday and holiday games but also suggests that the principle of leaving well alone in fact represented the majority opinion, even among the upper ranks and the middling sort. There was considerable variation from area to area and from parish to parish; but attempts to suppress games or even to regulate them were strikingly sporadic, and overall it can hardly be said that legal action amounted to a coherent 'reform of popular culture'.[69] It is well known that in some counties, such as Lancashire and Somerset, the justices of the peace issued orders to suppress ales, feasts and revels.[70] But this did not happen in Wiltshire, though very occasionally the quarter sessions dealt with individual cases, involving a special threat to the peace, on an *ad hoc* basis. Thus the organisers

[67] Samuel Rawson Gardiner (ed.), *The constitutional documents of the puritan revolution, 1625–1660*, 3rd edn (Oxford, 1906), pp. 99–103; 1 Car. I c. 1; Hill, *Society and puritanism*, pp. 192–3.

[68] Keith Thomas, *The perception of the past in early modern England*, University of London, Creighton Trust lecture (1983), pp. 21–3; Hill, *Society and puritanism*, pp. 193–4; William Hunt, *The puritan moment: the coming of revolution in an English county* (Cambridge, Mass., 1983), pp. 175, 253.

[69] Note, however, that local attacks on games and festivities did not necessarily involve recourse to the courts. The phrase 'reform of popular culture' derives from Peter Burke, *Popular culture in early modern Europe* (1978). The notion has been applied to puritan attacks on festivities in sixteenth- and seventeenth-century England by Jeremy Goring, *Godly exercises or the devil's dance? Puritanism and popular culture in pre-civil war England*, Friends of Dr Williams's Library lecture, 37 (1983).

[70] Thomas G. Barnes, 'County politics and a puritan cause célèbre: Somerset churchales, 1633', *Trans. Roy. Hist. Soc.*, 5th ser., 9 (1959), p. 109; Haigh, 'Puritan evangelism', pp. 51–5.

of a 'young men's ale' at Netheravon in 1628 were bound over because they had been wandering about Wiltshire and Hampshire begging for corn and intended to 'draw great company together'.[71] Church court cases did not invariably involve attempts to regulate or suppress games; the judges were sometimes called upon simply to adjudicate disputes about the cash raised by means of church ales.[72] The ecclesiastical authorities became more aggressive when festivities took place on church premises or disrupted services. Thus the churchwardens of Tisbury were prosecuted in 1615 for allowing ales to be kept in the yard of the chapel at Hatch, while in 1621 a number of individuals from Newton Tony were dealt with for holding a cockfight in the chancel. Cases of this type were however rare.[73] The stock form of prosecution was for missing prayers by playing or watching games. But alleged offenders often declared their conformity with the strict letter of the law, claiming that the sports took place *after* prayers and sometimes adding that what they did was 'no way contrary to his majesty's laws ecclesiastical' or that 'the king did allow of it by his book'.[74] Whether because the judges were satisfied that games did not significantly affect church attendance, or because they believed that excessive rigour was likely to be counter-productive, the courts themselves made little effort to ferret out offenders. The detection of unlawful players thus depended overwhelmingly on the vigilance of local churchwardens and ministers. But it is plain that these were often complaisant, and despite some increase in the frequency of prosecutions in the early seventeenth century the overall numbers of cases remained quite small. In Wiltshire, in the period 1615–29, an annual average of fewer than ten people appeared to answer for unlawful games. Moreover this figure, low as it is, in a sense gives an exaggerated impression of the degree of enforcement. When particularly zealous ministers or churchwardens did bother to detect players they tended to exhibit lengthy lists of offenders: the actual number of *occasions* on which action was taken was very small.[75] There is no reason to

71 W.R.O., QS/GR Trin. 1628/36–8, 44–5.
72 W.R.O., B/*Detecta* Bk 6, fol. 38; B/ABO 5, fol. 25v; B/Libels 4/26.
73 W.R.O., AS/ABO 11, 24/6/1615, *Office v. Gray and Scammell*; B/ABO 10, 26/9/1621, *Office v. Myles and Bundaie*.
74 W.R.O., D/AB 28, 26/1/1626, *Office v. Tompson*; B/ABO 8, 6/10/1618, *Office v. Fowler*.
75 For an extreme example, see the lists of football players and spectators presented by the minister of Great Bedwyn in 1619: W.R.O., D/Pres. 1619 (unnumbered).

suppose, moreover, that the experience of Wiltshire was in any way atypical in this respect: the pattern of prosecutions in Leicestershire, West Sussex and Cambridgeshire was very similar.[76]

Apart from work, games and the attractions of alehouse society, there were many pretexts on which people absented themselves from church, including sickness, lack of decent apparel and fear of arrest for debt.[77] But the most common reason was probably simple slackness. Thus Thomas Browne of Tockenham alleged in 1634 that 'he doth frequent his church as orderly as any parishioner but denieth not but that he may be absent upon some Sundays or holiday'; Elizabeth Reade of Wanborough, with nice ambiguity, declared in 1620 that 'she for her part cometh as often to service and sermon as any other of her neighbours'; while in 1627 the judge had to be content with Thomas Molens's limp promise that he would 'henceforward resort more often to the church when the weather is fair and that he hath not any extraordinary occasions to be absent'. An even more reluctant worshipper was Edward London of Great Wishford, whose excommunication around 1600 was said to make little difference since 'he never loved the church'.[78] It seems clear, moreover, that church attendance and participation in the sacraments were in many parishes regarded primarily as the duty of householders; servants, and perhaps young people generally, were neither expected nor encouraged to attend regularly. Thus at Great Bedwyn around 1608 it was presented that 'all the servants in most part general of the parish do not receive the communion thrice every year'; while John Taunton of Westbury allegedly opined in 1614 that if householders 'did send their people to prayers they were as good send their horses'.[79]

[76] For example, the very full quarterly presentments for the archdeaconry of Chichester in 1622 named only 10 people for playing unlawful games, and 8 of these came from a single parish (Boxgrove): Hilda Johnstone (ed.), *Churchwardens' presentments (17th century)*, 2 pts, Sussex Record Soc., 49–50 (Lewes, 1949–50), pt 1, pp. 27–9, 53. For prosecutions in Elizabethan Kent and Essex, see Collinson, *Religion of protestants*, pp. 206–7; Frederick G. Emmison, 'Tithes, perambulations and sabbath-breach in Elizabethan Essex', in Frederick G. Emmison and Roy Stephens (eds.), *Tribute to an antiquary: essays presented to Marc Fitch by some of his friends* (1976), pp. 199–206.

[77] W.R.O., AS/ABO 7, 14/2/1601, *Office v. Bathe*; AW/ABO 5, 14/11/1617, *Office v. Seaburne*; AW/ABO 6, 27/5/1624, *Office v. Grymes*.

[78] W.R.O., AW/ABO 7, 19/2/1634; AW/ABO 5, 20/6/1620; AW/ABO 6, 4/12/1627; QS/GR East. 1604/158. The case of Molens may be one of crypto-recusancy rather than simple slackness.

[79] W.R.O., D/Pres. 1607–9 (unnumbered); Precentor/Pres. 1614–40, Westbury, 17/10/1614; cf. D/Pres. 1611–12 (unnumbered), Hill Deverill.

Churchwardens and sidesmen were by no means necessarily immune to these attitudes; and even those who were keen to enforce religious observances may often have relied primarily on local chivvying, reporting only obdurate or persistent offenders to the courts. For these reasons, presentments for negligent attendance at church and failure to receive the communion undoubtedly under-represent the actual numbers of offenders. The spatial pattern of prosecutions is also a very uncertain guide to the real situation (especially on short time-scales, since detections from many parishes did not come in regularly but in periodic bursts, presumably the result of 'drives' by particularly zealous churchwardens or exasperated ministers). For what it is worth, the topographical distribution of prosecutions in Wiltshire reveals two main areas of possibly significant clustering. One was in certain of the densely populated towns and villages of the clothing areas in the north-west of the county, and probably reflects real difficulties of enforcing attendance in that region. The other was in some of the chalkland villages in the far south of Wiltshire; this may reflect a kind of recusant penumbra of reluctant churchgoers, or it may be that the authorities' increasing insistence on the identification of catholics made churchwardens in this region more sensitive to absence from church and more prone to report offenders. On the whole, however, regional variations in the pattern of prosecutions are less marked than differences between individual parishes, the latter presumably reflecting local traditions of enforcement as well as the actual numbers of offenders.[80]

What the pattern of prosecutions suggests more clearly is that over the period 1570–1640 the courts gradually increased their efforts to improve standards of religious observance and that, in alliance with local interests, they did achieve some success. In the archdeaconry of North Wiltshire in the late Elizabethan period, it appears that little attempt was made to enforce regular churchgoing, the court contenting itself with an annual drive to discover those

[80] Analysis of the spatial patterns of prosecutions is complicated by the fact that most of the office act books of the Wiltshire courts in the early seventeenth century only record offenders who actually appeared in court; but the conclusions offered here are based not only on these but also on the fuller late sixteenth-century materials and the files of presentments for parishes subject to the jurisdiction of the dean of Salisbury. For some general comments on the problems of interpreting prosecutions for non-attendance at church, see Marchant, *Church under the law*, pp. 218–20; Collinson, *Religion of protestants*, pp. 207–12.

who had failed to receive the communion at Easter. In 1593, for example, only 19 people were presented for neglecting church attendance, while 126 were named for not receiving the sacrament; in 1599 the figures were 3 and 109 respectively.[81] Analysis of prosecutions for the period 1615–29 indicates that the stress on the annual reception of the communion still remained, but by this time more effort was being directed towards the enforcement of regular weekly churchgoing. The figures are difficult to interpret, not least because of changes in the nature of the court records between the late sixteenth and the early seventeenth century,[82] but they do convey the distinct impression that regular attendance at church, and certainly annual participation in the communion, were far more widely accepted by the 1620s and 1630s than they had been in the middle years of Elizabeth's reign.[83] The impression is reinforced by comparison with the records of the church courts in the archdeaconries of Chichester and Leicester and in the diocese of Ely. With variations in the precise pattern of prosecutions, all these areas reveal a growing insistence on the part of the ecclesiastical authorities on regularity of worship; and the form of the resulting presentments (more revealing in this respect than the records of the Wiltshire courts) indicates a considerable measure of active co-operation in many parishes. Increasingly, for example, presentments specified precisely the date or dates on which offenders had absented themselves from church, suggesting careful local monitoring and perhaps the use of attendance registers.[84] And positive statements by churchwardens, more convincing in tone than the traditionally evasive 'all is well', indicate that some parishes did manage to achieve something close to the pattern of universal regular churchgoing prescribed by law. The churchwardens of Fernhurst (Sussex), for example, were able to report in 1622 that 'all the inhabitants do resort to church orderly' except for one named individual.[85]

It is one thing to enforce regular churchgoing, another to inculcate real devotion. Some historians have argued that, even when the

[81] W.R.O., AW/*Detecta* Bk, 1586–99, fols. 87–9, 92–8, 101–6, 139, 143v–4, 153–7v, 167v–8v, 170.
[82] See above, n. 80.
[83] For fuller discussion, see Ingram, 'Ecclesiastical justice in Wiltshire', pp. 91–2.
[84] For example, see L.M., 1 D 41/13/40, fols. 4–5, 8, 9v and *passim*. For an example of a Wiltshire attendance register, see D/Pres. 1611–12, Heytesbury, 17/9/1612.
[85] Johnstone (ed.), *Churchwardens' presentments*, pt 1, p. 40.

common people attended church, they often slept, spat, told jokes, and indulged in other forms of irreverence which turned the service into a 'travesty of what was intended'.[86] In point of fact, presentments for these forms of misbehaviour were very rare in most areas; of those that occurred, some were plainly instigated by particularly touchy ministers who would perhaps have done better to reflect on the most appropriate means of communicating with their rustic congregations.[87] Of course the paucity of reports of gross irreverence does not necessarily imply a high level of serious devotion, but the contrary view, which sees the tone of many congregations in this period as similar to that of 'a tiresome class of schoolboys', may well be an exaggeration.[88]

How strong were feelings of anticlericalism or of resentment towards the institutional aspects of church organisation in this period? Some historians have assumed that the increase in tithe litigation in the late sixteenth and early seventeenth centuries must have reflected or encouraged ill feeling towards the clergy.[89] But the growing numbers of tithe suits were merely part of a broader trend, the burgeoning of litigation over property in both the ecclesiastical and the secular courts; and lay people benefited from tithe rights – as impropriators, tithe-farmers, and collectors – to such an extent that the issues of tithe and clerical privilege could no longer be easily equated. (Nearly half the tithe suits in the Salisbury consistory court in 1640–1 were commenced by laymen.)[90] Whether brought by clergy or not, the great majority of tithe actions prove on examination to be in the nature of simple debt suits or to relate to specific disputes over tithing customs, compositions and the like. Very few reflect principled objections to, or anticlerical resentment of, the payment of tithes as such.[91] Rather similar considerations apply to other ecclesiastical exactions, such as the wages of parish clerks and church rates. Admittedly constant pressure from the authorities was

86 Thomas, *Religion and the decline of magic*, p. 161–2; Fletcher, *County community in peace and war*, p. 88.

87 For examples, see W.R.O., AS/ABO 1b, fol. 19; AW/*Detecta* Bk, 1586–99, fol. 77v; AW/ABO 6, 1/6/1630, *Office v. Hicks*; D/Pres. 1616–17/6. Cf. *The works of George Herbert*, ed. F. E. Hutchinson (Oxford, 1941), pp. 231–2.

88 Thomas, *Religion and the decline of magic*, p. 162.

89 See esp. O'Day, *English clergy*, pp. 191–8.

90 Based on analysis of W.R.O., B/Citations 5/20–280, collated with B/ABI 54.

91 For similar conclusions, see Marchant, *Church under the law*, p. 63; Christopher Haigh, *Reformation and resistance in Tudor Lancashire* (Cambridge, 1975), pp. 58–61.

needed to enforce the repair of churches and chapels and to ensure that they were properly supplied with liturgical furniture and books, but there is little evidence of serious opposition to these maintenance duties, irksome though they might be. People who failed to pay rates and wages were usually not numerous, and the majority of cases involved such issues as alleged overrating or, in times of economic recession, simple inability to pay; real defiance was rare.[92]

Inevitably ministers and the ministry occasionally attracted abuse from some of their parishioners, who drew on an age-old anticlerical tradition in framing their insults. Maurice Harman told the minister of Bishopstrow that 'when [he]...died he thought he should meet him riding on a black bull'; Thomas Dench of Enford wished 'that all professors that do not what they promise...were hanged...and said he meant all [ministers] to be naught'; Richard Fripp said of the vicar of Winterbourne Stoke that 'he was a base priest...and lived by other men's goods'; while John Cheyney railed at the curate of Everleigh 'for that he was but...a beggarly servingman'.[93] But such cases trickled into the courts (whether as presentments or as suits for 'opprobrious words against the clergy') in very small numbers indeed, and seem often to have resulted from particular tensions existing between the abuser and the minister concerned.[94] Only rarely is there evidence that ministers were at odds with a large number of their parishioners. Some of the clergy concerned were puritans whose self-righteousness or zeal outran their common-sense;[95] a few were misfits who were totally unsuited to their task. The most scandalous case of the latter type involved John Coren, vicar of Box around 1600, who was accused of a variety of offences including sexual immorality, drunkenness and blasphemy; deeply in debt, he had to go about accompanied by armed guards for fear of writs, was engaged in numerous lawsuits and was said to have cursed

[92] For examples of alleged overrating, etc., see W.R.O., B/ABO 12, fols. 1v, 13, 18, 20v, 22v. In the period 1615–29 an annual average of about 25 people appeared before the courts of the three main Wiltshire jurisdictions to answer for not paying rates or other dues; but this figure was inflated by unusually large numbers of cases occurring in 1619, 1620 and 1621, perhaps as a result of economic difficulties.

[93] W.R.O., AS/ABO 14, 8/7/1626, *Office v. Harman*; AS/ABO 12, 30/4/1618, *Office v. Dench*; B/DB 38, fol. 45v; B/DB 29, fol. 109.

[94] For example, Cheyney's outburst arose from the fact that the curate had been sent for to help draw up a bond to enforce the former's appearance on a writ: W.R.O., B/DB 29, fol. 114.

[95] For example, see W.R.O., B/DB 9, fols. 85–6; B/*Detecta* Bk 6, fol. 15.

his parishioners from the church porch. Undoubtedly a man of this sort could damage the reputation of the whole ministry and even encourage sectarianism: on Easter day 1603 there was a disturbance in Box church in which a weaver and a roughmason denied the Book of Common Prayer and impugned the ministrations not only of Coren but also of 'a thousand of like insufficiency'. But a case like this was in itself utterly exceptional.[96]

Evidence of resentment towards ministers must in any case be offset by considering *positive* sentiments and the beneficent functions of the clergy. George Herbert's account of the duties of a minister, based on his experience as rector of Fugglestone with Bemerton in the 1630s, is no doubt idealised; but his picture of the clergyman as one who laboured to achieve harmony in his parish is supported by frequent references in court records to the part which ministers played in helping to arbitrate lawsuits and reconcile the parties, and in striving in other ways to achieve the ideals of Christian charity between neighbours.[97] In fine, it would be misleading to exaggerate the importance of anticlerical feelings; a degree of such resentment is to be expected in any society in which clerics play a prominent role, but it could and did co-exist with other, more positive sentiments towards the clergy.

Irrespective of attitudes to ministers, attachment to the local church was undoubtedly nourished by the central role it played in parish life. Numerous references in court records and other sources indicate that church and churchyard were important as places where neighbours met not only to worship and for the *rites de passage*, but also to gossip and to transact parochial and personal business.[98] On occasion they also quarrelled there, and though the resulting brawls and scuffles may at first sight appear to reflect badly on the devotion of the people concerned, the fact that so many of these disputes centred on the possession of seats and pews testifies to the real social importance of the forms of religion. In most parishes the ranking of seats in church broadly reflected the social hierarchy, though the correspondence was rarely exact; demographic and social structural

[96] W.R.O., B/DB 29, fols. 68–70; P.R.O., STAC 8/98/20; *H.M.C.*, *Various collections*, vol. 1, pp. 71–2.

[97] Herbert, *Works*, ed. Hutchinson, pp. 236, 259–60; cf. W.R.O., B/DB 20, fol. 10; B/DB 41, fol. 15; *H.M.C.*, *Various collections*, vol. 1, p. 102.

[98] For examples, see W.R.O., AW/ABO 5, 17/3/1618, *Office v. Berrie*; B/ABO 8, 11/9/1616, *Office v. Harris*; AS/ABO 15, 30/7/1640, *Office v. Peirce*. References are innumerable.

changes gradually tended to create anomalies, especially since pew rights were often attached to particular houses or pieces of land irrespective of the actual social status of the current possessors. The result was sporadic tensions, which sooner or later would necessitate a total reallocation of seats – a process which could itself generate bitter feelings among people who had been downgraded. How fiercely rights to certain 'places' were cherished could be illustrated by numerous examples; but a case from Tisbury in 1637, albeit unusual in that it led to direct defiance of the church courts, is particularly striking. At the petition of the inhabitants the diocesan chancellor had redistributed the seating in the church to accommodate an increased population, and had allocated the places according to 'ranks, qualities and conditions'. Joan and Anne Scammell, the latter a widow, refused to leave their old places. Despite an admonition in court, the pair answered defiantly that 'notwithstanding ... they would sit in those seats as long as they live'; and when the judge excommunicated them for contempt, Anne Scammell broke out in court, 'by way of imprecation': 'blessed are they that do comfort the widows but cursed be they that do them wrong'.[99] The strength of feeling which underlay this and similar cases is an indication that, for established householders at least, prestige and status were intimately linked with the forms of religion, and to this extent attachment to the church was strong.

The role of religion in the communities of Elizabethan and early Stuart England, the nature of religious developments and the part that the church courts (in association with other legal institutions) played in enforcing conformity are in many ways best understood through the medium of individual parish histories. A valuable point of reference for such local perspectives is Wrightson and Levine's study of the village of Terling in Essex, since it embraces many of the themes pursued in this chapter and furthermore investigates their relationship to socio-economic developments. But, as was noted earlier, Terling was unusual for the strength and coherence of the 'godly' group which emerged there in the early seventeenth century; and for this and other reasons it displays an atypically striking convergence of economic and religious–cultural shifts. In late sixteenth-century Terling, Wrightson and Levine indicate, the 'better sort' (consisting of relatively prosperous yeoman and substantial husbandman and craftsman families) were already in wealth and

[99] W.R.O., AS/ABO 15, fols. 47v–8.

lifestyle drawing apart from the growing numbers of poorer inhabitants; and religious and cultural changes in the period *c.* 1580–*c.* 1640 both reflected and reinforced this process of social differentiation. The growth of literacy among the 'better sort' tended to align them with the values and outlook of the county magistracy and the committed protestant clergy, and in particular made them receptive to puritan piety and to the ideal of 'godly' discipline. In alliance with successive puritan incumbents, and motivated by a mixture of religious zeal and economic prudence, the parish notables of Terling mounted a vigorous attack – articulated through the secular and ecclesiastical courts – on lax religious observance, drunkenness and unlicensed aleselling, dancing and other festivities, and sexual immorality. By the 1630s these 'common country disorders' had been substantially reduced and, in so far as they did survive, become largely associated with the poorer, 'rougher' elements in the community. Terling was well on the way to becoming a model of godly discipline.[100]

The course of economic and demographic change in Keevil, and to a lesser extent that in Wylye, have affinities with Terling's history;[101] and, as will be seen, both places also witnessed in the early seventeenth century an intensification of discipline over sexual immorality. But their religious history presents something of a contrast to Terling. In these Wiltshire villages many of the changes stressed by Wrightson and Levine were visible only in a fleeting or fragmentary way; overall the religious situation emerges as less polarised and less dynamic, varieties of inconspicuous orthodoxy being far more important than signal piety. These features accord with the impression conveyed earlier in this chapter, and suggest that Wylye and Keevil were more representative of the majority of English parishes.

As in most Wiltshire villages in this period (in this respect as in Terling), witchcraft and magical beliefs appear to have been of only minor importance in everyday life. Over the years 1580–1640 there was only one known witchcraft prosecution in each place. In Keevil a woman, probably of humble status, was presented at the archdeacon's visitation in 1604 'for that she is suspected of witchcraft'.

[100] Wrightson and Levine, *Poverty and piety*, *passim*. For a more detailed summary of the argument, and critique thereof, see Ingram, 'Religion, communities and moral discipline', *passim*.

[101] See above, Chapter 2.

Apart from the fact that she denied the charge, virtually nothing more is known about her. More dramatically, in 1613 John Potticarie, one of the most prominent men in Wylye, accused a certain John Monday of bewitching his child, threatening that 'if that he die I will hang thee for it'. Apparently the child lived, but none the less Potticarie brought a charge at the quarter sessions. But Monday, a married labourer said to live on the alms of the parish, was supported by a testimonial signed by thirteen parishioners including the rector and was exonerated; and he retaliated by bringing a church court defamation suit against his accuser.[102]

The religious complexion of any village probably depended a good deal on the quality of pastoral care provided by the clergy. Not much is known about the early Elizabethan vicars of Keevil,[103] but it is plain that Francis Greatrakes (1588–1617) and his son Stephen (1617–40) were both diligent, constantly resident preaching ministers, though only the second was a graduate. There is no evidence that either was a puritan in any doctrinal sense, but they do seem to have laboured steadily to maintain and foster more than minimal standards of religious observance among their flock; on at least one occasion Francis Greatrakes rebuked a man from the pulpit for lack of concentration.[104]

Evidence about how the laity responded to these ministrations is perforce largely inferential. The majority of Keevil wills in the period *c.* 1590–*c.* 1615 were prefaced by the neutral formula 'I bequeath my soul to Almighty God', but there was a marked change thereafter. Elaborately worded, distinctively protestant preambles became much commoner and by the 1630s heavily predominated. Wrightson and Levine inferred the growth of protestant piety in Terling mainly from will evidence; and it might at first sight appear that a similar shift in religious attitudes occurred in Keevil, at least among the upper third of village society who made most of the wills.

[102] W.R.O., AS/ABO 8, 16/10/1604, *Office v. Isabel Gybbins alias Elton* (buried 22/3/1623); B/Misc. Ct papers 29/48, fols. 3–6v; QS/GR East. 1613/100, 214; Hadow (ed.), *Wylye registers*, pp. 14–16.

[103] Robert Yorke (1550–77) was neither a graduate nor a preacher, but was described as resident and 'moderately learned' in 1561: Corpus Christi College, Cambridge, MS 97, fol. 187v. There was a succession of short incumbencies in the period 1578–88.

[104] Inferred from W.R.O., D/AB 21, fol. 271v (*Office v. Harris*). On the Greatrakeses' qualifications, see W.R.O., B/Exhibit Bk, 1613, fol. 33; Joseph Foster, *Alumni Oxonienses: the members of the university of Oxford, 1500–1714*, 4 vols. (Oxford, 1891–2), vol. 2, p. 596.

But on close examination it emerges that the change in will formulae largely reflected the forms preferred respectively by Francis and Stephen Greatrakes, who were responsible for actually writing the majority of testaments. However, it does appear that by the 1620s and 1630s elaborate professions of faith, by no means entirely stereotyped, were regarded as the most desirable form and were likely to appear even in wills not penned by the minister. Thus, while the alteration in will formulae cannot be taken as firm evidence of a marked strengthening of protestant commitment in Keevil, it does suggest a measure of sensitivity to religious matters among testators and of what may be termed 'protestant drift'.[105]

Potential access to the fundamental text of protestantism, the Bible, was certainly growing in Keevil. Here, as in Terling and so many other English parishes, literacy became more widespread in the late sixteenth and early seventeenth centuries. The available evidence, derived mainly from probate records, is not easily quantifiable, but the main outlines are clear. Early in the reign of Elizabeth literacy in Keevil was largely confined to the minister and a few gentlemen and near-gentlemen. By the 1630s about half the Keevil yeomen and those of similar status could sign their names, as also could some husbandmen and craftsmen. Ownership of Bibles also increased, mainly among the wealthy yeomen and clothiers. Thus by the decades 1630–49 some 18 per cent of probate documents mentioned Bibles, compared with only 4 per cent in the years 1590–1629. These are, of course, minimum indications, since books – especially items of small intrinsic value such as cheap editions of the Bible intended for everyday use – were by no means always separately itemised in wills and inventories. To be sure, Bible ownership is in itself no certain evidence of personal piety, and indeed the Bibles mentioned in probate documents (evidently substantial volumes often located in or on ornamental cupboards) could well have served essentially as status objects.[106] But at the least the possession of Bibles must reflect the social importance of religious symbols among the higher strata of Keevil society.

A few wills from the period 1570–1640 do provide more positive evidence of exceptional piety. They are characterised by a particularly original or exceptionally elaborate religious preamble, and/

[105] For comments on the limitations of wills as evidence of personal religious belief and commitment, see Spufford, *Contrasting communities*, ch. 13.

[106] Cf. Cressy, *Literacy and the social order*, pp. 50–2.

or by indications (such as references to 'my well beloved friends in Christ') that the testator's religious sentiments extended to an unusual degree to social relations and everyday activities.[107] In contrast to the situation in Terling, however, these pious villagers were relatively few, quite widely scattered in the social scale, and as a group not particularly literate. Perhaps 'group' is a misleading term to use of them: they were scattered over time, apparently did not form a close-knit nexus in village society, and certainly did not dominate the structure of local office-holding. Whether they were more numerous than, or played a different social role from, exceptionally pious villagers who had presumably existed in earlier times can only be conjectured.

More typical of the village, and apparently as true of the poorer householders as of the wealthier inhabitants, was a stolid conformity which stopped well short of enthusiasm. Few parishioners made much demur about the payment of tithes or church dues; the occasional disputes which ended up in court were mainly of a technical nature, involving allegations of unfair assessment and the like.[108] Many testators made some small bequest towards the upkeep of the parish church or of Salisbury cathedral, and more than a third of wills in the period 1590–1640 included legacies to the minister.[109] Successive churchwardens, probably chosen by a rotation system from the middling to upper householders, were willing to co-operate with the church courts to the extent of presenting at least the most notorious cases of absence from church, misbehaviour in church or churchyard, and Sunday work; indeed the intensity of prosecutions, though hardly amounting to a crusade, did increase somewhat over the period.

There were prosecutions not only in the church courts but also in the quarter sessions and the local court leet for drunkenness and unlicensed aleselling. But action was sporadic, save for a certain bunching of cases in the early to mid-1620s (a time of severe economic difficulty), especially in the years 1624–5, when about fifteen men, mainly cottagers, poor undertenants and menservants,

[107] For example, see W.R.O., Archdeaconry court of Salisbury probate records, will of Christopher Gaffray, 4/5/1620.

[108] For example, see W.R.O., B/ABO 7, fol. 66.

[109] But some of the legacies may have been in the nature of payment for services, particularly the writing of the will; and some of the bequests to Keevil church were for graves.

were prosecuted for alehouse haunting and drunkenness.[110] As regards games and pastimes, the only activity which regularly generated prosecutions was bowling (forbidden to the lower orders by an act of 1542). The culprits were mostly recurrent offenders and included some of the wealthiest and most influential men in the village: even Stephen Greatrakes was presented on one occasion.[111] The tiny fines levied for this offence in the court leet cannot possibly have been of any deterrent value; they were in effect a bowling tax cheerfully paid by addicts. Dancing and summer festivities seem to have flourished in the village and only came under attack twice. In 1611 the manor court ordered the destruction of a 'king house' set up on the waste as a bower for dancing and revels.[112] That the minister was in some way responsible for this order, perhaps abetted by members of the prominent Blagden family, is suggested by the sequel: an obscene rhyme (a stock form of derision or protest in this period) accused Francis Greatrakes, his wife and daughters, and the wife of Robert Blagden of 'beshitting' the king's hall. The libel was apparently penned by the son of one of the wealthier inhabitants of the village, a reminder that neither literacy nor higher social status necessarily lead to godliness.[113] In 1624, in the context of the multi-court drive against alehouses and inebriety, five young men were prosecuted in the archdeacon's court for dancing in prayer time. They confessed to dancing 'in the company of divers men and women of Keevil in a bower in the midst of the town there at a dancing match', asserting that 'there is usually dancing in Keevil upon the Sabbath days after...evening prayer, which...is no otherwise than is allowed by the king's majesty'. These cases suggest that festivities were still thriving, despite the earlier attack; and the fact that one of the individuals prosecuted was the son of one of the most powerful men in the parish, while his companions were of various social ranks, indicates that participation in sports was by no means confined to the poor.[114]

110 W.R.O., QS/GR Trin. 1624/121; W.R.O., 288/1, view of frankpledge, 31 Mar. 1 Car. (1625).

111 W.R.O., 288/1, view of frankpledge, 18 Dec. 19 Jac. (1621). The act of 33 Hen. VIII c. 9 against unlawful games, including bowls, consolidated and extended the provisions of a number of earlier statutes.

112 W.R.O., 288/1, court baron, 4 Sept. 9 Jac. (1611).

113 W.R.O., QS/GR Mich. 1611/108. For further discussion of mocking rhymes, see below, p. 164.

114 W.R.O., AS/ABO 13, 22/7/1624, *Office v. Aneave, Blagden, Elliot and Foote*; B/ABO 11, 23/7/1625, *Office v. Harris* (apparently referring to dancing, etc. in the previous year).

There are indications that the choice of victims in the spate of prosecutions in 1624–5 was partly dictated by feuds among the parish notables. Specifically religious issues certainly figured in such feuds from time to time. In a dispute between two wealthy yeomen in 1625, both of them prominent in parish government, Roger Blagden caused John Ford and his associates to be prosecuted in the church courts for adultery, open quarrelling at the communion table and other matters. In a suit in the star chamber in 1619, Roger Blagden's brother Robert accused one of his opponents of rudely disturbing the minister during divine service and of defrauding the poor, another of tearing up briefs and reviling the minister and churchwardens as asses, knaves and fools; while in their turn his enemies charged him with setting up a tapster on a stool to preach a mock sermon in an inn, and with doubting whether the writings of the apostles and prophets were true. Whether these accusations and counter-accusations had any basis in truth is obviously doubtful; Robert Blagden was at any rate eventually to preface his will with an elaborate profession of faith and to leave a legacy of 13s. 4d. to 'Greatrakes, preacher of God['s] word in Keevil'. The significance of these quarrels is not in reflecting indifference to religion; it is in showing both that ecclesiastical and religious issues were of sufficient significance in social life to serve as a focus for parish rivalries, and that in so far as religious and moral issues were socially divisive the splits were as much vertical as horizontal.[115]

Religious developments in late Elizabethan and early Stuart Keevil may be summed up as slow progress towards better standards in at least the outward forms of religious observance, interrupted from time to time by unedifying wrangles among the parish notables and occasionally punctuated by fleeting drives against alehouses and festivities. The situation in Wylye was on the whole even more static, though the placidity of parish life was disturbed by one dramatic though short-lived attempt at moral and religious reformation in the early 1620s.

Between 1582 and 1619 the rector of Wylye was Thomas Bower, a graduate of Christ Church who also held the living of Pentridge in Dorset. He was succeeded by John Lee (1619–34), another pluralist who eventually became treasurer of the cathedral; and he in turn

[115] W.R.O., B/ABO 11, 31/10/1625, *Office v. Ford;* P.R.O., STAC 8/59/11, m. 2; W.R.O., Archdeaconry court of Salisbury probate records, will of Robert Blackden, senior, 16/11/1635.

was followed by Alexander Hyde (1634–46), cousin of the future earl of Clarendon and himself destined to become subdean of Salisbury (1637) and ultimately bishop (1665–7). For much of the period a good deal of the pastoral work of the parish was performed by a succession of curates and by Thomas Crockford (schoolmaster at Stockton, 1602–13, and vicar of Fisherton Delamere, 1613–34), who acted as 'coadjutor' in Wylye.[116] A high proportion of nuncupative wills suggests that at times there was no clergyman readily available on a day to day basis. Evidently there was some social contact, even intermarriage, between the family of Thomas Bower and a few of the leading sub-gentry parishioners. But lack of continuous clerical contact may have inhibited the formation of close bonds between the clergy and the mass of the inhabitants – it is noticeable that legacies to the church and to the minister were much rarer than in Keevil. On the other hand, there was apparently little trouble over the payment of tithes and dues. Will dedications, penned by many hands, were predictably various, and show no clear pattern of development over time; and although literacy was certainly becoming more widespread among the wealthier inhabitants, there is positive evidence of only one Bible in lay ownership by 1640.[117] As in Keevil, there was a scattering of particularly pious individuals, and conventional orthodoxy was probably general. When Thomas Starre alias Warminster, a tailor of modest substance, made oral disposition of his goods on his death-bed in 1620, his neighbours testified that he 'christianly committed his soul into the hands of Almighty God, with comfortable hope of His everlasting mercy'.[118]

In 1581 five men were prosecuted in the bishop's court for allegedly performing a mock marriage, but it turned out to be a harmless game at a Childermas party;[119] while in 1603–4 there was a small clutch of prosecutions for not attending church, at a time when there was plague in the village.[120] Otherwise there were few ecclesiastical court presentments for lax religious observance and similar

116 Hadow (ed.), *Wylye registers*, pp. v–vii.

117 W.R.O., Archdeaconry court of Salisbury probate records, inventory of goods of John Hilman, tailor, 18/11/1640.

118 W.R.O., Archdeaconry court of Salisbury probate records, will of Thomas Starre alias Warminster, 1/2/1621.

119 W.R.O., B/DB 8, fols. 83v–4; B/ABI 13, fols. 114v, 148v. 'Childermas' was the feast of the Holy Innocents (28 December), traditionally the occasion for inversionary pranks and burlesques.

120 W.R.O., AS/ABO 8, 28/1/1604, *Office v. Kent and wife*, *Office v. Dewe and wife*, *Office v. Randall and wife*, *Office v. Smith and wife*.

matters for upwards of forty years before 1620 (though there were sporadic quarter sessions prosecutions for unlicensed aleselling). That this dearth of presentments was due to the complaisance of successive churchwardens – drawn, as usual, from the middling ranks – rather than to exceptionally high religious standards emerged after the arrival of John Lee as rector in 1619. He and his son, who served as curate for several years, speedily mounted a moral and religious reform campaign. The effect on presentments for sexual offences will be considered in later chapters, but other aspects of the drive of 1620–1 were impressive enough. Two people were presented for not receiving the communion, one for not coming to church, another for not troubling to arrive until the service was half over. The last was also charged with unseemly behaviour in church; while his brother, prosecuted for the same offence, confessed that 'in the Christmas time he hath cloathen himself in maiden's apparel as it were in a masque' – a charge which, as the sequel showed, reflected the Lees' distaste for traditional festivities. Another man was presented for playing 'kittles' in service time. At least eight people, and possibly several more whose offences were not specified in the act books, were prosecuted for drunkenness, drinking during service time, or allowing drinking and ill rule in their houses. One man was presented as a common swearer, two for negligently deferring the baptism of their children; and three excommunicates were presented and induced to procure absolution. In all 23 people, drawn from all ranks of the social scale, are known to have been prosecuted for religious and non-sexual moral offences, the 19 men involved representing a very substantial proportion of the total adult male population of the village.[121]

The pattern of presentments for religious offences is revealing. It reflected not massive abstention or alienation from the church on the part of the inhabitants of Wylye, but simply a laxity which was anathema to the precisian Lees. The situation is further illuminated by a series of prosecutions which were brought in the bishop's court in 1624 against a certain Thomas Kent, who had recently served as churchwarden, and his son Thomas and daughter Susan. Kent senior, a literate yeoman of substance, was charged with absence

[121] Most of these prosecutions are recorded in W.R.O., B/ABO 10, 14/12/1620 and courts held in January 1621 (dates crumbled away). See also W.R.O., AS/ABO 13, 30/9/1620, *Office v. Potticary* and *Office v. Sop*, 12/5/1621, *Office v. Waile*; B/ABO 10, 7/3/1621 (second court that day), *Office v. Long*.

from church on Easter day; with negligent attendance at other times and with making an appearance, when he did come, only at the end of service; with failing to provide adequate supplies of bread and wine for the communion when he served as churchwarden; with aggressive mismanagement in allocating pews; and with quarrelling with the curate in the church. Further, he was charged with dissuading the people from strict religious observance. Allegedly he complained that Mr Lee's sermons were too long and that the parishioners, especially servants, were better employed at home looking after their beasts; that it was unreasonable to expect those who lived at a distance from the church to attend often; and that celebrations of the communion had become too frequent. He reckoned that the cost in bread and wine was a drain on parish finances, and apparently disliked what he saw as religious regimentation: 'I know by the canons we ought to have a week's warning... [of the celebration of communion]; it was not like a muster, no more but beat up the drum and come away; they ought to have more time.'

Susan Kent's sentiments were probably fairly characteristic of the young. She did not like Mr Lee's demand that all the parishioners, both young and old, should come regularly to hear the catechism: 'when once he...takes his green book in hand we shall have such a deal of bibble babble that I am weary to hear it, and I can then sit down in my seat and take a good nap'. Further, she resented the Lees' attacks on games and festivities and relied on her father to defend them, asserting that 'the king doth allow of it' and declaring that 'we had a good parson here before but now we have a puritan ... A plague or a pox in him that ever he did come hither, and I would we had kept our old parson for he did never dislike with [games and dances] ... These proud puritans are up at the top now but I hope they will have a time to come as fast down as ever they come up.' The bitterness of her feelings was intense. On one occasion, it was alleged, she declared that 'she would not stay prayers but would get her as far as she could out of the devil's clutches ... Yes! There lies Mr Lee the great devil in his den and I will go as far out of his reach as I can.' Her place of safety was a dancing match in the neighbouring village of Steeple Langford.[122]

122 The prosecutions against the Kents, with the extensive depositions summarised and quoted in these paragraphs, are found in W.R.O., B/ABO 11, fols. 35v–40, 41v–2.

Apparently the Kents were not hostile to the church and to religion as such. When the younger Thomas Kent died by accident in 1625, he was buried with special solemnity and a funeral sermon was preached by a minister from Hampshire; and Kent senior had elm trees planted from the east to the west end of the churchyard in 1636.[123] The family's objections were to unprecedentedly strict standards of conduct and religious observance demanded by the Lees. How far did the latter have willing allies among the other inhabitants of Wylye? Apart from the younger Lee, eleven people (including four women) deposed against the Kents, being drawn mainly from the middling ranks of village society but including some poorer individuals. Five of the seven men could sign their names. None of these witnesses had been prosecuted in the moral campaign of 1620–1, and they may have prided themselves on their respectability; and a husbandman named John Taylor was probably speaking for all of them when he claimed that Mr Lee's sermons, being 'not at any time above an hour...is thought well of by all the rest of the parish it being always performed in a very seasonable time'.[124] But the terms of this statement hardly suggest that Taylor and his co-witnesses found a self-consciously 'godly' group marked off from the rest of the inhabitants, and there is little evidence from other sources that they were marked by truly exceptional piety. In any case some of them had other reasons apart from moral and religious zeal for witnessing against the Kents. By their own admission Thomas Kent and his son were heavily indebted (they claimed that their frequent absences from church were due to fear of arrest), and this may have fuelled resentment against them. More specifically, John Taylor had been fellow-churchwarden with Kent senior and was plainly anxious to dissociate himself from his colleague's alleged misdoings; while Thomas Potticarie, another hostile witness, had along with other members of the parish been antagonised over the allocation of pews. (The church seating question was to be a live issue for the next twenty years.)[125] In fine these deponents emerge as

[123] Hadow (ed.), *Wylye registers*, pp. xii, 50. However, the will of Thomas Kent senior, proved in 1652, was unusual in lacking a religious preamble: P.R.O., P.C.C. 185 Bowyer.

[124] W.R.O., B/ABO 11, fol. 37.

[125] For manifestations of the later history of the church seating issue, see W.R.O., B/Citations 5/5, and an agreement (with details of the allotment of seats) dated 1664, located in the class 'Bishop: Miscellaneous papers and books' (Stewart, *Diocese of Salisbury: guide to the records*, p. 23).

solid conformists rather than religious activists, disapproving for various reasons of the Kents' behaviour but not necessarily wholly in tune with the precisian Lees. A lack of really strong principled support for the latter's puritanical reform programme is suggested by the fact that it rapidly ran out of steam; no spate of prosecutions comparable with those of 1620–1 and 1624 occurred again before the civil war.

Bearing in mind the experience of Keevil and Wylye, what generalisations can be made about the state of religious belief and observance in this period and the role the church courts played in enforcing conformity? There existed a minority of particularly pious individuals and, no doubt, a number of people who were virtually indifferent to religion. But most people fitted neither category, professing some degree of unspectacular orthodoxy. The notion that religious commitment was conditioned by social class must be treated with caution. The church and religion were probably least powerful in their hold on the young, especially transient servants – a life-cyclical distinction rather than a simple matter of economic standing. To established householders the church and religion were important as markers of status, respectability and belonging, if for nothing else; and though this may have been *most* true for the middle to upper strata of parish society (the groups from which churchwardens were usually recruited and which were most likely to possess family pews), it probably applied also to many 'honest householders' of the poorer sort, who had a definite, albeit modest stake in the community.

In any event, the centrality of church and religion in social life guaranteed a measure of support for the ecclesiastical courts in enforcing church attendance, communion reception and other observances. The ecclesiastical authorities, for their part, played a significant role in waging a war of attrition against catholic recusants and protestant sectaries, and in promoting improved clerical standards. In trying to raise standards of religious observance among the ordinary laity the courts were inclined to hasten slowly. They paid most attention to the basic matters of church attendance and communion reception and over time did achieve some success on these fronts. Aware of the difficulties involved, they trod much more warily in prosecuting such matters as holiday work, drunkenness and dancing – the pattern of presentments for these offences tended to reflect skirmishings in individual parishes. The church courts' approach may be summed up as broadly consensual, marching slightly in advance of popular attitudes so as to effect gradual improvement, but avoiding the contention which excessive innovation tended to arouse. As will be seen, they pursued a rather similar policy, with considerable success, in exercising discipline over marriage and sexual immorality.

4. *Sex and marriage: laws, ideals and popular practice*

In Elizabethan and early Stuart England, marriage and sexual morality were of more central social and political concern than they are today. Then as now, the family based on the conjugal couple was the primary matrix of procreation and of the socialisation – in contemporary terms, the 'education' – of the young. To a greater extent than at present, the family household was important as a unit of production and consumption, as a vehicle for the accumulation and transmission of property, and as the fundamental institution of social order and political authority. Tudor and Stuart philosophy regarded the rule or 'government' of the householder over his wife, children and servants as analogous to that of the prince over his subjects: royal and patriarchal authority were mutually validating reflections or natural manifestations of a divinely ordered hierarchy.

It followed that the decision to marry and establish a new household was conventionally seen as a matter which concerned not just the couple themselves but in some measure also their existing families and members of the wider society. Moreover the upholding of the marriage bond, once established, was a major social principle. Extramarital sexual activity of whatever kind was in social theory abhorred as hateful to God and a threat to the well-being of the commonwealth, and hence subject to legal penalty. Contrariwise, sexual 'honesty' and the status of married householder were important touchstones of respectability and stability. 'Necessary it is', observed the moralist William Gouge, 'that good order be first set in families: for as they were before other polities, so they are somewhat the more necessary: and good members of a family are like to make good members of church and commonwealth.'[1]

In essence these ideas were well established by 1500. But concern about marriage and sexuality intensified among the clerical and lay leaders of society from around the middle of the sixteenth century.

[1] William Gouge, *Of domesticall duties* (1622), Epistle, sig. 2v.

The economic and social changes of the period helped to stimulate a quest for order which re-emphasised the importance of the 'little commonwealth'.[2] At the same time, the government's concern to foster religious unity, and the zeal of a wide spectrum of churchmen and pious laymen to improve standards of religious belief, knowledge and practice led to greater stress on the role of the family household as the nursery of religion.[3] Among moralists and social commentators, these concerns coalesced into an insistence on the need for responsible, stable marriage and stricter standards of sexual morality – demands which the church courts were expected to meet.

The purposes of this chapter are threefold. The first is to sketch the moral assumptions which emerge from contemporary homilies, sermons, conduct books and other prescriptive discussions of marriage and sexuality. These concepts constituted the ideological framework within which the church courts worked and must be understood if the role of ecclesiastical justice is to be adequately appreciated. The second is to outline the inherited body of law on marriage and sexual conduct which constrained the church courts' conduct of business, and to discuss how far it was adapted to meet contemporary concerns and needs. The last is to discuss in general terms (in advance of the more detailed treatment of later chapters) how far the laws and ideals which governed the church courts' activities were congruent with popular attitudes and practices. In the following survey these themes are interwoven into a general review of marriage formation, marital relations and marital breakdown, and of the public control of illicit sexuality in early modern England.

What were the essential characteristics of the Tudor and Stuart 'family'? The great majority of family households were nuclear in form. Analysis of contemporary listings reveals that only about 10 per cent of households included resident kinsfolk other than the conjugal couple and their unmarried children. An even smaller proportion actually housed three generations of the same family; while to find two or more conjugal couples in co-residence (whether a

[2] For example, such ideas seem to underlie the statute of artificers (1563): R. H. Tawney and Eileen Power (eds.), *Tudor economic documents*, 3 vols. (1924), vol. 1, pp. 338–50, 353–63.

[3] Hill, *Society and puritanism*, ch. 13; cf. John Bossy, 'The counter-reformation and the people of catholic Europe', *Past and present*, no. 47 (May 1970), pp. 64–70.

parental couple with married children or two or more married siblings) was rare. Clearly the preferred norm was one conjugal couple per household.[4]

The majority of family households, especially among the poor, consisted simply of parents and children. But the households of the middling to upper ranks commonly included one or more living-in servants engaged in domestic work or farm labour, or resident apprentices learning their master's trade. They were regarded in law and social practice as part of the householder's 'family'. Indeed masters and mistresses were supposed to act *in loco parentis*, and servants (who were characteristically unmarried) owed them quasi-filial obedience and respect.[5]

Then as now, the idea of the 'family' could extend to kinsfolk and affines outside the household circle. The role of kinship in early modern England has so far not been fully researched. But limited information available from various English locales is sufficient to establish the main patterns; while analysis of wills, inventories and other sources from the parishes of Wylye and Keevil, together with scattered information from an assortment of other Wiltshire records, suggests that this county was in no way atypical. The method of reckoning kin was identical with the bilateral system familiar to us today: this meant that each individual had a unique set of kin reckoned through both the father and the mother, and as a result kin groupings tended to be flexible and impermanent. The aristocracy and gentry did often recognise and maintain more or less active relationships with a wide range of kinsfolk, and considerable pride was taken in ancestry. Interest in wider kin and pride in forebears also existed to some extent further down the social scale, especially among substantial yeoman families hovering near the brink of gentry status. But most people in the middling and lower ranks of society actually maintained effective relationships with only a narrow range of kin, largely confined within the circle closely related to the conjugal couple – grandparents, uncles and aunts, nephews and nieces, and in-laws. In everyday affairs, relationships with neighbours were usually of more practical importance than kin ties. Yet on occasion kinsfolk and affines (sometimes including quite remote relatives) could play a significant role, especially at times of family emergency: instances will crop up later in this book.[6]

[4] Laslett, *World we have lost further explored*, pp. 90–9.

[5] Kussmaul, *Servants in husbandry*, ch. 1 and *passim*.

[6] Available evidence on kinship in this period is surveyed in Wrightson, *English*

Thus the most intense and socially important kin relationships normally existed within nuclear family households, which were in effect the basic units of which the society was composed. Marriage normally meant leaving the parental home for good and the creation of such a new unit. It was hence a *rite de passage* of enormous social significance. Save at the poorest social levels, the marriage of a child was usually associated with the transfer of property across the generations, while wealthier and more influential families could hope to derive a variety of benefits from favourable alliances. Marriage also had important implications for the role played by the individual in the wider society. The status of married householder denoted adulthood and carried prestige. Equally (as was seen in the last chapter) it carried obligations and duties, marking an end to the irresponsibility of youth and implying the will and ability to perform the religious, social and political duties of adult members of the commonwealth.[7]

In view of the great public and family import of marriage, it was conventional wisdom that the matter could not be left wholly to the discretion of individual couples. Regulation was necessary. On the other hand, Christian principles prescribed that in important respects marriage was in the last resort the concern of two individuals, a state divinely ordained for the procreation of children, the avoidance of fornication, and the mutual society, help and comfort of the couple. What appear at first sight to be inconsistencies or even absurdities in contemporary laws and ideals concerning marriage formation were, in fact, designed to hold in balance the potentially conflicting principles of individual freedom and communal responsibility.

In theory it was possible for people to marry very young. The minimum legal ages for contracting a binding union were twelve for women and fourteen for men. Moreover, it was legally permissible for couples to be betrothed at the age of seven, with the right to dissent from and repudiate the engagement when they reached the age for full marriage.[8] Child 'marriages' of this sort may have been quite common in parts of north-west England at least as late as the

society, pp. 44–51; Ralph A. Houlbrooke, *The English family, 1450–1700* (1984), ch. 3. I hope to publish full details of the Wylye and Keevil material on another occasion.

[7] Laslett, *World we have lost further explored*, pp. 99–101.

[8] Sir Frederick Pollock and Frederic William Maitland, *The history of English law before the time of Edward I*, 2nd edn, 2 vols. (Cambridge, 1898), vol. 2, p. 390.

reign of Elizabeth, but were probably rare in most other parts of late sixteenth- and early seventeenth-century England; in Wiltshire, for example, only a tiny number of cases has come to light.[9] Even the minimum ages for full marriage were, in practice, of little social relevance: it was tacitly accepted throughout society that matrimony should be reserved for those of the age of discretion, and most people married much later than the legal threshold. In England as a whole the mean age of first marriage for both men and women was in the mid- to late twenties, with males generally marrying somewhat later than females. But there were fluctuations in marriage ages over time, and variations between communities and at different social levels.[10] Analysis of information from Wiltshire marriage licences, revealing mean ages of between 26 and 29 for grooms and around 24 for brides at various dates in the early seventeenth century, indicates that this county conformed to the normal pattern;[11] while study of stated marriage ages in the village of Wylye and the neighbouring parishes of Stockton and Fisherton Delamere in the period 1619–32 illustrates some variations. In these communities the mean age at first marriage for men was 29.7 (median 28.5) and 26.9 (median 27) for women. But there was a marked difference between the experience of females from yeoman and gentry families and those from poorer households: the former typically married in their late teens or early twenties, while the latter often did not get married till the late twenties or the thirties. Wealthy menfolk also tended to marry earlier than their poorer neighbours, but the disparity was less marked, and few men of whatever rank took a wife before the age of 25.[12]

Not law but social custom, internalised as a sense of what was 'fitting', thus largely governed marriage age. Incidental references

[9] Haigh, *Reformation and resistance*, pp. 48–9; Laslett, *World we have lost further explored*, pp. 86–8; W.R.O., AS/ABO 14, 28/8/1626, *Office v. Chambers*; P.R.O., STAC 8/59/11, m. 2.

[10] For an introduction to the growing literature on age of marriage, see Laslett, *World we have lost further explored*, pp. 82–4; R. B. Outhwaite, 'Age at marriage in England from the late seventeenth to the nineteenth century', *Trans. Roy. Hist. Soc.*, 5th ser., 23 (1973), pp. 55–70; Wrightson, *English society*, pp. 68–70; Houlbrooke, *English family*, pp. 63–8.

[11] Based on analysis of Wiltshire marriage licences for 1615–18 and 1636–7, abstracted by Edmund Nevill, 'Marriage licences of Salisbury', *Genealogist*, new ser., 24–38 (1908–22), *passim*.

[12] Based on analysis of Hadow (ed.), *Wylye registers*, pp. 3–7; W.R.O., 203/1, 522/1.

in church court records and other sources indicate that teenagers who projected marriage often faced opposition and, indeed, derision, and that their friends, neighbours and relatives questioned whether they were 'of sufficient knowledge and experience' or had 'wit enough' to choose a partner. When one Wiltshire girl, not yet 16, went to the vicar of Broad Hinton 'to know her age' with a view to getting married, the minister 'was angry with her and asked her whether she were in haste for a husband'.[13] But it should not be assumed that the majority of youngsters were constantly fretting to be wed or necessarily found the postponement of marriage long after puberty an intolerable burden. The freedom and irresponsibility of the single life doubtless had its attractions, while contrariwise the perception that marriage and householder status involved duties and burdens as well as benefits and privileges probably helped to reconcile young people to their unmarried state for a number of years after they reached physical maturity.

The need to accumulate the skills and resources necessary to maintain a viable household was probably an even more powerful inducement to postpone matrimony. But this was not merely a matter of personal prudence; a reasonable degree of economic competence was regarded virtually as an essential qualification for marriage. Thus the moralist William Whately urged that candidates for matrimony 'must have some honest calling, and will and ability to walk in the same faithfully, that reason may tell them, through God's blessing, there shall be something gotten to maintain a wife, though not richly, yet sufficiently'.[14] Although this principle naturally bore more hardly on poorer people, it was in all probability widely accepted so long as most people had a reasonable chance of eventually accumulating the necessary resources and was internalised in ethical terms even among those of humble status. A Wiltshire husbandman called John Gray, for example, rejected the prospect of marriage in 1622 on the grounds that 'it was not *fit* for him for he had no house to keep a wife in nor was not able to rent one'.[15] The issue became more contentious as the scale of poverty increased in the late sixteenth and early seventeenth centuries and as concern grew about the numbers of poor marriages. It was one thing to

[13] W.R.O., B/DB 5, fol. 14; B/DB 47, fols. 134, 136, 138; D/DB 5, fol. 29.

[14] William Whately, *A bride-bush: or, a direction for married persons* (1623 edn), p. 175.

[15] W.R.O., B/DB 38, fol. 154.

require people to *postpone* marriage until they could afford it; but, as Whately and others recognised, to deny absolutely the right to marry on the grounds of poverty contravened the Christian principle that marriage was lawful for all persons 'of what calling or condition soever'. Another moralist, Philip Stubbes, evaded the issue by assuming that poverty-stricken unions were largely the result of premature marriage, and proposed to solve the problem by raising the legal age for matrimony.[16] Parish officers and local ministers preferred direct action and increasingly tried to prevent the marriages of very poor people (of whatever age) lest they burdened the poor rates. Thus the minister of Nether Compton (Dorset) wrote of a certain Anne Russed in 1628: 'she hath no house nor home of her own and very like to bring charge on the parish, and therefore will hardly be suffered to marry in our parish'.[17]

To prevent the poor from marrying in this way was against the law of the church, but the ecclesiastical courts did little to halt the practice. Indeed it became quite common in various parts of England (including Wiltshire) by the reign of James I, and by the middle of the seventeenth century was beginning to excite literary comment.[18] The complaisance of the authorities and the apparent heartlessness of the wealthier sections of parish society are easy to condemn, but in contemporary terms their stance is readily understandable. As will be seen, the marriages of the very poor were often extremely vulnerable and could hardly survive without considerable parochial assistance. There are indications, moreover, that at least initially the prohibitions were applied selectively with some regard to morality and the circumstances of individual cases. Some of the earliest instances related to individuals who had borne or begotten one or more bastard children; they were probably perceived by their neighbours as having through their irresponsibility and immorality *forfeited* their right to marriage.[19]

The law relating to the actual formation of marriage, which had in essence been fixed in the twelfth century, reveals other ambiguities in

[16] Whately, *Bride-bush*, p. 175; Gouge, *Of domesticall duties*, p. 183; *Phillip Stubbes's anatomy of the abuses in England in Shakspere's youth, A.D. 1583*, ed. Frederick J. Furnivall, 2 vols. in 3, New Shakspere Soc., 6th ser., 4, 6, 12 (1877–82), vol. 1, p. 97.

[17] W.R.O., D/Pres. 1628 (unnumbered), John Clarke to John Johnson, 24 January.

[18] Wrightson, *English society*, p. 78; Hunt, *Puritan moment*, p. 74.

[19] For example, see W.R.O., B/DB 11, fols. 2v–3.

contemporary attitudes to matrimony. Shorn of complexities (some of which will be considered later) the basic position was as follows. An indissoluble union could be created solely by the consent of the two parties expressed in words of the present tense – a contract of marriage or spousals *per verba de praesenti*. (The ideal form of such a contract is still familiar to many people today in the carefully worded version embodied in the Anglican marriage service.) Neither solemnisation in church, nor the use of specially prescribed phrases, nor even the presence of witnesses, was essential to an act of marriage. These provisions had been originally intended to safeguard individual freedom of consent in marriage, but in practice they inevitably led to confusions and uncertainties, and late medieval churchmen and others complained of the evils arising from 'clandestine' contracts.[20] In catholic Europe the law was eventually rationalised by a decree of the council of Trent (1563) which invalidated marriages not performed in public before a parish priest, and there were rather similar changes in many continental protestant countries.[21] But in England, despite attempts at reform around the mid-sixteenth century, the law remained essentially unchanged until the passage of Lord Hardwicke's marriage act in 1753.[22]

Thus in Elizabethan and early Stuart England an informal declaration between a man and a woman was still sufficient in law to create a valid and binding marriage. But the practical significance of this situation should not be exaggerated. Over the centuries the church had done its best to inculcate – through pulpit, confessional and court action – the principle that marriages should be formalised and sanctified by ecclesiastical solemnisation. The church was aided in its task by decisions made by common lawyers, which made certain property rights dependent on proof of a church wedding, and by the commonsense recognition that all ranks of society (whether propertied or not) stood to benefit from the certainty of solemnisation. By the reign of Elizabeth, marriage was normally a much more formal and public act than the law of spousals would at first sight suggest; and when people of whatever social rank thought and spoke of 'marriage', they usually meant marriage in church.[23].

[20] Steven Ozment, *When fathers ruled: family life in Reformation Europe* (Cambridge, Mass., 1983), pp. 1–2, 25–8.

[21] H. J. Schroeder (ed.), *Canons and decrees of the council of Trent* (St Louis, Mo., 1960), pp. 183–4, 454–6; Ozment, *When fathers ruled*, pp. 29–37.

[22] Cardwell (ed.), *Reformation of ecclesiastical laws*, pp. 39–40; 26 Geo. II, c. 33.

[23] Martin Ingram, 'Spousals litigation in the English ecclesiastical courts, c.1350–

This did not necessarily preclude, however, the making of binding marriage contracts in advance of the church wedding. Indeed some sixteenth- and early seventeenth-century moralists positively recommended this practice, urging that such contracts were 'an ancient custom continued in all ages' which the Bible specifically sanctioned and which provided an opportunity for spiritual preparation between contract and solemnisation.[24] Among the less self-consciously pious sections of the population, moreover, the sheer inertia of social custom (especially in more conservative areas) was a powerful force which for a while helped to sustain the institution of spousals as a preliminary to marriage in church. Yet in the long term the custom was doomed to decline. Given the social and economic importance of marriage, it was desirable for all concerned that a single, incontrovertible act should signal entry into the married state; and the church ceremony, duly recorded in the parish registers, really made spousals redundant. By the early seventeenth century, according to William Gouge, the custom was more honoured in the breach than the observance; and by 1686 even the writer of the preface to Swinburne's treatise on marriage contracts was constrained to admit that 'spousals are now in great measure worn out of use'.[25]

The reign of Elizabeth, and to some extent the early seventeenth century, formed an uneasy transition period. Despite widespread acceptance of church marriage and the decline of spousals even as a preliminary to ecclesiastical solemnisation, the fact that an informal contract could still create a binding union entailed uncertainty, moral ambiguities and opportunities for deceit and fraud. In dealing with the resulting problems, the church courts were in a delicate situation. The letter of the law obliged them to uphold informal contracts at a time when such spousals were falling gradually into disuse and disfavour. As will be seen, the church courts walked this tightrope well. Their policies towards contract cases and related issues, far from running counter to social trends, reinforced these developments and helped to minimise uncertainty about what exactly constituted the formation of a marriage.[26]

c.1640', in R. B. Outhwaite (ed.), *Marriage and society: studies in the social history of marriage* (1981), pp. 38–40, 53–4.

24 Gouge, *Of domesticall duties*, pp. 196–202; Daniel Rogers, *Matrimoniall honour* (1642), pp. 118–21.

25 Gouge, *Of domesticall duties*, p. 202; Swinburne, *Treatise of spousals*, sig. A2v.

26 See below, Chapter 6.

But popular acceptance of the need for solemnisation did not wholly eliminate the problem of unregulated unions, and sixteenth- and early seventeenth-century commentators continued to bemoan the problem of 'clandestine' marriages. The concern now was with unions which were solemnised by a minister but took place more or less secretly, often in a parish remote from the couple's place of residence, evading the formalities of banns or licences. Such marriages were unquestionably valid; but to procure a clandestine ceremony had long been regarded as a great offence in ecclesiastical law, and those involved were subject to penalties.[27] Despite this, the problem seems to have been on the increase in the sixteenth century, presumably reflecting the enhanced social and legal importance of solemnisation, which made eloping couples eager to secure at least the semblance of a church wedding.[28]

The projected *Reformatio legum*, drawn up in the reign of Edward VI, would have eliminated the problem by making clandestine marriage ceremonies invalid.[29] In the aftermath of the failure of this scheme, public concern over such marriages gradually increased, and some interests in parliament accused the church of exacerbating the problem through the poorly regulated issue of marriage licences and the inadequate control of parish ministers. It was to meet such criticisms that the church enacted, in the canons of 1597 and 1604, more stringent regulations to govern the issue of licences and the conduct of weddings.[30] As will be seen, within the framework of this new legislation the church courts in the early seventeenth century were able, if not to eliminate the problem of clandestine marriage altogether, at least to contain it within acceptable limits.[31]

In England as in other parts of Europe, one of the most important issues underlying concern over irregular marriage was that of

[27] Ingram, 'Spousals litigation', pp. 39–40.

[28] Evidence on the incidence of clandestine ceremonies before about 1570 is limited, but see Sheehan, 'Formation and stability of marriage', pp. 240–3, 250; Frederick J. Furnivall (ed.), *Child-marriages, divorces, and ratifications, etc. in the diocese of Chester, A.D. 1561–6*, Early English Text Soc., original ser., 108 (1897), pp. lxii–lxiii, 140–1; Houlbrooke, *Church courts and the people*, p. 79. See also John R. Gillis, 'Conjugal settlements: resort to clandestine and common law marriage in England and Wales, 1650–1850', in Bossy (ed.), *Disputes and settlements*, p. 264.

[29] Cardwell (ed.), *Reformation of ecclesiastical laws*, pp. 39–40.

[30] Cardwell (ed.), *Synodalia*, vol. 1, pp. 152–4, 282–3, 286–7, 304–6; cf. Strype, *Life of Whitgift*, vol. 1, pp. 232, 365–6, vol. 2, pp. 373–7, 380–2, vol. 3, pp. 378–82.

[31] See below, Chapter 6.

parental influence. The traditional law of the church insisted that the mutual consent of the couple was alone necessary to make a marriage. Admittedly the implications of this idea were less individualistic than at first sight appears. The principle of freedom of consent, irrespective of the wishes of family, had been developed primarily to ensure freedom from positive compulsion: to prevent families from using their children as mere pawns in the game of dynastic aggrandisement or property accumulation. Medieval canon lawyers accepted that in normal circumstances children should respect parental guidance in choosing marriage partners and condemned marriages made in defiance of parental disapproval.[32] Nevertheless, by the early sixteenth century a powerful body of both clerical and lay commentators was urging that the existing law provided inadequate protection for family interests.[33]

The problem of balancing individual against family interests proved a knotty one, and in different parts of Europe attempts to change the law either foundered or produced a variety of uneasy compromises which rarely satisfied those interests which favoured strong family control.[34] In England, the abortive *Reformatio legum* would have rendered invalid marriages made without the knowledge or consent of parents or 'governors', save that couples faced with unreasonable family pressures could appeal to an ecclesiastical judge.[35] Despite continuing support for such a measure,[36] convocation in 1597 strongly reasserted the traditional principle that 'consent in marriage is the matter specially to be regarded, and credit of kindred, honour, wealth, contentment and pleasure of friends be rather matters of conveniency than necessity in matrimony'.[37] The apparently untidy provisions of the canons of 1604 should be seen as an attempt to steer between extremes. Children under the age of

[32] John T. Noonan, Jr, 'Power to choose', *Viator*, 4 (1973), pp. 419–34; Helmholz, *Marriage litigation*, p. 91; cf. Sheehan, 'Formation and stability of marriage', pp. 229, 263.

[33] Ozment, *When fathers ruled*, pp. 1–2, 25–8; Houlbrooke, *Church courts and the people*, pp. 62–3.

[34] Ozment, *When fathers ruled*, pp. 37–44; Charles Donahue, Jr, 'The canon law on the formation of marriage and social practice in the later middle ages', *Jl family history*, 8 (1983), p. 147.

[35] Cardwell (ed.), *Reformation of ecclesiastical laws*, p. 41.

[36] For example, see *The sermons of Edwin Sandys*, ed. John Ayre, Parker Soc. (Cambridge, 1842), pp. 50–1, 281–2, 325; Gouge, *Of domesticall duties*, pp. 446–53.

[37] Strype, *Life of Whitgift*, vol. 3, p. 380.

21 were forbidden to marry without the consent of their parents or guardians, while marriage by licence required proof of parental consent irrespective of the age of the parties; but marriages made in contravention of these regulations were not declared invalid.[38]

Not all contemporary moralists were entirely happy with these measures. But the weight of moralist opinion was broadly in agreement with the spirit of the law in urging a balance between parental and individual interests. It was universally agreed that children ought to marry only with the consent of their parents or guardians. While this applied pre-eminently to minors, many writers discussed the issue without reference to age, while some stressed the desirability of parental approbation even in the case of remarriage.[39] On the other hand, many moralists also emphasised that it was wrong for parents to force their offspring into marriages which were repugnant to them and denounced the practice of arranging marriages with an eye to profit or dynastic interest rather than the happiness and well-being of the couple.[40] Plainly the ideal was not parental dictation but the *multilateral* consent of the various interests involved in marriage formation, within the framework of respectful attention to parental guidance.

The criteria which moralists suggested for judging the reasonableness of proposed marriages reflect a similar notion of balance. Commentators recognised that there should be 'good liking', even love, between prospective spouses, but they warned against the fascination of mere outward beauty and urged attention to interior qualities.[41] Beyond that the essential yardstick was *equality* or at least comparability between the couple, especially in respect of religious commitment, virtue, age, birth and breeding, and wealth and estate.[42]

How relevant were these pious recommendations to actual practice? The subject of marriage formation in early modern England

[38] Canons 100–3.

[39] For example, *The works of William Perkins*, 3 vols. (Cambridge, 1616–18), vol. 3, p. 696. For a wide-ranging survey of moralist literature on marriage formation, see Richard L. Greaves, *Society and religion in Elizabethan England* (Minneapolis, 1981), chs. 3–4.

[40] For example, *The worckes of Thomas Becon*, 3 vols. (1560–4), vol. 1, fols. dcxviii–dcxix; Gouge, *Of domesticall duties*, pp. 563–5; John Dod and Robert Cleaver, *A godly forme of houshold government* (1630 edn), sig. H4.

[41] Gouge, *Of domesticall duties*, pp. 196–8; Dod and Cleaver, *Godly forme of houshold government*, sigs. G2v–6v.

[42] For example, *Works of Perkins*, vol. 3, p. 680; Gouge, *Of domesticall duties*, pp. 188–96.

has been intensively studied in recent years, but the issues remain to some extent controversial. According to Lawrence Stone, the nature of the family and family behaviour were shifting in this period, and amongst other changes this involved a modification of practices governing the selection of marriage partners. Stone suggests that up to the early sixteenth century the predominant family form was an 'open lineage' type characterised by extensive kin ties, disregard of individual autonomy and privacy within the family, and a low level of emotional attachment between family members. At least at the upper social levels, marriages were normally *arranged* 'by parents, kin and "friends", rather than by the bride and groom', and dynastic, financial and other practical considerations largely dictated the choice. In the later sixteenth and early seventeenth centuries, argues Stone, this type of family was gradually replaced by the 'restricted patriarchal nuclear family', less open to influences beyond the nuclear core and somewhat warmer in its domestic relationships. In upper-class families of this type, parental choice still dominated matchmaking, and romantic love between prospective spouses was regarded with disapproval. But, under the influence of puritan ideas which stressed the importance of love *within* marriage, children were gradually allowed some limited right of veto in cases where the proposed partner was utterly repugnant. It was not until the late seventeenth and the eighteenth centuries, however, that unions based primarily on personal selection became at all common among the aristocracy and gentry. Stone admits that at lower social levels (especially among the propertyless) there had always been greater freedom of choice, for the essentially negative reason that parents could not hope to derive financial or other benefits from their children's marriages. But even at this level love and personal attraction played little part in the matrimonial calculus – it was far more important to find a wife or husband who could work.[43]

Stone's analysis has been rightly criticised by Alan Macfarlane and others for being too schematic, unduly biased towards upper-class experience, and poorly related to the evidence.[44] In particular, there is no firm basis for the idea of a major shift in family forms in this period: continuity between the fifteenth and the seventeenth

[43] Stone, *Family, sex and marriage*, pp. 4–8, 180–94.

[44] Alan Macfarlane, review of Stone, *Family, sex and marriage*, in *History and theory*, 18 (1979), pp. 103–26.

centuries is far more striking than change.[45] Stone's analysis of the processes involved in matchmaking is in some points congruent with reality; but overall he exaggerates the strength of parental influence, underestimates the role of romantic love and gives inadequate attention to the middling groups who played such an important part in parish society.

There is no doubt that parental influence in matchmaking was often very strong among aristocratic and gentry families, especially when the marriage of heirs and heiresses was involved. However, marriages which were wholly 'arranged' for financial or dynastic reasons, with little or no reference to the wishes of the couple, were probably uncommon except in the very highest aristocratic circles or when the marriages of orphans under the jurisdiction of the court of wards were the subject of blatant speculation.[46] Even many substantial gentry families allowed the couple more than a minimal right of veto, and in some cases children (especially males) were allowed to take the initiative in finding mates.[47]

As regards the ranks below the gentry, Stone is correct to the extent that the children of labourers, poor artisans and others with little or no property were in almost complete control of their own marital destinies. Even at this level it was probably considered 'fitting' for children to secure their parents' 'goodwill' or 'blessing' before they actually solemnised marriage. But this was largely a matter of courtesy and hardly insisted on. Poor parents had little or nothing to gain from influencing the marriages of their offspring, and if they did harbour preferences they simply lacked the practical means to assert them. In any case, low expectation of life coupled with high marriage ages meant that many children had lost one or both parents by the time they came to contemplate matrimony; and those who had not were often in service, remote from parental persuasions.[48]

Demographic facts and the prevalence of service and apprentice-

[45] Kathleen M. Davies, 'Continuity and change in literary advice on marriage', in Outhwaite (ed.), *Marriage and society*, pp. 58–80; Wrightson, *English society*, pp. 103–4; Houlbrooke, *English family*, ch. 10 and *passim*.

[46] Joel Hurstfield, *The queen's wards: wardship and marriage under Elizabeth I* (1958), ch. 8.

[47] Houlbrooke, *English family*, pp. 68–73; Miriam Slater, *Family life in the seventeenth century: the Verneys of Claydon House* (1984), p. 145.

[48] Vivien Brodsky Elliott, 'Single women in the London marriage market: age, status and mobility, 1598–1619', in Outhwaite (ed.), *Marriage and society*, pp. 89–91.

ship also limited the possibilities of parental control in the middling ranks of yeoman, husbandman and substantial craftsman families. But irrespective of such factors, it is plain that at this social level young people of both sexes were commonly allowed a good deal of freedom in seeking out a potential mate. There were, however, exceptions. Some middling families (especially those of wealthy yeoman or similar status) seem to have conformed more closely to gentry practices, which involved considerable parental influence in marriage formation; while minors (especially daughters) in middle-rank families were likely to experience closer parental tutelage than children in the very lowest ranks of society.[49]

Although children of middling status were often allowed to take the initiative in finding a spouse, their parents did expect to be consulted – preferably before the matter had been finally clinched. Plainly many children respected this duty; indeed it was in their practical interests to do so if they expected their families to endow them with land or goods. In the last resort, parents who disapproved strongly of their offspring's choice of spouse might resort to moral, physical or – most commonly – financial pressure. (The effectiveness of economic sanctions did not depend entirely on the actual amount of property involved: even such things as household goods, of trivial value to modern eyes, could be important to an intending couple desperately trying to scrape together the wherewithal to set up house.) On the other hand, some children did try to defy their families. As will be seen, the evidence of marriage contract cases suggests that in cases of outright conflict parents usually won in the end; and other sources bear this out.[50] To this extent the strength of parental authority and influence over matchmaking among the middling ranks should not be underestimated.

In practice, too, influence over marriage choice was not always confined to parents. There seem to have been no prescriptive rules governing the involvement of kinsfolk; but if more remote kin like uncles or aunts intended to bequeath or otherwise transfer property to a particular individual, they might expect to be consulted about that person's matrimonial intentions or even to take a hand in matchmaking. Likewise, siblings might demand a say if a proposed marriage was likely to affect their condition or prospects. Again, if

[49] Wrightson, *English society*, pp. 74–8; Houlbrooke, *English family*, pp. 72–3; Elliott, 'Single women in the London marriage market', pp. 84–6, 90–1, 97–8.

[50] MacDonald, *Mystical bedlam*, pp. 94–6. See also below, Chapter 6.

either or both parents were dead, other relatives might step in and assume a quasi-parental role. Masters and mistresses sometimes exercised their rights as surrogate parents; and respected neighbours, godparents or the local minister also played a part on occasion, usually (though not invariably) when the candidate for marriage had lost one or both parents. Occasionally such arrangements were prescribed by parents in their wills. Thus in 1638, Thomas Taylor alias Wolford, a Keevil yeoman, bequeathed to his youngest daughter the sum of £100, to be paid to her at the age of 21 'if she match with the consent of her brother Thomas and my overseers'; the 'overseers' were two of the testator's 'loving friends and neighbours'.[51] It was such a wider network of interested kin, affines and confidants that contemporaries had in mind when they spoke of the role of 'friends' in marriage formation.

What, in practice, were the criteria for judging the suitability of proposed marriages? The moralists' stress on parity does seem to have had some basis in social life, being reflected in the use of the word 'match' to describe a satisfactory union. But this idea of equality was not a rigid imperative, while in everyday life the emphasis placed on various qualities differed somewhat from the ideals proposed in sermons and conduct books.

There was probably greatest flexibility with regard to the ages of the partners. Many couples were close in age, the man commonly somewhat older than the woman. But larger disparities were not unusual, and men seem to have had little compunction in marrying women older than themselves – including widows, who, if they had property, could be an attractive proposition to a bachelor keen to make his way in the world. On the other hand, widowers not infrequently married younger women.[52] There is some evidence of popular disapproval of marriages of the January and May variety, but hostility was apparently muted except when other circumstances combined to make the match unacceptable. Richard Guy of North Bradley claimed in 1618 that the local minister had refused to publish the banns of marriage because 'the parishioners were unwilling that he...being very old, vizt. of the age of three score and thirteen years and upwards, should marry with his now wife being but young'. But

[51] W.R.O., Archdeaconry court of Salisbury probate records, 3/5/1639. See also Wrightson, *English society*, pp. 75, 77–8.

[52] Laslett, *World we have lost further explored*, pp. 82–3; Elliott, 'Single women in the London marriage market', *passim*.

another reference to this case reveals that economic competence was basically at issue. Guy was not only very old but also poor, and the parishioners naturally feared that he would soon die and leave his widow on the parish.[53]

The wealth of the prospective bride or groom or, at lower social levels, the ability to work was clearly of major importance in the choice of spouse. In individual cases marriage could be a vehicle of social mobility: servants of modest means could nourish some hope of marrying their wealthy master or mistress or otherwise bettering themselves through matrimony. But on the whole the various economic groupings tended to be endogamous: marriage thus served to reinforce and perpetuate the distinctions of the social order. Yet social worth and eligibility as a marriage partner were not assessed wholly in terms of pounds, shillings and pence. Across a broad social spectrum, marriage candidates and their families also attached some weight to 'ancestry', 'breeding' and good reputation. Religious belief and commitment may also have been a factor in some cases, though its importance in everyday life was evidently much less than the moralists would have wished.[54]

On the other hand, personal attraction played a much more significant role in matchmaking than contemporary moralists recommended or modern historians like Lawrence Stone have supposed. Diaries, autobiographies, incidental references in court records and many other sources testify to the importance at all social levels of feelings which were closely approximate if not identical to modern notions of romantic love. There was a rich vocabulary to describe the feelings of the heart and the behaviour to which they gave rise: 'love', 'fancy', 'fantasy', 'delight', 'dalliance', 'gestures of lovely liking'.[55] Such sentiments could be regarded as destructive or 'diseased' if they overrode prudential considerations or if (as contemporaries believed to happen) an unrequited lover sickened and died of love.[56] On the other hand, it was widely accepted that the ideal marriage required a strong element of mutual magnetism. If a union was in other respects satisfactory, love was thus accepted as

[53] W.R.O., AS/ABO 12, 22/8/1618, *Office v. Guy*; B/ABO 8, 2/12/1617, *Office v. Hitch*. Cf. Keith Thomas, 'Age and authority in early modern England', *Proc. Brit. Acad.*, 62 (1976), pp. 41–2.

[54] Wrightson, *English society*, pp. 79–88; Houlbrooke, *English family*, pp. 73–6.

[55] W.R.O., B/Misc. Ct Papers 29/47 (unfoliated), depositions of Israel Webbe, Alice Wheeler, Nicholas Currington; B/DB 10, fol. 15v.

[56] MacDonald, *Mystical bedlam*, pp. 89–90.

a positive sentiment which even families with pretensions to gentry rank were willing to accommodate. In 1586, for example, a minor gentleman of Compton Chamberlayne gave approval to his daughter's choice of spouse to secure both 'the well bestowing of his daughter to live in the world as also the satisfaction of her own fantasy, seeing the same so firmly fastened'.[57]

What emerges from this survey of attitudes to marriage formation is their complexity and flexibility. Instead of any clear-cut pattern of 'arranged' or 'free' marriages, a more subtle system prevailed in which love had a part to play in combination with prudential considerations, the pressures of community values and (at middling- and upper-class levels) the interests of parents and sometimes other family members. The seventeenth-century moralist Matthew Griffith was probably correct in observing that this give and take system generally worked well: 'On all parts there is commonly a willing consent and promise of marriage; and that most an end [i.e. for the most part] with consent of parents, and parties, some few *Individuum Vagum*'s only excepted.'[58] The potential for conflict within the system should thus not be exaggerated; yet things *could* go wrong in marriage formation, and it was precisely with the individuum vagums that the church courts had to deal: the untoward results of poverty-stricken unions, runaway marriages, broken promises.

Once marriages were firmly established, the everyday relations between husbands and wives and their children were (except to a limited extent in probate and testamentary matters) of little direct concern to the church courts unless the circumstances involved sexual immorality or led to the actual breakdown of marriage. Yet family relationships were extensively discussed in sermons and conduct books by moralists who regarded the 'right ordering' of families as essential to the well-being of the commonwealth. Domestic relations were thus on the borders of public and private morality in this period – matters to be influenced by exhortation but not ordinarily by the exercise of formal discipline. They demand at least brief treatment here, both to provide essential background for later discussions, and as a reminder that there existed large and important

[57] W.R.O., B/DB 9, fol. 186v. On the role of love in marriage formation, see also Wrightson, *English society*, pp. 82–4; Houlbrooke, *English family*, pp. 76–8; MacDonald, *Mystical bedlam*, pp. 88–98.

[58] Matthew Griffith, *Bethel: or, a forme for families* (1633), p. 272.

areas of personal conduct outside the normal purviews of ecclesiastical justice.

Stone would argue that the Elizabethan and early Stuart family was an emotionally bleak and authoritarian institution. He admits that contemporary moralists stressed the need for 'love' between spouses and towards their children, but he argues that this did not produce what we today would recognise as caring and affectionate relationships; on the contrary, wives and children were firmly subjected to the patriarchal authority of the male head of the family and often subjected to harsh discipline and even abuse.[59]

This analysis is vitiated by a misunderstanding of contemporary ideals and a further confusion between legal and moral prescriptions and the realities of everyday life. In a broad sense the ideals governing family relationships in this period may be described as patriarchal and authoritarian. The conventional notion of a correspondence between royal and patriarchal authority was reinforced by the stress which sermons and conduct books laid on the governing role of the male householder and the duty of wife and children to submit themselves to him. 'He is the highest in the family', observed William Gouge, 'and hath...authority over all...He is as a king in his own house.'[60] Again, the common law was strongly biased in favour of the husband/father. Despite legal modifications based on decisions in equity, it was still essentially true that married women had no proprietary rights independent of their husbands; while the law prescribed that 'the husband hath...power and dominion over his wife, and may keep her by force within the bounds of duty, and may beat her' (albeit not in 'a violent and cruel manner').[61]

On the other hand, the patriarchal prescriptions of moralist writings were qualified to a much greater extent than Stone admits. The official homily on matrimony envisaged the ideal marriage as a yoke drawn 'in one accord of heart and mind' by spouses united by a 'pleasant and sweet love'; while even William Gouge, among the most authoritarian of seventeenth-century moralists, recognised that the marital relationship was 'the nearest to equality that may

[59] Stone, *Family, sex and marriage*, pp. 4–7, 135–41, 151–218.

[60] Gouge, *Of domesticall duties*, p. 258.

[61] Matthew Bacon, *A new abridgment of the law*, 4th edn, 5 vols. (1778), vol. 1, p. 285. On equity developments, see Maria L. Cioni, 'The Elizabethan chancery and women's rights', in Guth and McKenna (eds.), *Tudor rule and revolution*, pp. 159–82.

be…wherein man and wife are after a sort even fellows and partners'. And a host of writers strongly condemned wife-beating. 'God forbid that!', thundered the homily. 'For that is the greatest shame that can be, not so much to her that is beaten, but to him that doth the deed.'[62]

What was the nature of popular attitudes and practices? The custom of 'riding skimmington', well established in Wiltshire and other western counties and (with variations) in other parts of England, suggests widespread acceptance of the patriarchal ideal. These noisy, mocking demonstrations characteristically took place when a wife had beaten her husband, thus subverting the conventional ideal of 'right order' within the family. Yet close study of these customs suggests that equally they reflect the fact that the authoritarian ideal was much modified in everyday life. Skimmington rides stigmatised *extreme* violations of the patriarchal schema, but their psychology was more complex than that of a simple corrective response; rather, they represented a cathartic release of tensions arising from the continual conflict between the roles conventionally ascribed to wives and husbands and the more flexible marital relationships which existed in actual practice.[63] More direct evidence from diaries, autobiographies, letters, wills and other sources likewise supports the idea that family relationships in the middle and lower ranks of society were more affectionate and less authoritarian than Stone implies.[64]

It is important, however, not to go to the other extreme and idealise family life in this period. Court records and other sources reveal, in Wiltshire as in other areas, some brutal cases of child neglect and ferocious wife-beating; and no doubt tyrannical husbands were to some extent sustained by the stereotype of male dominance.[65] For these and other reasons, marriages could in some cases become 'a little hell'.[66] To be sure, unsatisfactory unions were more likely to be resolved by the early death of one of the parties

[62] *Sermons or homilies appointed to be read in churches in the time of queen Elizabeth* (Liverpool, 1799 edn), pp. 323, 328, 330; Gouge, *Of domesticall duties*, p. 356. For fuller discussion of moralists' prescriptions on marital relationships, see Davies, 'Continuity and change'.

[63] Martin Ingram, 'Ridings, rough music and the "reform of popular culture" in early modern England', *Past and present*, no. 105 (Nov. 1984), pp. 79–113.

[64] Wrightson, *English society*, ch. 4; Houlbrooke, *English family*, chs. 5–6.

[65] For example, W.R.O., QS/GR East. 1609/99; QS/GR Hil. 1615/193; QS/GR Mich. 1620/200; QS/GR Trin. 1640/82; Wrightson, *English society*, pp. 98–9, 117.

[66] Whately, *Bride-bush*, title page.

than is the case today, but, since the median duration of marriages in pre-industrial England may have been as high as twenty years, there was still much scope for marital misery.[67]

The potential avenues for escape were few and narrow. The traditional law of the church rigorously upheld the sanctity of the married state and the indissolubility of the conjugal bond, so that divorce in the modern sense – the termination of a valid marriage, enabling the partners to marry again – was not recognised. However, it was possible to secure an annulment (declaring that the union had never constituted a true state of marriage) if it could be proved that certain basic 'impediments' to matrimony had been violated. The most important grounds were the fact that one or both partners were under age; permanent frigidity or impotence; the existence of a prior contract of marriage, even if it had not been consummated or solemnised; and the fact that the couple were related within certain prohibited degrees of kinship or affinity.[68] An annulment left the erstwhile partners free to remarry, but the other legal effects could be dire: under English common law an annulment barred the woman from her dower rights (a share of the husband's estate after his decease) and bastardised any children born of the union.[69]

In the early and mid-sixteenth century these inherited rules came under attack from protestant reformers, in England and abroad, who argued that the annulment laws undermined the institution of marriage. Criticisms of the provisions concerning precontract were part and parcel of the wider concern over 'clandestine' or unsolemnised marriages,[70] while the rules of consanguinity and affinity were denounced as too complex and unreasonably extensive. The pre-Reformation canon law in fact forbade marriages within the fourth degree of kinship – that is, even between third cousins – and there were further restrictions based on 'spiritual' relationships between godparents and godchildren. Such rules were barely workable in practice. The reformers accused the catholic church of making money out of the resulting confusion by selling dispensations, and of

[67] Peter Laslett, *Family life and illicit love in earlier generations* (Cambridge, 1977), pp. 161–2, 184.

[68] Helmholz, *Marriage litigation*, pp. 74–100.

[69] Pollock and Maitland, *History of English law*, vol. 2, p. 394; Sir Edward Coke, *The first part of the institutes of the lawes of England* (1628), fols. 32, 33v, 235; Sir Edward Coke, *The third part of the institutes of the laws of England* (1644), p. 93.

[70] See above, p. 132.

corruptly using the regulations to furnish specious grounds for divorce.[71] But, whereas the protestant churches on the continent substantially reshaped the traditional law in the light of these and other criticisms,[72] in England the debate produced only one major change: by 1563 the range of prohibited degrees had been drastically reduced to something close to the situation which prevails today. The new rules were confirmed by the canons of 1604, which also took care to stress that unions within the newly specified degrees were void and that 'the parties so married shall by course of law be separated'.[73] However the new regulations were of little practical significance to ill-matched couples seeking an escape route from marriage. Despite what contemporary protestant reformers claimed and modern historians have until recently assumed, annulments based on the rules of kinship and affinity (or indeed on any other ground) were in actual practice very rare both before and after the Reformation.[74]

An alternative means of escape from an unsatisfactory marriage was a judicial separation 'from bed and board' (*a mensa et thoro*). This could be granted on proof of adultery or extreme cruelty on the part of either spouse, and unlike an annulment it did not in English law affect the wife's dower rights or the legal status of the children. The drawback was that the bond of matrimony remained undissolved, and hence the separated spouses were forbidden to remarry during each other's lifetime.[75] Again, the continental protestant reformers attacked these provisions. Lutherans argued that adultery dissolved the marriage bond and that at least the innocent party should have the right to remarry, while Zwingli and Bucer also allowed divorce and remarriage for wilful desertion and other causes[76]. In England, this more radical philosophy was embodied in the *Reformatio legum*, but these divorce proposals came to nothing when the scheme as a whole foundered. It is indeed highly doubtful whether there was at this time much support, even among relatively advanced English protestant theologians, for such a dramatically

[71] Ozment, *When fathers ruled*, pp. 44–7.
[72] *Ibid.*, pp. 47–9.
[73] Gibson, *Codex*, vol. 1, pp. 414–15. See also Jack Goody, *The development of the family and marriage in Europe* (Cambridge, 1983), pp. 168–82.
[74] Helmholz, *Marriage litigation*, pp. 77–87; Houlbrooke, *Church courts and the people*, pp. 71–5.
[75] Coke, *First institutes*, fols. 32, 33v, 235.
[76] Ozment, *When fathers ruled*, pp. 80–98.

sweeping revision of the law of divorce. However a considerable number of Elizabethan and early Stuart divines did continue to advocate full divorce in cases where adultery was at issue, while some writers entertained doubts whether a marriage contracted after a decree of separation was actually invalid.[77]

Two aristocratic *causes célèbres* in the middle decades of the sixteenth century highlighted these uncertainties and differences of opinion. The marquess of Northampton and Sir John Stawell, in 1552 and 1572 respectively, were able by dubious means to secure remarriages after divorcing their first wives for adultery.[78] The need for a firm restatement of the law became even more urgent with the publication of extremely radical views on divorce (total anathema to all shades of clerical opinion within the established church) by protestant sectaries.[79] It was against this background that the canons of 1604 strongly reaffirmed the traditional ban on remarriage after a decree of separation 'from bed and board', prescribed that separated spouses must enter into bonds not to contract new marriages, and laid down stricter rules for the handling and determination of both separation and annulment suits by the church courts.[80] Thus in England, unlike the situation in most continental protestant states, the ultimate effects of the Reformation debate on divorce were if anything to tighten rather than to slacken the bonds of marriage.

It is difficult to judge how far there existed a demand for divorce reform outside restricted theological and sectarian circles. Certainly there are few signs of any urgent wish for change. Some contemporaries believed, however, that marital breakdown was frequent and that the couples concerned often separated without recourse to the courts. Thus the homily on whoredom, written in 1547, lamented 'the divorces which nowadays be so commonly accustomed and used by men's private authority'; while a century later Daniel Rogers similarly bemoaned 'the separation of such in the country of all sorts, as depart from their yoke-fellows, abandoning each other by law, or lawless divorces'.[81]

77 Cardwell (ed.), *Reformation of ecclesiastical laws*, pp. 51–8; Sir Lewis Dibden and Sir Charles Chadwyck Healey, *English church law and divorce* (1912), pp. 22–48. Many of the opposing arguments in the controversy were rehearsed by Edmund Bunny, *Of divorce for adulterie, and marrying againe* (Oxford, 1610).

78 Dibden and Healey, *English church law and divorce*, pp. 62–9, 83–92.

79 Keith Thomas, 'Women and the civil war sects', *Past and present*, no. 13 (Apr. 1958), pp. 49–50.

80 Canons 105–8.

81 *Sermons or homilies*, p. 87; Rogers, *Matrimoniall honour*, p. 131.

But how accurate were these observations? The available evidence (independent of church court prosecutions, which will be considered later) suggests that marital breakdown was mostly confined to the extremes of the social scale. Stone found that in the period 1570–1659 about 10 per cent of all aristocratic marriages ended in annulment, separation or serious estrangement. The peerage, however, formed only a tiny proportion of the total population, and the actual *numbers* of cases were small.[82] At the other end of the social spectrum, the marriages of the very poor were also quite vulnerable. Over 8 per cent of the married women included in a survey of the poor in the city of Norwich around 1570 had allegedly been deserted by their husbands, and a similar problem, albeit on a lesser scale, was revealed in Salisbury in 1635.[83] Nor were deserted wives found only in the towns. In the small village of Wylye in the period 1615–35 there lived at least two, and possibly three, women whose husbands had left them.

Some of these broken marriages among the poor involved feckless husbands who had callously deserted their wives and disappeared for good. Such a one was Richard Williams of Wylye, described as a 'worthless runaway', who left his wife Joan, 'a poor woman, herself of blameless life', some time before 1623.[84] But in many instances the motives for separation were more complex, perhaps involving a joint decision by husband and wife in the face of adverse circumstances. A Wiltshire case, recounted incidentally in the court of star chamber in 1615, illustrates what was evidently a hazard of poor marriages in many parts of England at this time. A tailor of Lydiard Tregoze got married, but 'the world began to grow hard with them and charge began to come upon them'. Poverty and lack of work forced the couple into a decision to separate. The man went to Portsmouth to seek work as a labourer, while his wife went into service in Lydiard. They never saw each other again, and the woman later remarried when she had satisfied herself that her husband was dead. Even more pitiful were cases in which social pressures combined with financial difficulties to force couples apart. Marian Leighton was with child when she got married around 1630, but because

82 Stone, *Crisis of the aristocracy*, pp. 660–2.
83 John F. Pound (ed.), *The Norwich census of the poor, 1570*, Norfolk Record Soc., 40 (Norwich, 1971), pp. 19, 95; Paul Slack (ed.), *Poverty in early Stuart Salisbury*, Wilts. Record Soc., 31 (Devizes, 1975), pp. 77, 79.
84 Hadow (ed.), *Wylye registers*, pp. 45, 48.

the couple were very poor the parishioners of Great Bedwyn opposed their petition to the county justices for leave to erect a cottage. The husband had to remain as a household servant, while Marian was forced to 'wander up and down' and for a long time could find shelter only in a barn.[85]

Yet such evidence of separation must be kept in perspective. Even among the poor, only a minority of couples were affected; and the available evidence suggests that across a broad social spectrum, including the middling groups of lesser gentry, urban bourgeoisie, yeomen, and husbandmen and craftsmen of reasonable substance, marriages were generally very stable. Thus Richard Gough's account of Myddle (Shropshire) and neighbouring areas, compiled in 1700, mentions only a handful of broken marriages occurring over a period of fifty years or more among the families of middling rank which mainly concerned him. Apart from other considerations, marriage at these social levels was probably so important as an economic partnership that the couple would consider dismantling it only in the most extreme circumstances. Cases like that of Thomas Bennett of All Cannings, who left his wife around 1565 because 'they could not agree and for that she would not be obedient', taking care to draw up beforehand 'certain covenants touching the separation', were evidently very uncommon.[86]

A problem sometimes associated with marital breakdown was bigamy. Given high rates of mobility yet relatively poor communications, it was possible for men without too many ties of property or business to leave their wives, settle in some remote area and marry again. Some people certainly did contract bigamous marriages in this fashion, but there is no real evidence to support Stone's confident assertion that the practice was 'both easy and common'.[87] Nevertheless, a parliamentary committee of 1597 did identify this as one of the evils associated with clandestine marriage and the poorly regulated issue of marriage licences. The result was the passage of the bigamy act of 1604. Coinciding with the issue of new ecclesiastical canons to tighten up marriage regulations, this measure made it felony to marry again during the lifetime of the first

[85] P.R.O., STAC 8/269/7, m. 2; W.R.O., D/DB 11, fols 262, 263v-5, 267.

[86] Richard Gough, *The history of Myddle*, ed. David Hey (Harmondsworth, 1981), pp. 92–3, 125, 129, 151, 159, 166, 181, 198, 201, 228; W.R.O., B/DB 5, fol. 127v.

[87] Stone, *Family, sex and marriage*, p. 40.

spouse, unless the husband or wife had been absent for seven years, the parties to the first marriage had been under age, or the couple had been lawfully 'divorced' in an ecclesiastical court.[88]

The effect of this act was to transfer jurisdiction over most bigamy cases from the spiritual to the secular courts.[89] Apart from this restriction, the church courts continued to have full jurisdiction over matters concerning marital breakdown. This involved not only the hearing of petitions for annulment and separation, but also the prosecution of people who took it upon themselves to live apart without procuring a judicial order. This was bound to be a thankless task. Not only were marriage breakdown cases intrinsically difficult to handle, but also the classes most prone to marital breakdown – the very rich and the very poor – were those elements in society least amenable to ecclesiastical discipline. How the church courts fared in this matter will be seen in Chapter 5.

Two of the major issues so far discussed – the law of marriage formation and that of divorce – reveal a similar pattern: movements for reform visible in the early to mid-sixteenth century either petered out or were largely repelled, and by the early seventeenth century the traditional position had been reaffirmed with only relatively minor modifications. Contemporary debate on the laws against sexual immorality in some respects followed the same lines. An intensification of concern over sexual offences produced the familiar pattern of abortive attempts at reform on the question of how rigorously such offences should be punished – a question which was inextricably bound up with the issue of the boundaries between the secular and ecclesiastical jurisdictions.

A statute of 1286 assigned to the spiritual power the punishment of fornication, adultery and 'such like' offences.[90] By the early sixteenth century the scope of this vaguely defined but immensely wide jurisdiction had been subjected to certain minor limitations, while there was a number of imprecise areas of overlap between the secular and ecclesiastical courts. Rape and brothel-keeping were, as such, common law offences, though the church courts could punish the acts of unlawful copulation that these crimes implied. Justices of the peace (assisted by constables) also had discretionary powers to

[88] 1 Jac. I c. 11; cf. Strype, *Life of Whitgift*, vol. 2, p. 377, vol. 3, pp. 378–80.
[89] The church courts did retain a limited jurisdiction: see below, Chapter 5.
[90] 13 Edw. I (*Circumspecte agatis*).

deal with notorious cases of adultery or incontinence, especially those discovered by search of suspect houses. Some boroughs (including Salisbury, Devizes and Marlborough) and court leets also exercised jurisdiction over notorious sexual offenders, especially prostitutes, sometimes employing draconian punishments like branding, whipping or driving the culprits out of town with basins ringing before them.[91] But the scope of these secular remedies against sexual immorality, though not negligible, was on the whole limited: the punishment of sexual offenders was overwhelmingly left to the church courts.

The issue of jurisdiction became more urgent during the sixteenth century. One major reason for this was a growing demand in some educated circles for harsher punishments against sexual offenders. The movement began before the Reformation but in England became particularly associated with advanced protestants and, ultimately, with the more puritan-minded members of the church. These interests characteristically demanded that sexual offenders should be visited with severe physical sanctions; and a powerful body of writers urged that the sin of adultery, in particular, should carry the death penalty according to the dictates of Mosaic law.[92]

Plainly the church courts in their existing state could not satisfy such zealous opponents of sexual immorality; and it became a stock complaint among committed protestant reformers in mid-century and later puritans that public penance (or, worse still, a money payment in commutation of penance) was too light a punishment for heinous sins of the flesh.[93] One possible answer was to revise the penalties imposed by the church courts themselves; and the *Reformatio legum* proposed sanctions which, though stopping short of death, were none the less of great ferocity. Adultery, for example, was to be visited with perpetual imprisonment or exile, the forfeiture of all property rights gained by marriage and (in the case of the guilty husband) the surrender of half his goods to his wife.[94]

[91] Keith Thomas, 'The puritans and adultery: the act of 1650 reconsidered', in Donald Pennington and Keith Thomas (eds.), *Puritans and revolutionaries: essays in seventeenth-century history presented to Christopher Hill* (Oxford, 1978), pp. 265–6. For examples of draconian punishments, see C. H. Williams (ed.), *English historical documents, 1485–1558* (1967), pp. 967–8, 986.

[92] Thomas, 'Puritans and adultery', pp. 263–4, 269–71.

[93] W. H. Frere and C. E. Douglas (eds.), *Puritan manifestoes* (1954), p. 34; Stubbes, *Anatomy of abuses*, ed. Furnivall, vol. 1, p. 98.

[94] Cardwell (ed.), *Reformation of ecclesiastical laws*, pp. 49–51.

The failure of this scheme led would-be reformers (including at first some members of the church hierarchy) to pin their hopes on harsher secular laws enacted by parliament. The trail had already been blazed by an act of 1534 which, on the grounds that existing penalties were too mild, had made 'buggery committed with mankind or beast' a felony triable only in the secular courts.[95] Hence the reigns of Elizabeth and James I witnessed a long series of bills on adultery, fornication and bastardy, some of them supported by churchmen or paralleled in convocation by fearsome pronouncements against immorality. But the more wide-ranging of these proposals all foundered on legal difficulties, jurisdictional issues and reservations expressed by the mass of members of parliament – especially the fear that men of quality might be subjected to 'base' punishments for sexual transgressions.[96] The only substantive achievements were measures to ensure the maintenance of poor bastard children and the punishment of the guilty parents, these laws being enacted in the context of poor relief and vagrancy legislation in 1576 and 1610. The first of these acts gave justices a discretionary power to examine the circumstances of the birth of a bastard child which had either been left at the charge of the parish or was likely to become chargeable, to make an order for maintenance and to punish the offenders. The supplementary Jacobean act provided that the mothers of such bastards should be sent to the house of correction for one year. Neither act affected the rights of the church courts in bastardy cases, whether or not the justices had taken cognisance of the matter.[97]

These acts represented a significant hardening of the law against sexual offenders, and (as will be seen) they ultimately had an important impact on poor bastard-bearers. But they plainly fell far short of what the most vociferous advocates of moral reform were demanding. In time the members of the church hierarchy withdrew from the campaign for penal legislation, and the movement became associated with the more 'godly' or puritan elements in church and parliament.[98] By the reign of Charles I there were indeed signs that

[95] 25 Hen. VIII c. 6.

[96] Thomas, 'Puritans and adultery', pp. 272–5; Kent, 'Attitudes of members of the house of commons to the regulation of "personal conduct"', *passim*.

[97] 18 Eliz. I c. 3; 7 Jac. I c. 4.

[98] Kent, 'Attitudes of members of the house of commons to the regulation of "personal conduct"', pp. 41–2, 62; Thomas, 'Puritans and adultery', pp. 273–4.

such zealots were no longer being taken seriously:[99] most government officials, members of parliament, lawyers and churchmen were prepared to settle for the existing structure of sexual discipline run by the church courts. It was left to the Rump Parliament, when ecclesiastical discipline was no longer in operation, and in altered political circumstances, to enact a measure whereby incest and adultery became felonies punishable by death, while fornicators were liable to three months' imprisonment. But the more drastic provisions of this act proved largely a dead letter, and the whole measure was allowed to lapse in 1660 – a retrospective justification for the more cautious attitudes of Elizabethan and early Stuart legislators.[100]

The debate over the appropriate means of punishing sexual offenders should not obscure the fact that a broad spectrum of opinion among the clerical and lay leaders of society agreed on the heinousness of sexual sins and shared a growing concern with the problem. What lay behind this call for moral reformation? As part of a wider European phenomenon it was rooted in theological changes which stressed the depravity of man and the dangers of unbridled licence.[101] Increased reverence for the literal word of the scriptures also contributed. This is seen not only in proposals to enforce the Mosaic code against adulterers, but also in condemnations of incest. Moralists clearly felt constrained to denounce this sin in conventionally harsh terms, but the lack of extended discussion of the theme suggests that it was not really of major concern in contemporary social life.[102] Again, the discussion of immorality was often associated, either explicitly or implicitly, with the real or supposed doctrines of the Roman church: some of the energy spent in affirming the gravity of fornication, for example, was generated by the belief that the catholic church regarded it as a venial sin.[103]

But the mainspring of the moralists' attacks on 'whoredom' was

[99] Russell, *Parliaments and English politics*, p. 29.

[100] Thomas, 'Puritans and adultery', pp. 257–8 (and see also the references there cited), 275–80.

[101] For a brief introduction to these issues, see Steven Ozment, *The age of reform, 1250–1550* (New Haven, 1980), pp. 22–42; Bernard M. G. Reardon, *Religious thought in the Reformation* (1981), pp. 83–5, 100–2, 124, 190–1, 198, 307–12.

[102] For example, see Perkins, *Works*, vol. 3, p. 678; Gouge, *Of domesticall duties*, p. 186; Griffith, *Bethel*, pp. 247–8.

[103] For example, John Downame, *Foure treatises tending to diswade all Christians from swearing* (1609), p. 133; *The workes of Gervase Babington* (1615), pp. 74–5.

their conviction that many forms of sexual misconduct were rife and largely condoned by popular standards. The words of the official homily on whoredom, even in the device of citing a popular proverb to portray vulgar attitudes, are typical of much that was written: 'this vice...is counted no sin at all, but rather a pastime, a dalliance, and but a touch of youth: not rebuked, but winked at; not punished, but laughed at'. Many moralists claimed that the morals of men, in particular, were very lax, and attacked the idea of a 'double standard', which ran counter to the Christian principle that sexual immorality was equally reprehensible in men and women.[104] Reinforcing these ideas was concern over the practical and economic ill-effects of sexual misconduct. Adultery, it was argued, could result in the wasting of goods and the neglect of wives and children, while fornication harmed the commonwealth through the generation of poor bastards. Such economic ideas, developed most forcibly in Philip Stubbes's *Anatomie of abuses* (1583 and later editions), evidently appealed to practical-minded men in parliament and elsewhere, especially as the problem of poverty worsened in the later years of Elizabeth's reign and in the early seventeenth century; and plainly they helped the passage of the bastardy acts of 1576 and 1610.[105] But for the majority of moralists, economic concerns were subordinate to pastoral and theological considerations: their ultimate fear was that, if whoredom continued unchecked, a providential God would pour down his wrath upon the people and afflict the commonwealth with plagues and punishments.[106]

The moralists were, in general, forthright and uncompromising in their denunciations of sexual immorality; but there were certain areas where they recognised the existence of moral ambiguities. One of these was the issue of whether couples who had contracted themselves in words of the present tense – and were thus man and wife in the eyes of God – might enjoy sexual relations before the union was solemnised in church. Commentators recognised that such behaviour was not quite the same as barefaced adultery or fornication. Yet it would be wrong to exaggerate their scruples. Medieval lawyers

[104] *Sermons or homilies*, p. 82; Dent, *Plaine mans path-way*, pp. 61–9; Rogers, *Matrimoniall honour*, p. 12. See also Keith Thomas, 'The double standard', *Jl history of ideas*, 20 (1959), pp. 203–4.

[105] Kent, 'Attitudes of members of the house of commons to the regulation of "personal conduct"', p. 44.

[106] *Sermons or homilies*, pp. 88–90; Dent, *Plaine mans path-way*, pp. 227–8; Downame, *Foure treatises*, pp. 128–9.

and moralists had always strongly discouraged and sometimes explicitly condemned the consummation of marriage between contract and solemnisation; while in 1528 William Harrington plainly asserted that 'the man may not possess the woman as his wife nor the woman the man as her husband... afore such time as that matrimony be approved and solemnised by our mother holy church; and if they do indeed they sin deadly'. A century later John Downame likewise roundly condemned the practice as sinful; while even William Gouge, cited by Peter Laslett to support the idea that moralists were reluctant to condemn sexual intercourse after a binding contract, denounced such behaviour as 'unwarrantable and dishonest'.[107]

There was more hesitation on how far to condemn sexual contacts which fell short of full intercourse, and on the broader issue of how much freedom should be allowed to men and women to meet and interact. Puritan attacks on festivities, and the wider movement to regulate inns and alehouses, represented, in part, an attempt to limit opportunities for wanton dalliance. But Juan Luis Vives's book on the moral conduct of females, translated into English as *The instruction of a Christian woman* (?1529 and later editions), was unusual in urging a rigid code of personal behaviour which would have placed the unmarried girl under the strict tutelage of her parents and severely constrained her movements. These features, and indeed the tone of the whole book, betray its author's Spanish provenance. Native English moralists urged rather the need for personal discipline in the midst of social circumstances in which a good deal of contact between the sexes was normal. John Downame, for example, accepted that kissing and embracing could be lawful if used 'after a civil and honest manner to express our love one to another' in affectionate greeting; they were only to be avoided 'in wanton dalliance between those who are light and lascivious'. In listing ways by which to avoid fornication, moreover, he did not suggest that the sexes should be kept separate or that unmarried girls should be kept chaperoned.[108] The elder John Brinsley did urge that to avoid sexual sin it was not only necessary to shun filthy talk, foolish jesting, lascivious glances, wanton dalliance and dancing and lewd books,

[107] Henry Ansgar Kelly, 'Clandestine marriage and Chaucer's "Troilus"', *Viator*, 4 (1973), pp. 441–2; Chilton Latham Powell, *English domestic relations, 1487–1653* (New York, 1917), p. 233 (quoting Harrington); Laslett, *World we have lost further explored*, p. 172; Downame, *Foure treatises*, pp. 177–8.

[108] Downame, *Foure treatises*, pp. 195–201.

plays and pictures, but also to eschew private meetings with members of the opposite sex. Yet even he admitted that such private company could be 'both honest and intending no evil'.[109]

The fact is that the English moralists were urging a strict view of chastity in a society which was not organised towards a rigorous control of social relations between the sexes. Foreign visitors were often struck by the social freedom which women seemed to enjoy, and their observations are confirmed by a wealth of evidence from contemporary diaries, letters and autobiographies and many other sources.[110] The only area of public life in which women were regularly separated from men was in church – but throughout the period there were exceptions even to this rule, and the arrangement probably became less common over time.[111] In the economic sphere, it is plain that men and women, married and unmarried, mingled together in household service, in agricultural tasks and in the business of buying and selling in the market-place or elsewhere.[112] In domestic arrangements, again, there was no rigid segregation of the sexes: men- and maidservants were in constant proximity to their masters and mistresses and to each other, and even male and female sleeping areas were sometimes imperfectly demarcated.[113]

Notoriously the sexes mingled freely in the field of leisure. Married men probably predominated over married women in inns and alehouses, but there was evidently no absolute division, while such places were undoubtedly patronised by the young and unmarried of both sexes.[114] Men and women certainly mingled together freely at fairs and village festivities, and indeed these were important places for seeking out potential marriage partners. The case of Gabriel Miles of Woodford, who in 1609 went to 'see some dancing or other

[109] John Brinsley, Sr, *The true watch and rule of life*, 5th edn (1611), pp. 87–8; cf. Henry Scudder, *The Christians daily walke in holy securitie and peace*, 7th edn (1637), pp. 113–14.

[110] For example, see W. B. Rye (ed.), *England as seen by foreigners in the days of Elizabeth and James I* (1865), pp. 14, 72–3, 111. See also Wrightson, *English society*, pp. 73–6.

[111] Thomas, *Religion and the decline of magic*, p. 152; cf. the plan of seating arrangements in Corsley church, printed in M. F. Davies, *Life in an English village* (1909), pp. 295–8.

[112] Laslett, *World we have lost further explored*, p. 73; Houlbrooke, *English family*, p. 72. References in contemporary sources are numerous.

[113] For example, see W.R.O., AS/ABO 12, 9/3/1616, *Office v. Masye*; 20/2/1619, *Office v. Blanchard*.

[114] Clark, *English alehouse*, pp. 131–2.

sports' in the neighbouring village of Maddington with the intention of finding a wife, was wholly typical.[115] Puritan attacks on festivities, such as those described in the previous chapter, only slowly (if at all) eroded these patterns of behaviour in this period, and suggestions that dancing was itself immoral could arouse strong resentment. In 1602 Henry Hunt, curate of Winsley, urged from the pulpit the opinions of Calvin, Babington and others that 'dancing was a vainness and a provocation to uncleanness or adultery' and that 'for a maid to dance which is marriageable is a note of whorish wantonness'; but some of his parishioners took him to task for these strictures and prosecuted him in the bishop of Salisbury's court for his behaviour during the subsequent altercation.[116]

Were these social conditions associated with widespread sexual laxity, as contemporary moralists claimed? Independent of church court prosecutions there is virtually no reliable evidence on the incidence of incest, of adultery committed by married women, or of fornication or male adultery which did not result in conception. The analysis of parish registers can, however, provide some information about sexual activities which led to illicit pregnancies and bastard births. Such analysis certainly reveals that many couples had sexual intercourse before the solemnisation of marriage. Philip Hair found on the basis of samples from the registers of 77 parishes in 24 counties that bridal pregnancy was common throughout England in the late sixteenth and the seventeenth centuries. There were variations from community to community and from region to region, but overall about a fifth of all brides were pregnant by the time they got married in church.[117] Analysis of the registers of a variety of Wiltshire communities indicates that the situation in this county was roughly in conformity with the national pattern.[118]

Bastardy was much less common but by no means an unusual occurrence. The baptisms of illegitimates were often specified, or can be inferred, in parish register entries. Expressing the number of bastards as a percentage of total recorded baptisms provides the

115 W.R.O., D/DB 6, fol. 87.
116 W.R.O., B/ABI 31, fol. 311.
117 Philip E. H. Hair, 'Bridal pregnancy in rural England in earlier centuries', *Population studies*, 20 (1966), pp. 233–43; Philip E. H. Hair, 'Bridal pregnancy in earlier rural England further examined', *Population studies*, 24 (1970), pp. 59–70.
118 For further details, see below, Chapter 7.

so-called illegitimacy ratio, a demographically crude but nonetheless valuable index.[119] Peter Laslett's sample of 98 parishes in various parts of England suggests that the ratio was rising in the late sixteenth century to reach a peak around 1600. The precise figure varied between different communities, with relatively high rates tending to occur in the north and extreme west of the country. Overall the illegitimacy ratio averaged about 3 per cent at the end of Elizabeth's reign.[120] As with bridal pregnancy, the situation in Wiltshire was roughly congruent with the national pattern: analysis of the registers of nine sample parishes in various parts of the county yields an overall illegitimacy ratio of about 2.5 per cent in the decade 1601–10.[121]

While these illegitimacy figures, even at their peak, are low relative to nineteenth-century rates, they are by no means negligible;[122] and they do not necessarily imply a high level of chastity. The available figures are themselves underestimates of illegitimacy, since some bastard children were undoubtedly never baptised.[123] Account must also be taken of infanticide, contraception, abortion, and low levels of fertility. The first was probably fairly rare in England at this time,[124] while it is likely that contraception was also little practised. There is little evidence of the use of family limitation techniques (apart from prolonged lactation periods) even within marriage, and possible indications of contraceptive practices out of wedlock are rare and ambiguous. Edward Harper, a married man of Hilmarton, was said in 1617 to 'have to do with wenches when he list and would choose whether he would beget them with child or not'; while Jeremy Gibbens of Idmiston, accused in 1616 of begetting a bastard,

[119] On the shortcomings of the illegitimacy ratio, see Peter Laslett, 'Introduction: comparing illegitimacy over time and between cultures', in Peter Laslett, Karla Oosterveen and Richard M. Smith (eds.), *Bastardy and its comparative history* (1980), p. 15.

[120] Laslett, *Family life and illicit love*, ch. 3.

[121] For further details, see below, Chapter 8.

[122] Laslett, *Family life and illicit love*, p. 104.

[123] Laslett, 'Introduction: comparing illegitimacy', pp. 48–53; Ingram, 'Religion, communities and moral discipline', pp. 185–6.

[124] Keith Wrightson, 'Infanticide in earlier seventeenth-century England', *Local population studies*, 15 (1975), pp. 10–22; but cf. J. A. Sharpe, *Crime in seventeenth-century England: a county study* (Cambridge, 1983), pp. 135–7. Infanticide is discussed in a broader context in Peter C. Hoffer and N. E. Hull, *Murdering mothers: infanticide in England and New England, 1558–1803* (New York, 1981); and Keith Wrightson, 'Infanticide in European history', *Criminal justice history*, 3 (1982), pp. 1–20.

was said to have remarked to a friend that 'what he had done was as much as nothing'. Such statements *could* indicate knowledge of practices such as *coitus interruptus* or non-penetrative modes of intercourse, but they may well have been mere idle boasts.[125]

Abortion or attempted abortion was probably commoner. It is plain that in Wiltshire as in other parts of England the abortifacient qualities of the herb 'savin' (*Sabina cacumina*) were well known and, perhaps, widely employed; and there are other references to 'powders' and 'potions' of an unspecified nature which contemporaries clearly believed to be an effective means of destroying an unwanted foetus.[126] In any case, given prevailing poor standards of health and hygiene and inadequate levels of nutrition among the poorer sections of society, it is possible that a sizeable proportion of illicit pregnancies were terminated by natural miscarriages. Moreover, many casual sexual contacts could have occurred without leading to pregnancy at all. It has been estimated that, even in modern conditions within marriage, there is only about one chance in fifty that a single act of coitus will result in conception; in late Elizabethan and early Stuart England the chances were presumably even lower. Hence, as Laslett has emphasised, 'numbers of baptised bastards may well have to be multiplied fifty, seventy, or even a hundred times and more in order to guess at the number of sexual lapses which lay behind them'.[127]

The fact that we know so little of the actual occurrence of pre- and extra-marital sexual activity has allowed scope for widely divergent views on popular attitudes to illicit sex in this period. At one extreme, Geoffrey Quaife has portrayed – at least in early seventeenth-century Somerset, the focus of his detailed study – an amoral 'peasantry' besporting themselves lustily on every possible occasion. Quaife argues that only the wives and daughters of yeomen and gentry – a small minority of the population – adhered at all closely to Christian sexual morality. Men at this social level actively strove to enforce

125 W.R.O., B/ABO 8, 25/7/1617, *Office v. Stowte*; AS/ABO 12, 9/3/1616, *Office v. Gibbens*. For scattered indications of contraceptive practices in other areas, see E. A. Wrigley, *Population and history* (1969), p. 127; G. R. Quaife, *Wanton wenches and wayward wives*: *peasants and illicit sex in early seventeenth-century England* (1979), pp. 133–4, 171–2. On the limited significance of contraception within marriage, see Laslett, *World we have lost further explored*, pp. 117–18.

126 For examples, see W.R.O., QS/GR Mich. 1608/115; QS/GR Trin. 1614/166; QS/GR East. 1625/142; D/Pres. 1628/25; B/DB 9, fol. 164v; B/DB 36, fol. 142. See also Quaife, *Wanton wenches and wayward wives*, pp. 118–20.

127 Laslett, *World we have lost further explored*, pp. 163, 328.

such conformity among their own female family members, but themselves felt free to depart from the Christian moral code with the wives, daughters and widows of other people, especially those below them in social rank. No such double standard operated among the mass of the population below the rank of yeoman, for the simple reason that for them, men and women alike, 'sex was not a moral issue' and the church's rulings on fornication and adultery had no real importance. Extramarital sexual activity aroused disapproval only when it disrupted the peace of the community or had serious economic implications, most notably in the case of bastards born of poor parents. The fear of bearing or begetting a bastard was, in fact, one of the few constraints on unbridled licence. The result was that extramarital sexual activity was widespread, at least (among the unmarried) in the form of 'mutual heterosexual masturbation and heavy petting, and recourse to experienced village women'.[128]

This argument rests on dubious assumptions and in other respects also is open to serious objections. It is constructed from a highly impressionistic and selective reading of the available evidence, emphasising lurid instances of apparently immoral or amoral attitudes and behaviour with little regard to the question of how far they were typical. Further, Quaife seriously misreads the nature of contemporary attitudes. The distinction which he posits between 'economic' and 'moral' constraints was surely foreign to Elizabethan and early Stuart thinking: characteristically, economic ideas were suffused with moral values and conceived in ethical terms. The related assumption, that Christian principles had not penetrated to the mass of the population, appears equally questionable in the light both of the kinds of evidence presented in the previous chapter and of the work of other historians.[129] Even Lawrence Stone, whose account of late medieval attitudes to sexuality has affinities with Quaife's picture, does at least admit that by the late sixteenth and early seventeenth centuries the church had had considerable success in inculcating Christian values and a consciousness of sin among the lower ranks of society, and that its efforts to uphold Christian sexual morality were not wholly ineffectual.[130]

Lurking at the base of Quaife's argument appears to be yet another dubious assumption: that the relentless thrust of the libido

[128] Quaife, *Wanton wenches and wayward wives*, pp. 179, 247 and *passim*.
[129] See above, Chapter 3.
[130] Stone, *Family, sex and marriage*, pp. 143–6.

could not possibly be contained within the patterns of late marriage (and lifelong celibacy for some), premarital chastity and monogamy which prevailed or were supposed to prevail in this period, and that various forms of extramarital sexuality must therefore have been widespread. But it is known that the strength of sexual drives is not a biological constant but depends partly on socially inculcated expectations; and in any case sexual tensions may be released in many ways other than actual physical sexuality.[131] There are certainly indications that some contemporaries regarded continence as a difficult matter, but it is evident that the resulting frustrations were at least as likely to find expression in prurient talk or in other displacements as in real indulgence. Revealing in this respect is a case concerning a certain Isaac Chiverton of Yatesbury in 1628. He was in the company of a number of young men, when 'they in jesting manner said...that they marvelled how he lived so long without a wife and never spotted [i.e. accused of fornication] with any woman'; to which he replied 'that it may be when he was a young man as they were it might be he had played with some wenches'. Questioned before an ecclesiastical judge, he vigorously denied that he had ever committed fornication or adultery, and it does seem likely that this middle-aged man and the youngsters were doing no more than indulging each other's fantasies.[132]

At the opposite extreme from Quaife, Peter Laslett has argued that a strict system of 'personal discipline', including sexual continence outside marriage, operated in early modern England. Although roughly congruent with Christian moral values and reinforced by them, this system was primarily dictated by demographic facts and the need for social survival. Just as powerful external and internal controls operated against early marriage, so also (as a necessary corollary) pre- and extramarital sexuality were rigorously proscribed. Bridal pregnancy, though common, did not seriously undermine this system of social discipline because, in Laslett's view, sexual intercourse normally occurred only after the making of a solemn and binding contract, or at least where the couple had a clear intention to marry. As regards bastardy, Laslett has stressed its rarity in comparison with some other societies and with later periods of English history, and suggested that such illegitimate births as occurred were often associated with a small, bastardy-prone sub-

[131] *Ibid.*, pp. 15–16.
[132] W.R.O., D/AB 33, 11/6/1628, *Office v. Chiverton.*

society – women who produced a succession of illegitimate children, who were often related to other bearers or begetters of bastards, and who may in some cases have functioned as village whores.[133]

While convincing in some respects, this attempt almost to 'explain away' the evidence of illicit sexuality appears too extreme and mechanistic, lacks firm evidential support for the demographic inferences, and pays too little attention to variations in attitudes and behaviour at different social levels. To an extent Laslett has recognised these weaknesses and modified his views since their original formulation in 1965,[134] particularly in the light of work by Keith Wrightson. The latter shares Laslett's insight that unconscious attitudes shaped by demographic and social structures were a major determinant of sexual behaviour in early modern England and that their powerful logic worked against libertinism. But he is more sensitive than Laslett to the influences of law and religious beliefs, to the variety and flexibility of social customs, and to the subtleties and complexities of individual behaviour. Wrightson argues that sexual discipline was in general fairly strict. However, at least for the lower orders of society, 'the restraints upon sexual activity...crumbled once marriage was in sight'; couples with serious matrimonial intentions were allowed a good deal of licence in their courtship behaviour and often commenced sexual relations before they were wed. Such behaviour would account for the high proportion of brides pregnant at marriage, but it assumes neither a rigid system dependent on formal marriage contracts (such as Laslett postulates) nor moral laxity: 'popular attitudes, though far from loose, were simply more flexible than those of society's professional moralists'. Wrightson suggests, moreover, that illegitimacy can to a large extent be understood in a similar light. The great majority of unmarried mothers appear to have been of much the same age as the bulk of women bearing their first child in wedlock, though they tended to be poorer than average. Furthermore, many bastard-bearers claimed (sometimes with supporting evidence) that they had been promised marriage or had at least been in 'good hope' of matrimony, while some could demonstrate that their marriage plans were well advanced when some external catastrophe – the death of the intended spouse, his impressment into the army, the onset of economic reces-

133 Peter Laslett, *The world we have lost*, 2nd edn (1971), chs. 4, 6 *passim*; Laslett, *Family life and illicit love*, ch. 3 *passim*.

134 Laslett, *World we have lost further explored*, ch. 7.

sion – had intervened to shatter their hopes. Many unmarried mothers thus differed from pregnant brides only in that they had enjoyed worse luck. Of the remainder, some were victims of sexual exploitation by masters or other superiors. Others were 'bastardy-prone' women, though Wrightson attaches less importance to this group than Laslett did and is inclined to see them as a vulnerable, exploited and even demoralised element among the rural poor rather than as a deviant sub-culture.[135]

Wrightson has little to say about incest, adultery and acts of fornication which neither were followed by speedy marriage nor led to the birth of a bastard child. Moreover, he gives relatively little attention to sexual offenders who do not easily fit his stereotypes of 'unfortunate' or 'exploited' individuals; while arguably his portrayal of popular sexual *mores* is more true of England in the reign of Charles I than of the situation in the middle years of Elizabeth's reign.[136] But the general thrust of the argument is surely sound. Though not as stringent as in some human societies, and by no means wholly congruent with the stern and idealistic prescriptions of Tudor and Stuart moralists, popular attitudes to sexual morality in this period were certainly not as libertarian as either contemporary clerical commentators or some modern historians like Quaife have implied.

Popular customs which – independent of church and secular court sanctions, and indeed frowned upon by the authorities – were used to express hostility or derision towards blatant sexual immorality, or to exploit accusations of sexual misconduct as a damaging insult, shed further light on popular attitudes to illicit sexuality. Notorious fornicators or adulterers were sometimes visited with the discordant din of 'rough music', made by the beating of pots and pans and other household utensils. In 1586, for example, a certain Thomas Atkyns was 'rung about the town of Purton with basins for that he did live incontinently with the wife of Robert Pearce'.[137] Cuckolds (husbands whose wives had been unfaithful) were often savagely mocked: horns or antlers were hung up on their houses, or neighbours grimaced or made horn signs at them with their fingers. A man

[135] Wrightson, *English society*, pp. 84–6; Wrightson and Levine, *Poverty and piety*, pp. 126–33; David Levine and Keith Wrightson, 'The social context of illegitimacy in early modern England', in Laslett *et al.* (eds.), *Bastardy and its comparative history*, pp. 158–75.

[136] See below, Chapter 8.

[137] W.R.O., B/*Detecta* Bk 6, fol. 41v.

who married a woman of doubtful morals sometimes had to run the gauntlet of derision on his wedding-day. Thus in 1616, when Richard Tomes of Catcomb went 'with a great many young fellows in his company' to fetch his bride from a neighbouring parish, a buck's horn stuck with a wisp of hay and a 'picture of a woman's privities' were set up by the roadside to greet the bridal party on the way back.[138] Yet another practice was to compose derisive rhymes or other lampoons. One example of this genre, a reaction to attempts to put down festivities in the village of Keevil, has already been cited.[139] But adulterers, fornicators and cuckolds were far more commonly the target of such satire, and a case from Bremhill in 1618 aptly illustrates what the victims might have to endure:

Woe be thee, Michael Robins,
That ever thou wert born,
For Blancute makes thee cuckold
And thou must wear the horn.

He fetcheth the nurse
To give the child suck,
That he may have time
Thy wife for to fuck.

And so it went on for a further ten scurrilous verses.[140] These relatively formalised satires, moreover, were merely the most dramatic manifestations of a social environment in which sexual slanders, ranging from such abusive generalities as 'whore' and 'whoremaster' to highly specific accusations of immorality, were commonly bandied about, and in which neighbours and fellow-servants frequently engaged in ribald gossip about sexual misdeeds.

The background to the use of mocking rhymes, rough music and similar customs was, in practice, often complex, involving malicious motives or quarrels unrelated to the forms of behaviour ostensibly condemned; and the same is true of sexual slanders. They therefore cannot be taken *simply* as an index of sexual attitudes. Further, it is

[138] W.R.O., QS/GR Hil. 1617/92.
[139] See above, p. 117.
[140] P.R.O., STAC 8/164/18. For further discussion of the phenomena mentioned in this paragraph, see Ingram, 'Ridings, rough music and the "reform of popular culture"', pp. 87–90; Martin Ingram, 'Ridings, rough music and mocking rhymes in early modern England', in B. Reay (ed.), *Popular culture in seventeenth-century England* (1985), pp. 166–97.

plain that some of the ideas underlying these customs – notably the notion that the cuckolded husband was in some sense reprehensible and, more generally, ideas reflecting a double standard of morality for men and women – were not strictly in accord with Christian principles; while mocking rhymes and the like involved a prurient or even pornographic element which suggests that they sometimes served as a proxy form of sexual indulgence rather than a clear-cut condemnation of it. Fundamentally, however, these phenomena do indicate a degree of popular intolerance of blatant immorality which accords ill with contemporary moralists' assumptions that fornication and adultery were commonly regarded as 'no sin at all'. Indeed the authors of derisive lampoons sometimes aligned themselves firmly with the authorities and demanded that legal action should be taken against the offenders they were castigating. Thus a 'true bede-roll of the whores known in Warminster', fixed to the chancel door on Christmas Day 1603, listed the names of fourteen women and concluded: 'We would entreat you that be officers to look to it, for you shall answer for not doing your offices before God; we wish you well.'[141]

On the other hand, the fact that accusations of sexual misconduct (whether justified or not) clearly had considerable power to wound, and the consequent reactions of the victims of sexual slander and rough music, indicate the importance of sexual reputation. Thus the victims of the derisive rhyme at Bremhill complained that the effect had been to take away their 'good names and reputations' and to make them 'odious and contemptible persons'; while one Yorkshire woman, when she heard another defamed, commented that 'they might as well take her life as her good name from her'. Such utterances reflect the fact that sexual 'credit' and 'honesty' – the lower-class equivalents of gentry notions of honour – were an important touchstone of respectability, certainly among the middling ranks of yeomen, husbandmen and substantial craftsmen, and to an extent even lower down the social scale.[142] As will be seen, actions of defamation to provide redress against sexual slanders were among the most important social services offered by the church courts in Elizabethan and early Stuart England. Around 1570 such suits were

[141] W.R.O., QS/GR East. 1604/124, 147.

[142] P.R.O., STAC 8/164/18; J. A. Sharpe, *Defamation and sexual slander in early modern England: the church courts at York*, Borthwick papers, 58 (York, 1980), pp. 2–3.

already quite popular among the middling sort; they were to become even more numerous in the next fifty years or so.

This expansion of slander litigation could indicate increased concern over sexual reputation in this period and hence reflect a tightening of popular attitudes to illicit sexuality, at least at certain social levels.[143] There are a number of other indications to the same effect. Demographic studies have revealed that bridal pregnancy rates declined in some parishes in the early seventeenth century, as also did the incidence of bastardy. Laslett's 98-parish sample indicates that overall the illegitimacy ratio fell from over 3 per cent around 1600 to about 2 per cent in the 1630s; in the later seventeenth century it was to fall even further, to about 1.5 per cent.[144] Wrightson and Levine's detailed analysis of the village of Terling in Essex suggests that in part such changes represented a spontaneous demographic adjustment, one aspect of a broader pattern of increased restraint on fertility in response to harsher economic conditions after about 1600. But in part too it reflected a conscious shift in attitudes, especially among the wealthier sections of village society, a hardening stance towards prenuptial fornication and bastard-bearing. Similar shifts are visible in Wylye, Keevil and other Wiltshire communities, and indeed in many other parts of early seventeenth-century England.[145]

What caused this perceptible change in the moral climate? Wrightson and Levine argue that in Terling the main stimuli were puritan piety among some sections of village society (particularly the relatively prosperous, more literate yeoman and substantial husbandman elements) and, more generally, an increasing concern over the problems of poverty – which tended to sharpen moral outrage against bastardy and related sexual offences. As was seen in Chapter 3, the 'godly group' which emerged in Terling in this period was probably unusual for its strength and coherence; it is doubtful whether distinctively puritan principles played a really vital role in changing popular sexual *mores* in England as a whole in this period.

143 Sharpe, *Defamation and sexual slander*, pp. 24–6.

144 Laslett, *Family life and illicit love*, p. 119; Laslett, 'Introduction: comparing illegitimacy', pp. 14, 18, 20, 23–4.

145 Wrightson and Levine, *Poverty and piety*, pp. 126–33. See also Martin Ingram, 'The reform of popular culture? Sex and marriage in early modern England', in Reay (ed.), *Popular culture*, pp. 154–6.

Prudential considerations, albeit articulated in religious and ethical terms, would appear to have been of more general importance.[146]

This chapter has sketched some of the main ideas about marriage and illicit sexuality current in late sixteenth- and early seventeenth-century England and reviewed the nature of popular practices. On some issues there was diversity of opinion and attitude, and this produced some attempts (only very partially successful) to alter the law on marriage formation, divorce, the punishment of sexual immorality and related matters. Yet these debates and differences should not obscure the existence of a large area of consensus on major issues, a consensus shared not only by the clerical and lay leaders of society but also by many 'honest householders' in the parishes. A broad spectrum of opinion agreed on the need for responsible, stable marriage and on the heinousness of blatant sexual immorality; indeed these ideas grew stronger as the period progressed. What role did the church courts play, within the framework of existing law, in upholding and reinforcing these values? This question is pursued in the second part of this book.

[146] Wrightson and Levine, *Poverty and piety*, ch. 7 and *passim*. Cf. Ingram, 'Religion, communities and moral discipline', *passim*; Ingram, 'Reform of popular culture?', pp. 157–9.

Part 2

Sex and marriage : the pattern o
prosecutions

5. *Matrimonial causes: (i) the breakdown of marriage*

The pattern of matrimonial business dealt with by the ecclesiastical courts in late sixteenth- and early seventeenth-century England provides a telling index of differences between that society and the England of today. Nowadays the bulk of matrimonial litigation – no longer handled, of course, by the church courts, which lost their jurisdiction in this field in 1857 – relates to divorce. Four hundred years ago, the church's insistence on the indissolubility of marriage, and the relative stability of marriages in actual practice at most social levels, ensured that marital breakdown cases came much more rarely before the courts: far more common were marriage contract suits and other cases connected with the *formation* of marriage. Causes concerning separation, annulment and related matters were, however, regarded as of great gravity in ecclesiastical law, and in spite of their relatively small numbers were by no means devoid of social significance. It is the purpose of this chapter to assess the church courts' work in this field.

As was seen in Chapter 4, divorce in the modern sense was unrecognised, but erstwhile spouses could remarry if they managed to secure an annulment. But the grounds for action were narrowly defined, and indeed became even more restricted in the aftermath of the Reformation. Annulment also entailed drastic legal consequences, including the wife's loss of dower rights and the bastardising of any children born of the dissolved union. Furthermore, potential plaintiffs faced formidable problems of proof. All these factors conspired to minimise the numbers of cases brought before the courts.

Even before the Reformation (when, it has often been supposed, the very extensive prohibitions on marriage with kin and affines provided endless opportunities for specious 'divorces'), annulments were in point of fact quite rare.[1] In Elizabethan and early Stuart

[1] Helmholz, *Marriage litigation*, pp. 74–6; Houlbrooke, *Church courts and the people*, p. 75.

times the incidence of cases was minimal. Thus the records of the archdeaconry of Chichester for twelve sample years spread over the period 1580–1640 reveal only two nullity suits, both of which occurred in 1602.[2] At least in the late sixteenth century, such suits may have been *slightly* more common in the diocese of Ely: including a few doubtful cases – the Ely court books for this period do not always distinguish clearly between annulments and mere separation suits – there was a possible average of one nullity cause per annum in the 1580s. After 1600, however, annulment cases became as rare at Ely as they were at Chichester.[3] In Wiltshire they were very uncommon throughout the period 1560–1640. Thus there were no suits of this type at all in the Salisbury consistory court in the three years commencing September 1565 (though one case did crop up in October 1568). In the period 1581–90 only one nullity cause can be positively identified, though two or three others may have been registered under the ambiguous heading of 'divorce' suits. And close search of all the surviving records of the bishop and dean of Salisbury for the years 1601–40 reveals only eight nullity suits relating to Wiltshire.[4] In all probability annulment cases were likewise rare in the diocesan courts in other parts of England. Some additional suits, involving litigants of high social status, may have gone to the court of arches in London without passing through the local church courts; while the courts of high commission also dealt on occasion with matters of nullity. But the numbers of cases from any particular locality which these tribunals dealt with were no doubt minuscule.[5]

Houlbrooke's finding for Norwich and Winchester in the mid-sixteenth century, that some of the possible grounds for securing an annulment were scarcely ever used, applies equally to the church courts in the period 1570–1640.[6] This is hardly surprising in the case of impotence or frigidity, for however common such incapacity may have been it was extremely difficult to prove. The law demanded evidence that the condition was permanent and had prevented

[2] Based on search of proceedings for 1582/3–1584/5, 1601–2, 1619–21, 1631–2, 1639–40: W.S.R.O., Ep.I/10/15, Ep.I/10/21, Ep.I/10/33–4, Ep.I/10/39, Ep.I/10/45.

[3] Based on search of all surviving act books for Ely diocese, 1580–1640, listed in the Bibliography.

[4] Based on search of all surviving court records for the periods specified, listed in the Bibliography.

[5] Slatter, 'Records of the court of arches', p. 145; Usher, *Rise and fall of the high commission*, ed. Tyler, pp. 256, 279.

[6] Houlbrooke, *Church courts and the people*, pp. 71–5.

consummation. Some English courts in the fifteenth century had adopted the bizarre and apparently uncanonical practice of subjecting allegedly impotent males to the attentions of a group of women, whose task it was to try to excite their passion; but no trace of this practice has been found in later times.[7] According to conventional legal opinion in the sixteenth and seventeenth centuries, the law prescribed a trial period of at least three years' cohabitation before an action could be entertained. Then the defendant had to submit to examination by competent physicians, who had to be satisfied that the condition actually existed and that cure was impossible. A female litigant, whether acting as plaintiff or defendant, had to be declared *virgo intacta* by honest matrons.[8] Study of the church courts in Wiltshire and elsewhere in the period 1570–1640 reveals no case in which couples actually attempted to meet these legal requirements. In 1618 one woman did declare publicly in the court of the archdeacon of North Wiltshire that she intended to sue for nullity on the grounds of her husband's incapacity, but there is no evidence that she actually did so.[9]

A combination of legal complexities and social conditions explains why cases based on the fact that the couple were under age were exceedingly rare. Canon law prescribed that children of seven years and above could be betrothed in marriage, but the union was not binding till the girl was twelve and the boy fourteen. Espoused infants could, on reaching these ages, formally dissent from the contract and thus nullify it, a procedure which could be wholly uncontentious. The catch was that the contract became fully binding if, after coming of age, the couple 'consented' to the union either explicitly, or by 'deeds and tokens' signifying acceptance, or simply by having sexual relations. An individual who tried to break free from a marriage contracted in childhood might thus be met with the claim that he or she had tacitly consented; and in these circumstances the only recourse was a formal nullity suit to try the issue. An action of annulment was also necessary if marriages between children had been solemnised in church.[10]

The principle of tacit consent unfairly stacked the legal cards against young people who wished to dissent from child contracts; in

7 Helmholz, *Marriage litigation*, pp. 88–90.
8 Clarke, *Praxis*, p. 141.
9 W.R.O., AW/ABO 5, 17/3/1618, *Office v. Hedges*.
10 Clarke, *Praxis*, pp. 141–3.

any case, adolescents were likely to be under the tutelage of the parents or other kinsfolk who had arranged the marriage in the first place, and hence in a weak position to do anything about it.[11] But in practice these problems were of little concern to the great majority of people, since, as we have seen, the espousing of infants was itself uncommon in most areas in late Elizabethan and early Stuart England.[12] In any event the issue rarely came before the courts. Incidental references to the repudiation of child marriages are occasionally found; but the Wiltshire court records for the years 1565–8, 1581–90 and 1601–40 reveal only one formally recorded case of undisputed dissent from infant spousals,[13] and one formal annulment suit on the grounds of impuberty. The plaintiff in this case claimed to have been baptised in 1591 and married in 1600. The parish registers of Berwick St John (Wiltshire) and Gussage All Saints (Dorset) provided a straightforward means of proof, and since the girl was still below the canonical age for marriage when she commenced her suit in February 1602, no counter-allegation of post-pubertal consent was possible. Neither party was of gentry rank, but otherwise nothing is known of the social status of the litigants or of the circumstances of the case. The location of the case is, however, interesting in that the downlands on the southern fringe of Wiltshire were apparently a very conservative area where, as will be seen, some older marriage customs persisted longer than elsewhere in the county.[14]

The rarity of cases of annulment based on duress is again readily comprehensible. Given that all social ranks paid at least lip service to the principle that the consent of the couple was necessary to marriage, instances of blatant coercion were probably uncommon. Undoubtedly some individuals were subjected to considerable pressure to marry according to the wishes of their families – such circumstances sometimes crop up in other types of matrimonial cause and will be discussed later – but this did not necessarily provide the grounds for a nullity suit. From medieval times the courts had interpreted duress in a narrow sense, accepting cases only when they involved 'force and fear' sufficient to sway a 'constant' man or

[11] Houlbrooke, *Church courts and the people*, p. 73.
[12] See above, pp. 128–9.
[13] W.R.O., AW/ABO 6, 29/7/1626, *Office v. Nott*.
[14] W.R.O., B/ABI 31, fols. 83v, 99, 125v. On marriage customs, see below, p. 206.

woman.[15] The extreme rarity of such suits in late sixteenth- and early seventeenth-century England is reflected in the records of the Wiltshire courts, which reveal only one possible case. In 1617 William Pavie, guardian of his idiot brother John, alleged that the latter had been abducted by Christopher Bigges (a convicted recusant) and George Tettershall, both of Stapleford, and married to one of Bigges's servants called Edith Northover. The outcome of this case is unknown because the defence speedily entered an inhibition to remove the matter to another, unspecified court; indeed it is not even quite certain that the grounds for action were duress. What is known is that the social and legal background of this suit was highly complex and probably helps to explain how the matter came to court. The Pavies, Biggeses and Tettershalls were rival gentry families whose feuds around this time involved them in a frogspawn mass of litigation on a variety of issues in a multiplicity of courts.[16]

The church's restrictions on marriage between kin and affines, which had been drastically simplified by 1563, were likewise only rarely invoked as grounds for annulment in this period. The pattern in the Salisbury courts appears to have been typical. A few couples were ordered to separate after disciplinary investigations of incestuous marriages; but the circumstances of these cases were obviously different from normal nullity suits.[17] In 1633 Robert Bartlett of Chilton Foliat did commence such a cause on the grounds that his pretended wife of eight years' standing, who had given birth to three of his children, was his niece by a former marriage. The litigants were probably fairly low on the social scale, since the defendant's uncle and brother both described themselves as bricklayers. Beyond this the circumstances of the suit, including the final outcome, are unfortunately unknown; the most striking feature of the case is simply its isolation.[18]

The most common grounds for nullity proceedings in Elizabethan and early Stuart England was precontract – the prior existence of a binding union, whether or not it had been solemnised in church.[19] Historians have often criticised the fact that an established, solemn-

[15] Helmholz, *Marriage litigation*, pp. 90–1.

[16] W.R.O., B/ABI 43, fol. 219; B/ABI 44, fol. 35v. On the background, see Ingram, 'Communities and courts', pp. 120–1.

[17] See below, pp. 246–7.

[18] W.R.O., B/DB 51b, fols. 14v–16.

[19] The same was true of the mid-Tudor period: see Houlbrooke, *Church courts and the people*, p. 75.

ised marriage could be subverted by invoking an earlier, unsolemnised and perhaps even unconsummated union.[20] But study of the five Wiltshire cases recovered for the period 1601–40 shows that there was little cause for concern, not only because the number of suits was very small but also because such cases as there were usually did not challenge established marriages. In the first of these cases, in 1612, Anne Umble of Mere sued her husband of eight years' standing on the grounds that he had a former wife living in Calverton (Derbyshire). Only one witness was called, a man whom Anne and her mother had sent to Calverton to investigate. He confirmed that when the defendant married Anne he already had a wife living, but he produced a certificate of burial to prove that the latter had since died. In view of the former wife's decease, the judge gave sentence at Anne's petition in favour of the later marriage. The suit may well have been collusive. Suspicion had apparently grown up among the Umbles' neighbours that their marriage was bigamous; Anne's real motive in going to court was probably not to secure an annulment but to get judicial confirmation of her present marriage and so quell local gossip.[21]

Sentences of annulment were granted in each of the other four suits. But in at least three of these cases the dissolved marriages had scarcely existed as a social reality. Amy Cooke, the daughter of a shoemaker, had apparently been forced by her mother into marriage with a 'lewd idle fellow', but the couple had never lived together or consummated their union. Joan Boarer claimed that she was 'through the importunity of divers of her friends and against her own full allowance and approbation' married to Alexander Strugnell, but the pair had separated after a fortnight and her husband had left Wiltshire. This was some 20 years previously and Joan believed that he was dead; his sudden, embarrassing reappearance brought her to court to secure an annulment. Rather different circumstances underlay the suit of Robert Herne alias Starr, a substantial man of an established Bremhill family. His marriage had existed for 18 years at the time of litigation and had definitely been consummated, but his wife admitted that she had spent little time in his company during that period. She confessed that she had had a child by another man some 14 years previously, and the records of

[20] For example, see Pollock and Maitland, *History of English law*, vol. 2, pp. 367–71; Ozment, *When fathers ruled*, pp. 44–5.

[21] W.R.O., D/DB 6, fol. 44; D/Citations 6/59; D/AB 24, fols. 31, 34, 38, 46.

the archdeacon of North Wiltshire reveal that she had also been presented for sexual incontinence with yet another man. Perhaps because of her promiscuity, she and her husband had been repeatedly delated by the churchwardens of Bremhill for the offence of living apart without lawful order; and it may have been this harassment which eventually induced Herne to bring a nullity suit to lay the ghost of a long-dead marriage.[22]

One possible criticism of the church courts is that their handling of evidence in nullity causes of this kind was sometimes rather dubious. The prior unions alleged by suitors in Wiltshire and elsewhere were mostly unsolemnised contracts which had supposedly occurred years previously and were naturally difficult to prove satisfactorily. In the late sixteenth century, the courts sometimes granted annulments essentially on the unsupported testimony of the parties themselves. This practice, which obviously facilitated collusion, was explicitly forbidden in the canons of 1604 and became much less common thereafter.[23] However, the courts still proved willing to accept some highly questionable hearsay evidence in precontract cases. If the number of suits had been large, or if there had been the remotest chance that the couple seeking an annulment would accept each other as man and wife, such legal laxity would have been reprehensible. As it was, the flexibility which the judges displayed can be justified on the grounds of commonsense and humanity.

Very occasionally precontract suits were used to annul marriages which had a real existence – at least in the sense that up till the time of litigation the couple had lived together as man and wife and even had children. These were not cynical divorces, however, but cases involving real bigamy. Around 1612 Elizabeth Ambrose of Ely was 'much abashed' to hear a stranger call her husband by another name. Tongues began to wag, the husband decamped, and on making inquiries Elizabeth discovered that he had another wife living in Yorkshire. A case before the Salisbury consistory court in 1585 was even more pathetic in that both the parties had apparently married in good faith. The defendant, Bridget Selbye of Corsham, confessed that 24 years previously she had married a certain John Werret, lived with him for seven years and had four children. Werret

[22] W.R.O., B/ABI 50, fols. 155v, 179v; B/DB 42, fols. 168v–76; B/DB 43, fols. 2–3; B/ABI 48, fols. 114v–15v, 132v–3; B/DB 38, fols. 116v–19v; B/ABI 35, fols. lv, 145, 184v; B/DB 25, fols. 33v–5, 48–9; AW/ABO 1, 15/2/1603, *Office v. Milles*; P.R.O., E 179/199/356, m. 1.

[23] Canon 105.

eventually left her and disappeared. After many years and fruitless efforts to locate him, Bridget assumed that he was dead and finally married John Selbye. But two and a half years later Werret turned up, whereupon John and Bridget immediately separated 'for that they knew their said marriage to be unlawful'.[24]

In cases like this, though one or other of the marriage partners took the initiative in bringing the matter to court, the suit took the form of a 'promoted office' prosecution to signify that it had disciplinary connotations and that the defendant was in theory liable to penance.[25] At least before the bigamy act of 1604, the courts also mounted 'mere office' or straightforward disciplinary prosecutions against bigamists. Such cases occurred regularly, but in fairly small numbers. Thus there were two such prosecutions in the archdeaconry of Leicester in 1586, two in the Cambridgeshire portion of the diocese of Ely in 1590–1, and one in the archdeaconry of Chichester in 1594.[26] The detailed episcopal visitation of Salisbury diocese in 1585 revealed only two Wiltshire cases (involving five people in all); while 28 visitations of the archdeaconry of North Wiltshire in the period 1586–99 uncovered a total of seven cases. To take a very local perspective, no cases of bigamy were reported from the parish of Keevil in the period after 1590; but there was one case in Wylye in 1599.[27]

A prosecution brought in the Salisbury consistory court in 1590, though unusual in involving double bigamy, illustrates the characteristic features of most bigamy cases in late Elizabethan England: the fairly low social status of the people involved, migration (often long-distance), and problems caused by poor communications. Sibil Carpenter of Fisherton Anger confessed that 26 years previously she had married an itinerant minstrel who died within five years at Cherry Hinton near Cambridge. She then went into service in Bristol, but eventually married a certain Richard Catser and lived with him in the Bristol area for about a decade. One night, about two o'clock in the morning, he announced that 'he must needs go to his first wife' who was still living at Prees in Shropshire. After a brief reappearance two weeks later to try to take away his 'household stuff',

[24] C.U.L., Ely D.R., D/2/31, fols. 68, 106v–7; W.R.O., B/DB 9, fol. 148.
[25] See above, p. 43.
[26] Based on search of L.M., 1 D 41/13/12; C.U.L., Ely D.R., B/2/11, fols. 42–222; W.S.R.O., Ep.I/17/8, fols. 139v–228v.
[27] Based on search of W.R.O., B/*Detecta* Bk 6; AW/*Detecta Bk*, 1586–99; B/ABO 1–5; AS/ABO 4–8. For the Wylye bigamy case, see AS/ABO 3, fol. 238.

Catser disappeared for good. Subsequently a linenweaver named Ralph Carpenter 'fell in love with her' and married her at Wolverhampton. The couple eventually moved to the crowded suburb of Fisherton Anger near Salisbury, only to attract the attention of the ecclesiastical authorities.[28]

For church court officials a worrying feature of some bigamy cases around this time was that the offence had been facilitated by uncertainties and confusions over the meaning of 'divorces' pronounced in the ecclesiastical courts; evidently some people acted as though a separation from bed and board allowed the parties to remarry.[29] But it is plain that the late Elizabethan ecclesiastical authorities were doing all they could to nullify this impression (which may have been encouraged by the mid-century debate on divorce) and were vigilant in the pursuit of witting or unwitting bigamists. Thus in a case from south Wiltshire in 1586, one party to a bigamous arrangement was, in spite of repeated migrations, eventually apprehended by the officers of the bishop of London, while another was disciplined by the archdeacon of Salisbury. At least in some cases the efforts of the courts were supported by strong local opinion: it was said of a couple living bigamously at Castle Combe in 1594 that 'all the country thereabouts for the most part crieth out thereat, for that they are suffered to live so offensively'. Moreover detected offenders were dealt with rigorously: bigamous couples were ordered to separate and the guilty parties enjoined severe penances.[30] Overall the evidence of prosecutions suggests that, certainly by the end of the sixteenth century, the offence was neither so easy nor so common as historians like Lawrence Stone have sometimes supposed, and that the impact of the church courts in this sphere was by no means negligible.[31]

The bigamy act of 1604 made the offence a felony but did not *entirely* destroy the spiritual courts' jurisdiction over unlawful remarriage. Owing to an ambiguously worded saving clause, they could still hear cases involving individuals who had remarried after a church court separation 'from bed and board'.[32] Indeed some

[28] W.R.O., B/DB 11, fols. 59v–60.

[29] For example, see W.R.O., AS/ABO 2, fol. 69; AS/ABO 3, fols. 55v–6; cf. B/DB 12, fols. 58v–9.

[30] W.R.O., AS/ABO 3, fols. 55v–6; B/DB 12, fols. 42v–3 (cf. B/DB 8, fols. 128v–30); B/DB 12, fol. 69.

[31] Cf. Stone, *Family, sex and marriage*, p. 40.

[32] John Godolphin, *Repertorium canonicum: or, an abridgement of the ecclesiastical laws of this realm* (1678), pp. 421–2.

post-1604 visitation articles continued (probably as a result of administrative inertia) to inquire more generally about people 'voiced, noted and credibly reputed and accused to have two wives living, or two husbands'.[33] But church court prosecutions for bigamy in whatever form were very rare after 1604.[34] How effective, on the other hand, was the bigamy act? It is impossible to say how many Wiltshire cases were dealt with by the secular courts, since the relevant assize records are lost; though it is known that a bigamist was hanged after indictment at the Wiltshire quarter sessions in 1617.[35] Studies of criminal records in other areas suggest that bigamy prosecutions were quite rare in early Stuart England and that the offence was not a matter of urgent concern to either judges or jurors.[36]

Apart from matters of nullity, the church courts had to deal with marriages which were of unquestionable validity but which had run into difficulties. Occasionally they received presentments about marital disharmony before relations between husband and wife had actually reached breaking-point. In 1592, for example, the court of the archdeaconry of Chichester heard that Thomas Kent of Lodsworth 'beateth his wife in such sort that they are in doubt he will kill her'; while the bishop of Ely's court was informed in 1590 that Mary Wright of Whittlesey 'did misuse her husband with undecent words and...did scratch him by the face'.[37] But such cases were everywhere rare and in some areas (including Wiltshire) virtually unknown. Regular interference by the church courts in everyday marital relations would probably have been resented. In any case, the judges probably saw routine marriage guidance as the responsibility of parish ministers. Incidental references occasionally reveal the local clergy actually performing this role: it was said in 1609, for example, that the vicar of Wootton Rivers had 'often blamed' one of his parishioners for beating his wife. Ordinary neighbours also intervened on occasion. When Richard Greene of Downton continually ill-treated his wife around 1623, 'all the street cried shame at him'.[38]

[33] For example, see the articles of Townson (1620) and Davenant (1622 and 1628), listed in the Bibliography under 'England, church of'.
[34] For an isolated instance, see W.R.O., B/ABO 11, 9/6/1628, *Office v. Barber*.
[35] W.R.O., QS/GR Mich. 1617/99.
[36] Sharpe, *Crime in early modern England*, p. 54; Sharpe, *Crime in seventeenth-century England*, pp. 67–8.
[37] W.S.R.O., Ep.I/17/8, fol. 20; C.U.L., Ely D.R., D/2/18, fol. 104.
[38] W.R.O., QS/GR East. 1609/99; B/DB 40, fol. 39.

When marital disharmony came before the church courts, it was usually when the marriage was on the point of breakdown or the couple had actually split up. A variety of party and party remedies were available to meet these circumstances. The most important was an action to secure a judicial separation 'from bed and board' on the grounds of either cruelty or adultery. Separated wives could also sue for alimony. A husband whose wife had been induced to leave home by some third party – whether lover, relative, or anyone else – could bring an action of 'detention of wife'. Deserted wives or husbands could also sue for restitution of conjugal rights. In practice, restitution suits often proceeded in similar fashion to (or were superseded by) separation causes: the errant partner counter-alleged cruelty or adultery and petitioned for licence to live apart. The existence of these overlapping remedies meant that marital disharmony sometimes translated itself into a veritable battle of cross-suits.[39]

The high commissioners in London handled some matrimonial causes of these types, especially those involving gentry or aristocracy. But to judge from surviving high commission act books for the years 1634–6, the amount of litigation which by-passed the local church courts was, from the perspective of any single county, inconsiderable. The cases found in diocesan records mainly sprang from the middling ranks of society. Since marriages were usually very stable at this social level,[40] and since the most the courts could do to relieve marital unhappiness was to license a separation with no right of remarriage, it is not surprising to find that suits were not very common. Indeed they become fewer as time wore on. This decline may actually have reflected a declining incidence of marital breakdown, or it may have been conditioned by legal changes: the canons of 1604 insisted on stricter standards of proof in separation cases and strongly reaffirmed the ban on remarriage.[41]

A few statistics will suffice to illustrate the main patterns of litigation. In the archdeaconry of Chichester, in twelve sample years between 1580 and 1640, there were in all only three separation causes, two restitution suits and one alimony case. In the diocese of Ely in the 1580s, there were one or two separation or restitution cases each year, plus an occasional detention suit; cases were even fewer in the early seventeenth century.[42] In Wiltshire, in the years

[39] Clarke, *Praxis*, pp. 144–53.

[40] See above, p. 149.

[41] Canons 105–8.

[42] For the sources on which these statements are based, see above, notes 2 and 3.

1565–8, there were in all three separation and three restitution suits. Twenty years later there were already markedly fewer cases, and the incidence of litigation was even lower in the early seventeenth century: only nine separation causes and three restitution suits can be identified in the period 1601–40.[43]

Cases which were brought before the judges tended to involve intractable circumstances. Downright marital incompatibility was essentially at issue in some restitution causes. In 1565 John Bennet claimed that, despite his extensive negotiations with his wife's stepfather and other 'friends' she refused to live with him. When he tried to get into bed with her, she 'did suddenly rise out of her bed and refused to company with him...saying that she was the worse when she saw him'. In 1588, Julian Cordwell explained that Henry Cordwell of Corsley had been keen to marry her, but she could never 'find in her heart to fancy him'; nevertheless, 'by means of the importunity, suit and earnest soliciting of him unto her friends, viz. her father and mother, her master and her lady and mistress with other of her dear friends, who altogether thereupon did so menace and evil intreat her', she eventually submitted to marry him. She regretted it immediately, however, and utterly refused to live with her husband.[44]

Adultery underlay only a minority of separation suits, though it not uncommonly figured as a counter-allegation in restitution causes. Probably adultery was not generally regarded, in itself, as sufficient reason to seek a separation; and in any case it was difficult to prove satisfactorily.[45] Plaintiffs suing on account of infidelity had to possess both an obdurate nature and hard evidence. Thomas Gascoigne, a substantial householder of Marlborough, did sue his wife in 1566 on the grounds of what was evidently a long-standing liaison with a certain Robert Hall. A servant in the house had become aware of the couple's 'evil and lewd behaviour' and told her fellow-servants and various neighbours. A Mistress Godwine, at the request of Agnes Gascoigne's mother, urged silence 'to make the best of the said matter'. But a group of neighbours and servants spied on the couple and eventually caught them in the act, whereupon Thomas Gascoigne 'kept no company with his wife after he had heard of her usage'.[46] An even more clear-cut case occurred in 1602, when the

[43] Based on W.R.O., B/ABI 3 and all surviving records of the bishop of Salisbury's consistory court in the periods 1581–90, 1601–40, listed in the Bibliography.
[44] W.R.O., B/DB 5, fols. 30, 36; B/DB 10, fols. 17v–18.
[45] This point is discussed fully below, Chapter 8.
[46] W.R.O., B/DB 5, fols. 58v–63.

rector of Orcheston St George alleged that his wife had been enjoined penance for having a child by another man; a certified copy of the relevant acts of the archdeacon of Salisbury's court provided ample proof.[47] In contrast to these cases, some of the counter-allegations of adultery which were made in restitution suits were more dubious. Mary Martin, seeking to regain her conjugal rights in 1582, denied her husband's charges of immorality. Her story was that her husband allowed or procured her abduction in the streets of Gloucester by one Parker, who thereupon kept her prisoner for over six months until she eventually managed to escape to the house of her stepfather.[48]

As in earlier periods, cruelty usually formed the grounds for action in separation suits in the late sixteenth and early seventeenth centuries, and it was sometimes alleged as a justification for desertion in restitution causes.[49] Though termagant wives were not unknown, a man who tried to sue his wife for ill-treatment would no doubt have been regarded as a laughing-stock;[50] and it is not surprising to find that it was invariably the wife who claimed cruelty. Since in common law a husband had the right to beat his spouse, the church courts had perforce to interpret cruelty in a strict sense; and plaintiffs normally claimed that they had suffered abuse sufficient to endanger their well-being or even their life.[51] Close study of depositions suggests that witnesses often found it difficult to remember incidents which quite matched the enormities alleged by the prosecution, but sympathetically did their best. Certainly the women concerned had suffered injury: there was ample evidence of blows, neglect and unreasonable treatment sufficient to make conjugal life extremely uncomfortable.

A group of five well-recorded Wiltshire cases (including one restitution suit and four separation suits) from the early seventeenth century provides valuable insights into the underlying circumstances. All the husbands involved showed signs of mental disturbance or instability. William Passion of Salisbury, for example, was apparently obsessed with guilt for marrying while he had a former wife living,

47 W.R.O., B/ABI 31, fols. 142v, 257v, 274.

48 W.R.O., B/DB 9, fols. 8v, 22–3. The husband's basic allegation in this case was that Mary was precontracted to Parker. For the woman's subsequent matrimonial adventures, see B/DB 12, fols. 58v–9.

49 Helmholz, *Marriage litigation*, p. 101; but cf. Houlbrooke, *Church courts and the people*, p. 68.

50 On termagant wives, dominated husbands, and popular reactions to them, see Ingram, 'Ridings, rough music and the "reform of popular culture"', *passim*.

51 J. M. Biggs, *The concept of matrimonial cruelty* (1962), pp. 21–2.

'wishing his throat cut that ever he left his true wife'. Another defendant, Geoffrey Benger of Fyfield, was described by witnesses as someone who broke out at times like a man 'frantic', not caring what he said or did in his fury; and he seems to have been prey to obscene fantasies.[52] Such psychological traits may have been linked with another general factor, the decaying economic position of the menfolk concerned. Geoffrey Benger, though born a gentleman, was said to be living in base condition; William Passion believed that 'he could not prosper'; Richard Greene of Downton was heavily in debt; while George Churchouse was a failed goldsmith reduced to living on the charity of his wife's uncle – who was none other than Dr Henry Seward, canon of Salisbury.[53] These financial difficulties bred or reinforced marital tensions. The menfolk clung to their wives for economic reasons, while at the same time resenting and ill-treating them and flinging odium on their relatives. George Churchouse, for example, was said to have fallen into hatred towards his spouse, 'telling her that he thought her uncle and she would have him a prentice boy again'. On the other hand the wives, aided by their kinsfolk, became increasingly desperate to safeguard themselves and salvage some of their property. Henry Seward in fact eventually withdrew his support from Churchouse, the latter's credit collapsed, and the citation which summoned him to hear sentence in the consistory court bears a note that it had to be delivered to 'the door of the gaol in Sarum where he now liveth'.[54] Such tangled circumstances, going beyond mere personal incompatibility or gratuitous cruelty, are very reminiscent of some of the cases of broken marriage recorded by Gough in the Shropshire village of Myddle.[55] Clearly it was only in dire circumstances that couples from the middling ranks in early modern England would resort to legal separation.

How were cases handled by the courts? In the late middle ages, according to Richard Helmholz, the main goal of the judges in handling separation suits (especially cruelty cases) was to bring the couple to concord and agreement. If attempts at reconciliation

[52] W.R.O., B/DB 25, fols. 60v–1; B/DB 25, fols. 65–7.
[53] W.R.O., B/DB 25, fol. 66; B/DB 25, fol. 60v; B/DB 40, fols. 44–7, 128v, 129v; B/DB 48, fols. 60–1.
[54] W.R.O., B/DB 48, fol. 79; B/Citations 2/97. For a different perspective on the Churchouse case, especially Seward's role in it, see *H.M.C.*, *Fourth report*, appendix, pp. 130, 135.
[55] Gough, *History of Myddle*, ed. Hey, pp. 166, 198, 228.

failed, the courts were prepared to arrange separations on an informal basis without involving the couple in the trouble and expense of calling witnesses. Only if these expedients proved unacceptable were cases tried formally according to strict rules of evidence. Ralph Houlbrooke found that procedure was generally more formal and legally rigorous in the mid-sixteenth century;[56] and this stricter approach seems to have prevailed later. In Elizabeth's reign the courts were sometimes willing to grant sentences of separation or formal licences to live apart on the mere declaration of the parties, without the calling of witnesses;[57] but such 'quickie' divorces were explicitly forbidden by the canons of 1604 on the grounds that they facilitated collusion, and the practice all but ceased after that date.[58] Most cases were handled quite rigorously, and separations were granted only on very good evidence. Well-documented adultery cases, like those discussed earlier, resulted in speedy sentences of separation; but the complexity of the issues involved in cruelty cases made the outcome more hazardous. The wife of George Churchouse was successful in securing a separation; in *Passion v. Passion*, on the other hand, the couple was ordered to resume conjugal life after the husband had given 'bond and oath' for the security and good treatment of his wife.[59]

The shift from the flexible approach of the medieval courts to the stricter and more rigorous attitude of later judges should be seen as part and parcel of the church's growing insistence on the sanctity of marriage and of increasing public control over matrimony. It may also be, as suggested earlier, that the predominantly lay officials of the post-Reformation courts felt that informal efforts to reconcile quarrelling couples were best left to the parish clergy. In any case the decline of judicial efforts at reconciliation can only have been of marginal social significance, since even in the late middle ages separation suits came before the courts only in very small numbers.[60]

Some couples split up without bothering to bring a separation or annulment suit. This made them liable to disciplinary prosecution;

[56] Helmholz, *Marriage litigation*, pp. 101–7; Houlbrooke, *Church courts and the people*, pp. 68, 84.

[57] For example, see W.R.O., B/ABI 3, fol. 98; C.U.L., Ely D.R., D/2/12, fols. 21v, 29v, 33v; D/2/18a, fols. 291, 295, 297v.

[58] Canon 105. But see C.U.L., Ely D.R., D/2/24, fol. 159a.

[59] *H.M.C., Fourth report*, appendix, pp. 130, 135; W.R.O., B/ABI 36, fols. 142v, 143v.

[60] Helmholz, *Marriage litigation*, p. 101.

but detections for this offence in late Elizabethan and early Stuart England were generally few in number. The pattern found in Wiltshire appears to have been fairly typical. A detailed episcopal visitation of Salisbury diocese in 1585 revealed only five Wiltshire cases; while the visitations of the archdeacon of North Wiltshire between 1586 and 1599 turned up, on average, only one or two cases a year. The appearance books of the three main Wiltshire jurisdictions for the period 1615–29 record a total of 25 cases – an average of fewer than two per annum. Even making generous allowance for non-appearers, whose cases were not entered in the appearance books, it is obvious that the number of detections at this period cannot have been large.[61]

Given that, in all probability, marriages were mostly very stable in the late sixteenth and early seventeenth centuries, substantial numbers of prosecutions for unlawful separation are not to be expected. Nevertheless it is plain that the recorded cases by no means represent all the instances of broken marriage which actually occurred. Local records and incidental references in a variety of other sources sometimes reveal informal separations which apparently never led to prosecution. For example, there were at least two wives living on their own in the village of Wylye in the period 1615–35, but there is no evidence that either was detected to the church courts.[62]

Evidently churchwardens and court officials exercised a certain discretion. The marital problems of aristocrats and gentry were probably for the most part discreetly ignored – though the high commission sometimes took up these cases, while churchwardens did occasionally pluck up the courage to present to the local courts such personages as Sir Robert Tirrell of Shudy Camps (Cambridgeshire), 'by public fame separated from his lady'.[63] At the other end of the social spectrum, there was little point in presenting poor, deserted wives (like those of Wylye) if the women themselves were blameless and their husbands had obviously gone for good. Separated couples were most likely to become 'offensive' to churchwardens and other respectable inhabitants, and hence liable to be detected, when either

[61] Based on search of W.R.O., B/*Detecta* Bk 6; AW/*Detecta* Bk, 1586–99; B/ABO 7–11; AW/ABO 5–6; AS/ABO 11–14. Extensive sampling of the records of the archdeaconries of Chichester and Leicester and of the diocese of Ely indicates rather similar levels of prosecution in those areas.

[62] Hadow (ed.), *Wylye registers*, pp. 45, 48.

[63] C.U.L., Ely D.R., B/2/36, fol. 163.

or both spouses were suspected of 'lewdness', when a husband wilfully failed to support his wife and so burdened the poor rates, or more generally when couples were apparently living apart without 'any just cause... but only a wayward humour'.[64]

Cases which came before the courts were for the most part briefly recorded, and it is often impossible to determine just why the marriage had broken down. The better-documented cases illustrate a variety of causes or major symptoms of marital tension, including adultery by either partner, cruelty, impotence, disagreements over children and property, and sundry unspecified 'quarrels' and 'discontents'.[65] More striking is the fact that in over 40 per cent of the more detailed cases the sheer pressure of poverty rather than actual marital disharmony was the reason why the couple had separated – a stark reflection of the vulnerability of marriage among the indigent in this period, and a reminder of why the 'better sort' in parish society were sometimes reluctant to let very poor people get married in the first place. Some of these couples made pathetic efforts to keep their marriages going. The husband of Anne Noble of Idmiston, for example, 'being a labouring man', lived away from her on weekdays but managed to spend some time with her on Sundays; and though a couple in Little Hinton had been separated for four years because the husband was in service, his wife claimed that 'he goeth home to her sometimes'. Edith Miles of Bulford would have been ready to live with her husband 'if that he had wherewithal to maintain her', but his poverty forced her to dwell with her father who allowed her 'that maintenance which she hath'.[66] Even in cases where poverty was not the ostensible reason for marital breakdown it may often have been a contributory factor. It is evident from fee-notes and other details that a high proportion (perhaps two-thirds) of the defendants in separation prosecutions were very poor. Moreover the numbers of cases tended to rise somewhat in harsh economic conditions: for example, in the wake of depression in the cloth trade and bad harvests, the archdeacon of North Wiltshire's Michaelmas

[64] W.R.O., AW/ABO 5, 9/12/1618, *Office v. Jones*; B/ABO 11, 11/7/1625, *Office v. Porter*; D/Pres. 1606–8 (unnumbered), Gt Bedwyn, 17/10/1605 [*sic*]; AW/ABO 4, 30/10/1610, *Office v. Kinge*.

[65] W.R.O., AS/ABO 14, 8/7/1626, *Office v. Smith*; B/ABO 5, 22/2/1603, *Office v. Walker*; AW/ABO 5, 17/3/1618, *Office v. Hedges*; B/ABO 10, 22/12/1620, *Office v. Beedle*; AS/ABO 14, 4/7/1629, *Office v. Twiford*.

[66] W.R.O., B/ABO 11, 14/12/1622, *Office v. Noble*; B/DB 37, fol. 158v; B/ABO 11, 20/12/1622, *Office v. Miles*.

visitation in 1586 yielded an exceptional total of six separation cases.[67]

The judges dealt with these poor people with realistic tolerance, usually dismissing them with or without an admonition, and often waiving the court fees. They also tended to dismiss other wives or husbands who had reasonable grounds for living separately, such as cruel usage or the blatant adultery of one partner; but in these cases they strove to reform or punished with penance the guilty spouse. They sometimes ordered quarrelling couples to live together again, though how far these injunctions were backed up by constructive advice or counselling is unknown. In the last resort, when the couple was bitterly at odds, there was little that the judges – or indeed anyone else – could do.

In assessing the church courts' work in the sphere of marital breakdown, it is important to remember that marriages across a broad social spectrum were probably mostly stable and that broken marriages were far less socially acceptable than they are today. In offering only limited grounds for separation and annulment, and in pursuing at least the more 'offensive' cases of unlawful separation, the church courts were simply reinforcing these features of early modern English society in a way which most people regarded as perfectly acceptable. Cases which came before the courts were inevitably few in number. As a corollary, the cases which did come to the judges' attention often involved dire circumstances and were hence not easy to handle; while it was obviously beyond the power of the courts to remedy marital difficulties arising from the sheer pressure of poverty. Perhaps the judges could have done more to counsel quarrelling couples, but otherwise the courts coped as well as could reasonably be expected.

67 W.R.O., AW/*Detecta* Bk, 1586–99, fols. 2, 4–5. On the economic background, see Sharp, *In contempt of all authority*, pp. 13–17.

6. *Matrimonial causes: (ii) marriage formation*

The bulk of matrimonial business in this period was concerned with marriage formation, including party and party suits over disputed marriage contracts and disciplinary prosecutions for irregular or 'clandestine' marriages. Historians have often been critical of the church courts' work in this sphere, on the grounds that the ecclesiastical law of marriage was complex, confusing and riddled with anomalies; but such judgements are largely unjust.[1] It is true that the church's law on marriage formation did include complex and ambiguous elements; but it would be wrong to exaggerate their importance, and the canons of 1604 went some way towards clarifying matters.[2] Moreover, study of what ecclesiastical lawyers actually did within the confines of existing law reveals that the courts worked fairly consistently to minimise popular uncertainties about marriage entry and to stress the necessity of the properly publicised solemnisation of marriage in church. At the same time, they carefully balanced the conflicting claims of individual and family interests in marriage, conforming with the widely accepted principle that the ideal union was based on the multilateral consent of all the parties involved. In this light the work of the courts appears eminently sensible and in accord with the values of the wider society.

Traditionally the most prominent type of matrimonial business was marriage contract litigation. Such cases were, at least in theory, of great social significance, since what was generally at issue was not mere breach of promise, but whether or not the couple was actually man and wife. It will be recalled that the essential requisite for a legally binding union was not the formal solemnisation of marriage in church but a *contract* – called, in popular usage, 'spousals', 'making sure' or 'handfasting' – by which the couple took each

[1] For example, see Pollock and Maitland, *History of English law*, vol. 2, pp. 367–72; Stone, *Family, sex and marriage*, pp. 30–4.

[2] See above, pp. 134–6.

other as husband and wife using words of the present tense (*per verba de praesenti*).[3] In order to be fully licit in the eyes of the church and of the society as a whole, the law prescribed that contracts should be publicised by the calling of banns and solemnised in open church; and marriage in church was undoubtedly normal practice in the late sixteenth and the seventeenth centuries.[4] But an unsolemnised or unwitnessed union, though irregular, might nonetheless be fully binding.

Canon law recognised, however, other forms of marriage contract which were not immediately binding and irrevocable. Spousals in words of the future tense (*per verba de futuro*) constituted a contract *to marry* rather than a contract *of marriage*. Such an agreement could be dissolved by mutual consent, or even repudiated unilaterally in certain circumstances. *Conditional* contracts were rather similar. The couple accepted each other as man and wife subject to the fulfilment of specified provisions such as the consent of parents or an adequate financial settlement, and normally the union only became fully binding when these conditions were met. The law recognised, of course, that betrothed individuals could not be expected to wait for ever for future or conditional promises to be performed. Hence it was held that a future or conditional promise could be superseded by a subsequent *de praesenti* contract with someone else. On the other hand, if couples betrothed by conditional or future contracts had sexual intercourse their union became immediately and irrevocably binding.[5]

At its simplest, an action over a disputed contract involved only two parties. But sometimes more than one individual claimed a marriage contract with a certain person. In these three- or multi-cornered cases the judges had to decide which of the alleged contracts (if any) was valid and which null: the prime rule was that the first of two absolute contracts was binding, even if the second had been solemnised in church. These suits were referred to as causes of 'spousals and nullity' or 'marriage and divorce' – but they were quite unlike modern divorce suits, since marital unhappiness was not

[3] On popular terminology, see Griffith, *Bethel*, p. 269; A. Percival Moore, 'Marriage contracts or espousals in the reign of queen Elizabeth', *Reports and papers of associated architectural societies*, 30 (1909), pp. 261–73.

[4] See above, p. 132.

[5] For the English reader the most convenient authoritative text setting forth the law of spousals is Swinburne, *Treatise of spousals*. The best brief modern commentary is Helmholz, *Marriage litigation*, pp. 26–57.

involved, and, indeed, in most cases the controverted marriages had not really got going when the cases came to court.[6]

There were various other types of suit concerned with marriage contracts and related matters. Causes of 'jactitation of matrimony' reversed the normal roles of the parties: the plaintiff complained against someone who untruly 'boasted and affirmed' that a contract existed. A successful action, which was closely akin to a defamation suit, was supposed to dispose of all claim to and fame of the pretended marriage, and the defeated defendant was ordered to keep perpetual silence on the matter. A cause of 'impediment of marriage' could be brought against a third party (characteristically a father or other relative) who unjustly prevented a marriage from being solemnised. 'Probation of marriage' causes were formal proceedings to establish, usually for legal reasons, that a marriage had duly taken place. Finally, in certain circumstances it was possible to bring a church court action for the payment of a dowry. These subsidiary types of matrimonial litigation were relatively unusual and, when they did occur, were often begun in tandem with straightforward contract suits.[7]

Spousals suits were usually prosecuted as 'instance' actions between parties. But, since marriage contracts concerned matters of public morality, the courts sometimes intervened directly on the basis of detections sent in by churchwardens or of information from court officers or an interested party. The usual targets of such disciplinary proceedings were couples who were in dispute over banns or spousals, who appeared to be reneging on contracts, or who unduly delayed the solemnisation of their marriage. Depending on the circumstances, such cases might be handled summarily, or they might develop into formal causes similar to those initiated by instance procedure.

The legal principles outlined here were qualified by many detailed provisions; and commentators have often stressed that even the all-important distinction between 'present' and 'future' contracts was

[6] Helmholz, *Marriage litigation*, pp. 57–9; Houlbrooke, *Church courts and the people*, p. 59.

[7] Clarke, *Praxis*, pp. 143, 145–7 (on jactitation). On dowry suits, see Helmholz, *Marriage litigation*, p. 110. For examples of 'impediment' suits, see W.R.O., B/ABI 3, fol. 65; Norfolk and Norwich R.O., ACT 21/24a (stray Ely act book, 1588–90), 7/6/1589, *Office promoted by Agnes Brocke v. George Skiner*. For examples of 'probation' suits, see W.R.O., B/ABI 33a, fol. 165; B/ABI 33b, fol. 21.

not always easy to recognise in practice. If there was as a result widespread uncertainty among lay people about what exactly constituted entry into a binding union, one would expect to find a high incidence of suits over marriage contracts and related matters coming before the courts. In the fourteenth century spousals cases did indeed occur in significantly large numbers, but by the middle decades of the sixteenth century they were far less common. It would seem that the church's laws on matrimonial contracts, complex and anomalous though they may appear to modern eyes, were actually giving rise to relatively few disputes by the early years of Elizabeth's reign.[8]

In the period 1570–1640 the flow of marriage contract cases was further reduced from a fairly low incidence to the merest trickle. Every diocese and jurisdiction which has so far been examined tells the same story. In the diocese of Ely in the 1580s, the consistory court dealt with an annual average of about nine cases recorded in the instance act books, while a significant number of additional cases cropped up in the registers of disciplinary prosecutions. By the early seventeenth century, private litigants commenced on average fewer than three contract suits each year, and disciplinary prosecutions had become far less common.[9] In the archdeaconry of Chichester there was an average of about seven contract suits per annum in the legal years 1582/3 – 1584/5; forty years later the average had dropped to below two.[10] In the archdeaconry of Leicester in 1588 there were five spousals suits; in 1632 there were none at all.[11] A similar pattern of decline has been found in the dioceses of Exeter, Norwich and Canterbury, and in the huge diocese of York, which covered much of northern England.[12]

The pattern can be traced in more detail for the Wiltshire portion of Salisbury diocese. Table 4 shows that there were normally fewer than ten spousals suits in any year throughout the period 1565–1640. The figures for the 1580s show a slight increase over those for twenty years earlier, but since the population was growing at this time the change is hardly significant. More striking is the fact that, despite further population increases in the late sixteenth and early seven-

[8] Ingram, 'Spousals litigation', pp. 42–3 and the references there cited.
[9] *Ibid.*, pp. 42–3.
[10] Based on search of W.S.R.O., Ep. I/10/15, 21, 33–4, 39, 45.
[11] Based on search of L.M., 1 D 41/11/21, 65.
[12] Ingram, 'Spousals litigation', pp. 42–3 and the references there cited; B.L., Egerton MS 2631 (on Exeter diocese).

Table 4 *Wiltshire spousals suits before the bishop of Salisbury's consistory court in selected years, 1565-1640*

1565/6*	4	1618	2
1566/7*	4	1619	3
1567/8*	6	1620	2
1587	5	1628	0
1588	3	1629	2
1589	8+1 *caveat***	1630	1
1607	6	1638	1
1608	4	1639	2
1609	3	1640	2

* Legal years September–August.

** Court order entered at the petition of a certain party to prevent someone from solemnising marriage on the grounds that that person was already contracted to the petitioner. Such *caveat*s were normally followed up by spousals proceedings, but in the case in 1589 the matter was probably settled out of court.

teenth centuries, there was a definite drop in the numbers of contract suits under the early Stuarts. After about 1610 the number of causes handled each year by the consistory court was normally well under five. This evidence of a decline in spousals litigation is reinforced if disciplinary prosecutions relating to marriage contracts and banns are taken into account. Such prosecutions were never very numerous in Wiltshire in this period, but their numbers were at least appreciable in the late sixteenth century. Soon after 1600, however, they became very rare indeed.

The decline in marriage contract litigation is a reflection of the trends outlined in Chapter 4. Over the centuries there was a growing acceptance of the principle that solemnisation in church was the only satisfactory mode of entry into marriage, and a corresponding decline in the custom of contracting binding spousals even as a preliminary to the church wedding.[13] The policy of ecclesiastical judges in handling marriage contract cases contributed to these developments, as did the courts' activities in punishing antenuptial fornication, and a variety of other social, administrative and legal developments. These points will be developed later in this and subsequent chapters. Meanwhile, let us consider spousals litigation in more detail. What kinds of people were involved in marriage contract suits in the late sixteenth and early seventeenth centuries, and in what social circumstances did such cases occur? The following discussion

[13] Ingram, 'Spousals litigation', pp. 54–5.

is based primarily on Wiltshire material; but the analysis is supplemented by data from other dioceses, and many of the conclusions would appear to have wider relevance.

The prosecution of marriage contract suits was not the prerogative of either sex, but in most areas in this period male plaintiffs seem to have predominated. In the diocese of Ely, for example, males outnumbered females in a ratio of over 2:1. Wiltshire showed a similar pattern in the late sixteenth century, but the situation was reversed in the early seventeenth when women plaintiffs outnumbered men in a ratio of about 3:2. The significance of this change is not entirely clear; but, as will be seen, it may in part have been related to the especially swift decline of the custom of spousals in large parts of Wiltshire in this period and, more particularly, to a decline in the association of marriage contracts with property transfer arrangements.[14]

Everywhere the litigants in spousals suits were mostly bachelors and spinsters. In Wiltshire over the period 1580–1640 only about 3 per cent of female plaintiffs and 8 per cent of female defendants were widows. Fewer than 2 per cent of male plaintiffs and 5 per cent of male defendants can be positively identified as widowers, though these figures are no doubt underestimates since the marital status of males was not consistently recorded. As regards age, there is in a few cases direct or inferential evidence that the defendant was under twenty-one, while a handful of litigants (including some of the widows and widowers) were described as being relatively old or even 'aged'.[15] But the overwhelming impression is that the great bulk of litigants were in their twenties or early thirties – within the normal range for those contemplating marriage for the first time. Some of the female plaintiffs, but apparently only a small minority, were pregnant, a fact which gave added urgency to their suits.

The records do not consistently indicate the social status of the parties, but it is plain that most ranks of society were represented among litigants, except for the very rich and the desperately poor. There was a sprinkling of people from lesser gentry families and an occasional clergyman, but most litigants came from the middling ranks of yeomen, husbandmen, tradesmen and craftsmen. Predict-

[14] See below, pp. 205–6.

[15] For example, see W.R.O., B/DB 5, fol. 10, D/DB 5, fol. 26v, B/DB 47, fols. 134, 136 (female minors); B/DB 24, fols. 106–7v, B/DB 48, fol. 90 (male minors); B/DB 51a, fols. 121, 123–4 (aged).

ably, in view of the age-profile and social background of the parties, a significant proportion was or had recently been in service. These generalisations are supported by analysis of Wiltshire depositions for the period 1601–40 (when the documentation is exceptionally rich), which provide more specific information on the wealth and standing of about a third of all the known marriage contract litigants in that period. Few of the males represented were really poor, and the rest ranged fairly evenly from the lower levels of the tradesman/husbandman class into the ranks of men who could call themselves 'yeoman' or even, in a few instances, 'gentleman'. A handful, with incomes or expectations of over £100 per annum, would have been regarded as fairly wealthy in early seventeenth-century society. The females were, on average, somewhat less well off. About two-fifths were said to be worth 'little or nothing'. This did not mean that they were utterly destitute, but implied that they had no significant property of their own and could not expect much in the way of dowry; they were, apparently, mostly from families at or below the level of modest husbandman or craftsman. Another fifth were better provided for, from families in the solid husbandman range. The remainder came from substantial families, including a few which had pretensions to gentry rank. Predictably enough, there was some tendency for plaintiffs (whether male or female) to be rather poorer than defendants, and in a few cases the disparity was very marked.

These Elizabethan and early Stuart spousals suits conformed to a pattern which had been well established in England since the high middle ages.[16] Although plaintiffs might have to backtrack later and concede that a contract had been in conditional or future form, they almost invariably started off by alleging that the parties were man and wife by virtue of a marriage contract in words of the present tense. Normally these alleged marriages had not been solemnised, and suitors had the task of trying to convince the judges that none the less they fulfilled the requirements for a valid and binding union.

It was precisely to facilitate proof in cases of dispute that the church tried to insist that contracts made in advance of solemnisation should be adequately publicised and witnessed. But plaintiffs had commonly been negligent in this respect. Only a minority of cases illustrate what was conventionally regarded as the ideal pro-

[16] Donahue, 'Canon law on the formation of marriage', pp. 147–51.

cedure for making a contract. Preliminary marriage negotiations were 'ended' at a prearranged meeting, in the presence of impartial witnesses, between the couple, members of their families and other interested parties (the issue of family involvement in contract cases will be discussed in more detail later). Matters of property might be thrashed out and agreements made either verbally or – especially at higher social levels, and increasingly over time – in writing. A relative, a respected neighbour or sometimes a minister then undertook to contract the couple. This was evidently regarded as a responsible task demanding special expertise: in a case in 1565 the 25-year-old Evan ApJohn Owen at first refused the role of master of ceremonies on the grounds that he was 'unskilful therein'.[17] The recognised procedure was first to admonish the couple about the gravity of what they were about to do, and then to make sure that both parties were fully consenting. When assured that all was well the officiant got the couple to join hands and voice the words of contract. The spousals were characteristically sealed with the exchange of tokens, a 'loving kiss', mutual pledging in wine or beer, and sometimes a celebratory meal. Plainly it was assumed that marriage in church would follow as soon as possible, and sometimes the contracted couple took immediate steps to publish the banns or obtain a licence.[18]

In most cases before the courts, the circumstances fell far short of this ideal pattern. Often the contract (if it existed at all) had been made quite without witnesses, or with only a single witness present. Much trouble arose from failure to consult parents or other interested parties, and from precipitate action in unsatisfactory circumstances. Sometimes spousals were made on the spur of the moment, in barns, streets or fields. In 1583, for example, an Amesbury servant called Christian Veriat paid a surprise visit on her lover, Thomas Sharpe, a weaver dwelling with his master at Durrington. That night, as Sharpe and his master were walking her home, Christian allegedly took it into her head to become contracted immediately. The older man advised that 'the matter required no such haste but might be done afterward some time when she had made her friends privy thereunto and by their consents'. But Christian would brook no such delay, and, according to Thomas Sharpe's story, they were

[17] W.R.O., B/DB 5, fol. 83.

[18] For examples of cases which exhibit the features mentioned in this paragraph, see W.R.O., B/DB 8, fols. 130v–2; B/DB 9, fols. 111v–12; B/DB 10, fols. 14v–15v; B/DB 36, fols. 32v–3v; B/DB 46, fols. 197–9.

contracted on the spot 'on the road between Durrington and Amesbury'.[19]

Even when they could produce witnesses, plaintiffs often had difficulty in establishing the words of contract. In stating their case they invariably declared that an unequivocal formula was used, often closely modelled on the form prescribed in the Book of Common Prayer. The witnesses sometimes supported this, occasionally adding that the defendant had embroidered the words of contract with elaborate protestations or 'deep oaths'.[20] Very commonly, however, the declarations reported by witnesses were vague and woolly: if the couple had seriously intended to make themselves man and wife they had taken little trouble to make this plain.[21]

In legal theory and popular estimation, symbols, ritual actions and various forms of circumstantial evidence could partially support the allegation that a contract existed. Plaintiffs appealed to rings and other gifts exchanged as 'tokens of marriage' at the time of contract and beforehand during courtship – 'a little gold ring enamelled in blue with the inscription "to express my love"'; 'a piece of gold of ten shillings'; 'a gilded nutmeg'; 'a silver bodkin with a point in it knit in a true lover's knot'.[22] They also claimed that the couple had 'acknowledged' the contract to others and called each other husband and wife; that they had taken practical steps in preparation for marriage, such as putting the proposed conjugal dwelling into good repair or buying wedding clothes; or that the defendant had behaved in ways which suggested that he or she was already part of the plaintiff's family. Thus it was sometimes alleged that men had 'manured' (i.e. worked) a farm in expectation of taking it over; while in one case the fact that a woman went to a man's house, sat by the fire and began to knit was cited as evidence that she regarded herself as his contracted wife. On the basis of such circumstances it was often claimed that a 'common fame' had developed that the couple were 'man and wife marriage only in the church excepted', and that they 'should marry together'.[23]

19 W.R.O., B/DB 9, fols. 41–2.

20 For example, see W.R.O., B/DB 51a, fol. 120; B/DB 54, fol. 35v.

21 For example, compare the elaborate words of contract alleged by the plaintiff in *Salter v. Chevers alias Cheverell* (1615) with the deposition evidence: W.R.O., B/Libels 1/10; B/DB 30, fols. 37–9.

22 W.R.O., D/Libels 12/58; B/DB 11, fol. 49; D/Libels 13/31.

23 For examples of cases which illustrate these features, see W.R.O., B/DB 9, fols. 19v–20; B/Misc. Ct Papers 29/47 (unfoliated), depositions in *Mockridge v.*

These symbols and so forth buttressed contracts which were relatively formal and adequately witnessed. 'Well noted and observed' by servants and others, they enhanced the solemnity of spousals and furthered their publication. But as supports for unwitnessed or poorly witnessed contracts their evidential power was slight. The exchange of gifts was an especially slippery form of evidence, since defendants often claimed that these were not 'tokens of marriage' but merely 'tokens of goodwill' or 'fairings' which had no matrimonial significance whatever.[24]

What train of circumstances had brought these plaintiffs to court, often with only weak evidence of a contract? Unfortunately the background to many suits is very obscure, especially in cases where no witnesses were forthcoming. Even extensive depositions often give only a very incomplete impression of what had happened, since the recorded evidence was limited to particular points at issue. However, about three-fifths of the Wiltshire cases can be very tentatively grouped into categories which probably fairly represent the main varieties of social situation which underlay marriage contract litigation.

Some plaintiffs, perhaps as many as one in five, had no shadow of a real case. It is fairly clear from the surviving evidence that no contract had ever been made and, in most instances, that there had never been any serious prospect of marriage. Such litigants were naively persistent, scheming or (especially in the case of women made pregnant by their lovers) desperate. In 1584, as Alice Gurd rode in company with Tristram Bartlet, she sang a song about love. Bartlet tried to draw personal inferences from this, but she firmly rejected him. Undaunted or perhaps piqued, he continued to press his suit and eventually began a matrimonial cause. More sinister was a case brought by Gabriel Jefferies of Calne in 1609. Perhaps instigated by his father, he had tried to inveigle into making a contract a rather simple-minded teenager called Jane Tuck, an orphan whose parents had left her a good portion. But the defence was able to prove that Jefferies's witnesses were from the dregs of Calne society, and the suit foundered. Dorothy Hobs may have had a better moral case in 1629. A poor girl who sometimes worked for a substantial

Lansdale, Nov. 1586; B/DB 26, fols. 72v–3; B/DB 38, fols. 167, 170, 172; D/Libels 13/31.

[24] For example, see W.R.O., B/DB 5, fol. 8; B/DB 9, fol. 128; B/DB 28, fol. 1.

Wylye yeoman, she found herself pregnant by him after dalliance at the clerk's ale. But she could produce no evidence of a promise of marriage, and it is most unlikely that he ever made one.[25]

Dorothy Hobs's suit is narrowly distinguishable from those in the next category (representing about 10 per cent of the better recorded cases), in which the defendant had probably made some kind of promise of marriage, but insincerely or with fraudulent intention. The usual motive was seduction. Cecily Chisleton, fellow-servant with Robert Maundrell in the house of Sir John Ernle at Whetham around 1620, allowed him to have sex with her after he had promised her marriage and given her a variety of tokens, including a 'kind loving letter with a pair of gloves in it'. But he soon cooled off after she became pregnant. 'How these women do hang about one', he remarked to a friend. Lady Ernle clearly believed Cecily's story and tried to browbeat Maundrell into marrying her. But he never did so, coolly alleging in court that he had merely kissed and embraced her 'as he did other of my lady's maids and no otherwise'.[26]

In the bulk of cases the talk of marriage had apparently been sincere on both sides. The defendants had committed themselves, or come close to doing so, but had subsequently withdrawn. In a minority of instances (about 20 per cent of all the better-recorded cases) this withdrawal was as far as can be seen a purely personal matter, neither dictated by nor in reaction to family pressures. In a few cases, defendants had changed their minds in the light of altered circumstances or better information. In 1633, for example, a widow with a child by a former union was on the point of marrying Thomas Eyres when she heard that he had ill-treated his first wife and was heavily indebted. Discussions to safeguard her child's 'stock' (inheritance) in the event of marriage apparently foundered, the woman broke off the match, and Eyres began a spousals suit.[27] More commonly, individual withdrawals seem to have been the result simply of a change of heart, though they were sometimes justified on prudential grounds. A Salisbury widow, sued by a certain Richard Lovibone in 1606, was said to be 'wavering and unconstant'. Only the previous year she had herself unsuccessfully sued another man for matrimony, and she speedily married yet a third individual when

[25] W.R.O., B/DB 9, fols. 117v–18; D/DB 6, fols. 68–80v, *passim*; B/DB 43, fols. 27v–9, 57v.
[26] W.R.O., B/DB 36, fols. 125–6, 134–40, 149–50v, *passim*.
[27] W.R.O., D/Libels 11/92, 113.

Lovibone commenced legal action. In 1635 Henry Barrow of Berwick St John eventually decided that financial considerations should outweigh sentiment. Rebecca Burt's mistress warned him that the girl had nothing, but Barrow professed that this did not matter and affirmed an idiosyncratic desire for her 'because she was very well like his first wife'. He later changed his mind, declaring that 'she must have money though it were but twenty pounds'.[28]

Many cases (more than half the better-documented suits) arose out of a conflict between individual choice in marriage formation and the pressure of family and other interests. There was probably nothing unusual in the degree of family involvement in marriage contract cases, and the range of kinsfolk and other 'friends' who played a part in events was likewise normal. Parents, step-parents and occasionally masters and mistresses acting *in loco parentis* were predictably most prominent. Uncles and occasionally aunts played a role either when they intended to bequeath property to their nephew or niece or if they were acting as 'tutors' or guardians of youngsters who had lost one or both parents.[29] Siblings were occasionally involved, usually when brothers had been directed by their father's will to hold the portion and oversee the marriage of younger sisters.[30] In some cases respected 'friends' from outside the family (including godparents on occasion) were also in evidence, either to reinforce parental advice or, again, when they had been designated to act as tutors or guardians. A typical example was Edmund Mathewe, a middle-aged gentleman of Downton, who had the 'tuition and government of...[Mary Hooper] and...a special care in carefully bestowing her for her preferment in marriage according to her portion and degree'.[31]

A certain tension between individual and family interests in marriage formation was, especially at higher social levels, normal in early modern English society. But, whereas most unions presumably resolved the issues to the reasonable satisfaction of all concerned, the controverted marriages in contract litigation were often cases where things had gone wrong – where the usual interplay of interests had exploded into conflict.

[28] W.R.O., B/DB 24, fols. 66–7, 73v–4; B/DB 52, fols. 198v–203.

[29] For example, see W.R.O., B/DB 8, fol. 130v; B/DB 9, fols. 13–20 *passim*; D/DB 5, fols. 14v–16, 24–31 *passim*.

[30] For example, see W.R.O., B/DB 9, fols. 96v–7; B/DB 42, fol. 13v; B/DB 48, fols. 24v–5.

[31] W.R.O., B/DB 8, fol. 97v.

A small minority of these 'familial' cases concerned marriages which had been actively promoted, if not actually 'arranged', by the defendant's own family. Most of the families involved were relatively wealthy, and the individuals concerned were invariably females, sometimes below the age of 21. These young women had not actually been *forced* into unwelcome unions: in most cases the evidence makes plain that parents or others had at least consulted them and secured their consent. But, under parental or other family tutelage, they clearly had only limited room for manoeuvre. Nevertheless, they had eventually refused to marry the designated man, commonly aided by altered circumstances such as the death of one or both parents before the marriage could be solemnised, or by a split of opinion among the various family members involved in the match-making. Mary Flower, for example, daughter of a minor gentleman, had around 1615 agreed to a betrothal to Francis Hussy, the young son of her father's close confidante and possible mistress. After her father's death she refused to honour the contract, apparently supported by her brother, who was incensed that a farm had been bequeathed to Mistress Hussy. It was in vain that the latter used moral blackmail against Mary, saying that 'it was wonder of God that her father did not rise out of the pit again for her naughtiness'.[32] Joan Ogbourne's father was already dead when her mother arranged a match with William Burden. The matter was all but settled when the mother died too, and for decency's sake the marriage was postponed. In the interim this 17-year-old girl of doubtful wit turned against Burden and entangled herself with another man, aided and abetted by the 'friends in trust' who had been appointed to administer her goods.[33]

In the majority of 'familial' cases, the defendants (including both men and women) had conformed to what was probably the norm at middling and lower social levels: they had themselves taken the initiative in finding, or responding to the advances of, a potential marriage partner. But when they referred back to their 'friends' they faced disapproval and opposition, and the match was broken off or thrown into jeopardy. In these circumstances plaintiffs often claimed that the defendant remained faithful at heart but was unable to honour his or her promise because of family pressures. In cases like this the judge could order defendants to be 'sequestrated' (usually in

[32] W.R.O., B/DB 30, fols. 50–5v, 90–5, 97v–102, 123v–32v, *passim*.
[33] W.R.O., B/DB 46, fols. 197–205; B/DB 47, fols. 132–9, *passim*.

the house of a court official or of a minister) to ensure that their answers were made freely. Whether or not this procedure was employed, confessions were rarely forthcoming. Mostly defendants had bowed to the wishes of their families, and by the time the case came to court were themselves firmly unwilling to acknowledge the alleged contract.

The circumstances which underlay such behaviour are a reminder of how strong the negative influence of parents over their children's choice of spouse could sometimes be. Some defendants were coerced physically into dishonouring their promise. Edith Parker of All Cannings was beaten by her father when she revealed that she had entangled herself with a neighbour's servant; Robert Nicholas of Compton Chamberlayne was probably flogged to put him in a better frame of mind, and hastily married off to someone more to his family's liking; while Alice Bush of North Bradley was 'conveyed away' by her father and uncle and married in Somerset to a certain Mr Rice Phillips.[34] More commonly, parents and other family members relied on moral pressure, threats of disinheritance, or occasionally a combination of financial threats and blandishments. Katherine Imber's mother 'did take the matter so grievously that it would be her death', and Katherine was upbraided by a friend of the family for having 'brought her father and her mother into that heaviness wherein they were'. William Head's father, on hearing that his son proposed to wed a servant girl, declared that 'if he have her he shall never have a penny of me'; while in somewhat similar circumstances Joan Pile's uncle laconically advised her to 'make merry with that you have already for you get nothing else'. More positively, John Gray's uncle 'promised him eighty pounds to forsake' Katherine Boyce; the rest of his 'friends' warned him that he should 'go a-begging with her'.[35]

It was not always necessary for families to resort to explicit threats. For some defendants, the mere fact that their families disapproved was sufficient to make them withdraw from a proposed match. The defence often claimed, indeed, that if any promise of marriage had been made it had been contingent on the approval of friends: in other words, that it was a *conditional* rather than an absolute con-

[34] W.R.O., B/DB 11, fol. 66; B/DB 24, fol. 108; B/DB 11, fols. 20–1; B/ABI 17, fols. 64–162 *passim*; B/ABI 18, fols. 4–63v *passim*.

[35] W.R.O., B/DB 5, fol. 91; B/DB 30, fol. 93; B/DB 26, fol. 169; B/DB 38, fols. 167v, 170v.

tract. Plaintiffs tried to forestall or counter this kind of defence by alleging that defendants had explicitly declared their independence or their willingness to brave family disapproval. According to Richard Browne in 1584, Emma Harrolde said she would marry him 'though all her friends would say nay thereunto and [they] should go a-begging together'; while in 1623 Margaret White claimed that William Kilson declared that 'he would never be driven from or forsake her whilst he lived for all the friends he had, had he so many more as he had'.[36]

Occasionally, cases involving family conflict were further complicated by pregnancy. A man who got a woman with child could find himself amid a turmoil of conflicting pressures. The woman and her family might have the support of important elements in the community in trying to force him into marriage, while his own family tried to dissuade him from what they regarded as an imprudent match. Robert Nicholas, who was probably under 21, saw no solution but to marry the woman he had seduced: 'What will you have me do else?' His father took a more brutal line: 'Why, man, cannot...a man fall into a turd but must bind him to his nose as long as...he liveth?'[37]

The reasons why families objected to particular matches highlight the important (though by no means exclusive) role played by prudential considerations in marriage formation. Almost invariably the problem was that the plaintiff was too poor or too lowly. Indeed the defence often claimed that the disparity between the parties was so great that the allegation that a contract had been made was completely preposterous. In *Catherine Nicholls v. John Wilde* (1616), for example, it was alleged that there was 'great disparity betwixt the said parties...as well in respect of birth and descent as of estate and livelihood'. On interrogation the witnesses debated the issues, incidentally shedding light on the criteria of status which people in the middling ranks of society evidently thought important. Catherine Nicholls's father was said to have been 'a good liver and had a living worth forty marks per annum'. Wilde's mother was denigrated because she 'liveth poorly and receiveth alms'. His father, on the other hand, was 'a good liver's son' and would have enjoyed a 'living' of £20 a year had he survived longer, though in the event he died poor. The phrase 'a good liver' is elucidated by a witness who

36 W.R.O., B/DB 9, fol. 116; B/DB 39, fol. 104.
37 W.R.O., B/DB 24, fol. 94v.

claimed that 'Ambrose Wilde [John Wilde's uncle] is a man of good estate and living and liveth in a very good fashion', contrasting him with another interested party whose 'living is worth fifty pounds per annum but he liveth poorly'. Clearly something more than mere wealth was at issue here – the quality of 'port', the ability to maintain an appropriate style of life. Morality and 'breeding', in the sense of belonging to a respectable family and enjoying the benefits of education and accomplishment, were also of concern. John Wilde was said to 'descend of honest parentage' and was 'of good friends...of honest life and conversation'.[38]

As can be seen from this case, attempts to prove disparity of wealth and status were often contradicted by the opposing party. Nonetheless, it is plain that one of the main reasons for these matrimonial disputes was that defendants had got involved with people outside the range of those who would normally be considered eligible – the principle of equality so stressed by contemporary commentators had been breached.[39] How had this happened? John Gray justified his wayward choice on prudential grounds, declaring: 'I must have one that can work and not a fine wife'. A West Harnham man claimed he had been bewitched. Katherine Imber was simply desperate for freedom, wishing 'that she might be gone away from her father's house for that she was weary to be kept as she was', and so succumbed to an ardent manservant.[40] But the most common reason for *mésalliance* was simply physical and emotional attraction; the importance of romantic love, with all its heartaches and inconstancies, emerges strongly from the depositions in contract suits, balancing the emphasis on financial prudence and family influence. Even in the semi-arranged matches, which in any case figured in only a minority of suits, sentiment was not totally neglected. In 1619, Alice Nippered's father (a husbandman of Fonthill Giffard) assured himself of his daughter's feelings before contracting her to Thomas Langley: 'Now you have been long enough together to know one another's mind. How say you, daughter, can you find in your heart to love this man and to forsake all other, and are you contented to have this man to be your husband?' In a case in 1588, in response to a similar question, the couple were able to reply that 'they did well fancy one the other'.[41] Often love emerges as an even more powerful

[38] W.R.O., B/DB 30, fols. 132v–3, 147v; B/DB 31, fols. 63, 66v–7, 77, 120v–1.
[39] See above, p. 136.
[40] W.R.O., B/DB 38, fol. 172; B/DB 12, fol. 96v; B/DB 5, fol. 82v.
[41] W.R.O., B/DB 36, fol. 32v; B/DB 10, fol. 15v.

force. In 1586, Richard Morse was said to be 'greatly inflamed with love'. In 1615, Abigail Smith was 'sicklow...for love' of William Head, a form of indisposition not confined to females. When David Nayler was in love with Edith Mills in 1565 it was believed that 'the sickness wherewith...[he] was troubled came for her sake'.[42]

Love, prudence, individual choice, family interest – all these ingredients were present in marriage contract litigation throughout the period from the late sixteenth century to the eve of the civil war. How far were there, within this overall framework of continuity, changes in the circumstances underlying spousals suits? The issues are obscured by the inherent limitations of the deposition evidence and by uncertainties arising from the relatively small numbers of cases involved; but certain shifts may be very tentatively identified on the basis of the Wiltshire materials. Cases involving purely personal decisions to withdraw from engagements may have increased somewhat towards the end of the period; and there was an absolute and proportional decline in the incidence of cases involving a conflict between family and individual. Cutting across these categories another change is discernible. Cases where contracts were allegedly linked to the transfer of substantial amounts of property, quite common in the late sixteenth century, tended to disappear in the early seventeenth – a shift which may help to explain the change in the sex ratio among plaintiffs, since these 'property' suits were characteristically brought by men.[43]

These changes should not be taken as evidence that family involvement in marriage formation or property transactions associated with marriage declined over this period. Rather, they reflect the fact that fewer families and individuals were willing to put their trust in extra-ecclesiastical marriage contracts. Whether from a personal or a property point of view, it was safer for all concerned to make arrangements and expectations contingent on the certainty of marriage in church. The shifts serve to underline, in fact, the message conveyed by the overall drop in the numbers of spousals suits: that informal marriage contracts were declining as a significant social institution.

The decline of marriage contracts was undoubtedly a country-

[42] W.R.O., B/Misc. Ct Papers 29/47, deposition of Israel Webbe, 14/2/1586/7; B/DB 30, fol. 95; B/DB 5, fol. 23v.

[43] For clear-cut examples of such 'property' suits, see W.R.O., B/DB 9, fols. 13–20, 22v; B/Misc. Ct Papers 29/47, depositions, etc. in *Mockridge v. Lansdale*, Nov. 1586; B/DB 10, fols. 14v–15v.

wide phenomenon. However, the fact that in early seventeenth-century Wiltshire the sex ratio among plaintiffs was apparently different from that found in the diocese of Ely and the archdeaconry of Chichester alerts us to the possibility that the speed or nature of the decline did vary from area to area. In church court cases other than spousals suits in the early seventeenth century, especially bridal pregnancy prosecutions, references to marriage contracts appear to have been more common in Cambridgeshire, Leicestershire and West Sussex than in Wiltshire, and it may well be that the custom was declining somewhat less swiftly in those regions. Moreover, variations *within* the county of Wiltshire are apparent from detailed analysis of the records of contract litigation. Spousals suits did arise in all parts of the county, including chalk and cheese countries, clothing and non-clothing areas, town and country. But cases which genuinely involved relatively formal contracts, characterised by the careful exchange of consent, the gift of rings and tokens and other rituals, mostly came from the chalk areas of south and south-east Wiltshire. In these comparatively conservative, socially stratified parishes older ways perhaps died hard. As will be seen, it was precisely in these areas that the church courts had least success in mounting prosecutions for bridal pregnancy.[44] In most of the spousals cases from other parts of Wiltshire, especially after about 1600, the alleged 'contracts' appear in actuality to have been mere engagements, legally formless *promises* to marry which were simply preliminary to marriage in church.

Given that the letter of the law still prescribed that a mere verbal declaration could constitute a valid marriage, the decline of spousals as a social phenomenon placed ecclesiastical lawyers in a potentially awkward position. It is clear that the officials of the church courts did not resist the forces of social change; on the contrary, in their handling of spousals suits they tended by and large to reinforce the shift. One indication of this was their willingness, by the early seventeenth century, to allow many contract suits to be settled out of court. In theory spousals causes (unlike most other types of litigation) could not be compromised or allowed to remain indeterminate. For disciplinary and moral reasons the relationship between the couple had to be clarified. In practice church court judges were never wholly inflexible in this matter, but studies of marriage contract litigation in the late middle ages indicate that the proportion of

[44] See below, Chapter 7.

cases which were judicially determined was very high.[45] It was still impressive (over 70 per cent) in Ely diocese, and likewise in the archdeaconry of Chichester, in the 1580s. In late sixteenth-century Wiltshire, however, it was already common practice to allow many suits to be abandoned without coming to sentence, and after around 1600 a similar pattern is found in other areas too. Both at Ely and at Salisbury in the early seventeenth century, fewer than 40 per cent of causes were brought to a definite conclusion.

What happened in these abandoned suits? In a few cases, the commencement of legal proceedings rapidly brought the defendant to heel, and the couple proceeded to get married without bothering to procure a formal sentence; or the same result was achieved by negotiation between the 'friends' of the parties. The last act book entry in a Wiltshire case in 1588, for example, bears the note *in tractatu pacis pro matrimonio* (negotiations for marriage by mutual agreement).[46] But most indeterminate cases apparently did not end in marriage. Some were simply dropped, others were compromised: after informal out-of-court negotiations the plaintiffs relinquished their claim either freely or in return for an apology or a payment in money or goods. Traditionally the church had been hostile to such transactions, and before about 1600 sometimes prosecuted people for 'selling' contracted wives in this fashion.[47] By the seventeenth century the issue seems to have aroused less concern, and the compromising of marriage suits was reported in court records without fear of the judges' displeasure. Depositions in a case in 1631, for example, reveal that the suit was referred by the parties to the vicar of Warminster, who determined that the defendant, Joshua Abathe, should pay all Anne Middlecot's legal fees and a sum of ten shillings in compensation; the woman in fact declared that she scorned to enrich herself at his expense and would give the money to the poor. In 1609 the uncle of another plaintiff, Mary Matravers, was less highminded: at a meeting of 'friends' to 'make an end' of the suit he initially demanded forty pounds in compensation and declared

[45] Ingram, 'Spousals litigation', pp. 51–2 and the references there cited.

[46] W.R.O., B/ABI 17, fols. 99, 105.

[47] For Wiltshire examples, see W.R.O., B/DB 8, fol. 161; B/DB 16, fol. 92; and for a striking Cambridgeshire case, see C.U.L., Ely D.R., K/2/50. The sale of wives after a marriage had actually been solemnised appears to have been very rare if not totally unknown in England in this period, contrary to the impression conveyed in Samuel Pyeatt Menefee, *Wives for sale: an ethnographic study of British popular divorce* (Oxford, 1981), pp. 2, 31, 211–12.

that 'under twenty pounds there should be no end'.[48] The practice of settling causes for cash invites comparison with the common law action of breach of promise of marriage. The earliest precedents for this action apparently date from the sixteenth century, but suits became more common in the seventeenth, as marriage contract litigation declined in the church courts.[49]

In their growing willingness to allow spousals suits to be abandoned or compromised, church court judges were helping to undermine the credibility of extra-ecclesiastical marriage contracts. Changes in policy in giving sentence in cases which *were* judicially determined also facilitated the decline of spousals. As time wore on, judges became increasingly reluctant to pronounce in favour of disputed contracts. In the diocese of Ely in the 1370s and 1380s, over 50 per cent of plaintiffs in cases which came to sentence were successful in securing a confirmatory decree; in the same diocese in the 1580s, barely more than 20 per cent of sentences were in favour of plaintiffs, and the proportion fell even lower in the early seventeenth century.[50] In Wiltshire, confirmatory sentences were already uncommon in the late sixteenth century, and they became even more rare after 1600. Of 26 spousals causes which proceeded to a formal sentence in the period 1601–40, only one was determined in the plaintiff's favour.[51] Even this isolated success depended on special circumstances. George Maton was apparently willing to acknowledge a contract with Margaret Plimpton, but his family objected to the union. After sequestration Maton confessed, sentence was given against him, the court conceded a licence despite the lack of parental consent, and the couple was ordered to solemnise their marriage in Milston church on a given date. There is no relevant entry in the parish registers, however, and it may be that Maton's family were after all successful in frustrating the match.[52]

It might be argued that the declining proportion of confirmatory sentences simply reflected the fact that fewer soundly based suits were being brought. Changes of this sort may have affected the

[48] W.R.O., B/DB 46, fol. 196v; D/DB 6, fol. 88.

[49] S. F. C. Milsom, *Historical foundations of the common law* (1969), p. 289. It was, however, probably not until the late seventeenth and the eighteenth centuries that actions of this type became really well established.

[50] Ingram, 'Spousals litigation', p. 52 and the references there cited.

[51] In some of these cases, however, the defendant was ordered to pay the plaintiff's costs, signifying that the latter had a very strong case: for example, see W.R.O., B/ABI 43, fol. 144.

[52] W.R.O., B/ABI 45, fol. 131v; B/ABI 46, fols. 59v, 109.

statistics to some degree, but it seems likely that the attitudes of the judges were more important. Close study of individual cases suggests that early seventeenth-century judges subjected the evidence in marriage contract suits to the most searching scrutiny. Moreover, they showed a marked tendency to favour a solemnised marriage over a prior unsolemnised contract, even when the extra-ecclesiastical union was well substantiated. This is most strikingly evident in certain cases where defendants, in order to prejudice the outcome of spousals suits, rapidly got married in church to a third party. This practice was naturally forbidden[53] and the courts punished offenders for their contempt; but they nonetheless tended to regard the solemnised union as definitive.[54]

These judicial developments suggest that ecclesiastical lawyers were, in practice, gradually turning their backs on the ancient law of spousals and coming to regard unsolemnised contracts as well-nigh unenforceable. This stance may have been influenced by continental developments, but more probably was simply contingent on the long-term success of the English church in fostering widespread acceptance of church weddings as the recognised mode of entry into the married state. In the high middle ages there had probably existed among laymen some reluctance to accept the church's claims to jurisdiction over marriage and considerable uncertainty among the population at large about what acts constituted a valid union.[55] In these circumstances (which generated a relatively high incidence of spousals suits) it was appropriate for church court judges to adjudicate in favour of a high proportion of disputed contracts and to insist that suits should not be left undetermined. By the seventeenth century, widespread recognition of solemnisation in church as the essential guarantee of a socially and legally acceptable marriage narrowed the opportunities for confusion and uncertainty and made it reasonable for the courts to pronounce in favour of unsolemnised unions only in exceptional circumstances. The courts' attitude both reflected and hastened the decline of the custom of spousals, further limited uncertainties about marriage entry and helped to reduce the numbers of marriage contract suits to the very low level observable on the eve of the civil war.

[53] Cardwell (ed.), *Synodalia*, vol. 1, pp. 162, 305; Clarke, *Praxis*, p. 140.
[54] For example, see W.R.O., B/DB 24, fols. 92v–4v, 105–8, 111–12; B/DB 25, fol. 56; B/ABI 35, fol. 67v; B/ABI 36, fols. 2, 32, 57, 65 (*Waterman v. Nicholas and Jeay*, 1607).
[55] Helmholz, *Marriage litigation*, pp. 4–5, 27–33, 59.

The legal developments of the period raise other interesting issues concerning the relationship between the values administered in the church courts and those of the wider society. The church's matrimonial law had always been fairly tender towards individual self-determination, insisting that the consent of the couple was essential to marriage; and this principle was in a sense underlined by the judges' growing reluctance to pronounce in favour of disputed contracts. But not everyone in early modern England was equally scrupulous about the morality of forced marriages. Some spousals suits reveal attempts to by-pass the church courts by using strong-arm methods to compel recalcitrants to honour promises of marriage. In a Wiltshire case in 1609, Mary Matravers's father threatened to have Gabriel Miles hanged if he would not marry his daughter – though this only aroused in Miles the will to resist.[56] Women made pregnant by their lovers were in a better moral position to attempt coercion, and it is plain that employers, the woman's family or the community at large were sometimes able and willing to force seducers into marriage.[57] Pregnant women or their families could also appeal to the justices of the peace, who were sometimes willing to 'persuade' the menfolk involved to accept marriage as an alternative to being dealt with under the bastardy statutes. Richard Foster of Imber, who had fathered a child on Anne Slie, recounted how in 1619 he was 'by her procurement ... served with a warrant and brought before Sir Edmund Ludlow ... before whom ... [his] father Brian Foster and his master John Matthew ... did undertake that he ... should marry her'. As Foster ruefully remarked, 'he should never love her but he must of necessity do it'. In 1637, William Upton of Woodborough likewise agreed to marry Alice Jud when 'he was threatened to be sent to the gaol'. Thomas Barter of Salisbury, with a shade more fortitude, 'seemed not to accept thereof but went away to prison', but he later changed his mind and did marry the woman. This last case (which came before the church courts in the rare form of a dowry suit) is of particular interest because it suggests that the justices did not always confine their powers of compulsion to the very poor: Barter had expected the woman to

[56] W.R.O., D/DB 6, fol. 87v.

[57] For examples of successful or attempted coercion, see W.R.O., B/ABI 31, fol. 40; B/ABI 38, fols. 80, 88, 96, 106; B/DB 36, fols. 125v, 137v, 139; D/AB 28, fol. 53; D/AB 32, fol. 5v.

bring a not inconsiderable dowry of 'twenty or thirty pounds'. However, these cases of marriage by magisterial dictation do not seem to have been very common; nor were they necessarily regarded with popular favour. The sequel to Richard Foster's interview with the justice is revealing in this respect. A local gentleman took Foster's part, saying that it was the 'worst way to marry her', and the Warminster petty sessions freed him from the obligation to marry Anne Slie on condition that the bastard child did not become a charge on the poor rates.[58]

Another issue raised by spousals suits is the relationship between the church courts' rulings and family influence in marriage formation. As can be seen from some of the cases already quoted, the courts were on occasion willing to adjudicate in favour of contracts made against the wishes of the defendant's family. On the other hand, the practical effect of absolutory sentences was often to confirm the negative control of families over young people's choice of spouse; and the records give the strong impression (though the point cannot be proved conclusively) that judges bore such family interests very much in mind when giving sentence.[59] Moreover, in granting marriage licences the courts almost invariably insisted, as the law required, on proof of parental consent. In effect the officials of the church courts walked a tightrope between the claims of individualism and of family influence – a tightrope which was characteristic of the society as a whole.

To take a broader view, is it possible to argue that the growing difficulty of obtaining sentences to confirm disputed contracts tended towards greater individual freedom in marriage formation? John Bossy has argued that this is what happened in France: the matrimonial reforms of the council of Trent, by invalidating extra-ecclesiastical marriage contracts or *fiançailles*, undermined kin influences.[60] But this argument ignores the fact that family interests in marriage could be just as (or more) easily organised around the ceremony of solemnisation in church; and indeed Bossy's interpretation seems misguided since contemporary fears that unsolemnised unions *threatened* family influence were among the factors which led to the Tridentine reforms.[61] In England, the decline of spousals in

[58] W.R.O., B/ABO 9, 19/7/1619, *Office v. Foster*; AW/ABO 7, 13/7/1637, *Office v. Upton*; B/DB 38, fols. 25v–6v.
[59] Cf. Houlbrooke, *Church courts and the people*, pp. 63–4.
[60] Bossy, 'Counter-reformation and the people of catholic Europe', pp. 56–7.
[61] Donahue, 'Canon law on the formation of marriage', p. 147.

the late sixteenth and the seventeenth centuries represented merely the culmination of a long development, and it is highly doubtful whether the changes of the period 1570–1640 altered the balance between individual and family interests to any significant extent.

It is possible, however, that the church's efforts to punish clandestine marriage ceremonies, and to exercise tighter control over the issue of marriage licences, did do something to strengthen the hand of parents who wished to influence their children's choice of marriage partner, and may also have made it more difficult for poor people to get married in the face of parochial opposition.[62] As was noted in Chapter 4, concern over clandestine marriage ceremonies grew in the sixteenth century (eclipsing earlier worries over unsolemnised unions), as did disquiet over marriage licences.

In practice the scale of these problems varied from area to area. More compact jurisdictions like the archdeaconry of Chichester and the diocese of Ely, where it was relatively easy for the ecclesiastical authorities to exercise control, seem to have been little troubled; in these areas prosecutions for clandestine marriage were always few in number throughout the period 1570–1640. The Wiltshire portion of Salisbury diocese in the late sixteenth century was experiencing greater problems. The numerous peculiar jurisdictions within the county could serve as havens for the performance of clandestine ceremonies and the unregulated issue of licences, and the consequent difficulties were compounded by chicanery on the part of William Watkins, official of the archdeacon of North Wiltshire.[63] It was precisely to combat abuses like this that convocation enacted new canons in 1597 and 1604 to tighten procedures in the conduct of weddings and the granting of licences;[64] and action at the national level was reinforced by changes at Salisbury. By 1601 William Wilkinson had become the official not only of the bishop and archdeacon of Salisbury but also of the archdeacon of North Wiltshire.[65] This enabled him to secure an episcopal monopoly in the issue of marriage licences throughout Wiltshire, save in the peculiar jurisdictions. Correspondingly, in many of these exempt areas marriage licence business was gradually monopolised by the court of the dean of Salisbury.[66] Of course, this policy served the self-interest of the

[62] For the obstruction of poor marriages, see above, p. 131.
[63] W.R.O., B/ABO 2, fols. 30v–1.
[64] Cardwell (ed.), *Synodalia*, vol. 1, pp. 161–3, 282–3, 304–6.
[65] *H.M.C.*, *Salisbury MSS*, vol. 11, p. 437.
[66] *H.M.C.*, *Fourth report*, appendix, p. 133.

officials both of the bishop and of the dean, since the issue of marriage licences was a valuable perquisite; but it also had public and disciplinary significance in minimising the danger of corrupt dealings. From around 1600, moreover, the previously haphazard registration of marriage licences was gradually systematised: eventually the bishop's court developed a series of special registers for this purpose which survive from 1615.[67] Finally, the various Wiltshire courts (including the archidiaconal ones) stepped up prosecutions for clandestinely performed marriages. A trickle of cases already came before the courts in the late sixteenth century: in 1585, for example, the bishop's visitation revealed seven allegedly clandestine unions in Wiltshire.[68] But the pursuit of offenders became more systematic in the early seventeenth century.

Precisely what was at issue in these cases? A marriage ceremony was regarded as 'clandestine' when it neglected one or more of the canonical regulations governing the solemnisation of matrimony. After 1604 this meant a marriage without the threefold publication of banns or the issue of a valid licence, a ceremony conducted outside the diocese in which the couple dwelt, or a marriage performed during certain prohibited seasons or outside certain set hours, or in any circumstances save within a lawful church or chapel and in the presence of a properly constituted minister of the church of England.[69]

Traditionally the church had prohibited marriages at certain times of the year, principally the penitential seasons of Advent and Lent.[70] Partly because such prohibitions were anathema to some protestants, these rules were not included in the successive versions of the Book of Common Prayer or in post-Reformation canons, nor were they mentioned in any of the sets of visitation articles issued by the bishops of Salisbury in the early seventeenth century. Yet about 15 per cent of Wiltshire clandestine marriage cases in the period 1615–29 were primarily concerned with weddings held during the prohibited seasons. The main periods of prohibition were probably well known, and parish register analysis commonly reveals a slump

[67] Described in Stewart, *Diocese of Salisbury: guide to the records*, p. 55. From about 1600 to 1615 marriage licence allegations were registered in the instance act books.

[68] W.R.O., B/*Detecta* Bk 6, fols. 6v, 9, 13v, 20v, 30, 42.

[69] Gibson, *Codex*, vol. 1, pp. 424–5, 428–30.

[70] *Ibid.*, p. 430. For an interesting discussion of the significance of the prohibited seasons, see also Thomas, *Religion and the decline of magic*, pp. 620–1.

in weddings in December and March. But the cases before the courts suggest that ministers and laymen were sometimes hazy about the lesser periods of prohibition, so that defendants could plead ignorance with a good chance of a sympathetic hearing.[71]

The various other provisions about the conduct of weddings were more obviously related to the social regulation of marriage. Unfortunately, in recording cases court officials were principally concerned to establish the exact circumstances of the clandestine ceremony itself, and the underlying motives which impelled couples to procure a secret wedding were often left obscure. About 20 per cent of couples confessed that the bride was pregnant. This figure is close to the normal proportion of brides pregnant at marriage, but it is none the less plain that the fact of pregnancy was sometimes the reason why the couple had resorted to a clandestine ceremony, either to evade publicity or simply because the woman was so far gone that speed was essential.[72] Scattered references indicate a variety of alternative or complementary motives. As we have seen, where contract litigation was being considered or had actually been commenced, the defendant sometimes procured a clandestine marriage to prejudice the plaintiff's case or to deter him or her from further action. More often, clandestine ceremonies were sought when the couple could not get the consent of parents or other family members. In 1617, for example, Nicholas Caiford of Warminster explained that 'being a suitor to his now wife Amy Parrett in the way of marriage and having acquainted her friends therewith, and perceiving them very unwilling but she the said Amy willing', he decided to procure a secret ceremony.[73] In contrast to such relatively innocent elopements, a small number of cases involved what look like sinister or exploitative circumstances. In 1623, for example, Joan Pridye confessed that she had been secretly married to an idiot in her father's house in Purton.[74]

In a few instances, it was explicitly stated that poor people had resorted to a clandestine ceremony to evade parochial opposition to

[71] For example, see W.R.O., B/ABO 10, 7/3/1621 (second court that day), *Office v. Robert Adams*, 27/9/1621, *Office v. Elizabeth Bloye*; D/AB 33, fol. 37. On the seasonal pattern of weddings, see Wrigley and Schofield, *Population history of England*, pp. 298, 519–21.

[72] For example, see W.R.O., B/ABO 8, 28/9/1618, *Office v. Penny*.

[73] W.R.O., B/ABO 8, 14/10/1617, *Office v. Caiford*; and, for similar cases, see B/ABO 8, 14/9/1616, *Office v. Cole, Collier and Aprice alias Collier*; B/ABI 42, fols. 66v–7.

[74] W.R.O., B/ABO 11, 19/3/1623, *Office v. Pridye*.

their getting married in case they burdened the poor rates.[75] More generally, it seems likely that the concern of local parishioners to regulate marriages and check the influx of newcomers underlay a good many prosecutions. While some cases were reported to the courts either by apparitors or by parish ministers annoyed by the loss of marriage fees,[76] many did come in from churchwardens' detections; and the form in which these presentments were often made – couples were 'living together as man and wife but whether they be married we know not' – was redolent of local anxieties. It is striking, moreover, that cases increased in times of economic hardship. Thus the years of bad harvests and trade depression from 1621 to 1625 account for well over half the total number of known prosecutions in Wiltshire in the 15-year period 1615–29, with a peak figure of 22 cases in the especially bad year of 1623 (Table 5a). A link with economic pressure is likewise indicated by the topographical distribution of cases: the clothing and pastoral areas of north-west Wiltshire, badly hit by the slump in the cloth trade in the second and third decades of the seventeenth century, were disproportionately represented. (Precisely the same areas yielded the majority of prosecutions for bridal pregnancy, which, as will be seen, equally reflected parochial concern over the control of marriage entry.)[77] In the village of Keevil a clutch of clandestine marriage cases in 1622, involving a number of poor cottagers and undertenants, coincided with measures taken in the local manor court to restrict immigration and control subletting.[78]

Church court prosecutions for clandestine marriage were thus nourished by local needs, and articulated the concerns of 'honest householders' in the parishes. How did court officials treat such cases? The law prescribed that clandestine marriages, though irregular, were valid and binding and, unless some basic impediment to matrimony existed, could never be broken at the behest of family or community interests. But offenders were subject to punishment: ministers who conducted clandestine ceremonies were liable to the severe penalty of suspension from office for three years, while

[75] W.R.O., B/ABO 8, 2/12/1617, *Office v. Hitch*; cf. B/ABO 7, 11/1/1615, *Office v. Townsend*; AW/ABO 6, 8/12/1629, *Office v. Southernewood.*
[76] W.R.O., B/ABI 41, fol. 131v.
[77] See below, Chapter 7.
[78] W.R.O., B/ABO 10, 24/4/1622, *Office v. Greatrex*, *Office v. Bayly*, *Office v. Burges and Hancocke alias Burges*, *Office v. Masklyne*; cf. W.R.O., 288/1, view of frankpledge, 29 Sept. 21 Jac. I.

Table 5 *Clandestine marriage cases tried by the courts of the bishop of Salisbury* and the archdeacons of Salisbury and North Wiltshire, 1615–29*

(a) Incidence of cases by year

1615	8	1620	2	1625	13
1616	4	1621	15	1626	13
1617	3	1622	12	1627	8
1618	2	1623	22	1628	8
1619	4	1624	21	1629	13

(b) Treatment of offenders

	Principals (couples)	Officiating ministers	Others present
Dismissed	22	5	4
To prove regular marriage	11	—	—
Excommunicated**/absolved	32	4	29
Excommunicated**	58	3	10
Penance	6	—	2
No recorded sentence	19	7	10
Total	*148*	*19*	*55*

* Excluding Berkshire cases.
** Suspension from office in the case of officiating clergymen.

laymen who procured or abetted secret marriages incurred the sentence of greater excommunication – a punishment which could entail serious civil disabilities as well as exclusion from the church.[79]

Table 5b summarises the actual treatment of offenders before the courts of the bishop of Salisbury and of the two Wiltshire archdeacons in the period 1615–29. Couples who had procured clandestine ceremonies were dealt with fairly rigorously. The dismissals (about 15 per cent of the total) are largely accounted for by defendants whose sudden appearance as a married couple had excited suspicion, but who were able to prove that they had been married in due form, and by culprits guilty only of minor infringements of the regulations. Most defendants proved guilty of planned evasion of

[79] See above, p. 53; and on the effectiveness of excommunication, see below, Chapter 11.

the law were excommunicated, a few enjoined penance. However in some cases (categorised in the table as 'excommunicated/absolved') the sentence of excommunication was almost immediately lifted on payment of the appropriate fees, usually because the culprits were able to plead extenuating circumstances.

Sensibly, the courts dealt fairly leniently with layfolk accused of abetting clandestine ceremonies, especially if their offence consisted merely in being present at a secret marriage. The numbers of prosecutions were not high, and those who were decreed excommunicate according to the strict letter of the law stood a good chance of securing immediate absolution. Far more important was to strike at ministers who actually conducted clandestine ceremonies; but unfortunately this posed problems. Couples who wanted to get married privately often went outside the diocese or into peculiar jurisdictions exempt from episcopal or archidiaconal discipline: the royal peculiar of Ansty, totally free of control from Salisbury, was particularly popular in south Wiltshire. To take effective action against the ministers of these 'lawless' churches was virtually impossible. Moreover, some ministers of non-exempt parishes were able to engage regularly in clandestine marriage business, mulcting their clients of substantial sums. One of the most notorious in this period was William Harpe, curate of Ashton Keynes, a remote parish on the Wiltshire–Gloucestershire border. The courts had to tread warily in such cases, since the practical effect of suspending a minister from office might be to deprive his parish of pastoral care. None the less, the judges did sometimes make an example of particular ministers by inflicting this penalty.

How effective were these measures? Plainly the sanctions and safeguards against clandestine marriage were insufficient to deter a really determined couple. Yet the number of prosecuted cases does not suggest a large-scale problem. The figures in Table 5 need to be inflated to take account of non-appearers, whose cases were not recorded in the Wiltshire act books in this period; but, even if generous allowance is made for the contumacious, it remains true that prosecutions were few in relation to the large numbers of legal marriages performed annually.[80] Admittedly it is unknown what proportion of offenders escaped detection; but independent evidence, albeit from a different area of England, does suggest that clandestine marriages were not very common in the early seventeenth

[80] On the nature of the Wiltshire act books at this period, see above, pp. 22–3.

century,[81] and some of those which did occur may have served as a useful safety valve whereby unreasonable family or community pressures could be evaded. A serious problem did develop after the Restoration, the result partly of the disruption of the established system of regulating marriages during the civil war and interregnum, partly of the growing availability of private ceremonies in the Fleet prison and elsewhere. But these changes, which were ultimately to lead to Lord Hardwicke's marriage act of 1753, could not have been foreseen before 1640.[82]

The ecclesiastical law of marriage formation has provoked adverse criticism from historians on the grounds that it was irrational and anomalous; spousals suits have attracted attention because of their vividness and the light they appear to shed on popular marriage customs. But these approaches obscure how much the church had achieved over the centuries in promoting widespread popular acceptance of the solemnisation of matrimony. In late sixteenth- and early seventeenth-century England marriage contracts were of rapidly diminishing significance both to the officials of the church courts and to society at large; and, far from trying to arrest the decline of spousals, ecclesiastical judges reinforced the trend by the manner in which they handled the falling numbers of cases which came before them. The prime concern of the church courts was to enforce the solemnisation of marriage in due form, a policy which accorded with the concerns of parish householders. The courts pursued this aim both through the regulation of marriage licences and through the prosecution of people involved in clandestine marriages; and, though they were unable to stamp out such ceremonies entirely, their activities were probably sufficient to contain the problem. In any event the contentious marriage business of the church courts must be seen in perspective; the true monument to the ecclesiastical regulation of marriage entry lies in the thousands upon thousands of parish register entries of weddings performed, whether by licence or after the publication of banns, according to the rites and ceremonies of the church of England.

[81] MacDonald, *Mystical bedlam*, p. 95.

[82] Roger Lee Brown, 'The rise and fall of the Fleet marriages', in Outhwaite (ed.), *Marriage and society*, pp. 117–36; Gillis, 'Conjugal settlements', pp. 261–71.

7. *Prenuptial fornication and bridal pregnancy*

In handling marriage contract cases, it has been shown, the church courts laid increasing stress on solemnisation in church as the only guarantee of a socially and legally acceptable marriage. An important complementary development in the period *c.* 1570–1640 was that the courts, by stepping up disciplinary prosecutions for prenuptial fornication and bridal pregnancy, tried more firmly to insist that betrothed couples should remain chaste before they were married in church: that a properly solemnised marriage alone made sexual relations licit. This policy ran counter to popular customs and attitudes, which were fairly tolerant of sexual contact between couples who were courting seriously, and it is not surprising that the ecclesiastical authorities were never wholly successful in ensuring that the offence was regularly and consistently presented, far less in suppressing bridal pregnancy itself. But the courts' increasing rigour was actively supported by some parochial interests, especially in areas under economic pressure, and many churchwardens did cooperate in prosecuting guilty couples. The church courts' work in this field probably reinforced the pre-existing trend towards the decline of marriage contracts, re-emphasised the importance of a church wedding as the only acceptable mode of entry into the privileges and responsibilities of marriage, and may even have helped to produce the decline in bridal pregnancy rates visible in some parishes in the early seventeenth century.

The demographic facts about bridal pregnancy were outlined earlier. In early modern England generally, at least a fifth of all brides were with child by the time they got married in church; but rates varied between communities and in some places declined from the late sixteenth to the early seventeenth century.[1] Some of the variations are illustrated in Table 6a, which presents bridal pregnancy rates for the period 1601–40 in six parishes of various sizes

[1] See above, p. 157.

Table 6 *Bridal pregnancy in late Elizabethan and early Stuart Wiltshire*

(a) Bridal pregnancy in six Wiltshire parishes, 1601–40

		A	B	%
All Cannings	1601–40	98	30	31
Alvediston	1601–35	10	5	50
Broad Chalke	1601–40	70	19	27
Keevil	1604–35	127	13	10
Steeple Ashton	1601–35	166	37	22
Wylye	1604–40	25	5	20
Aggregate		*496*	*109*	*22*

(b) Bridal pregnancy in two Wiltshire parishes by 15-year periods, 1591–1635

		A	B	%
Steeple Ashton	1591–1605	81	21	26
	1606–1620	75	18	24
	1621–1635	66	12	18
Broad Chalke	1591–1605*	29	9	31
	1606–1620	28	6	21
	1621–1635	22	5	23

A = No. of brides traced to first offspring.
B = No. of traced brides pregnant at marriage.
* Period 1596–1600 not included, on account of imperfect data.

scattered over the county of Wiltshire.[2] The sample yields an aggregate rate of about 22 per cent, but between individual parishes the figure varied from 10 to 50 per cent. The highest rate comes from Alvediston in south Wiltshire, a village so small that one bridal pregnancy more or less could have a disproportionate percentage effect. But it is noticeable that all the chalk country/agricultural parishes – All Cannings, Broad Chalke and Alvediston – yield high figures in comparison with the cheese country/clothworking villages of Steeple Ashton and Keevil and also with Wylye, the last being a somewhat anomalous case in that it was located on the chalk but

[2] The original registers were used for Keevil, Steeple Ashton and Alvediston: W.R.O., 653/1, 730/1–2, 1052/1. Printed versions were used for the other parishes: Hadow (ed.), *Wylye registers*; C. G. Moore (ed.), *The registers of Broad Chalke, Co. Wilts.* (1881); J. H. Parry (ed.), *The registers of Allcannings and Etchilhampton* (Devizes, 1905). The exact time-span analysed within the period 1601–40 depended on the peculiarities of the individual registers.

was to some extent involved in clothmaking. However, as Table 6b reveals, in both the chalk and the cheese countries there was some decline in bridal pregnancy rates after 1600.

How far were these demographic patterns reflected in or affected by activities in the church courts? In theory moralists and legal commentators had always, though with varying degrees of rigour, disapproved of sexual intercourse between intending marriage partners even when the couple had been contracted before witnesses.[3] Yet before the later part of Elizabeth's reign, church court action against prenuptial fornicators was in practice fitful. Houlbrooke found that in Winchester diocese in the 1520s the judges took a rigorous view and frequently punished antenuptial incontinence. Yet such prosecutions were rare in the diocese of Norwich in the mid-sixteenth century, and as late as the 1560s couples detected of fornication were often dismissed without punishment if they got married.[4] Evidence from a wide range of dioceses indicates overall that the policy of the church courts became increasingly rigorous towards the end of the sixteenth and in the early seventeenth century. There were, however, variations from area to area. In the archdeaconry of Chichester, prosecutions for prenuptial incontinence never became very frequent: there were only seven presentments for this offence in 1622, the same number as in 1587.[5] In the diocese of Ely, in contrast, prenuptial fornication cases were already a prominent item of court business in the 1580s, and this pattern simply continued into the early seventeenth century.[6] In most areas of England, prosecutions tended to be fairly rare up to about 1585, gradually increased in the closing years of Elizabeth's reign, and had become commonplace by the death of James I. Thus Marchant found that presentments for prenuptial immorality were unusual in the diocese of York before 1590 but 'gradually began to flow in' thereafter, and a rather similar evolution is known to have occurred in the diocese of Oxford, the archdeaconry of Leicester and at least parts of Kent (Canterbury diocese) and of Essex (archdeaconries of Colchester and Essex). To cite figures for but one of these areas, there were only 11 prosecutions for antenuptial fornication in the

[3] See above, pp. 154–5.
[4] Houlbrooke, *Church courts and the people*, p. 78.
[5] Based on search of Johnstone (ed.), *Churchwardens' presentments (17th century)*, pt 1, pp. 27–59; W.S.R.O., Ep.I/17/6.
[6] For example, see C.U.L., Ely D.R., D/2/18, *passim*.

Table 7 *Prenuptial incontinence cases tried by the courts of the bishop of Salisbury* and the archdeacons of Salisbury and North Wiltshire, 1615–29*

1615	[30]**	1620	43	1625	36
1616	30	1621	81	1626	60
1617	48	1622	65	1627	60
1618	65	1623	52	1628	44
1619	40	1624	54	1629	63

* Excluding Berkshire cases.
** Record for the court of the archdeacon of North Wiltshire lacking.

archdeaconry of Leicester in 1586; in the legal year 1615–16 there were 55.[7]

A similar pattern is found in Wiltshire. Prosecutions for antenuptial incontinence were by no means unknown in the late sixteenth century, but the total numbers were small. Thus only three cases came before the court of the archdeaconry of Salisbury in 1573; the bishop's visitation of the whole county in 1585 yielded only five presentments; and in the archdeaconry of North Wiltshire in the late 1580s and early 1590s an annual average of fewer than six cases were detected. The turning-point came around 1600. Twenty-three cases were reported in the archdeaconry of North Wiltshire in 1599, while in the county as a whole (excluding the peculiar jurisdictions) there were over thirty cases in 1602 and over forty in 1603. By the second and third decades of the seventeenth century prenuptial incontinence had become a staple of court business. Table 7 reveals an annual average of over fifty cases before the courts of the three major Wiltshire jurisdictions in the period 1615–29; and this figure, based on appearances to answer charges, and therefore excluding the contumacious, is undoubtedly an underestimate of the actual number of prosecutions.[8]

[7] Marchant, *Church under the law*, p. 137; Jones, 'Ecclesiastical courts before and after the civil war', p. 167 (Table 6.2); cf. Brinkworth (ed.), *Archdeacon's court*, *passim*; Patrick Collinson, 'Cranbrook and the Fletchers: popular and unpopular religion in the Kentish Weald', in Peter Newman Brooks (ed.), *Reformation principle and practice* (1980), pp. 184; Wrightson and Levine, *Poverty and piety*, pp. 126–7; L.M., 1 D 41/13/12, 40, *passim*.

[8] Based on search of W.R.O., AS/ABO la; B/*Detecta* Bk 6; AW/*Detecta* Bk, 1586–99; AW/ABO 1, 5, 6; AS/ABO 7, 8, 11–14; B/ABO 5, 8–11. On the issue of contumacy, see above, pp. 22–3, and below, Chapter 11.

The charges brought against accused couples were expressed in a variety of ways. In the earlier years, such presentments as there were often included explanatory details of the offence and especially of blatant circumstances. Thus it was reported at Woodborough in 1591 that 'Henry Cantry was taken in bed with Agnes Cantry before they were married', and at Highway in 1592 that 'Agnes Hellier alias Bowdler the wife of Roger Hellier was delivered of a child within a month after they were married'. Later the charges tended to become less colourful, including such routine formulae as 'for incontinent living before they were married' or 'for fornication before marriage'.[9] Though this was often not made clear at the outset, it is plain from subsequent court proceedings or from local records that in most cases the bride was actually pregnant at marriage or (exceptionally) had even given birth before the wedding. In some instances the original presentment simply charged the couple with fornication, but the fact that they had since married emerged when the matter came to court. Such cases were quite prominent early on – they accounted for nearly 18 per cent of prenuptial incontinence detections before the archdeacon of North Wiltshire in 1602 and 1603 – but later became rare, as also did prosecutions involving couples who were still unmarried when they appeared in court but declared their intention of solemnising their union in the near future. Cases of this type, on the margins between prenuptial incontinence and ordinary fornication, had never been very numerous and all but disappeared shortly after 1600. Only 34 were recorded in the act books of the three main Wiltshire jurisdictions in the period 1615–29, and in 17 of these the parties had not been presented but appeared voluntarily before the court, usually to obtain a marriage licence.[10] These changes may be seen as complementary to the main trend of cases, reflecting a growing recognition of prenuptial incontinence as a distinct category of punishable offence.

Not all prosecutions for antenuptial fornication involved simple bridal pregnancy. In a few cases there was doubt as to the real father of the child. In 1617 the churchwardens of Mere presented that 'Elizabeth the wife of William Viggars was with child before that she

[9] W.R.O., AW/*Detecta* Bk, 1586–99, fols. 57, 77v; cf. Collinson, 'Cranbrook and the Fletchers', pp. 184, 186.

[10] For examples of these kinds of case, see W.R.O., AW/ABO 1, 5/11/1602, *Office v. Allis and Fisher*; AS/ABO 12, 8/11/1617, *Office v. Gray*; B/ABO 7, 10/3/1615, *Office v. Furnell alias Rogers and Stephens*.

was married and that the fame goeth that she was with child by John Crumpe junior and that the said William Viggars hath put her away upon this fame'.[11] In this instance Viggars had evidently married his wife in ignorance of the fact that the child she was bearing was of doubtful paternity, or even perhaps of her being pregnant at all. But some men, if adequately rewarded, were willing to marry a woman whom they did know to be carrying another man's child. The courts investigated such cases very thoroughly, both to discover the real father (often someone of relatively high social status) and because men who 'covered' the faults of others in this way were liable to punishment for the offence of *lenocinium* or pandering.[12] Indeed even in routine bridal pregnancy cases the Wiltshire judges often interrogated couples to establish that the male party was indeed the real father.

Another aggravating circumstance was actual cohabitation in anticipation of marriage, but such behaviour was evidently rare throughout the period, and prosecutions were correspondingly few. In 1624 Debora Bisse of Tisbury denied incontinence, but admitted living for three months in the house of her prospective father-in-law pending the conclusion of marriage settlement negotiations; this unusual arrangement was sanctioned by the church court judge, albeit with reluctance. A less innocent case was reported from Shorncote in 1621. Margaret Greene explained that she was contracted to a man called John Prater and that the banns had been published in church. But a certain Jane Haskins 'forbade' the banns, claiming that John was promised to her. Margaret therefore allowed Prater to have sexual relations with her, bore his child, and confessed that 'she doth live in the house with the said Prater and purposeth forthwith to be married'.[13] Cohabitation may have been marginally less rare in cases of *remarriage*: there were obvious reasons why it might be convenient for a man to move in with a widow or a woman with a widower to take on household duties before the wedding. However, such arrangements seem to have been regarded with marked disfavour by fellow-parishioners. Thus when Richard Greeneway, a widower of West Kington, entertained his intended wife in his house

[11] W.R.O., D/Pres. 1617, Mere, 1/11/1617.
[12] See below, Chapter 9.
[13] W.R.O., AS/ABO 13, 26/6/1624, *Office v. Bisse*; AW/ABO 5, 2/6/1621, *Office v. Greene*. Cf. C.U.L., Ely D.R., B/2/34, fol. 104; D/2/18, fol. 33.

for three months in 1608 he was hauled up before the justices as well as being prosecuted in the church courts.[14]

Another complication is the likelihood that in certain cases marriage had been more or less forced on one or both the partners. Some couples had probably had no thought of marriage until pregnancy occurred; and occasionally the woman may have deliberately sought to become pregnant to induce the man to marry her. Thus Thomas Rowden of Steeple Langford claimed in 1612 that Katherine Graunt had 'often and many times provoked him to lust and incontinence for to have gotten him to marry her that she might have an estate in his living'.[15] The pressures which could impel men to agree to marriage against their desires – the promptings of conscience, the pressure of gossip and general social disapproval, the persuasions of the woman's family, or coercion by justices of the peace or others in positions of authority – have already been discussed.[16] But it is hard to say how many prenuptial fornication prosecutions related to such 'shotgun' marriages; explicit indications are rare.[17] Some (but certainly not all) cases in which a bastard child had been born to the parents before they got married, or in which the original presentment implied that the couple were ordinary fornicators, may well have masked 'unintended' unions; but cases of these kinds were in themselves relatively unusual. Taking all the evidence into account, it seems likely that only a small proportion of prosecutions involved what can truly be described as forced marriages – although, as will be seen, it is probably unrealistic to draw too rigid a distinction between voluntary and involuntary weddings.

The great majority of prenuptial fornication cases simply involved betrothed or seriously courting couples who had allowed themselves to enjoy sexual relations before they got married in church and set up house together. The bridal pregnancy statistics prove clearly that such licence was in practice widespread. But precisely what patterns of attitude and behaviour underlay this situation? The general context was one in which courting couples were customarily allowed a good deal of freedom not only to meet and talk but also to enjoy a

[14] W.R.O., AW/ABO 3, 14/6/1608, *Office v. Brewer and Greeneway*; B/DB 26, fols. 89v–90; B/ABI 37, fol. 46. Cf. W.S.R.O., Ep.I/17/8, fol. 146; C.U.L., Ely D.R., D/2/18, fol. 29v.

[15] W.R.O., AS/ABO 11, 21/11/1612, *Office v. Rowden*; cf. Laslett, *Family life and illicit love*, p. 129.

[16] See above, pp. 210–11.

[17] For an example, see W.R.O., AW/ABO 7, 13/7/1637, *Office v. Upton*.

measure of physical contact. Witnesses in matrimonial and other types of cause often described how couples were 'familiar together and loving one towards the other', frequenting each other's company at all hours. A good deal of kissing and cuddling went on, often in private or semi-private, and couples sometimes spent whole nights together, perhaps before the fire in the hall of the house where the woman lived with her parents or employers, in an inn or alehouse, or (in summer) in the open air.[18] Some witnesses even reported that couples stayed together overnight in the same bedchamber, though it was usually specified in such cases that they did not share the same bed and that others slept in the same room as well. Thus in 1594 it was deposed that Alexander Best, a gentleman's servant, and Alice Weaver, sister-in-law of a Whiteparish yeoman, 'have eftsoons used and frequented each one the other's company in very friendly and familiar sort, both early and late, yea sometimes all night in this deponent's company, in so much that she... Alice Weaver hath been contented to admit him to her bedside, where they have talked together almost all the night, and she this deponent being her bed-fellow hath risen from her bed and opened the doors to let him in'.[19]

These courtship patterns were evidently widespread among young people from a broad social spectrum ranging from substantial yeoman and near-gentry families down to the lowest levels of society. Throughout the period they rarely, in themselves, furnished matter for presentment and seem to have been widely tolerated on the understanding that the couple had serious matrimonial intentions. The conditional nature of such licence is well illustrated by a case from Potterne in 1615, where it was noted that a couple were together so often that 'the churchwardens would have presented them for such their meetings but that they thought they would have been married together'. And a case from South Burcombe in 1603 indicates that couples were expected to conclude their match within a reasonable time: Richard Brassher was presented 'for that he was thought to be in love with one Mary Hallett there and hath continued

[18] For examples, see W.R.O., B/Misc. Ct Papers 29/47 (unfoliated), 11/7/1587, depositions in case of *Wheler v. Myntey*; B/DB 30, fols. 37–9; B/DB 36, fols. 14, 35v; B/DB 38, fols. 162v–4; B/DB 39, fol. 105; AS/ABO 12, 30/10/1619, *Office v. Gunning*.

[19] W.R.O., B/DB 12, fol. 34v; see also B/DB 30, fol. 53; but cf. AW/ABO 6, 6/12/1627, *Office v. Looker*.

his love these twelve months, by means whereof suspicion of incontinency is like to grow'.[20]

Peter Laslett has suggested that tolerance extended further when couples were actually contracted: that popular custom in some areas explicitly sanctioned sexual intercourse between espoused couples, either on a regular basis or as a 'token' to seal the match before the marriage was solemnised in church. In support he cites a spousals case from Hoby and Waltham in Leicestershire in 1598, when a certain Robert Hubbard alleged that Elizabeth Cawnt, after espousing herself to him, 'in the nights following kindly received him into her house and treated him in all things as her husband'; he claimed further that 'the common use and custom within the county of Leicester, specially in and about the towns before mentioned' was that 'if the said marriage be concluded and contracted then the man doth most commonly remain in the house where the woman doth abide the night next following after such contract, otherwise he doth depart without staying there the night'.[21]

Laslett himself admits that the form of this allegation is extremely unusual and possibly unique. It cannot safely be taken at face value but should be understood in relation to the legal context. Plaintiffs in lawsuits of all kinds (not just marriage contract cases) often alleged non-existent customs to buttress a weak case. In the lawsuit in question, the 'words of contract' which Hubbard alleged were from a legal point of view very imperfect, representing at most a future promise. In order to have any chance of securing a successful sentence, it was vital for him to prove not only that that promise had been made but also that it had been rendered absolute by subsequent sexual relations.[22]

The idea that local custom definitely permitted sexual relations between contracted couples is thus very insecurely based. The reality of the situation was much more ambiguous. Throughout the period some people certainly believed that familiarity should have its limits. In a case from Wootton Bassett in 1632, when John Parker kept Margaret Webb alone in a chamber for too long, her uncle reported

[20] W.R.O., B/DB 30, fol. 37v; AS/ABO 8, fol. 133v.

[21] Laslett, *World we have lost*, pp. 150–1; cf. Laslett, *World we have lost further explored*, pp. 168–9. For the actual case, see Moore, 'Marriage contracts or espousals', pp. 290–1.

[22] For the words of contract, see Moore, 'Marriage contracts or espousals', p. 291; on the relevant law of marriage contracts, see above, p. 190.

the matter to her brother, 'conceiving her said brother would not like well thereof'; and in 1631 when George Cooke of Bremhill announced to the woman he was betrothed to marry 'Let every man go to bed with his own wife; come, Anne, let you and I go to bed together', the master of the house – who was Anne's uncle – asserted his notions of propriety and refused to let them sleep together.[23] In a case from Potterne in 1587, the woman herself set firm limits on intimacy. James Myntey was trying to persuade Alice Wheeler to yield to him on the grounds that they were contracted: '"Why," quoth he, "thou knowest that thou art my wife, why then wilt not thou suffer me to have my pleasure of thee, I being thy husband?" Whereto she then answered, "I know...that I am your wife and you my husband, yet until such time as we are married [in church] you shall not have the use of my body."'[24]

The other side of the coin was that many individuals were less scrupulous than Alice Wheeler, and undoubtedly couples often assumed that betrothal, even in the form of an unwitnessed promise, offered an excuse if not a total justification for sexual relations before the church wedding. Sometimes there were special circumstances to give added force to the argument. Thus Thomas Trepocke of Teffont Evias explained in 1641 that he had been contracted to Elizabeth Macy for four years and had tried to obtain a licence to marry, but had been unable to do so since he could not secure the consent of some of Elizabeth's 'friends'. Therefore, he confessed, 'they two being...sure together in marriage and man and wife save only the outward solemnisation thereof in the church did since they were so contracted and sure the one to the other lie together'. But couples often employed similar reasoning even when there was no particular obstacle to their marriage. Thus in 1615 Elizabeth Evered of Fifield, having been promised marriage by Henry Blake and apparently secure in the knowledge that his father approved of the match, consented to have sex with him 'in respect that he the said Blake was her husband before God'.[25]

Defendants in court often pleaded prior intention to marry in mitigation of their offence, and in principle these allegations should indicate just how many couples could claim that they were betrothed

23 W.R.O., B/DB 48, fols. 27v–8; B/DB 46, fol. 50.
24 W.R.O., B/Misc. Ct Papers 29/47 (unfoliated), 11/7/1587, deposition of John Gillet. For a similar case, see Houlbrooke, *English family*, p. 81.
25 W.R.O., B/Citations 5/15; B/ABO 8, 18/11/1615, *Office v. Evered.*

before they proceeded to have intercourse. In practice the proportion of cases in which such pleas were recorded varied very considerably from year to year and from jurisdiction to jurisdiction, probably reflecting how much detail different scribes bothered to write down rather than social realities. It is, however, striking that allegations of prior intention to marry were noted in as many as 70 per cent of cases in the court of the archdeacon of Salisbury in the years 1627–9. But just how firmly engaged were such couples? In Wiltshire defendants very rarely alleged that they had been formally contracted before witnesses.[26] Indeed the term 'contract' was specifically used in only a minority of instances and, predictably in view of the continuing decline of formal spousals, such references become rarer over time.[27] By the third and fourth decades of the seventeenth century, most of the promises alleged by couples were probably no more than private, formless undertakings to marry.

Throughout the period by no means all couples accused of prenuptial incontinence could appeal even to an informal promise, and it may be that some of those who did were stretching the truth. As might be expected, the behaviour of courting couples did not always conform rigidly to the notion that a definite promise should precede intercourse. Some of the subtleties of behaviour and motivation are suggested by the case of Miliard Davies of Plaitford in 1602, though she was actually prosecuted not for bridal pregnancy but for having a bastard by Christopher Vincent. She confessed that 'in regard the said Christopher and she were both born in one parish and neighbours' children, and she had at his persuasion and request yielded unto him to be carnally known, she was in good hope that he would have married her' even though she could not in truth challenge a definite promise.[28] It seems likely that if her candour was unusual the basic situation was not, and that sometimes – perhaps often – sexual intercourse and pregnancy did not so much follow the definite choice of marriage partner as actually help to determine that choice. In other words, increasing intimacy, the normal concomitant of courtship, was both the result of and a further stimulus to a growing sense

[26] For examples, see W.R.O., AW/ABO 1, fol. 84v; AS/ABO 11, 25/11/1615, *Office v. Woodyer*.

[27] For examples of specific references to contracts, see W.R.O., B/ABO 10, 27/9/1621, *Office v. Mighell and wife*; B/ABO 11, 26/8/1623, *Office v. Rowden*; AS/ABO 15, 9/2/1639, *Office v. Reeve*. On the decline of spousals, see above, Chapter 6; and see also Marchant, *Church under the law*, p. 137.

[28] W.R.O., B/ABO 5, fol. 21v.

of commitment. If all went well the couple were indeed 'sure together' by the time pregnancy occurred, and marriage in church speedily followed. But, as will be seen in Chapter 8, Miliard Davies was by no means the only woman who emerged unluckily from this process and became an unmarried mother rather than a pregnant bride.[29]

Attitudes to antenuptial fornication are best summed up as ambivalent but, especially before the end of Elizabeth's reign, tending towards tolerance. The variety of circumstances and motives involved, and the fact that in the last resort there was only a narrow dividing line between bridal pregnancy and bastardy, made it impossible for local communities to regard sex before marriage in church as wholly licit. On the other hand, since a good deal of familiarity and even physical contact between courting couples was taken for granted, it must have been tacitly accepted that many couples would take the opportunity to consummate their relationship with or without the justification that they were betrothed or 'husband and wife before God'. Very little shame or disgrace seems to have attached to bridal pregnancy. Brides far gone with child occasionally sought the privacy of a clandestine marriage ceremony, perhaps to avoid ribald comments; but slanders accusing women of being pregnant at marriage were throughout the period rare, suggesting that the charge had little power to wound or insult.[30]

The build-up of prosecutions in many areas of England after about 1600, while not entailing a massive re-orientation of attitudes, did depend on a partial erosion of the more tolerant vein in popular thinking and a corresponding reinforcement of the ideal of premarital chastity. However, the pattern of change was not uniform, and regional and local variations in the intensity of prosecutions apparently reflect not only the amount of pressure applied by the ecclesiastical authorities themselves but also different degrees of receptivity to change among the churchwardens and other local officers responsible for making presentments. The social processes underlying the rise of bridal pregnancy prosecutions were in fact complex and are hard to elucidate and document. But the following

[29] See below, pp. 267–8.

[30] For rare examples, see W.R.O., B/DB 25, fol. 41v; B/DB 46, fol. 43v. Women were sometimes slandered with being pregnant at marriage, but on examination most of these cases turn out to involve the implication that the father of the child was not the woman's eventual husband; in other words, the matter at issue was not simple bridal pregnancy.

analysis, based mainly on Wiltshire evidence supplemented by indications from other dioceses, does provide some suggestive clues about what was happening.

Much of the initiative towards the more rigorous treatment of prenuptial fornicators undoubtedly came from the church courts themselves. But, to judge from the Wiltshire situation, the authorities did not make use of visitation articles as a means of educating parish officers into new attitudes: none of the extant sets of articles for Salisbury diocese makes special mention of antenuptial incontinence.[31] Probably this means that the relevant policy decisions were taken not at the episcopal level but by judges and registrars, who had at their disposal two main means of expanding the numbers of bridal pregnancy prosecutions. The first was to apply informal pressure at visitations, when churchwardens and sidesmen were quizzed before making presentments. The second was to initiate disciplinary proceedings on the basis of information from apparitors or from some other source apart from churchwardens' reports, such cases serving not only to bring particular offenders to book but also to build up local awareness of prenuptial fornication as a punishable offence and hence, in time, to encourage parochial presentments. The former process has by its very nature left few traces; the latter can be better documented, and it does seem to have affected the intensity of prosecutions in different jurisdictions. In the archdeaconry of Chichester, the relative paucity of antenuptial fornication cases was partly due to the fact that the court relied almost exclusively on churchwardens' presentments and rarely brought prosecutions based on informations. In the diocese of Ely, in contrast, the use of informations was commonplace, and this helps to explain why bridal pregnancy prosecutions were already quite frequent in the Ely courts by the 1580s.[32] In the archdeaconry of Leicester, informations were increasingly used in the early seventeenth century and were clearly a significant factor in the build-up of prosecutions: court officials identified some of the culprits by the simple expedient of comparing marriage and baptism dates in the parish register transcripts returned annually by churchwardens.[33] The role of informations is less easy to establish in the Wiltshire

[31] The visitation articles consulted are listed in the Bibliography under 'England, church of'.
[32] Owen, *Ely records*, p. 20.
[33] For examples, see L.M., 1 D 41/13/64, fols. 90v, 157v, 158, 158v, 159.

courts, but it is certain that at least some cases were based on apparitors' and ministers' reports, while others were initiated by court officers after they had interrogated couples seeking marriage licences.[34]

Despite the importance of these forms of prosecution, the pursuit of prenuptial fornicators did depend to a large extent on parochial presentments; and the precise pattern of prosecutions within a particular area like the county of Wiltshire reflected how far churchwardens in different parishes were prepared to co-operate with the courts. Puritan-minded ministers sometimes played a role in prodding local officers into taking action. For example, the detection of eight men for 'committing adultery with their wives before they were married' in the village of West Kington in 1599 was no doubt instigated by Benjamin Russell, the newly arrived rector.[35] But probably the willingness of churchwardens to make presentments was affected less by individual influences of this nature than by broader socio-economic factors. Analysis of the distribution of cases in Wiltshire in the period 1615–29 reveals some suggestive clustering. Detections were most numerous in certain areas, located mainly in the western half of the county: in a group of parishes near the middle of the shire, centring on Market Lavington and Urchfont; in some of the villages in the lower Wylye valley north-west of Salisbury; and, most noticeably, in a broad strip of north-western Wiltshire extending from Warminster, through places like Steeple Ashton, Corsham, Lacock and Bromham, to Wootton Bassett.[36] In contrast, prosecutions were distinctly less in evidence in most parishes in the far south and in the east of the county. To an extent these variations merely reflected population density, but they cannot be explained wholly in these terms: there were in fact marked variations in the *intensity* of prosecutions in different areas. Such variations may be illustrated for particular parishes by checking how many of the bridal pregnancy cases identifiable by parish register analysis were detected to the church courts. Table 8 presents the results for five communities, of which two (Keevil and Steeple Ashton) were located

[34] For examples, see W.R.O., B/ABO 8, 15/9/1617, *Office v. Humfries*; D/Pres. 1633, John Pytt to John Johnson, 17/9/1633; D/AB 28, 4/9/1626, *Office v. Biggs*.

[35] W.R.O., AW/*Detecta* Bk, 1586–99, fol. 139v. On Russell, see Foster, *Alumni Oxonienses*, vol. 3, p. 1290.

[36] For further details, see Ingram, 'Ecclesiastical justice in Wiltshire', pp. 183–5, 197.

Table 8 *Prosecution of prenuptial incontinence in five Wiltshire parishes*

		A	B	%	C	D
Keevil	1604–29*	11	8	*73*	3	14
Steeple Ashton	1600–29	30	18	*60*	11	41
Wylye	1600–29	6	3	*50*	2	8
Broad Chalke	1600–29	14	1	*7*	2	16
Alvediston	1600–29	3	0	*0*	0	3

A No. of cases of prenuptial incontinence derived from parish register analysis.
B No./percentage of cases in category A which led to church court prosecutions.
C Additional cases known from prosecution evidence only.
D Total no. of cases known.
* Period 1600–3 not used on account of imperfect data.

in the main area of relatively dense prosecution and two (Broad Chalke and Alvediston) in a part of south Wiltshire where cases were much rarer; the village of Wylye represents an intermediate situation. In none of these parishes were cases of bridal pregnancy invariably detected to the church courts in the early seventeenth century; but the rate of prosecution was notably higher in Keevil and Steeple Ashton (73 and 60 per cent respectively) than in Broad Chalke (7 per cent) and in Alvediston (where there were no prosecutions whatever). In Wylye the prosecution rate was moderate (50 per cent).

The social and economic characteristics of different parts of the county help to explain these variations. The areas of sparse prosecution largely corresponded to the socially stratified and economically fairly stable chalklands, a conservative social environment which seems to have encouraged the persistence of traditional attitudes to marriage and marriage formation. As we have seen, it was precisely in these areas that formal marriage contracts or spousals (though on the decline even here) lingered on longest; and it is not surprising to find coupled with this a robust survival of largely tolerant views on sexual relations in advance of the church wedding. An Imber man who declared in 1637 that bridal pregnancy was 'but a small matter to be called up to the court for' was expressing an opinion which undoubtedly remained very widespread in the chalklands.[37] The areas where prosecutions had become quite common, in contrast,

[37] W.R.O., AS/ABO 15, 11/2/1637, *Office v. Munday and wife.*

largely corresponded to the pastoral, clothmaking regions of the county, where resources were coming under increasing strain in the early seventeenth century. It may be inferred that economic pressures, which made local interests sensitive to the setting-up of new households (especially by poor people) and to forms of popular behaviour which could easily lead to a bastard birth, had gradually eroded erstwhile tolerant attitudes and encouraged churchwardens to detect cases of bridal pregnancy. Such a background of parochial vigilance is glimpsed in a case from Steeple Ashton in 1627. Anthony Nashe confessed that his bride was pregnant at marriage, but protested that they would have been married earlier but for the opposition of their fellow-parishioners; his status, and the probable reason for local hostility to the marriage, are indicated by the laconic marginal entry 'pauper'.[38]

A link between bridal pregnancy prosecutions and economic concerns is further suggested by some of the short-term fluctuations observable within the overall pattern of a gradual build-up of detections.[39] The first sizeable cluster of cases in the archdeaconry of North Wiltshire occurred in 1599, in the wake of a disastrous series of bad harvests.[40] In the county as a whole there was another noticeable jump in prosecutions in 1603, perhaps reflecting the difficulties which the Wiltshire cloth industry faced in that year: at the Michaelmas quarter sessions the justices of the peace issued apprenticeship orders which included a measure specifically 'to avoid young marriages and the increase of poor people'.[41] And the bad years from 1620 to 1624, when harvest failure combined with industrial dislocation to produce widespread misery and acute concern over the problem of poverty within the county, were marked by an unusually large total of over eighty prosecutions in 1621 and fairly high numbers in the following three years (Table 7).[42] This upsurge of cases in the early 1620s recalls the bulge in clandestine marriage prosecutions around the same time (Table 5a): both phenomena, it

[38] W.R.O., AS/ABO 14, 22/6/1627, *Office v. Nashe*; cf. AS/ABO 11, 22/7/1615, *Office v. Williams*; B/ABO 9, 22/6/1619, *Office v. Stokes alias Ferris*.

[39] Short-term fluctuations were the product of numerous factors and interpretation of them must be tentative. For a somewhat fuller discussion, *inter alia* taking account of changes in the incidence of marriages, see Ingram, 'Ecclesiastical justice in Wiltshire', pp. 183–6, 197–8.

[40] For the effects of the bad harvests of the later 1590s in the west of England, see Sharp, *In contempt of all authority*, pp. 17–18. See also above, pp. 78, 79, 81.

[41] *H.M.C.*, *Various collections*, vol. 1, p. 75.

[42] For fuller details of economic conditions in these years, see above, pp. 78, 80, 81–2.

may be inferred, reflected parochial anxiety about marriage entry during years of severe economic stress.[43]

How far are these themes reflected in local studies? The experience of both Wylye and Keevil from the 1590s to the 1630s illustrates the gradual build-up of prosecutions over time, while developments in Keevil in particular re-emphasise the likely importance of economic pressure in stimulating a more rigorous attitude to prosecution on the part of parish officers. In Wylye the first detection for prenuptial incontinence occurred in 1610, and there were four others by 1630. The male culprits included a tailor and a blacksmith, each of moderate substance, a labourer and a poor Irish immigrant; the fifth, Robert Lock, was described as a labourer (*operarius*) in 1618, when he married another labourer's daughter, but he was later to attain the status of substantial husbandman.[44] These instances may be compared with those of three other men whose brides are known (from parish register analysis) to have been pregnant at marriage, but who apparently escaped prosecution in the church courts. Of these, one was a substantial village husbandman who was taxed in the subsidies, while the others were labourers, including a man who by the time of his death was receiving alms from the parish.[45] These data indicate that offenders were drawn from a fairly wide social spectrum; otherwise they reveal no clear pattern of any great significance. The information from Keevil, on the other hand, is rather more suggestive. In this village the first clear-cut presentment for antenuptial incontinence occurred in 1599.[46] In the three decades 1600–29 a further thirteen couples were prosecuted, and it is striking that eight of these cases occurred in the 1620s, when Keevil, like other parishes situated in the clothmaking region of Wiltshire, was under considerable economic pressure. Two of the menfolk involved were of substantial status (though one of these, Hugh Bollin, was not actually presented but appeared voluntarily before the court).[47]

[43] See above, p. 215.

[44] W.R.O., AS/ABO 12, 30/1/1619, *Office v. Lock*; Hadow (ed.), *Wylye registers*, pp. 3, 10, 18, 20, 22, 27; Kerridge (ed.), *Pembroke surveys*, pp. 87, 90–1.

[45] Thomas Bellie: P.R.O., E 179/198/329, m. 5; W.R.O., Archdeaconry court of Salisbury probate records, will and inventory of Thomas Belley, 29/9/1640; Hadow (ed.), *Wylye registers*, pp. 2, 13–14, 54, 56; Kerridge (ed.), *Pembroke surveys*, pp. 92–3. John Baker: Hadow (ed.), *Wylye registers*, pp. 2, 14–17, 46, 50. Thomas Wadland: Hadow (ed.), *Wylye registers*, pp. 5, 13, 20, 22, 26, 30, 47.

[46] W.R.O., B/ABO 4, fol. 40. Earlier there had been a few cases of the marginal type, where the couple got married after originally being presented for ordinary fornication: W.R.O., AS/ABO 4, fols. 133, 137, 140; AS/ABO 5, fol. 39v.

[47] W.R.O., B/ABO 6, fol. 98v.

The parties involved in a further three cases have left few traces in the records: they were evidently transient residents, in all probability of low status. The remaining eight bridegrooms can be identified as cottagers and undertenants, men who were not among the poorest of the parish but not of solid status either. The records of Keevil manor in the 1620s show that the proliferation of families of this type was a source of considerable concern to the better-established residents: it is hence not surprising that parish officers readily co-operated with the courts in prosecuting such individuals.[48] As for the few people who are known from parish register analysis to have committed antenuptial fornication, but for whom no record of prosecution can be traced, they appear to have come from the same social strata as most of the other culprits; just why they escaped prosecution is unclear.

How did the judges treat offenders, whether in Wiltshire or in other parts of England? Although the courts were growing more rigorous in the sense of stepping up prosecutions for antenuptial incontinence, churchmen and court officials continued to recognise a difference between this offence – the understandable if regrettable result of strong passions between courting couples – and unmitigated adultery and fornication.[49] Culprits were generally spared the full rigour of public penance and allowed instead to confess their offence in their ordinary clothes or even in semi-private before the minister and churchwardens: such a generally moderate sentencing policy operated in all the Wiltshire courts, the archdeaconries of Chichester and Leicester and the courts of the diocese of Ely. Guilty couples could not absolutely rely on such indulgence, however. In all jurisdictions individual offenders were occasionally singled out for special punishment, while Marchant found that some of the courts of the diocese of York regularly imposed formal public penance in a white sheet.[50] Whatever the form of penance, it was frequently supplemented by a sizeable burden of fees: in early seventeenth-century Wiltshire the husbands of pregnant brides were commonly mulcted of 8s. 4d., no mean sum for a poor man.

How far prosecutions actually affected patterns of premarital sexual behaviour is inevitably hard to determine. It will be recalled

[48] See esp. W.R.O., 288/1, view of frankpledge, 29 Sept. 21 Jac. I (1623).
[49] For further comments on this issue, see Ingram, 'Reform of popular culture?', p. 148.
[50] Marchant, *Church under the law*, p. 137.

that the demographic findings of Laslett and others indicate a fall in bridal pregnancy rates in the early seventeenth century, while the Wiltshire evidence suggests a similar trend. It is tempting to assume that the fall was directly or indirectly linked with the build-up of church court prosecutions after about 1600, but the existence and precise nature of such a linkage could only be satisfactorily established (if indeed at all) on the basis of far more extensive samples of material and more sophisticated methods of statistical analysis than can be deployed here. The limited data presented in Tables 6 and 8 are equivocal on this issue. They suggest that in parishes where prosecution was relatively intense in the early seventeenth century bridal pregnancy rates were low; on the other hand, parishes where prosecutions were infrequent experienced relatively high levels of prenuptial pregnancy. This correlation might indicate that court action did have a deterrent effect. On the other hand, the data reveal no obvious link between the intensity of prosecution in different parishes and changes in bridal pregnancy rates over time: the downland parish of Broad Chalke, where prosecutions remained rare throughout the period, experienced a fall in bridal pregnancy rates similar to that which occurred in Steeple Ashton, where prosecutions were being stepped up in the early seventeenth century.

Irrespective of whether they actually helped to stimulate a fall in the incidence of bridal pregnancy, church court prosecutions for antenuptial incontinence were by no means devoid of social significance. Even in areas where presentments remained sparse, the emergence of prenuptial fornication as a distinct category of punishable offence helped to drive home the message that sexual relations were only fully licit after marriage in church. In turn this probably served to reinforce the decline in extra-ecclesiastical marriage contracts, which had long been in train and continued apace in this period. In areas of denser prosecution, the detection and punishment of bridal pregnancy articulated the concerns of middling and substantial householders, who felt themselves hard pressed by problems arising from poverty and population growth – concerns which, as will be seen in the next chapter, also led to a harsher attitude towards bastard-bearing. The rise of prosecutions for prenuptial incontinence in the church courts of late Elizabethan and early Stuart England thus fitted into a broader pattern of the strengthening of public control over marriage entry and of the hardening of attitudes towards sexual immorality.

8. *Incest, adultery and fornication*

The major sexual sins had traditionally been a staple of disciplinary prosecutions in the church courts. This pattern continued under Elizabeth and the early Stuarts, apparently with a large measure of support from local interests and in accord with the wide spectrum of lay and clerical opinion which held that the public discipline of sexual offenders was essential to the well-being of the commonwealth. But not all sexual offences were equally liable to prosecution, while within the broad pattern of continuity some changes are visible in this field in the period 1570–1640. The following analysis establishes the range of ecclesiastical discipline over sexual offences, discusses the nature of the cases which did come before the courts, and traces trends over time in the volume of prosecutions. After rising to a peak in the reign of James I, cases diminished in the two decades preceding the civil war, a decline which reflected a real fall in the incidence of bastardy cases and, probably, other sexual offences. The exercise of ecclesiastical discipline was by no means the only factor involved; but the church courts can claim some credit for helping to bring about this perceptible shift in the moral climate.

Brian Woodcock wrote of the 'great weight of cases of immorality which burdened the courts' in the diocese of Canterbury in the fifteenth century.[1] The same remark could be applied to any church court jurisdiction in England in the late sixteenth and early seventeenth centuries. Thus in the archdeaconry of North Wiltshire alone, some 60–90 cases of sexual incontinence (apart from bridal pregnancy) were detected annually in the 1590s.[2] The abundance of such cases is hardly surprising. Whatever the state of Christian belief and observance, it was inevitable that a sizeable minority of people would indulge in sins of the flesh. On the other hand, the church

[1] Woodcock, *Medieval ecclesiastical courts*, p. 82.
[2] Based on detailed analysis of W.R.O., AW/*Detecta* Bk, 1586–99.

courts' jurisdiction over sexual offences had suffered little encroachment from the temporal courts, and its scope, at least in theory, was immensely broad. Thus the canons of 1604 required churchwardens to present not only cases of 'adultery, whoredom, incest' but also 'any other uncleanness and wickedness of life'.[3]

The catch-all nature of the church's jurisdiction discouraged the development of a sophisticated legal vocabulary to distinguish clearly between various kinds of sexual offence, though legal commentators and moralists did make limited efforts in this direction. Fornication, adultery and incest were sometimes ranked in ascending order of gravity, while some writers distinguished between 'double' and 'single' adultery, depending on whether both or only one of the partners had a living spouse.[4] But the nomenclature used in presentments and in court records tended to be very imprecise. Incest was generally specified as such; but the terms 'adultery' and 'fornication' were sometimes used interchangeably, while the blanket word 'incontinence' was used to cover a multitude of sins. Moreover, many cases of immorality were reported not as known fact but on the basis of 'common fame' or 'vehement suspicion'; it was often left unclear just what circumstances and forms of behaviour had given rise to charges of this kind.

Such imprecision obscures the exact range of ecclesiastical discipline over sexual immorality and has led some historians, apparently mesmerised by page after page of incontinence cases, to exaggerate its scope in practice. Thus Lawrence Stone assumes that the church courts regularly pried into the most intimate details of private life, while Christopher Hill asserts that the exercise of such intrusive discipline was a 'continual source of irritation'.[5] Detailed analysis of regular court proceedings reveals that ecclesiastical jurisdiction over sexual immorality was more discriminating than at first sight appears: the authorities largely concentrated on notorious cases which most respectable householders would have regarded as worthy of discipline.

The courts made virtually no effort to punish autoerotic activities and sexual irregularities which took place between husband and wife

[3] Canon 109.

[4] Thomas, 'Puritans and adultery', pp. 259–60 and the references there cited; Downame, *Foure treatises*, p. 179; Ayliffe, *Parergon*, pp. 42–3.

[5] Stone, *Family, sex and marriage*, pp. 144–5; Hill, *Society and puritanism*, p. 305.

in the marriage-bed. Before the Reformation such matters may have been dealt with by confessors; they had probably never been subject to public discipline, and the post-Reformation church courts did not commit the folly of trying to bring them into their orbit after the practice of compulsory auricular confession had been abolished.[6] Likewise the judges showed relatively little interest in extramarital sexual activities which fell short of full intercourse. Admittedly a man could be prosecuted for 'soliciting the chastity' of a woman, and some such cases turned out to involve merely coarse suggestions or similar unseemliness.[7] Thus William Lock of Wylye, a husbandman accused in 1618 of attempting the chastity of Susan Kent, confessed that 'he foolishly told her he must feel her etc. [*sic*]'.[8] But the essence of the offence of 'soliciting' was in making determined efforts to have actual intercourse, and some cases were tantamount to attempted rape.[9] In any event, cases of this nature were never very common.

In theory the church courts could bring prosecutions for immodest behaviour as such, but prevailing social conditions and judicial caution ensured that these powers were very sparingly used. Although the licence to enjoy advanced physical intimacy which popular custom tacitly accorded seriously courting or affianced couples was not extended to others, local society did tolerate a certain amount of kissing and touching between adolescent youngsters and even between single and married people, especially at dances and festivities. Such sexual horseplay occasionally attracted the attention of the authorities when the proceedings got badly out of hand, as happened in 1625 at Steeple Langford, where the dancers were said to have stripped naked, and at a nocturnal dancing match at a mill in Broad Chalke in 1639, when the door was locked, the candles put out, and a certain Catherine Sangar set on her head and 'bishopped'.[10] But normally the church courts turned a blind eye to festive dalliance, and indeed it was something of a stock defence among

[6] Thomas N. Tentler, *Sin and confession on the eve of the Reformation* (Princeton, 1977), pp. 162–232.

[7] Sir Edward Coke, *The second part of the institutes of the laws of England*, 3rd edn (1669), p. 488.

[8] W.R.O., AS/ABO 12, 19/1/1618, *Office v. Lock*.

[9] For examples, see W.S.R.O., Ep. I/17/21, fols. 40, 52v.

[10] W.R.O., AS/ABO 14, 15/1/1625, *Office v. Ayles alias Hickes, Office v. Merriot*; B. H. Cunnington (ed.), *Records of the county of Wilts*. (Devizes, 1932), pp. 131–2.

men accused of fornication that they had done no more than indulge in such acceptable forms of intimacy. Richard Goddyn of Hardenhuish, for example, successfully denying a charge of incontinence with Maud Brewer in 1601, protested that he had merely kept her company 'as well in dancing as other sports and pastimes as he doth other maidens'.[11] Just how much licence such pleas assumed is suggested by the testimony in slander suits which turned on the very question of the limits of decent behaviour. A gentleman of Compton Chamberlayne opined in 1615 that he 'never at any time knew any honest maidens to be groped' – that is, he considered it indecent for a man to put his hand up a young woman's skirt – 'but other dallying gesture may be used to maidens without offence'. At Barford St Martin in 1622, William Cowdrey (one of the newly elected churchwardens) urged as a matter for presentment that 'Margaret Kettle and Edward Page [a married man]...did kiss and coll together', but the existing churchwardens refused to regard this as a sufficient 'fame of incontinence'. In the course of the defamation suit subsequently brought by the woman, the rector of the parish deposed that at Christmas and 'other merry times' he had seen Page and Kettle 'in their dancing to kiss, and so he hath seen many others of the parish to kiss her', but none the less he considered that she had done nothing which did not become 'the modesty of a maid'. Margaret Kettle's behaviour apparently provoked a certain amount of rough jesting in the village but – apart from the insinuations of Cowdrey, which were apparently motivated by malice towards Edward Page – the most that was said against her was that she was 'somewhat wanton'. Her behaviour was never actually presented to the church courts for disciplinary action, and she won her defamation suit.[12]

The cases so far discussed involved single women. But prosecutions for immodest behaviour on the part of married females were also strikingly rare and, when they occurred, were dealt with leniently by the church courts. In 1591 John Grigge of Balsham (Cambridgeshire) was cited for 'kissing Joan the wife of Robert Grigge...eight or nine times together very suspiciously, his back being towards the south and her back towards the north, and he hath divers times both before and since very suspiciously resorted and kept company with her'; but on his denial the judge dismissed

11 W.R.O., AW/ABO 1, fol. 27v.

12 W.R.O., B/DB 30, fol. 46; B/DB 38, fols. 90, 132–3; B/DB 39, fols. 77–81v; B/ABI 49, 13/1/1624, *Kettle v. Cowdrey*.

the charge.[13] In Wiltshire, Thomas Whatley of Steeple Ashton was presented in 1605 for 'being taken kissing, playing and groping with Joan the wife of Anthony Stileman'; while Richard Tench of Bromham, accused in 1623 of unseemly behaviour with the wife of Robert Chaundler, admitted kissing her and handling her breasts, though he denied any 'evil intent'. Both men were let off with a caution.[14]

Cases presented as *suspected* immorality raise the question of what circumstances were accepted by the courts and by local officers as reasonable grounds for prosecution. On the basis of evidence from Somerset (diocese of Bath and Wells), G. R. Quaife has suggested that quite casual contacts, such as a couple riding together on horseback, and private meetings of any sort were sufficient to raise a presentable 'fame'.[15] Any series of church court records will yield cases which appear at first sight to bear this out. Thus in Wiltshire, Thomas Leere of Warminster was accused in 1616 of adultery with William Edwardes's wife because he 'did once bring her behind him on horseback'; Alice Smith of Devizes was suspected of immorality in 1602 when a man went into her house to drink; while John Hallet, a Burcombe shepherd, was presented for immorality in 1601 when he sheltered from the lightning for an hour or so in the house of Elizabeth Stokes.[16] But, in view of the abundant independent evidence that the lives of men and women in early modern England were not rigorously segregated and that social contacts between the sexes were commonplace, it is obvious that casual encounters alone could not possibly have constituted *normal* grounds for presentment: the courts would have been swamped with poorly based accusations.[17] Cases which seem to suggest the contrary were either isolated instances of excessive zeal on the part of individual churchwardens, involved more incriminating circumstances than appears at first sight, or resulted from circumstances in which for one reason or another third parties had seized upon and publicised incidents which would normally pass unnoticed. Thus Thomas Leere (mentioned above) claimed that the horseback incident had been deliberately exaggerated by 'some of his malevolent neighbours'; while William Smith of Fonthill Bishops got into trouble in 1600 not simply be-

[13] C.U.L., Ely D.R., B/2/11, fol. 176.
[14] W.R.O., B/ABO 5, fol. 62; B/ABO 11, 21/2/1623, *Office v. Tench*.
[15] Quaife, *Wanton wenches and wayward wives*, pp. 48–50.
[16] W.R.O., AS/ABO 12, 18/12/1616, *Office v. Leere*; B/ABO 5, fol. 45; AS/ABO 7, fol. 92v.
[17] See above, pp. 156–7.

cause he gave some herbs out of his garden to William Ford's wife, but rather because his own wife thereupon grew jealous and accused him of adultery, while his daughter foolishly talked about the matter in the village and so stimulated gossip.[18]

To be sure, certain types of contact were regarded as suspicious and likely to generate a 'fame'. This was true of private meetings which took place at night, especially in bedchambers or secluded spots, and also of daytime trysts if the couple were observed to lock the door against intrusion or otherwise behaved in surreptitious fashion.[19] Reasonable suspicions could also be aroused if couples haunted each other's company with conspicuous frequency: thus in 1603 Nicholas Brooke of Easton Grey was suspected of immorality with Joan Hort 'by means of...[his] oftener resorting to the house of the said Hort than to others his neighbours'.[20] Understandably enough, the actual sharing of a dwelling tended to generate grave apprehensions of misbehaviour; though it is interesting that at Steeple Ashton in 1638 the fact that a man was living in the same house as a widow whose lands he rented led to a long discussion among the churchwardens and sidesmen as to whether the circumstances were in themselves presentable or not.[21] Indeed none of these forms of suspicious behaviour necessarily led to immediate presentment: it often took a *combination* of questionable signs to create a really definite fame sufficient to stir churchwardens into action. The ecclesiastical authorities, for their part, were not interested in accusations based on idle gossip, the unsupported assertions of individuals or weak forms of circumstantial evidence; if such cases got into court at all they were usually summarily dismissed.[22] In fine, the great majority of suspected immorality prosecutions were based not on mere rumour but on carefully considered evidence. The only significant exception, which itself proves the rule, was in the case of

[18] W.R.O., AS/ABO 12, 18/12/1616, *Office v. Leere*; cf. *ibid.*, 13/1/1617, *Office v. Elizabeth Edwardes*; AS/ABO 7, fol. 90v; cf. AS/ABO 11, 5/5/1615, *Office v. William Andrewes*.

[19] W.R.O., AW/ABO 5, 10/11/1618, *Office v. Harget*; cf. *ibid.*, 9/12/1618, *Office v. Bishop*; AW/ABO 6, 1/6/1630, *Office v. Hobbs*; AS/ABO 12, 3/3/1617, *Office v. Ficketts*; AS/ABO 13, 1/7/1620, *Office v. Chandler*; AS/ABO 13, 26/6/1624, *Office v. Coffin*.

[20] W.R.O., AW/ABO 1, 15/2/1603, *Office v. Brooke and Hort*.

[21] W.R.O., B/DB 55, fols. 26v–7, 36; cf. AW/ABO 4, 22/6/1610, *Office v. Brine*; AW/ABO 4, 30/10/1610, *Office v. Bullock*.

[22] For examples, see W.R.O., AS/ABO 12, 13/1/1617, *Office v. Edwardes*; *ibid.*, 15/1/1617, *Office v. Bartlett*; B/ABO 11, 14/12/1622, *Office v. Read*.

people who had already been in trouble for sexual offences. Couples who had successfully undergone the process of compurgation were normally ordered to avoid each other's company in future 'except in open and public places' such as church or market. Thereafter the simple fact of meeting in private was in law accepted as tantamount to proof of immorality and subject to disciplinary proceedings – though in practice, even in cases like this churchwardens were sometimes prepared to allow the couple a certain amount of leeway.[23]

The care with which circumstantial evidence was assessed reflects the fact that clear proof of immorality was by no means easy to obtain. Certain historians, arguing the contrary case, have been impressed by instances in which churchwardens or other local officers, neighbours or even fellow-servants actively spied on other people's sexual misdoings through window panes or chinks in walls or doors, often taking turns to peer, calling others to look too, and sometimes ending up by bursting in to confront the couple with their 'lewdness'. According to Keith Thomas, such behaviour implies that much of the modern concept of privacy was lacking in early modern England, while Quaife suggests that it was (in part) a voyeuristic response to sexual repression. Both authors would see the phenomenon as evidence of very close moral surveillance.[24]

Such cases can certainly be found in any series of church court records, though they can hardly be described as frequent. On examination they mostly reveal a common pattern: some individual, or occasionally the community at large, had a particularly strong interest in convicting the couple concerned of sexual immorality. Sometimes the offenders had a history of sexual offences and of repeated appearances in court to answer charges: the patience of local officials, or of neighbours in general, finally snapped and determined efforts were made to bring the couple to book.[25] Sometimes these episodes were maliciously motivated: individuals tried to convict their enemies of immorality in the context of parochial feuds over land or status or of other quarrels.[26] Quite often the woman

[23] For examples, see W.R.O., B/DB 8, fol. 163; AS/ABO 12, 5/5/1617, *Office v. Cotten*; *ibid.*, 6/12/1617, *Office v. Haswell.*

[24] Thomas, *Religion and the decline of magic*, p. 527; Quaife, *Wanton wenches and wayward wives*, pp. 50–2.

[25] For examples, see W.R.O., B/DB 5, fol. 108; B/DB 9, fols. 87, 153v–4, 207v–8.

[26] For examples, see W.R.O., AS/ABO 12, 15/1/1617, *Office v. Bartlett*, cf. B/DB 31, fols. 156v–7; AS/ABO 12, 9/12/1616, *Office v. Tolley*, *ibid.*, 1/2/1617, *Office v. Donnynge* (the Tolley–Donnynge case apparently reflected jealousies among servants in a gentleman's household).

accused of incontinence was a widow holding lands by manorial customs which specified that her rights lasted only so long as she remained 'chaste and sole'; the accuser was usually someone who stood to benefit if the widow forfeited her holding.[27] All these situations demanded incontrovertible proof of immorality, to make it impossible for the accused person to rebut charges by means of compurgation. The various activities such as peering through a window or bringing witnesses to look too were specifically laid down in canon law as acceptable modes of proof.[28] In short, these spying cases did not represent normal, spontaneous, neighbourly behaviour but carefully planned, *legally purposeful* activity; they were the early modern equivalent of the private detective bursting into a hotel bedroom to secure photographic proof of adultery in divorce proceedings. They give a wholly misleading impression both of lack of privacy and the closeness of moral surveillance. While the right to privacy was certainly not as well established as in modern western society, it did exist. Local communities did not normally intrude themselves into people's lives to seek out cases of immorality: they usually waited until the circumstances became blatant or a matter of common knowledge and insistent gossip.[29]

The practical limitations on the church courts' activities concerning sexual immorality, and the evidential barriers to prosecution, were thus much greater than is generally realised. These constraints inevitably affected the nature of the church courts' case load. As the following analysis shows, there were in addition a variety of other factors which conditioned the make-up of the courts' agenda, including the differing frequency of various kinds of sexual immorality and variations in the gravity with which they were regarded by local opinion.

Prosecutions for incest were comparatively rare. In thirty visitations of the archdeaconry of North Wiltshire in the period 1586–99, only 4 charges of incest were specified.[30] The appearance books of the three main Wiltshire jurisdictions for the years 1615–29 reveal only

[27] For examples, see W.R.O., B/DB 9, fols. 38, 80v, 81v, 167–8v; cf. B/Misc. Ct Papers 29/47, deposition of William Curteis in *Office v. Margaret Hurle, widow and John Baker*.

[28] Ayliffe, *Parergon*, p. 51.

[29] Cf. Houlbrooke, *English family*, p. 23; D. H. Flaherty, *Privacy in colonial New England* (Charlottesville, Va, 1972), pp. 92–7, 164–218.

[30] Based on search of W.R.O., AW/*Detecta* Bk, 1586–99.

28 cases, an average of less than 2 per annum. The real total was greater, since some couples were presumably presented but did not make an appearance; but even making generous allowance for the contumacious, it is unlikely that the number of prosecutions exceeded an average of 5 per annum.[31] Sampling of the records of disciplinary proceedings in the diocese of Ely and the archdeaconries of Chichester and Leicester reveals a similar pattern: prosecutions were sparse, and in some years there were none at all.[32] The courts of high commission also handled incest charges, but, from the perspective of any single county, the number of cases was minuscule.[33]

Accusations of 'incest' could include both simple sexual relations within the prohibited degrees and cases where the couple had procured or tried to procure a solemnised marriage.[34] The latter were far less common: the Wiltshire records for the period 1615–29, for example, reveal only four such cases. A Marlborough man had married his father's sister and had treated her as his wife for thirteen years. John Sawyer of Minety had married his mother's brother's widow, alleging that Mr Samuel Hudson, minister of Chesterton in Oxfordshire, had assured him that the union was lawful. Tristram Wattes of Warminster likewise alleged ignorance of the law. He had made suit of marriage to his deceased wife's sister's daughter and had had sexual relations with her, though he denied that the union had actually been solemnised; his partner explained that her aunt had brought her up 'lovingly' and on her death-bed persuaded her to marry Wattes. Roger Mowdie of Downton claimed that he had contracted himself to his deceased wife's sister, consummated the union and arranged for the calling of banns, all in ignorance that the marriage was unlawful; it was only when a neighbour informed the minister of the nature of the relationship between the couple that Mowdie was disabused. In a case before the London court of high commission in 1634, a Seend yeoman called Charles Hardikin likewise pleaded ignorance: a 'weak old man', he had married his brother's daughter's daughter. These protestations of ignorance have the ring of truth, especially in the case of Hardikin, since his marriage was not *explicitly* forbidden in the official table of kindred

[31] Based on search of W.R.O., B/ABO 7–11; AS/ABO 11–14; AW/ABO 5–6. On contumacy, see below, pp. 340–61.
[32] Based on search of C.U.L., Ely D.R., B/2/11, 37; W.S.R.O., Ep. I/17/8, 21, 25; L.M., 1 D 41/13/12, 40, 64.
[33] Based on search of P.R.O., SP 16/261, 324.
[34] Gibson, *Codex*, vol. 1, pp. 414–15.

and affinity but was held to be unlawful 'by necessary consequence'.[35] Some lay people evidently depended for their knowledge of the more remote prohibitions on expert clerical advice, and if this was for some reason not forthcoming they could fall into error. But the small number of cases of incestuous marriage would indicate that the main prohibitions were both well known and well observed.

The 24 known prosecutions for incestuous sexual relations in Wiltshire in the period 1615–29 included three cases of father/daughter and two of mother/son incest, and one brother/sister liaison. Beyond these the range of incestuous relationships was fairly wide and, save that offences between blood-kin were outnumbered by those between affines, no significant groupings are discernible. Several of the accusations of incest between close kin were in any case denied, usually with the explanation that the defendant was simply unable to provide separate accommodation for family members. Thus John Mercer of Donhead St Mary claimed that he admitted his brother's daughter into his bed 'in respect of necessity of lodging', while John Page of Fonthill Giffard pleaded that 'his daughter (he having no other place to lodge her in) did for many years past lie with him at his feet in the same bed'. In each case the excuse was accepted by the judge.[36] Similar cases occurred in other parts of England. Thus in 1625 Thomas Court of Westhampnett (Sussex) was dismissed with a simple admonition when he pleaded that he and his sister 'did lie together about Christmas last, their house being torn by tempest of weather and little other room in the house to keep them dry'.[37]

Did the paucity of prosecutions for incest reflect a low level of offence, difficulties of detection, lax attitudes to offenders locally or a combination of these factors? (Modern studies indicate that cases of incest known to official agencies represent only a small proportion of those that actually occur.)[38] The fact that some churchwardens

[35] W.R.O., B/ABO 8, 21/2/1616. *Office v. Walfar alias Sturley alias Pearce*; *ibid.*, 14/1/1618, *Office v. Sawyer*; B/ABO 11, 12/12/1622, *Office v. Wattes*; *ibid.*, 4/3/1623, *Office v. Elinor Withers*; B/ABO 8, 25/2/1618, *Office v. Mowdie*, *Office v. Gillian Levier alias Dier*; P.R.O., SP 16/261, fols. 134v, 189v, 222, 231, 236v, 263v.

[36] W.R.O., AS/ABO 12, 2/5/1617, *Office v. Mercer*; *ibid.*, 24/2/1616, *Office v. Page*; see also *ibid.*, 15/12/1617, *Office v. Skynner*.

[37] W.S.R.O., Ep. I/17/21, fol. 85.

[38] See, for example, Herbert Maisch, *Incest*, trans. Colin Bearne (1973), pp. 86–7; Blair Justice and Rita Justice, *The broken taboo: sex in the family* (1980), pp. 15–18.

and offenders themselves used expressions like 'the most wicked sin of incest' suggests that the offence, once discovered, was regarded as a serious matter in local society.[39] But, unlike the situation in some societies studied by anthropologists, incest does not seem to have loomed large in the minds of the inhabitants of early modern England. As we have seen, even clerical moralists usually devoted little attention to the subject.[40] At the popular level, it is striking that accusations of incest rarely figured in defamatory insults, and that there was no colloquial expression equivalent to 'whore' or 'whoremaster' to express the sense of 'incestuous person'.[41] People do not seem to have spent much time or energy searching out suspected cases of incest, and there is no evidence of savage informal penalties directed specifically against incestuous couples.

This lack of strong, active interest in incest was doubtless of long standing and had complex historical roots.[42] But it is hardly surprising in view of other salient features of early modern English society. Muted concern with incest and the relative weakness of kinship ties which was characteristic of sixteenth- and early seventeenth-century England may be seen as two sides of the same coin.[43] Moreover, as Alan Macfarlane has argued, the widespread practice of sending adolescent children away from home as servants or apprentices limited the opportunities and temptations for the occurrence of incest within the nuclear family.[44]

In these circumstances it is not surprising that the provisions of the act of 1650, which made incest a felony punishable by death, were to prove virtually a dead letter: such an extreme penalty was neither necessary nor desirable in seventeenth-century England.[45] The strict but not draconian penalties imposed by the church courts were in better accord with social attitudes. Defendants who denied the offence but had no persuasive defence to offer were ordered to undergo compurgation, usually with between four and seven neigh-

[39] For examples, see W.R.O., AS/ABO 11, March 1614 (exact date unspecified), *Office v. William Dew of Broad Chalke*; W.S.R.O., Ep. I/17/12, fol. 117; C.U.L., Ely D.R., B/2/35, fol. 22.

[40] See above, p. 153.

[41] Sharpe, *Defamation and sexual slander*, p. 15.

[42] Pollock and Maitland, *History of English law*, vol. 2, pp. 543–4; Goody, *Development of the family and marriage*, *passim*.

[43] Cf. Robin Fox, *Kinship and marriage* (Harmondsworth, 1967), pp. 71–2.

[44] Alan Macfarlane, *The family life of Ralph Josselin: a seventeenth-century clergyman* (Cambridge, 1970), p. 205.

[45] Thomas, 'Puritans and adultery', pp. 257–8, 278–80.

bours, but sometimes with as many as nine – a searching test of local opinion. Convicted offenders were enjoined severe penances. These usually involved repeated public confessions in church or market-place in the penitential white sheet, and some culprits had to submit to additional humiliations such as appearing bare-legged or wearing a placard marked 'for incest'. On at least one occasion, the bishop of Salisbury used his powers as a justice of the peace to make sure that the penance was performed.[46] Penalties of this type were quite sufficient to reinforce the principle that incest was a grave offence, and they may well have had considerable deterrent effect.

Prosecutions for adultery involving married women were a good deal commoner than for incest but still formed only a minority of incontinence cases. Samples from Ely diocese, the archdeaconries of Chichester and Leicester and the main Wiltshire jurisdictions at various dates between 1570 and 1640 indicate that the proportion of cases in which the involvement of a married woman was specified ranged from about 5 per cent (episcopal visitation of Wiltshire, 1585) to 26 per cent (visitation of Ely diocese, 1619), the norm being around 10 per cent.[47] Admittedly such figures tend to underestimate the incidence of female adultery cases, since churchwardens in their presentments and court scribes in writing up the record sometimes failed to specify that accused women were married. But studies of particular parishes, where the information contained in the court records can be supplemented by data from local sources, confirm that cases of female adultery were normally in the minority. The parishes of Wylye and Keevil in the period 1591–1630 yield a total of 85 immorality cases in which the marital status of the accused female can be positively ascertained: married women were involved in 18 instances, or about 21 per cent of the total.[48] Studies of other villages would probably yield even smaller proportions, since, as will

[46] W.R.O., QS/GR East. 1617/166, 201.

[47] The specified percentages are based on analysis of W.R.O., B/*Detecta* Bk 6; C.U.L., Ely D.R., B/2/37. A wide range of records from the various jurisdictions on which this study is based were sampled to estimate the norm.

[48] These figures of course exclude cases of bridal pregnancy/prenuptial fornication. The totals are computed on the basis of 'liaison': i.e. a relationship, whether fleeting or prolonged, between a given couple; certain individuals were involved in more than one liaison, while some liaisons gave rise to repeated church court prosecutions. The total sample includes a few cases from the period 1631–40 involving individuals who had already been in trouble for sexual immorality in earlier decades.

be seen, in both Wylye and Keevil there were unusual circumstances which tended to inflate the numbers of prosecutions involving married women.

Independent evidence of the actual incidence of adultery by married women (as opposed to the incidence of *prosecutions*) is not available. But it would probably be mistaken to assume that the offence was widespread or generally condoned. Admittedly there are occasional indications of tolerant attitudes. When Thomas Oven saw John Bathe, a yeoman of Christian Malford, having sex with Arthur Hodgkins's wife under a hedge one night in 1627, he bade them as he passed 'grind on' and later promised Bathe that he would be 'as secret as his confessor', adding the generous sentiment that 'if he could make no sport he should mar none'.[49] But the other side of the coin in this case was that the couple evidently feared exposure, and there is no doubt that immorality involving married women was conventionally regarded with considerable disfavour. In describing such behaviour, churchwardens and witnesses not uncommonly used expressions, such as 'filthy', 'very lewd and lascivious', 'to the great offence of all honest and civil people', strongly redolent of moral indignation.[50] And the evidence of slander suits, examined in detail in Chapter 10, indicates that, at least in the middling ranks of yeomen, husbandmen and craftsmen, married women were highly sensitive to aspersions of sexual immorality and clearly valued their reputation for sexual 'credit' or 'honesty'. Their menfolk were sensitive to imputations of cuckoldry and may be assumed to have taken reasonable care to ensure that their wives remained chaste.

None the less some women did engage in adulterous behaviour. The impression conveyed by the records of church court prosecutions, confirmed by the more detailed evidence available for Wylye and Keevil, is that they and their partners spanned the social spectrum.[51] But the precise circumstances in which wives were unfaithful are in most cases obscure, since culprits only rarely made full confessions (the majority of convictions were secured through the procedure of compurgation). A minority of better-documented cases does, however, give some insight into the social context. It is evident, for example, that there were often special circumstances involved

[49] W.R.O., QS/GR Mich. 1627/225.
[50] W.R.O., B/DB 30, fols. 126v–7; QS/GR Mich. 1627/209; B/ABO 2, fol. 34; B/ABO 9, 2/7/1619, *Office v. Cecily Springbat*.
[51] Illustrative cases from both Wylye and Keevil are quoted in succeeding pages.

when married women of reasonable substance were tempted to adultery. Anne Downe, second wife of a wealthy yeoman of Orcheston St Mary and possibly much younger than he, was left alone a good deal in a 'farm house' remote from her husband's 'dwelling house'; small wonder that she formed a liaison with her stepson's resident schoolmaster. A certain Lyming's wife of Marlborough was also left too much to her own devices, drank to excess and around 1590 indulged in at least one intoxicated bout of adultery with a lover named Trubshawe. She was still drunk when her husband returned home, and confessed all after vomiting over him in bed. A case from Fisherton Anger in 1615 was rather different. The woman justified her adultery by asserting a precontract with her lover: 'he is mine for he was my husband by right before I married with Aunsell my now husband'. At Chilmark in 1622, a man tried to persuade a woman to adultery under cover of a Hock Tuesday custom whereby men were allowed to chase and tie up women. He told her 'that he must bind her' and that then 'they would do as their forefathers had done' – but the invitation was refused. An even more unusual case occurred at Melksham in 1622, where a pair of religious radicals called Henry Cheevers and Mary Banfield had made a written covenant to forsake their present spouses and live as man and wife, 'David and Jonathan'. Cheevers claimed that if she refused him her body she was not doing the duty of a wife, and the couple called their legitimate children bastards because their legal spouses were not 'converted to the faith and were not in the state of regeneration'. Cheevers planned, 'if this country would not suffer them to live together', to sell his goods, put fifty pounds in his purse and make a fresh start elsewhere, leaving 'his own wife a base scab as he found her'.[52]

The hardships and vicissitudes suffered by poor and very poor wives sometimes made them vulnerable to bribery or trickery practised by wealthier men. In 1588 James Wheler alias Knave of North Bradley had sex with a beggar woman in the presence of her husband, presumably in return for alms, and he had also committed adultery with the wife of a poor tailor who was absent at work in another village. In 1592 Robert Blagden, scion of one of the wealthiest families in Keevil and later to become a dominant figure in village

52 W.R.O., B/DB 5, fols. 80–1; B/DB 11, fols. 67v–9; B/DB 30, fols. 126v–7; B/ABO 10, 9/5/1622, examination of Edith Lane; AS/ABO 13, 23/3/1622, *Office v. Cheevers*; *ibid.*, 11/5/1622, *Office v. Banfield* and *Office v. John Neele.*

life, apparently tricked a poor woman called Susan Passion into adultery. According to her story, he came 'bearing in hand' the false news that her husband, absent in Ireland, was dead, and offered to marry her himself. In the same village in 1617, it was said that 'John Wattes...gave Gough's wife...six pence to lie with her'; the woman was a cottager's wife, while Wattes was a miller's servant with good expectations. However, it cannot be assumed that poverty was inconsistent with sexual honesty or that female adultery was taken lightly among the poor wage-labourers and cottagers at the bottom of settled society. According to Alice Gough's story (accepted as true by the church court judge), she had firmly rejected Wattes's assault on her honesty: 'I had rather say to my husband "Go, poor knave" than "poor cuckold".'[53]

There were, however, a few habitual adulteresses, mostly poor and often involved in other criminal or quasi-criminal activities. An innkeeper's wife from the crowded suburb of Fisherton Anger, in trouble in 1588, was perhaps a part-time prostitute. In 1604 the wife of Richard Battyn of Corsham was accused of keeping an unlicensed tippling house and of 'lewd life' with her customers, while in 1627 a married woman of Collingbourne Kingston entertained servants and children against the will of their masters and parents, allowed her house to be a centre for drunkenness and pilfering, and was in addition 'very much defamed of body' with numerous persons including three named young men. More sinister circumstances were revealed in a case in 1616. A Brinkworth husbandman claimed that the wife of Robert Blake alias Jacques of Purton (a slum-strewn parish in Braydon Forest) enticed him into her house, entered into familiar talk and 'did...kiss him offering him kindness'. As soon as he tried to make love to her, however, her husband jumped out of concealment, threatened him with a knife, and forced him to sign a bond to pay him forty shillings a year for five years.[54]

While it is likely that female adultery was not very common at most social levels, it is certain that by no means all the cases which did occur led to prosecution in the church courts. Discovery and proof were no easy matter. Determined lovers could engage in illicit meetings under the cloak of such acceptable, day-to-day transactions

[53] W.R.O., B/DB 13, fol. 13; B/ABO 2, fols. 22v, 29v; B/DB 32, fols. 128v–33v.
[54] W.R.O., B/DB 10, fol. 6v; QS/GR East. 1604/157; QS/GR Mich. 1627/201; B/ABO 8, 5/9/1616, *Office v. John Frye*.

as taking corn to the miller, visiting farmers' wives to buy grain or eggs, or receiving visits from a tailor.[55] If the liaison led to pregnancy, the child could usually be passed off as the normal fruit of marital relations; to be sure, the infant might grow up to look suspiciously like someone other than the woman's husband, but that was a matter for mere gossip rather than serious grounds for legal proceedings.[56] Even quite strong suspicions did not necessarily lead to delation. Since no bastard birth was involved, the offence did not ordinarily threaten the poor rates, so there was no sharp financial spur to reinforce the sense of moral indignation. On the other hand, there were more positive considerations which inclined churchwardens to let sleeping dogs lie. Female adultery was probably regarded locally as primarily a matter of household discipline. It was the husband's duty to restrain his wife's behaviour, and local officers were inclined to allow him ample opportunity to do so before resorting to legal action. The latter could indeed be counter-productive. If there was mere suspicion of adultery and no real proof, and if the husband was in real or feigned ignorance or biding his time before taking action, a presentment might have the effect of precipitating scandal, strife or violence; and in extreme cases, where the husband reacted by turning his wife out or deserting the home, the poor rates might be jeopardised after all.

A number of well-documented cases illustrate the various barriers to presentment and the circumstances in which the misdeeds of adulterous wives finally came out into the open and led to court action. In 1616 a promoted office suit was begun against Edward Wacham and Christopher Moody, churchwardens of Boyton, and a certain Alexander Knight on the grounds that a fame of adultery between Knight and Moody's wife had not been presented. Wacham acknowledged that Knight had frequented Moody's house 'early and late', but he claimed that this did not constitute adequate grounds for presentment. Moody, not unnaturally, was unwilling to detect his own wife. The affair became scandalous through the intervention of a certain Richard Ambrose, who, as the evidence

[55] For examples, see W.R.O., B/ABO 7, 16/7/1613, *Office v. Joseph Hancock*; B/ABO 8, 22/3/1616, *Office v. Giles Norton*; *ibid.*, 10/4/1616, *Office v. John Pepler*; B/ABO 10, 9/5/1622, examination of Edith Lane.

[56] W.R.O., B/DB 9, fol. 156; B/ABI 45, fols. 100v–1. See also Houlbrooke, *Church courts and the people*, p. 77 n. 74.

revealed, had ulterior motives connected with an inheritance for wishing to discredit Judith Moody. He stirred up local gossip, hung cuckold's horns on Moody's gate, confronted him with allegations of his wife's adultery and reported the matter to Sir William Jorden, the local justice. The latter interviewed Knight and warned him that 'he might have done well to have forborne' his visits when he saw that they were leading to trouble. But Knight was deaf to admonition and advice, claiming that he had legitimate reasons to visit Moody's house. According to one account, he boasted that even if Moody actually found the couple in bed together he could do nothing without witnesses. In this impasse, with suspicions rife but no hard evidence available, the prevailing local feeling seems to have been one of embarrassment coupled with considerable irritation towards Ambrose for stirring up trouble. Even the prosecution of the churchwardens did not entirely overcome their reluctance to accuse Knight, and the presentment that was eventually framed against him was studied in its accuracy: 'a fame of using too much the company of Judith Moody'. But local opinion seems to have backlashed against the woman, and other adultery charges were subsequently brought against her.[57]

Another revealing case occurred in 1619. It eventually emerged that, over a period of about six months, Edward Peinton of Collingbourne Ducis had frequented the house of John Earle of Collingbourne Kingston and had sexual relations with his wife Agnes. At length 'some suspicion did grow', and Peinton was 'wished by some friends to forbear her house and company'. But these attempts to compose the matter failed because Agnes Earle urged him 'that whereas he came once he should come thrice'. Peinton, however, eventually had an attack of conscience and confessed the adultery to a friend, who thereupon told the minister. The latter examined the couple and induced them to confess, promising not to reveal the matter; but the affair became scandalous when he decided not to admit Peinton to the communion. It was this formal, public act that crystallised local suspicions and made it impossible for the churchwardens to turn a blind eye, and the couple were duly presented to the court of the bishop of Salisbury. At root it was Peinton's folly that had led to prosecution: as a local shepherd commented ironi-

[57] W.R.O., B/DB 30, fols. 123–5, 148–56; B/DB 32, fols. 2–30; B/ABO 8, 30/9/1616, *Office v. Knight*; *ibid.*, 8/2/1617, *Office v. Judith Moody*; AS/ABO 12, 10/2/1616, *Office v. Edward Wakeham* (*or Wacham*) *and Christopher Moody*.

cally, he was 'a wiseman to say that he had lain with ... Agnes Earle and to tell of it'.[58]

Ill-advised confessions by the adulterous couple themselves; discovery by the husband, followed by quarrels, public revelations or the expulsion of the wife; the intervention of an outside party who stirred up trouble for reasons of personal enmity – it was things like this that turned suspicion into public scandal and precipitated prosecution. With luck, strong nerves and tight lips, couples could pursue liaisons without getting caught out. In 1593 Thomas Messenger of Cricklade was finally brought to court, where he confessed a series of illicit relationships over the previous fifteen years. Two of them were affairs with married women, 'never before perfectly known nor confessed...until this day, yet nevertheless suspected of many'.[59]

The evidential and social factors discussed in preceding paragraphs account for the broad pattern of prosecutions involving married women, but certain spatial and chronological variations remain to be explored. The topographical distribution of prosecutions mainly reflected population density. This meant that cases cropped up quite regularly (albeit in small numbers) in major urban centres, whereas many country parishes yielded no detections whatsoever for years on end. However, some villages did witness above-average numbers of prosecutions on a semi-regular basis, while sudden clusters of cases sometimes occurred in particular parishes over a short period. Such aberrations, and the special local circumstances which produced them, are well illustrated by events in the villages of Keevil and Wylye.

In Keevil the tally of female adultery prosecutions was boosted by a number of vexatious or poorly substantiated charges, arising from the interpersonal tensions characteristic of this community among the householders of middling to upper rank.[60] As we have seen, the yeoman Robert Blagden was in his youth justly convicted of adultery. Years later, in 1609, the matter was again raked up against him, apparently at the instigation of members of the Jones family, with whom Blagden was in endemic conflict. The prosecution of William Jones in 1606 for adultery with Alice Rasie, a weaver's wife,

[58] W.R.O., B/DB 34, fols. 149–51v, 157v–8; B/DB 35, fols. 16v–17v, 43v–7; B/DB 36, fols. 46v–7; B/Libels 2/28; B/ABO 9, 9/7/1619, *Office v. Peinton*; *ibid.*, 3/10/1619, *Office v. Agnes Earle*.

[59] W.R.O., B/ABO 2, fol. 33.

[60] The social milieu in Keevil is described above, pp. 81–2.

was perhaps more soundly based, but this case also may have been related to the Blagden/Jones feud, which around this time was generating a multiplicity of suits and prosecutions in various local and central courts.[61] In 1619 the prosecution of Alice, wife of Thomas Gough, resulted from a malicious slander against her alleged lover; while in the same year a prosecution against the wife of James Cratchley was also based on slander. She was in fact the victim of local hostility against her husband, a weaver who was accused not only of fathering a bastard, but also of sheepstealing, assault and legal chicanery.[62] These vexatious charges represented about a third of all the known female adultery prosecutions in Keevil in the period 1591–1630, but the way in which they were handled dispels any notion that the courts could be easily manipulated for malicious purposes: after brief hearings which established the flimsy nature of the evidence, the cases were summarily dismissed.

In Wylye there were suspicions of malicious intent in one of the eight known prosecutions for female adultery in the forty years after 1590, though the case was by no means entirely without foundation and the same couple were in trouble in both earlier and later years.[63] Of the other cases, four occurred in the context of the short-lived moral reform campaign which followed the institution of John Lee as rector in 1619. As was seen in Chapter 3, the new incumbent was characterised as a puritan who immediately set his face against lax religious observance, dancing and festivities, drunkenness – and sexual immorality. The married women and their alleged lovers prosecuted in 1619–21 varied in status from middling to low, and most of them had connections with the village's inns and alehouses. John Sopp, for example, a shepherd accused of adultery with two of the women, was a notorious drunkard; Grace Hill was the wife of a husbandman–tailor who also kept an inn; Alice Girdler's husband, a man of some substance who ran a grist and tucking mill, was several times prosecuted for drunkenness, and she herself may have been fond of a drink. These people may in their cups have indulged in undue familiarity, but they were probably not the notorious

[61] W.R.O., D/AB 21, fol. 275; AS/ABO 9, 17/5/1606, *Office v. Jones*; cf. B/DB 24, fols. 60–75v, *passim*; P.R.O., STAC 8/59/11.

[62] W.R.O., AS/ABO 12, 10/4/1619, *Office v. Gough*; B/DB 32, fols. 128v–33; AS/ABO 12, 10/4/1619, *Office v. Edith Cratchley*; B/DB 35, fols. 40v–4.

[63] W.R.O., AS/ABO 8, 22/6/1603 and 28/1/1604, *Office v. Humphrey Furnell.*

sinners who normally figured in female adultery cases; and in the event only Sopp was put to penance.[64]

Clusters of cases like this, or a series of charges such as that brought against Judith Moody of Boyton when her adulterous behaviour was finally brought out into the open, could significantly inflate the numbers of cases heard by the courts in particular years and thus help to explain annual fluctuations in female adultery prosecutions. There are also signs that in certain years the bishop of Salisbury's officers took special pains to ferret out offenders, as in 1616 and 1621 (the primary visitations of respectively Robert Abbot and Robert Townson).[65] But to a large extent interannual fluctuations were simply a random effect of sporadic prosecution. Of greater interest are longer-term trends in the incidence of cases. Sampling of the surviving Wiltshire materials suggests that the numbers of detections rose between the middle years of Elizabeth's reign and the later years of James I's (Tables 9 and 10). Much of this expansion was probably due simply to population growth, but there may have been some increase in the *intensity* of prosecution. In the later 1620s and the 1630s, on the other hand, there was a fall in the numbers of cases, which could well reflect a decline in the actual incidence of female adultery comparable to the decline in illegitimacy revealed by parish register analysis.[66]

If immorality involving married women did indeed become less common, this was probably due more to broad shifts in social attitudes – the growing attractions of respectability and good reputation, for example, some evidence for which is discussed in Chapter 10 – than to actual fear of punishment by the church courts. For most defendants the main hazards of presentment were the shame of public exposure, possible reprisals from the husband and the trouble and expense of court proceedings. To be sure, convicted defendants were normally ordered to perform formal public penances in a white sheet on one or more Sundays during service time – no doubt a

[64] W.R.O., AS/ABO 12, 19/1/1618, *Office v. Sopp*; *ibid.*, 30/10/1619, *Office v. Sopp*; B/ABO 10, Jan. 1621 (exact date crumbled away), *Office v. Sopp and wife*; B/ABO 10, Jan. 1621 and 22/1/1621, *Office v. Grace Hill*; B/ABO 10, 14/12/1620, *Office v. Joel Girdler and Alice Girdler*; B/ABO 11, 11/7/1625, *Office v. Joel Girdler*; Hadow (ed.), *Wylye registers*, pp. 2, 7, 16–18, 23.

[65] Inferred from the pattern of prosecutions in these years (cf. Table 10), but I have not found direct evidence that these bishops personally took an especial interest in the prosecution of adulteresses.

[66] See below, pp. 276–7.

Table 9 *Fornication/adultery cases* in Elizabethan Wiltshire*

(a) Court of the archdeacon of Salisbury: sample years

1573	39 (3)	1586	39 (3)	1602	45 (5)
1574	31 (4)	1587	42 (3)	1603	44 (2)

(b) Bishop of Salisbury (*visitation presentments*)

1585	110 (6)

(c) Archdeacon of North Wiltshire (*visitation presentments*)*: sample years*

1587	50 (3)	1594	82 (8)
1590	74 (5)	1599	64 (5)

Note: Bracketed figures indicate numbers of cases specified as involving married women.

* Characteristically though not invariably involving *two* specified individuals.

Table 10 *Fornication/adultery cases* in Jacobean and Caroline Wiltshire*

(a) Cases tried by the courts of the bishop of Salisbury and the archdeacons of Salisbury and North Wiltshire, 1615–29: combined totals

1615	[49 (5)]**	1620	92 (8)	1625	42 (3)
1616	102 (26)	1621	137 (22)	1626	43 (7)
1617	94 (6)	1622	101 (15)	1627	46 (7)
1618	108 (12)	1623	42 (11)	1628	33 (4)
1619	121 (15)	1624	58 (4)	1629	72 (4)

(b) Dean of Salisbury (*visitation presentments*)*: sample years*

1622	24 (3)	1631	14 (1)
1625	15 (0)	1634	12 (0)
1628	23 (0)	1638	14 (1)

Note: Bracketed figures indicate numbers of cases specified as involving married women.

* Characteristically though not invariably involving *two* specified individuals.

** Record lacking for archdeaconry of North Wiltshire.

deeply humiliating experience, especially for established householders. But convictions were difficult to obtain. As was noted earlier, few defendants were prepared to make a confession. The majority who denied were usually ordered to undergo compurgation with between four and seven neighbours, and most were able eventually to secure a dismissal. As a result both of the relatively small numbers of detections and of the low conviction rate, it was rare to see married women and their lovers do penance for adultery.

While it would thus be wrong to overemphasise the impact of ecclesiastical justice in this sphere, it would be equally mistaken to write it off as a total failure. Its limits must be understood in context. They were the symptom not of contempt for the courts but of basic social structural features which facilitated contact between the sexes (thus making adultery difficult to detect) and of the due regard shown by both the courts and local officers for sensible rules of evidence. In these conditions the punishment of each and every case of adultery was quite out of the question. Nor would it have been seen as desirable by most people. Throughout the period the offence was probably fairly uncommon, and when cases did occur communities preferred if possible to deal with them by admonition and advice rather than legal action. The courts served as a longstop for the power of public disapproval, usually resorted to only when couples blatantly defied the rules of propriety. Even then the chief desire was probably to bring the affair to an end rather than to subject the couple to punishment; and this need was adequately met by the fact that prosecuted couples, whether convicted or not, were henceforth subject to narrow scrutiny and liable to immediate representment if they stepped out of line. The system may appear haphazard, but it made sense in the social conditions of early modern England. The alternative provisions of the adultery act of 1650, which made the offence a felony prosecuted on indictment and punishable by death, were to prove totally ineffective.[67]

The bulk of incontinence cases dealt with by the church courts in this period involved unmarried women – spinsters and widows. Yet evidential and social factors limited the intensity of prosecution even in this sphere of sexual immorality. Since young, unmarried people, especially servants, enjoyed such a large measure of personal freedom in their leisure and courtship activities, it was impossible for the courts themselves or for local officers to supervise their lives at all rigorously. Moreover female servants were often in close physical proximity to their masters and to the householder's male relatives and friends: what ensued from this in halls, bedchambers, barns and cowhouses was only very partially open to the scrutiny of neighbours and churchwardens. Proverbially widows enjoyed a wide measure of

[67] Thomas, 'Puritans and adultery', pp. 258, 278–80.

liberty, and this was especially true of those who were fortunate enough to be householders in their own right.

In these circumstances unmarried women could pursue quite sustained relationships before they were discovered. Defendants in court were sometimes asked to state how often they had had illicit intercourse and over what period, and the results are revealing. In a sample of 47 well-recorded cases before the bishop of Salisbury's court in the period 1615–21, 11 culprits claimed to have had sex only once, while a further 11 alleged that intercourse had occurred only two or three times; but most confessed to frequent coupling, using expressions like 'often times' or 'divers and sundry times'. Of defendants before the archdeacon of Salisbury's court in the 1580s who reported the duration of their relationships, most confessed to periods of several months (characteristically beginning in the spring and extending into or through the summer). A few even admitted relationships lasting a year or more: Elizabeth Cully and Michael Cooper of West Grimstead had apparently pursued a liaison for three years before they were finally detected in 1586.[68]

Many liaisons were only discovered when the woman became visibly pregnant, and such cases were always very prominent in incontinence presentments involving unmarried females. Analysis of prosecutions from the Wiltshire jurisdictions, the diocese of Ely and the archdeaconry of Chichester at various dates in the late sixteenth and early seventeenth centuries reveals that the proportion of bastardy/illicit pregnancy cases was normally well over 50 per cent, rising as high as 78 per cent in Chichester archdeaconry in 1625. The archdeaconry of Leicester reveals somewhat lower proportions (55 per cent in 1586 and 37 per cent in 1615–16), but this was due partly to the scribal practice of recording cases simply as 'for fornication' or 'for incontinence' without bothering to specify whether or not an illicit pregnancy had occurred. The importance of illegitimacy cases is driven home by detailed parish studies: in 44 of the 67 cases of sexual incontinence involving unmarried women in the villages of Wylye and Keevil in the period 1591–1630, bastardy or illicit pregnancy was certainly at issue.[69] As a corollary, it is reasonable to assume that a considerable number of barren relationships, especially fleeting ones which had a low chance of leading to pregnancy,

[68] W.R.O., AS/ABO 2, fol. 80v.

[69] These cases are discussed more fully later in this chapter.

were never detected.[70] Some of those which did result in prosecution had been revealed by drunken boasts or foolish confessions by the couple themselves, drawing attention to circumstances which would otherwise have passed unnoticed.[71]

It is plain why illicit pregnancies and bastard births were so important in the eyes of churchwardens and other presenting officers. A 'great belly' not only provided proof positive of sexual immorality but also crystallised a sense of moral outrage. Hostility to bastardy, at least at the level of publicly expressed attitudes, was no new thing among the 'honest householders' of middling rank who served as churchwardens and sidesmen; and such hostility became even more intense in the late sixteenth and early seventeenth centuries. As we have seen, illegitimacy was on the increase in the later part of Elizabeth's reign, while growing problems of poverty and the effects of economic dislocations increased the financial and administrative burden of poor relief. Some detailed presentments and petitions vividly reveal the mixture of moral indignation and financial concern that bastard births evoked in these circumstances. A presentment from Calne in 1601 listed the names of a number of bastard-bearing women and went on: 'These all we most humbly beseech you to see punished, that it may be a terrifying to others to fall in the like vice; we already are overpressed with too many poor bastard children.' More dramatically, a petition from Castle Combe in 1606 (presumably penned by the local minister but also signed by the churchwardens, constables, overseers of the poor, and other inhabitants) complained of a woman's 'filthy act of whoredom...by the which licentious life of hers not only God's wrath may be poured down upon us inhabitants of the town, but also her evil example may so greatly corrupt others that great and extraordinary charge for the maintenance of baseborn children may be imposed upon us'.[72]

Of all forms of sexual immorality, liaisons involving bastardy were the least likely to be passed over by churchwardens. Cross-checking between court records and parish register entries for Wylye, Keevil and other parishes indicates that throughout the period 1570–1640 bastardy cases were almost invariably reported to

[70] Cf. Laslett, *World we have lost further explored*, pp. 163, 328.

[71] For examples, see W.R.O., AS/ABO 3, fols. 83v, 102v; AS/ABO 4, fol. 13; AS/ABO 5, fol. 121v.

[72] W.R.O., D/Pres. 1600–2, Calne, Jan. 1601; QS/GR East. 1606/134.

the ecclesiastical authorities, at least to the extent of naming the woman concerned.[73] However, churchwardens were more circumspect in nominating a father. One reason for this was that, in the society generally, the role of the man was often regarded with greater tolerance. Thus in 1607, when Anthony Starr of Bremhill was accused of fathering a bastard, his nephew made light of the matter, openly admitting that he himself had once been in trouble about 'getting a wench with child'; while in 1629 Joan Cull of Broad Blunsdon, knowing that process was out for the apprehension of a certain Richard Fry on a paternity charge, held up her rake to him when she saw him in the fields and 'did then bid him beware or else he would be taken'.[74] Irrespective of such double standards, there were obvious evidential problems involved in identifying the fathers of bastards, and this inevitably affected the pattern of presentments.

Even the most zealous churchwardens were inclined to specify carefully that a certain man was the 'reputed' father 'as the common fame goeth' or 'as she [the bastard's mother] saith': they were well aware that women, for a variety of reasons, sometimes made false accusations.[75] And a proportion of presentments passed over the question of paternity in complete silence or rehearsed a formula like 'the father whereof we know not'. Such cases of evasion were, however, on the decline in this period. At the visitations of the archdeaconry of North Wiltshire in the 1590s, the fathers of bastards were specified in only about 60 per cent of cases; by the 1620s the proportion had risen to over 80 per cent. The church courts themselves played some part in effecting this change, summoning churchwardens who had neglected to name the reputed father and chivvying them into investigating the circumstances more closely. (Such proceedings were recorded with exceptional care in the archdeaconry of Chichester, but it is plain that the procedure as such was not confined to that area.)[76] But growing concern over poverty and the burden of poor relief was probably an even greater spur towards the identification of the fathers of bastards, so that they could be made to pay

[73] For similar findings, see Wrightson and Levine, *Poverty and piety*, pp. 126–7.
[74] W.R.O., QS/GR Mich. 1607/99; QS/GR Mich. 1629/119.
[75] For the sceptical comments of a contemporary J.P., see W.R.O., QS/GR East. 1638/192.
[76] For examples of formal proceedings to induce churchwardens to specify the father's name, see W.S.R.O., Ep. I/17/21, fols. 87, 93v; Ep. I/17/26, fols. 253, 307v.

maintenance. A number of well-established methods were used to elicit the facts. Pregnant maidservants were often examined and, if necessary, browbeaten by their masters and mistresses until they had confessed the truth.[77] Moreover midwives and 'honest neighbours' commonly interrogated the woman at the very moment of birth, refusing to aid the delivery if she refused to name the father and invoking fears of death, judgement and hell if she was thought to be making a false accusation. Thus in 1616, when Margaret Wheeler of Downton was 'in great pain and travail and almost beyond hope of life', the midwife 'did charge her that as she hoped to have God's favour to deliver her of her pains, that she should truly tell...who was the father...who answered in these words, vizt. I pray God never to deliver me of my child and I pray God let me not live if it be not the child of Thomas Poulden...'.[78] If such methods failed or could not be applied, parish ministers sometimes tried to elicit the required information by refusing to church the woman or to baptise her child – though the latter practice was technically illegal.[79]

The presentments made by churchwardens usually reveal little about the precise circumstances underlying bastardy and other fornication cases and about the social characteristics of the individuals concerned. Moreover the examinations of offenders in court were often very briefly recorded, amounting to little more than a bare statement of denial or confession. For certain periods the records of the Wiltshire jurisdictions do include some very detailed confessions containing a mass of circumstantial detail; but, since particular items of important information were not *consistently* recorded, and since it is in any case impossible to be sure that the minority of better-recorded cases were representative of the general run of prosecutions, there is no truly satisfactory means of analysing this material. The generalisations which follow are best described as semi-quantitative impressions. They are informed by a wide reading of Elizabethan and early Stuart church court records, and are based in particular on sets of well-recorded cases in the bishop of Salisbury's court for the periods 1581–90 (49 cases) and 1615–21 (77 cases),

[77] For examples, see W.R.O., B/ABO 8, 10/7/1617, *Office v. Mr William Small*; AS/ABO 12, 15/12/1617, *Office v. William Legg*.

[78] W.R.O., QS/GR East. 1616/179; cf. QS/GR Hil. 1620/185. Numerous examples could be cited of this practice, which was already well established by the mid-sixteenth century: see Houlbrooke, *Church courts and the people*, p. 77.

[79] W.R.O., AS/ABO 8, fol. 107v; B/ABO 9, 27/9/1619, *Office v. Agnes Coffyn*; D/AB 32, fol. 14v; cf. canon 68 (1604).

cross-checked with the archidiaconal records for the same years.[80] But they are not precise enough to justify tabular presentation.[81] The available information is in any case heavily biased towards prosecutions involving bastardy, for the simple reason that women who were accused of sexual immorality but had not become pregnant were far less likely to make a detailed confession.

Only a small proportion of cases, perhaps one in twenty overall, involved widows. The great majority of the women who found themselves in trouble were spinsters and, predictably enough, few were householders in their own right. Many were in fact domestic servants – perhaps as many as 70 per cent in the 1580s. There were some women from substantial families, but it is plain that overall the social standing of female offenders was fairly low and that some were very poor indeed. The seventeenth-century material indicates that nearly one in five was too poor to pay any court fees, and then and earlier there are in some cases direct references to dire poverty. In 1588, for example, Margaret Phelpes of Wroughton described how she had 'maintained herself by her hard labour', save that she was occasionally relieved by 'the devotion of well disposed people thereabouts'.[82]

The menfolk involved were drawn from a rather wider social spectrum. Unfortunately 'styles' or occupations were specified in only a minority even of the better-recorded cases. Those mentioned in the 1580s were very diverse, including a gentleman, two men who claimed the courtesy title of 'master', two clergymen, a physician, a scrivener, a husbandman, a woodward, an ostler and a shepherd. In the period 1615–21, reference was made to three gentlemen, a poor and ignorant minister, a schoolmaster, two yeomen, eight husbandmen, three tailors, three weavers, a tucker, an awlmaker, a parchmentmaker, one haberdasher, a baker, a cook and a warrener. A significant minority of the accused men, perhaps as many as 40 per cent in the 1580s but rather fewer later, were householders in their own right. On the other hand, servants were also fairly prominent:

[80] These sets of well-recorded cases were obtained by search of W.R.O., B/ABI 13–18, 41–51; B/ABO 8–10; B/DB 8–11; collated with AW/ABO 5, AS/ABO 1b–3, 11–13 and with surviving Wiltshire quarter sessions records. I abstracted all cases in which at least one of the parties made a confession consisting of more than merely a bare admission (with no further information about the circumstances) of incontinence/illicit pregnancy.

[81] Some of this material has been tabulated in Ingram, 'Ecclesiastical justice in Wiltshire', p. 225 (Table 13).

[82] W.R.O., B/DB 10, fol. 21v.

they figured in at least 27 per cent of the better-recorded cases in the bishop of Salisbury's court in the period 1615–21. Unfortunately marital status was not consistently recorded. It is evident, however, that a large majority of the accused men were unmarried, bachelors heavily predominating over widowers. But a sizeable minority, perhaps one in five overall, had a spouse living at the time of the alleged offence.

In what circumstances had these illicit relationships occurred? In a few instances the parties were strangers or only very casually acquainted with each other. Three women tried in the period 1615–21 claimed to have been raped by men totally unknown to them, one while she was in a state of drunken sleep at an alehouse. In 1592 William Yong alias Milles of Chippenham confessed that 'as he travelled on London way betwixt Bath and Chippenham...he happened to fall in company with a certain strange woman who after some little acquaintance with her allured him...unto lewdness'; while in 1619 Richard Foster of Imber confessed intercourse with a certain Anne Slie, 'to whom he remembreth not that he had spoken two words before but thinketh that he had some time danced before in her company'.[83]

Characteristically the couples were well known to each other before they became lovers. The great majority were fellow-parishioners, and a few miles at most separated nearly all the others. In many cases the couple actually lived under the same roof. Throughout the period, relationships between female servants and their masters (or, less commonly, the son, male relative or friend of the householder) and liaisons between fellow-servants were very prominent among sex cases involving single women. It would appear, however, that master/servant relationships became less common as time wore on, perhaps a reflection of the stricter attitudes to bastardy and related offences which developed in the early seventeenth century. Some householders managed to sustain quite lengthy relationships with women (whether servants or not) living under their roof; but permanent concubinage arrangements were very rare and evidently aroused massive local hostility. In 1604 Thomas Hill alias Butcher of Westbury swore that he would 'keep whores in the despite of his neighbours', but is doubtful if this was a realistic proposition. In 1616, when William Vaughan of Stapleford wished to establish an irregular ménage, he was forced to leave his wife, move to the

[83] W.R.O., B/ABO 2, fol. 21; B/ABO 9, 19/7/1619, *Office v. Foster*.

crowded suburb of Fisherton Anger and change his name. Even so the couple were detected and enjoined a series of severe penances for this 'grave sin'.[84]

Many of the liaisons between married men and unmarried women appear to have been opportunistic. In 1582, for example, Richard Blubeane of Salisbury confessed that while his wife was away he tried to have his pleasure of his servant, Frances Sotwell, while she lay in bed with another of his maids. The temptations of even more promiscuous sleeping arrangements were vividly revealed in a case from Bishopstone in 1616, when William Masye confessed trying to have sex with his twenty-year-old maidservant. It emerged that for the past six years he had regularly slept in the same bed as the girl – his wife lying between them – apparently for lack of house-room and furniture.[85] Regrettably there are only a few other indications of the specific circumstances and motives which impelled married men into adultery. It was conventional wisdom that the best safeguard against temptation was a lusty wife: thus a witness in a defamation suit in 1616 opined that an accusation of adultery against a certain William Hacker was 'very unlikely for that...[he] hath many children by his wife'. But such fecundity provided a stumbling-block to Humphrey Cox of Tilshead in 1602, who explained to the servant he was trying to seduce that he could get no satisfaction from his wife because 'her belly is so big I cannot come at her'.[86]

Unmarried women who succumbed to incontinence with married men were impelled by a variety of pressures and motives. Servants in household were in a vulnerable position and were sometimes seduced only after considerable harassment and even the use of force. In 1592 Mary Mountegne of Barford St Martin claimed that she had long resisted her master's solicitations, but 'in the end her said master did beat her and so by foul means...obtained his desire'.[87] Such 'magisterial exploitation' may well account, as Keith Wrightson has suggested, for a sizeable proportion of bastardy cases involving married men.[88] Yet it is plain that some servants and other

[84] W.R.O., QS/GR Trin. 1604/96; AS/ABO 12, 24/2/1616, *Office v. Alice Smith*; *ibid.*, 3/4/1616 and 20/4/1616, *Office v. Vaughan.*

[85] W.R.O., B/DB 8, fol. 137v; AS/ABO 12, 9/3/1616, *Office v. Masye*; cf. AS/ABO 3, fol. 127.

[86] W.R.O., B/DB 31, fol. 118; B/ABO 5, fols. 30, 32.

[87] W.R.O., B/ABO 2, fol. 24v.

[88] Wrightson and Levine, *Poverty and piety*, p. 128; Wrightson, *English society*, p. 84.

women played a willing role in these relationships, demanding if anything only the flimsiest reassurances or paltry gifts. Christian Myle, a Lacock widow, was convinced by Robert Collet's promise that he would marry her if his wife died, while Joan Speering of Donhead St Mary was seduced by her master's more candid if more modest proffer of a pair of gloves.[89] If these women were exploited, it was in the sense that their low social position minimised their marriage chances and condemned them to settle for what they could get. Even more tragic was the case of Elinor Welch, who may simply have been carried away by infatuation. In 1619 she left her father's house in Sodbury, went to lodge at an alehouse, spent several periods of a few days each in debauchery with a certain Richard Blanchard, and eventually accompanied him on an expedition to Biddestone which ended in a murder for which he was condemned to death.[90]

Undoubtedly the single most important reason why unmarried women were prepared to commit fornication was with marriage in mind. Both in the 1580s and in the late 1610s between 30 and 40 per cent of the female offenders in the better-recorded cases before the bishop of Salisbury's court claimed some kind of promise or expectation of marriage; and the proportion rises even higher if cases involving married men are excluded. Admittedly these pleas need to be treated with some caution. They were legally purposeful *allegations*, some of them probably false, representing a last-ditch attempt to induce the man to agree to marriage or designed to secure lenient treatment from the courts.[91] Moreover some of the alleged promises were (if they had been made at all) so flimsy as scarcely to justify the risk of an illicit pregnancy. Thus in 1590 Elizabeth Bedford foolishly agreed to spend the night at a Salisbury inn with an itinerant yarn-buyer who 'having before that time promised her marriage she was the more easily persuaded thereunto'; in 1582 Joan Grindal of Edington was prepared to sleep with Nicholas Harris merely 'in hope of marriage'; while Cicily Tilton of Pewsey ruefully admitted in 1589 that she had been seduced by 'vain promises of marriage'.[92] But if some of the women were disingenuous or ought to have known better than to take limp promises at face value, others found

[89] W.R.O., B/ABO 8, 28/9/1616, *Office v. Myle*; B/ABI 41, fol. 241.
[90] W.R.O., B/ABO 9, 26/2/1620, *Office v. Welch*.
[91] Some of these allegations were strongly denied by the menfolk concerned: for example, see W.R.O., B/DB 10, fol. 24v; B/DB 11, fol. 17v.
[92] W.R.O., B/ABI 18, fol. 67; B/DB 8, fol. 143; B/DB 11, fol. 2v.

themselves in the role of bastard-bearer rather than pregnant bride simply through ill luck or, at most, misjudgement. Some of the defendants were able to describe all the usual stages of courtship, sometimes involving the consultation of 'friends' and the exchange of tokens and pledges, or even to claim that all the wedding preparations had been made and the banns called before the man jilted them.[93] A few women had had their hopes shattered by external circumstances: Joan Buckland pathetically affirmed in 1588 that Robert Killinbeck 'had made her promise of marriage and would surely have performed the same had not the Almighty taken him to His mercy'; Elizabeth Dolman's lover had been pressed for a soldier; Thomas Sharp and Agnes Deacon of Pewsey claimed in 1589 that they were 'kept back from solemnisation...by the parishioners for that they were poor people' and so 'fell together in lewdness of life' – though the force of this plea was somewhat marred by Agnes's confession that she had borne two bastards previously.[94]

Agnes Deacon was among a substantial minority of female defendants – as many as 15–20 per cent in the 1580s, but rather fewer by the later years of James I – who were accused of, and sometimes confessed to, having had sexual relations with more than one man. Extreme cases included Joan Burton of Netherhampton in 1615, who quieted her partner's fears of an unwanted pregnancy with the assurance that she had recently had intercourse with an Ugford man and with 'two at the Green Dragon' without ill-effects, and Alice Dashe of Hilmarton in 1617, who had borne three bastards and was said to be a common harlot.[95] An even more inveterate bastard-bearer was Edith Brethers of Tidworth, who in the course of the 1580s bore three illegitimate children each begotten by a different man. Her activities have not been traced through the 1590s, but in 1603 she or a namesake of similar habits appeared from Fonthill Giffard, on the other side of the county, and confessed giving birth

93 For examples, see W.R.O., B/ABO 8, 30/9/1616, *Office v. Joan Combes*; *ibid.*, 20/3/1617, *Office v. Elinor Bugden*; AS/ABO 12, 7/12/1616, *Office v. Alice Huffe*.

94 W.R.O., B/ABI 17, fol. 72v; AW/ABO 2, 10/10/1606, *Office v. Dolman*; B/DB 11, fols. 2v–3. For similar cases of 'frustrated marriage', see Wrightson, *English society*, pp. 84–5; Ingram, 'Reform of popular culture?', p. 151.

95 W.R.O., B/ABO 7, 7/6/1615, *Office v. John Hibbert*; B/ABO 8, 25/7/1617, *Office v. Robert Stowte*; B/ABO 9, 14/10/1619, *Office v. Dashe*.

to two bastards by different men in the past three years.[96] Whether such women should be seen, as Peter Laslett has suggested, as members of a distinctive 'bastardy prone sub-society' is a question far too complex to pursue here. But the willingness of some of them to appear in court and submit to penance suggests that they were not necessarily total nonconformists.[97]

A smaller proportion of the men (well under 10 per cent) were accused of multiple sexual contacts, but it would be unsafe to conclude that they were actually less promiscuous. More probably the disparity reflected the evidential and social biases which tended to shield men from detection. Those who *were* accused of having illicit sex with more than one woman included youthful sowers of wild oats, householders who were over-susceptible to the attractions of their female servants, and a few notorious lechers like Thomas Whitehead of Marlborough, presented in 1616 for being 'famously reported to be a filthy person with many women and maids having a wife of his own'.[98]

Parish studies by and large corroborate these impressions derived from examinations, and offer additional insights, especially into the social standing of accused persons. In Keevil in the period 1591–1630 there were 44 alleged liaisons involving single women or widows, in Wylye 23: a combined total of 67.[99] ('Liaison' denotes a relationship, whether fleeting or prolonged, between a given couple; certain individuals were involved in more than one liaison, while some liaisons gave rise to repeated prosecutions and, in certain cases, produced multiple bastard births.) In a few instances one partner was of Keevil or Wylye while the other dwelt elsewhere, but mostly the couples were fellow-parishioners at the time of the alleged offence. The overall figures, considered in relation to the total population of these parishes, are consistent with the assumption that sexual immorality was by no means rampant in this period;[100] but of

96 W.R.O., AS/ABO 1b, fol. 27v; AS/ABO 2, fols. 16v, 68v; AS/ABO 3, fols. 77v, 99, 105; AS/ABO 8, fol. 91v; B/*Detecta* Bk 6, fol. 7v.

97 The concept of the 'bastardy prone sub-society' is extensively discussed in Laslett *et al.* (eds)., *Bastardy and its comparative history*, ch. 8 and *passim*.

98 W.R.O., B/ABO 8, 23/10/1616, *Office v. Whitehead.*

99 For completeness' sake, the total includes a few cases from the period 1631–40 involving individuals who had already been in trouble for sexual immorality in earlier decades.

100 On the population of Keevil and Wylye and other aspects of the social context, see above, pp. 78–82.

course they also reflect the bias of prosecutions towards the most notorious and/or most visible offences. As was noted earlier, at least two-thirds of these liaisons led to bastardy or illicit pregnancy.

Of the males involved, at least 19 (approaching 30 per cent) were married, a rather higher proportion than that suggested by the analysis of examinations. There were in addition 9 widowers. Regrettably the ages of the accused men can be ascertained in only a minority of cases: the available information indicates a fairly wide range, from around the normal age of marriage through and beyond middle life. Thus of 9 single men, 7 were in their twenties, one in his thirties, the last aged 44; two widowers were respectively in the thirties and the fifties; while of 8 married men, one was in his late twenties, 4 were in the thirties, and 3 were around 50 years old. Two other men were described as being very old, but their exact ages are not known.[101]

The Keevil men came from a broad social spectrum. At one extreme were five men of prominent status, including a minor gentleman and two of the wealthiest yeomen in the parish.[102] At the other were half a dozen transient residents, some of whom were certainly servants. But the majority of the accused men were middling and middling-to-poor husbandmen and husbandmen–craftsmen, including a miller, a blacksmith, a carpenter and several weavers. The social profile of the Wylye men was much the same; the most prominent among them was John Potticarie, a gentleman-clothier who figured largely in parish life in the first two decades of the seventeenth century and was accused (but not convicted) of begetting a bastard on one of his maidservants in 1611.[103]

The men from these two villages were again typical of the general run of male sexual offenders in the church courts, in that only a small proportion were accused of incontinence with more than one woman. The most notable cases of promiscuity occurred in Keevil in

101 Other records indicate advanced ages for both of these men, but in each case there may have been an element of exaggeration. Robert Jones of Keevil, in trouble in 1595, claimed to be 66 years old in a court of requests case in 1589: P.R.O., REQ 2/117/46, m. 4. Humphrey Furnell of Wylye, in trouble in 1619, was described as 80 years old in a parish register entry of 1620: Hadow (ed.), *Wylye registers*, p. 4.

102 Included in this category is Robert Jones, described as a weaver in a lawsuit of 1589 but a scion of the powerful Jones family; in 1598 he was represented in court by his kinsman William Jones, gentleman: W.R.O., B/ABO 4, fol. 9.

103 W.R.O., B/ABO 6, fol. 124; cf. *ibid.*, fols. 86, 98v. Potticarie's career is discussed above, pp. 79, 114.

the 1590s. William Cundett, a married husbandman of reasonable substance, confessed begetting a bastard on a poor woman in 1593; four years later he was in trouble for a similar offence. In 1597 John Flower, a wealthy yeoman, was accused of begetting bastards on two of his maidservants; he admitted that he had pursued an adulterous liaison with one of them during his wife's lifetime and had had sexual relations with the other only two or three weeks after his spouse's death. He did show some contrition, however, weeping in court as he related these events.[104]

Rather more common than notorious promiscuity among these men was a record of at least some involvement in other forms of disorderly activity. John Potticarie of Wylye, for example, was repeatedly prosecuted for unlicensed aleselling and for allowing ill rule and unlawful games; John Vynce (or Vennye) of Keevil was prosecuted for drunkenness as well as for fathering a bastard; Humphrey Furnell of Wylye, a married man several times accused of incontinence with a widow, was also brought to court as a common swearer; while James Cratchley of Keevil, who vehemently denied begetting an illegitimate child in 1620, had made himself unpopular with a variety of criminal and semi-criminal activities.[105] It would be wrong, however, to equate the sphere of male involvement in bastardy/fornication with any kind of criminal underworld. The majority of the accused men were *not* notorious for other crimes; conversely, many of the petty criminals of these villages were never brought in question for sexual immorality.

The liaisons under discussion involved forty Keevil women of whom two were widows; the great majority were accused of incontinence with only one man, though there were several cases of promiscuity or multiple bastard-bearing in the 1590s and one in the 1620s. About half the accused women did not belong to resident Keevil families, at least eight being servants. Most of the remaining women came from middling to poor families, and overall were certainly poorer than the accused males. However, four of the accused women were daughters of men who were reasonably sub-

104 W.R.O., AS/ABO 4, fols. 147v, 163v; AS/ABO 5, fols. 130, 185v; *ibid.*, fols. 158v, 169.

105 On Potticarie, see W.R.O., QS/GR Hil. 1608/120; QS/GR Hil. 1610/97; QS/GR Hil. 1611/84; QS/GR Hil. 1613/132; QS/GR Hil. 1614/82; QS/GR Hil. 1617/142. On Vynce, see W.R.O., AS/ABO 9, 17/5/1606, *Office v. Vennice*. On Furnell, see W.R.O., B/ABO 10, Jan. 1621 (exact date crumbled away), *Office v. Furnell*. On Cratchley, see W.R.O., QS/GR East. 1620/231.

stantial though not among the wealthiest inhabitants of the parish. Interestingly, three of these better-off women were relatively young (aged 18, 19 and 20 respectively); the majority of spinsters involved in these bastardy/fornication cases were, predictably in the light of other studies, in the mid- to late twenties or early thirties.[106]

In Wylye, apart from two women who lived in other parishes, sixteen unmarried females were brought in question, several of them repeatedly. The total included two widows of poor to middling status. Two of the single women, on the other hand, were daughters of wealthy parishioners. Of these Susan Kent, whose objections to the puritan ministrations of a newly arrived rector were discussed in Chapter 3, plausibly claimed that a husbandman–alehousekeeper had 'prevailed not' when he tried to persuade her to incontinence.[107] But Anne Potticarie, daughter of the wealthy Mr John Potticarie, actually bore a bastard whose father was never revealed.[108] Of the remaining single women, five were transient members of the parish – at least two were servants – of whom several were certainly poor; while the women from resident families included the daughter of a labourer and four others of very lowly status.

Two of these poor local women correspond closely to Laslett's stereotype of the 'bastardy prone'.[109] Elizabeth Long or Longenough was the daughter of a poor tiler who was himself accused of incontinence with a widow in 1610 and 1612, and two of her siblings were excommunicates; she produced three illegitimate children between 1611 and 1620. Susan Baker likewise bore three bastards between 1626 and 1634; described as a 'poor maidservant' (*ancilla paupercula*), she may have been related to Christabel Baker or Batter, another poverty-stricken bastard-bearer. The fathers of two of Elizabeth Long's bastards are unknown, while Susan Baker's illegitimates were begotten by three different men. These 'repeaters' may well have served as village whores – Elizabeth Long was described as 'whore' (*meretricula*) in the parish register – providing extramarital sex to a wider range of men than appears in the records. But they may have started out with matrimonial aspirations similar to other girls; and indeed after a fashion these ambitions were eventually

106 Cf. Levine and Wrightson, 'Social context of illegitimacy', pp. 161–2.
107 W.R.O., AS/ABO 12, 19/1/1618, *Office v. Kente*.
108 W.R.O., AS/Excommunications, 1607–33/38; cf. Hadow (ed.), *Wylye registers*, pp. 12, 26, 51.
109 Laslett, *Family life and illicit love*, pp. 147–51.

achieved. Elizabeth Long claimed that she had stoutly defended her chastity against the father of her second bastard, a labourer from another parish currently living as a servant in Wylye, and had only submitted on faithful promise of marriage. At length she was to marry the father of her fourth child, a semi-vagrant labourer from Fisherton Delamere. Susan Baker claimed that the father of her first bastard, a husbandman named Henry Belly, had promised to marry her; and eventually in 1640 she did find a husband (who of course got her with child before the wedding) in the person of James Long, one of Elizabeth Long's illegitimate offspring.[110]

There was only one other case from either Wylye or Keevil in which a promise of marriage was actually alleged in court. It featured a labourer's daughter, nineteen years old, who was probably sincere but hopelessly naive in supposing that the holiday attentions of one of the most prosperous bachelors in Wylye represented an offer of matrimony.[111] However, several of the single men and widowers did, some months or years after they had been called to court, finally marry the women with whom they were accused; in one instance it was said that the couple would have married earlier had they not both stood excommunicate and been forced to delay until they could procure absolution.[112] The most striking of these cases of eventual marriage involved William Prior, a Keevil husbandman or lesser yeoman, and his maidservant Welthian Vaughan. Following the death of his wife in or around 1590, Prior begot three bastard children on this woman, whom he was evidently keeping as his concubine. Such blatant disregard for conventional morality was as rare in Keevil as elsewhere, and plainly aroused immense resentment among the parishioners. The couple were detected to the church

[110] On Long, see W.R.O., B/ABO 8, 28/2/1617, *Office v. Elizabeth Longynowe*; AS/ABO 13, 12/5/1621, *Office v. Elizabeth Long*; AS/ABO 10, 8/12/1610, *Office v. David Longe*; AS/ABO 11, 17/5/1613, *Office v. David Longenow*; AS/Excommunications, 1607–33/13, 41, 95; QS/GR Hil. 1618/190; Hadow (ed.), *Wylye registers*, pp. 16, 19, 27–8. On Baker, see W.R.O., AS/Citations *quorum nomina*, 1630–6/16, 20; AS/Excommunications, 1607–33/27; AS/ABO 14, 27/1/1627, *Office v. Henry Belly*; AS/ABO 15, 25/1/1640, *Office v. James Long and Susan Baker alias Long*; QS/GR Mich. 1626/144; QS/GR Hil. 1627/135; QS/GR Trin. 1627/124; QS/GR Hil. 1635/26; QS/GR Trin. 1635/162; Hadow (ed.), *Wylye registers*, pp. 26, 30–1.

[111] Dorothy Hobs in fact brought a spousals suit against her seducer, but the evidence she adduced was inconsequential: see W.R.O., AS/ABO 14, 18/7/1629, *Office v. Hobs*; B/DB 43, fols. 27v–9, 57v; B/ABI 51, fol. 19v; Hadow (ed.), *Wylye registers*, p. 15 (Hobs), pp. 5, 7, 9, 45–7 (Lock).

[112] W.R.O., QS/GR Mich. 1609/104.

courts at every visitation for several years, with the result that Prior finally married the woman and went on to produce more offspring in lawful wedlock.[113]

Even some of the women involved with married men were eventually to wed their lovers, though whether they had realistic hopes of this at the outset is hard to say. Thus in Wylye, Humphrey Furnell – 'to avoid all future suspicion' – married the widow with whom he had earlier been accused of adultery, when his wife died in 1620. Likewise a wealthy Keevil yeoman, accused of adultery with a widow in 1623, married her the following year after his wife's timely decease.[114] Some of the other women accused with married men, including several servants and two girls of respectable local families, may have been the victims of harassment and exploitation; but there are positive indications of this in only one case, and in that instance the woman seems to have resisted successfully.[115] On the other hand, there is evidence that some of the married men encountered little or no resistance from the women they seduced. These included Joan Velles of Wylye, described on her death in 1627 as a 'poor old almswoman' (*vetula paupercula eleemosynaria*): in 1599 she confessed that she was pregnant by a married tailor called John Clarke, who had come to her house three times by night and 'promised her the making of a petticoat to yield unto his request'. An even more willing partner was Catherine Jones, a non-native Keevil servant, who in 1620 accused a married weaver of being the father of her bastard child: she was said to have drunk to 'all the merry conceits' which had passed between them.[116] Such cases emphasise the importance, in the last resort, of the complexity of individual circumstances and the variety of personal character and

[113] W.R.O., AS/ABO 4, fol. 62 and *passim*; AS/ABO 5, fol. 46v and *passim*; P.R.O., C 85/152/26 (signification of excommunication); W.R.O., 653/1 (Keevil parish register, 1559–1664), numerous entries. Prior's marriage to Welthian Vaughan does not appear in the register but may be inferred from baptismal and burial entries and from a reference to 'Welthian Prior' in W.R.O., QS/GR East. 1611/115.

[114] W.R.O., B/ABO 9, 24/5/1619, *Office v. Furnill*; AS/ABO 13, 18/11/1620 and 2/12/1620, *Office v. Furnill*; Hadow (ed.), *Wylye registers*, pp. 4, 45. W.R.O., B/ABO 11, 11/1/1623, *Office v. John Gasford*; AS/ABO 14, 5/10/1624, *Office v. John Gaysford*; cf. W.R.O., 653/1, 17/9/1623, burial of 'Alice the wife of John Gaisford'.

[115] W.R.O., AS/ABO 12, 19/1/1618, *Office v. Lock* and *Office v. Kente*.

[116] W.R.O., AS/ABO 5, fol. 250; Hadow (ed.), *Wylye registers*, p. 52; W.R.O., QS/GR East. 1620/231.

motivation among the individuals involved in bastardy and fornication prosecutions.

We shall shortly return to Wylye and Keevil in discussing changes over time in the incidence of bastardy/fornication cases. Meanwhile let us briefly review the topographical distribution of prosecutions in Wiltshire as a whole. Ubiquity is the chief impression. The high proportion of cases involving bastardy or illicit pregnancy, which churchwardens almost everywhere were assiduous in reporting, muted topographical variations resulting from differences in the *intensity* of prosecution. There is little sign that the completeness of parochial reporting was much affected by such factors as the strength or otherwise of manorial institutions, the presence or absence of resident gentry, the distribution of catholic recusancy, or even the activities of particularly zealous ministers. Thus in Wylye, the moral reform campaign inaugurated by the puritan John Lee around 1620, which as we have seen did produce an unusual spate of detections for lax religious observance, drunkenness, adultery and other matters, hardly influenced the pattern of bastardy/fornication prosecutions.[117] In large measure, therefore, the parish-by-parish distribution of cases simply reflected the actual incidence of illegitimacy, which in turn was a function of a complex set of variables of which population size and density and the scale of local poverty were probably the most important. Analysis of prosecutions in Wiltshire for the period 1615–29 indicates that cases were most numerous in the populous, partly industrialised and – increasingly during the early seventeenth century – impoverished areas in parts of the Wylye valley and in north-west Wiltshire. Places like Wylye, Keevil, Seend, Bromham, Lacock, Castle Combe and Christian Malford, and the urban centres of Warminster, Bradford, Melksham and Malmesbury with Westport, were generating a substantial proportion of the bastardy/fornication cases around this time. The sheep and corn downlands, in contrast, yielded fewer such detections – not because churchwardens there turned a blind eye to bastardy and related sexual offences, but because there were fewer cases to report.[118]

[117] See above, pp. 120–3, 256–7.
[118] For a somewhat fuller discussion, see Ingram, 'Ecclesiastical justice in Wiltshire', pp. 243–8.

Demographic factors linked with the problem of poverty were likewise important in conditioning changes over time in the volume of court business. Although the chronological pattern is obscured by the deficiencies and complexities of the surviving records of Salisbury diocese, the indications are that in Wiltshire (as in other areas of England) the tally of bastardy/fornication cases increased in the late sixteenth century to reach a ceiling in the reign of James I.[119] In the early 1620s, however, a sharp decline set in. There may have been a partial rally towards the end of the decade, but available records for the 1630s (regrettably fragmentary) suggest that by then the flow of cases was dwindling considerably (Tables 9 and 10).[120] These variations over the period 1570–1640 clearly reflect the shape of the illegitimacy curve. It will be recalled that the incidence of bastardy increased in the later years of Elizabeth's reign and the early years of James I's, a phenomenon which has been plausibly related to social structural changes and to the economic vicissitudes associated with rising population.[121] However, a turnabout rapidly occurred. The increasing scale of poverty in many parishes, and concern over the administrative and financial burdens associated with it, encouraged a more rigorous attitude to bastard-bearing and bastard-begetting, which – probably in combination with spontaneous demographic adjustments – led to a significant fall in the incidence of illegitimacy in the course of the early seventeenth century.[122] Thus Laslett's 98-parish sample shows that in England as a whole the

[119] For example, in the archdeaconry of Leicester there were 60 such cases in 1586 and 111 in the legal year 1615–16: L.M., 1 D 41/13/12, 40. See also Wrightson and Levine, *Poverty and piety*, pp. 125–7.

[120] The bishop of Salisbury's office (disciplinary) act books for the period 1635–40 have perished. Surviving records of the two Wiltshire archdeaconries yield a combined total of only 32 bastardy/fornication cases in 1637 and only 17 in 1639, though, since these totals are based on act books which record only cases in which at least one of the parties made an appearance in court, they may seriously underestimate the numbers of presentments. However, the picture of a decline in the numbers of bastardy/fornication cases from the 1620s to the 1630s is supported by figures of presentments in the Wiltshire parishes subject to the dean of Salisbury (Table 10). Similarly in the archdeaconry of Chichester, there were 28 bastardy/fornication cases in 1625 but only 19 in 1636 (based on search of W.S.R.O., Ep. I/17/21, fols. 29v–120; Ep. I/17/26, fols. 29v–333).

[121] Levine and Wrightson, 'Social context of illegitimacy', pp. 170–2. Note, however, that the model which these authors propose to explain the pattern of illegitimacy in Terling (Essex) may not *in detail* hold for other communities: cf. Ingram, 'Religion, communities and moral discipline', pp. 185, 193 n. 35.

[122] Levine and Wrightson, 'Social context of illegitimacy', pp. 172–4; Wrightson and Levine, *Poverty and piety*, pp. 125–33.

Table 11 *Illegitimacy in nine Wiltshire parishes, 1601–40, as revealed by parish register analysis*

(a) Illegitimacy ratios

	1601–20			1621–40		
	A	B	%	A	B	%
All Cannings	9	317	2.8	3	380	0.8
Broad Chalke	9	275	3.3	4	274	1.5
Bromham	12	666	1.8	12	685	1.8
Idmiston	8	241	3.3	7	218	3.2
Keevil	9	499	1.8	4	502	0.8
Kington St Michael	10	355	2.8	5	379	1.3
Latton	4	123	3.3	4	135	3.0
Steeple Ashton	15	651	2.3	19	682	2.8
Wylye	6	110	5.5	5	220	2.3
Aggregate	*82*	*3237*	*2.5*	*63*	*3475*	*1.8*

A = Illegitimate baptisms B = Total baptisms

(b) Incidence of illegitimate baptisms by decade (aggregate)

1601–10	41	1621–30	34
1611–20	41	1631–40	29

illegitimacy ratio (percentage of baptisms recorded as or inferred to be illegitimate) declined from over 3 per cent around 1600 to below 2 per cent in the 1630s.[123] Analysis of the registers of nine parishes of various sizes scattered over the county of Wiltshire reveals, with local variations, a similar trend. In five of these parishes the illegitimacy ratio was markedly lower in the years 1621–40 than in the first two decades of the seventeenth century, marginally lower or roughly the same in three others, and higher (but not markedly so) in only one; while overall the ratio fell from about 2.5 to 1.8 per cent. Of more direct relevance to the numbers of bastardy/fornication cases likely to come before the courts, there was a corresponding decline in the absolute incidence of registered illegitimacy in these nine parishes, from 41 bastards in the decade 1601–10 to 29 in the years 1631–40 (Table 11).[124]

123 Laslett, *Family life and illicit love*, p. 119; Laslett, 'Introduction: comparing illegitimacy', pp. 14, 18.

124 Figures based on analysis of Hadow (ed.), *Wylye registers*; Moore (ed.), *Broad Chalke registers*; Parry (ed.), *Registers of Allcannings and Etchilhampton*; W.R.O., 518/1 (Bromham); 1098/1 (Idmiston); 653/1 (Keevil); 1187/1–2 (Kington St Michael); 633/11 (Latton); 730/1–2 (Steeple Ashton).

Some of the local variations and aberrations concealed by the broad trend may be illustrated by the histories of Wylye and Keevil; in addition, the experience of these villages offers insights into the significance within the parish context of changes in the incidence of fornication and bastardy cases, and into the relationship between such changes and other social and economic shifts. If events in Wylye are viewed on the time-scale 1591–1640, and when parish register entries of illegitimate births are supplemented by the records of the ecclesiastical courts, it emerges that this village, contrary to the general trend, was experiencing an increase in illegitimacy/fornication cases in the years around 1620. Whereas only seven liaisons involving unmarried women or widows were reported to the bishop or archdeacon in the decades 1591–1610, sixteen were brought to light in the succeeding twenty years. This increase is only partly accounted for by the presence of two multiple bastard-bearers in the village after 1610, and in any case their presence at that time may not have been due merely to chance but could itself have been contingent on economic and social changes. As was seen in Chapter 2, the economy of Wylye was fairly stable in late Elizabethan and early Jacobean times. However by about 1620 population pressure was creating strains and stresses which may well have encouraged the incidence of illegitimacy, for example by disrupting the marriage opportunities of poorer women.[125] Reaction, in the form of harsher attitudes to offenders, came too late to prevent the village from experiencing a cluster of bastard births unprecedented in local living memory – though the problem did eventually recede in the 1630s.[126]

The pattern of development in Keevil, with a clear decline in illegitimacy and related offences in the early seventeenth century, was more typical of Wiltshire as a whole and indeed of England generally. In this parish 32 liaisons were reported in the period 1591–1610 and only 12 in the decades 1611–30, and in important respects the contrast between the two periods was even more marked than these figures suggest. The most blatant cases of immorality, involving promiscuity, concubinage, multiple bastard-bearing, and the seduction of maidservants by their masters, mostly occurred before 1610. The clear impression is that by the 1620s a perceptible shift in the moral climate had occurred, and the indications are that

[125] Cf. Levine and Wrightson, 'Social context of illegitimacy', pp. 170–2.

[126] On the punishment of bastard-bearers in Wylye around this time, see below, pp. 339–40.

of particular importance were alterations in attitude and behaviour in the ranks of wealthier householders – the yeomen, clothiers and substantial husbandmen who socially and economically dominated the parish. Whereas individuals of this type had been strikingly prominent in the more notorious cases of illicit sexuality in the late years of Elizabeth's reign, by the accession of Charles I they were far less in evidence. This change may well have had a religious dimension, though, unlike the situation in Terling in Essex, studied by Wrightson and Levine, there is no evidence of any *major* re-orientation of religious ideas or values.[127] More obvious is a link with economic circumstances. The key period of shift was in the 1610s and 1620s, when the village was experiencing increasing problems of poverty caused by a decline in resources (particularly the decay of the cloth industry) occurring at a time when the population was swollen by immigration and natural increase. In earlier chapters we have seen some of the adjustments which these conditions stimulated. The wealthier inhabitants took steps to close the village to newcomers and clamped down on the granting of subtenancies and the erection of cottages, while efforts were made to regulate marriage entry by stepping up prosecutions for bridal pregnancy and clandestine marriage. A stricter, more intolerant attitude to bastard-bearing and related offences was a logical concomitant of these developments.

The church courts' pursuit of unmarried mothers and other fornicators was thus in close, and indeed increasing, accord with the attitudes of 'honest householders' in the parishes, and meshed tightly with local interests and concerns. But how far prosecutions directly affected the level of illicit sexuality among unmarried women and their potential partners is another, more complex question, to which no certain answer can be given. The kinds of adjustment in attitude and behaviour with which we are concerned were not, of course, necessarily conditioned by fear of punishment. Even if it is assumed that legal deterrence did play some part in moulding behaviour, there is a further complication in assessing the role of the church courts, in that some cases of illegitimacy were handled by the justices of the peace with power to impose corporal penalties – though, as will be seen in Chapter 11, for most of the period the secular punishment of bastard-bearers was probably too sporadic to

[127] The comparison between Keevil and Terling is elaborated in Ingram, 'Religion, communities and moral discipline', *passim*.

have had much deterrent effect. Yet another complication is that many individuals detected to the church courts for fornication failed to appear, often because they had fled or simply moved away from the parish where the offence occurred; usually they were excommunicated, but suffered no other immediate penalty. Even in the case of people who *were* directly amenable to discipline, the impact of ecclesiastical justice is not easy to assess. According to their lights the judges certainly dealt with them strictly. In court the bulk of accused men denied the charges against them; female denials were naturally less common since many of the women had been incriminated by illicit pregnancies. But however much they protested their innocence, it was very rare for accused individuals to be summarily dismissed: the few who secured this favour were usually able to show that the charge against them was wholly spurious, or had come to court armed with certificates of innocence signed by their ministers and fellow-parishioners. Most defendants who denied the charges were ordered to undergo compurgation, usually with from four to seven 'hands' – a moderately stiff test of local credit-worthiness. People who failed in the purgation and defendants who had confessed their guilt were normally ordered to perform public penance in church on at least one occasion, sometimes two or more; some offenders were even sentenced to do penance in the market-place of a neighbouring town. Certainly among middling householders, who so valued their reputation and standing among their neighbours, such penalties could well have had a real deterrent effect.[128]

But the most important way in which the church courts contributed to changing attitudes was perhaps not in their impact on individual offenders, but more broadly in articulating ideals and over time gradually inculcating stricter standards of sexual morality. In visitation after visitation, year after year, generation after generation, the ecclesiastical authorities called for the detection of bastard-bearers and other fornicators; month after month they processed the resulting presentments, examining suspects, organising compurgation proceedings, awarding penances, excommunicating defaulters. The process had been going on for centuries, and it is hardly surprising that even the humblest servant-girls internalised the conviction that sex without marriage in view was reprehensible: in court they abjectly accused themselves and their partners of

[128] For further discussion, see below, pp. 334–40.

'wickedness', 'lewdness of life' and 'filthy lust'.[129] Irrespective of their direct deterrent impact, the church courts were clearly important in creating and maintaining the moral frame of reference in which the kind of shift towards stricter attitudes discernible in the early seventeenth century could occur.

[129] W.R.O., B/DB 11, fols. 1, 2v–3, 36.

9. *Aiding and abetting sexual offences*

In theory the church courts punished not only actual sexual offenders but also 'bawds, harbourers or receivers of such persons' – in other words, anyone who aided and abetted sexual immorality.[1] But the moral issues involved in such cases were often complex, the detection of offenders frequently difficult; and many forms of 'bawdry' led to only occasional prosecutions. Local communities were chiefly concerned about the sheltering of pregnant women (especially 'strangers' from other parishes) lest they became a burden on the poor rates, and it was cases of this type that furnished the majority of detections. Overall, prosecutions for aiding and abetting were never very numerous throughout the period, but they did occur in appreciable numbers in late Elizabethan and Jacobean times; they declined as the incidence of bastardy diminished in the two decades preceding the civil war.

In contemporary usage, a 'bawd' was an individual of either sex who procured or pandered to immorality. One serious form of bawdry which occasionally came before the courts was when a man was bribed to marry a woman who was with child by a third party. Most of these rigged marriages were engineered by gentlemen or substantial yeomen who, having pursued liaisons with women of lower status than themselves, were wholly unwilling to marry them when they became pregnant and also did not want their own reputations besmirched by bastardy proceedings. They were sometimes willing to pay handsomely to secure the necessary substitute. Thus in 1603 Alice Graie of Malmesbury recounted how Mr Richard St John, after getting her with child, had induced a certain Francis Smith to marry her by promising to provide the couple with diet for three years; while in 1616 Anthony Looker of Chisledon confessed

[1] *Articles to be enquired of within the diocese of Sarisbury, in the first visitation of...Martin* [*Fotherby*] (1619), sig. B4. Most other sets of visitation articles included similar queries.

that Mr John Pleydall of Shrivenham in Berkshire had given him £35 to marry a woman made pregnant by Pleydall's son.[2] It can only be conjectured how many cases of this sort went undetected. When informed that something was amiss, the church courts were certainly assiduous in trying to elicit the truth, citing everyone who had a hand in the affair and imposing penances on all the guilty parties.

Marriages rigged primarily for the benefit of the female were decidedly uncommon. Parents or relatives did sometimes try to procure a husband for a woman of good standing who had had the misfortune to become pregnant out of wedlock, but the option was not an attractive one since the men available for such service were usually of impossibly low status; in any case, the predicament itself was relatively unusual among women of substance. Thus cases of this nature came before the courts only very rarely. In 1628 a Ramsbury man, evidently almost a pauper, confessed that a woman had offered him twenty pounds and 'some other benefit in diet and apparel' to induce him to marry her daughter. Probably there were special circumstances which impelled this desperate attempt to procure a marriage at all costs: the girl had refused to name the father of her illegitimate child, and it may well be that the secret was an exceptionally shameful one.[3]

Another form of bawdry occurred when a husband agreed to tolerate and conceal his wife's adultery. Straightforward complaisance was probably uncommon, but there was slightly more scope for court action in the deals which injured husbands were sometimes willing to strike with adulterers to bring affairs to a private conclusion. As was seen in Chapter 8, however, it was probably widely accepted locally that husbands should be given every opportunity to settle their own matrimonial troubles in the way they thought best, and local officers were reluctant to bring cases of female adultery to court unless the affair had become a matter of public scandal. Hence prosecutions for the concealment of adultery were rare, and those that occurred tended to involve especially blatant circumstances. In 1609 it was revealed that Thomas Alexander of Upavon had found a certain Bartholomew Browne in the very act of adultery with his wife, who to make matters worse

[2] W.R.O., B/ABO 5, 16/2/1603, *Office v. Graie*; B/ABO 8, 25/9/1616, *Office v. Anthony Looker*; *ibid.*, 7/8/1617, *Office v. Pleodall*; *ibid.*, 15/9/1617, *Office v. Humfries*; *ibid.*, 23/9/1617, *Office v. Margaret Looker*.

[3] W.R.O., D/AB 31, fol. 65. For a rather different case, see B/DB 9, fol. 177.

happened to be the daughter of Browne's own spouse. Alexander had assaulted Browne, cut his leg, and locked him in the house; but 'farmer Pincknie' had come by and 'used means to make them friends', persuading Alexander to accept twenty pounds in composition for the adultery. In a sense this settlement foreshadowed the common law remedy of an action for criminal conversation, whereby a man could recover damages against his wife's lover (the leading cases in the emergence of this action occurred around 1619). But the archdeacon of Salisbury's court viewed it as a case of bawdry aggravated by extortion, and Alexander was put to penance.[4]

Keeping a house of bawdry was properly a common law offence, and in any case organised prostitution was probably rare outside the metropolis and a few other major urban centres.[5] Nevertheless cases which certainly or probably involved brothel-keeping did occasionally come before the local church courts, either in the form of condonation of adultery prosecutions or in some other guise. Thus in 1581 Robert Whittocke of North Bradley was presented for 'that he hath harboured and received harlots into his house and otherwise maintained suspected persons and such as have suspiciously frequented unto his wife'.[6] The existence of a 'whorehouse' was explicitly presented at Westbury in 1630; the matter was partly within the church courts' jurisdiction in that the brothel-keeper was accused of lying with the two whores himself. In 1637 Elizabeth Fenne of Tisbury was detected for keeping ill rule in her house on Easter day, and the presentment added that the place was suspected to be a house of bawdry; but Fenne denied this, as did two people prosecuted for being there.[7]

Occasionally parents were prosecuted for acting as bawds to their own children, by deliberately allowing them to fornicate under the parental roof. They usually answered indignantly that they were merely allowing honest courtship; and clearly, given the nature of popular courting customs, the church could not hope to enforce a strict line in this matter.[8] Such presentments as occurred were the

[4] W.R.O., AS/ABO 10, 6/5/1609, *Office v. Browne*; *ibid.*, 17/6/1609, *Office v. Alexander*. On the emergence of the action of criminal conversation, see J. H. Baker, *An introduction to English legal history*, 2nd edn (1979), pp. 382–3.

[5] Cf. Stone, *Family, sex and marriage*, pp. 615–19; Quaife, *Wanton wenches and wayward wives*, pp. 146–52.

[6] W.R.O., AS/ABO 1b, fol. 27.

[7] W.R.O., Precentor/Pres. 1614–40, Westbury, 14/6/1630; AS/ABO 15, 20/5/1637, *Office v. Fenne, Easton and Ball*.

[8] See above, pp. 225–7.

result of excessive zeal or misunderstanding on the part of individual churchwardens or ministers, exceptionally blatant circumstances or the local unpopularity of the individuals concerned. At Ashton Keynes in 1610, William Gilford heard the sound of a door opening while he was in bed, and on going into his stepdaughter's chamber found her in the arms of a certain Thomas Simons. At first he was angry, but Simons's 'great oaths and protestations' that the couple were contracted and intended to marry induced Gilford to 'permit them to lie together until the next morning'. But this explicit collusion with premarital sex seems to have excited considerable scandal locally, and Gilford was presented to the church courts and ordered to perform public penance. In a case from Keevil in 1606, Anthony Hooper and Thomas Harold, respectively a weaver and a labourer, were charged with acting as bawds to Anthony's daughter Agnes and a certain Philip Harvord; they denied the offence as such, but admitted that the justices of the peace had taken steps to stop the couple keeping company together. Whatever other considerations may have impelled the churchwardens to report this matter, there was probably local ill feeling against Harvord because he was an incomer of very dubious standing: he had recently come from Rugby as an indebted wooljobber, renting a piece of land and part of Harold's cottage in Keevil.[9]

Most aiding and abetting charges boiled down to giving unlawful assistance in cases of bastardy and illicit pregnancy, but not all forms of assistance were equally liable to prosecution. Presentments for nursing illegitimate children without revealing the parents were rare, probably because such behaviour was itself uncommon.[10] Also rare were charges that people had shielded the *fathers* of bastards or allowed them to escape without punishment; male sexual offenders, and those who assisted them, enjoyed the benefit of the doubt.[11] Slightly more common were prosecutions for helping to 'convey' away pregnant women and for allowing daughters or servants to depart without punishment when they were discovered to be with child; but, given that it was evidently stock practice for masters to

[9] W.R.O., AW/ABO 4, 22/5/1610, *Office v. William Gilford alias Willis and Elizabeth Willis alias Gilford*; B/ABO 6, fol. 4v; QS/GR Trin. 1606/42–3, 112.

[10] For examples, see W.R.O., AS/ABO 1a, fol. 17v; B/DB 9, fol. 146; AS/ABO 2, fol. 77v.

[11] For example, see W.R.O., AW/ABO 5, 29/1/1622, *Office v. Simon Parsons, senior*.

turn off servants in this condition as soon as possible,[12] it is obvious that many offences of this nature must have gone unpresented. The fact is that most local officers were only too glad when potential bastard-bearers disappeared from the parish; when cases *were* reported to the courts, it was sometimes because the householder himself was suspected of getting the woman into trouble.[13]

What aroused most parochial concern, and accounted for the great majority of prosecutions, was 'harbouring' pregnant women, especially females from other parishes: that is, receiving them, giving them shelter until they had given birth and (in some cases) eventually allowing them to depart unpunished or without naming the father of the child. Presentments often made clear that women were harboured 'to the dislike of the neighbours', and the use of terms like 'harlot' and 'whore' indicates that such hostility involved an element of moral condemnation.[14] But the basic source of parochial concern was the fear that the bastard child, and perhaps the mother as well, would burden the poor rates. Thus a certain John Pike was presented from Little Bedwyn in 1610 'for harbouring a stranger in his house that came to him from Gloucester great with child...We desire that the said Pike and the woman may be cited to court that the father of the child may be known and the parish discharged.'[15]

Underlying these harbouring cases was a great deal of human misery, the result of a variety of social pressures which often forced unmarried pregnant women to leave the place where they had been got with child and to take to the roads. Pregnant servant-girls were in an especially vulnerable position; often dismissed by their masters, they had to try to return to their homes or find some other place of shelter for their delivery. Women made pregnant in their native parish were generally in a more favourable situation, and were often able to give birth in their parents' house or otherwise among friends. But some were turned out by scandalised parents and either left to fend for themselves or hurried away to some place of concealment. Thus around 1620, when Edward Scutt of Warminster heard that his

[12] For indications of this practice, see W.R.O., B/DB 8, fol. 163; AS/ABO 3, fol. 127v; AW/ABO 1, fol. 72v; AW/ABO 5, 20/6/1620, *Office v. John Clarke*.

[13] For examples, see W.R.O., B/DB 8, fol. 94v; AW/ABO 6, 15/3/1626, *Office v. Henry Haman*; AS/ABO 12, 15/12/1617, *Office v. William Legg*.

[14] For examples, see W.R.O., AS/ABO 1b, fol. 26v; AS/ABO 2, fols. 72v, 95 (reference to '*meretricula*', i.e. 'whore'); AW/ABO 1, fol. 112; B/ABO 5, fol. 45v.

[15] W.R.O., D/Pres. 1610 (unnumbered file). See also B/ABO 5, fol. 31v.

stepdaughter was with child, he was 'greatly displeased and discontented...that his house might be abused and scandalised thereby', asserting that 'if she groan in my house I will sell all that I have and get out of the country'. Less harshly, a Longbridge Deverill alehousekeeper in 1585 was 'loth to leave his daughter an open gaze to the view of the world' and took steps to have her harboured elsewhere.[16] Some women, especially those of better status, moved on their own initiative, from a personal sense of shame. Thus Elinor Bugden, a widow of means, told in 1617 how 'finding herself...to be with child, intending to hide her folly and shame, she withdrew herself from her dwelling house'.[17] And, of course, some pregnant women decamped simply to avoid punishment, especially when they had been got with child in parishes where attitudes to bastardy were especially strict and there was a danger that they might be whipped.[18]

Once on the road, with or without an escort, pregnant women could cover considerable distances. In the harbouring cases recorded in the act books of the three main Wiltshire jurisdictions in the period 1615–29, the place where the woman had come from was specified in 39 instances. Nineteen women had come from places outside Wiltshire, mostly from adjacent counties but including two from London, one from 'beyond Somerset' and one from Montgomeryshire. One of them was ultimately destined for London, another for Taunton. Sixteen women had moved within Wiltshire, the distances varying from the neighbouring parish to the other end of the county, with many gradations in between. Only four of the women were harboured in the parish where they had actually been got with child.

It was no easy matter for a pregnant woman to find a place to give birth and someone to 'stand her friend in her misery'; and on her travels she was liable to be constantly 'troubled and molested' by local officers.[19] What sort of people were prepared to provide the necessary aid, and what motivated them to do so? Not surprisingly, harbourers were likely to live in a market town, a victualling centre or some other populous and well-frequented location. As regards social position, the three men accused of harbouring pregnant

[16] P.R.O., STAC 8/296/22, mm. 4, 9; W.R.O., B/DB 9, fol. 130v; cf. B/ABO 12, fol. 8.

[17] W.R.O., B/ABO 8, 20/3/1617, *Office v. Bugden*; cf. *ibid.*, 28/9/1616, *Office v. Christian Myle, widow*.

[18] On the physical punishment of bastard-bearers, see below, pp. 338–40.

[19] W.R.O., QS/GR East. 1620/205; B/DB 11, fol. 10v.

women in Wylye in the period 1591–1630 (there were no such cases in Keevil) were probably fairly typical. William Oliver (1592) and Jeremy Smithe (1599), respectively a husbandman and a tailor by trade, both kept alehouses. Richard Hadling or Wadling (1611) was a weaver of modest substance; more crucially, his spouse was the local midwife.[20]

Analysis of the examinations of defendants reveals something about the motives of harbourers. In Wiltshire in the period 1615–29 more than one in six were prepared to admit that they had sheltered women in return for cash; the real proportion was probably higher, since the ecclesiastical authorities evidently regarded the taking of financial profit as an aggravating circumstance, and culprits were naturally inclined to be reticent on this point. The charges could be quite substantial. Around 1626 Richard Staples of Warminster exacted three pounds for a month's stay, though admittedly he was lodging a gentlewoman; John Grove, a Malmesbury innkeeper, charged 6s. 8d. a week in 1627; while even the price of 3s. 4d. a week charged in 1615 by a Hankerton carrier must have given him something worthwhile for his trouble at a time when a labourer's daily wage was less than a shilling.[21]

A variety of alternative or complementary considerations was revealed in examinations. Some defendants were acting under authorisation, having received inmates at the request or direction of churchwardens, justices of the peace or borough officials;[22] while a few had received from people of high social status offers which in a deferential society could hardly be refused. Thus in 1592 William Oliver of Wylye confessed that, 'about the time that her majesty was in progress in harvest last past', a man brought to his house an unmarried gentlewoman who was shortly after delivered of child;

[20] Oliver: W.R.O., B/ABO 2, fol. 27; H. C. Johnson (ed.), *Wiltshire county records: minutes of proceedings in sessions, 1563 and 1574 to 1592*, Wilts. Archaeol. and Natural History Soc.: Records Branch, 4 (Devizes, 1949), pp. 81, 91. Smithe: W.R.O., AS/ABO 5, fol. 249; QS/GR Hil. 1610/97; Hadow (ed.), *Wylye registers*, p. 14; Kerridge (ed.), *Pembroke surveys*, p. 96. Hadling: W.R.O., B/ABO 6, fols. 86, 98v; QS/GR Trin. 1635/162; Hadow (ed.), *Wylye registers*, pp. 13, 47.

[21] W.R.O., AS/ABO 14, 4/10/1626, *Office v. Staples*; AW/ABO 6, 6/12/1627, *Office v. Grove alias Arnold*; B/ABO 7, 1/2/1615, *Office v. John James*. For wage-rates in Wiltshire around this time, see *H.M.C.*, *Various collections*, vol. 1, pp. 162–9.

[22] For examples, see W.R.O., AS/ABO 3, fol. 110; AS/ABO 12, 29/9/1618, *Office v. Francis Pitney, Thomas Hardin and wife* and *John Bartlett*.

'and as he hath heard tell a gentleman, one of the Paulets, was the father thereof;...[and] he hath heard say that he was of kin unto the lord marquess of Winchester and...was towards her majesty'.[23]

More positively benevolent sentiments were by no means absent. A few defendants claimed to have acted out of mere compassion, and some of these pleas were circumstantial enough to carry conviction. In 1610, for example, Anne Frie of Broad Hinton told how, on finding a 'walking woman...in travail of child in the open street', she took her in 'for womanhood's sake'.[24] In 1624 Richard Curtis of Downton helped a pregnant woman on the familiar neighbourly understanding that the father of the child would 'do him a good turn in exchange'.[25] More important were family sentiments and duties, a typical case being that of Nicholas Gilbert of Shrewton who in 1617 harboured a woman 'only in love to his...brother in law'.[26] In fact, in over a third of harbouring cases in Wiltshire in the period 1615–29 some relationship of kindred or affinity was said to exist between the defendant and the woman he sheltered, or between him and an individual who conveyed her. Most commonly, the harbourer was the woman's father: this was true in nearly one in every three cases in which family ties are known to have existed. For the rest, a wide range of specified and unspecified links of kindred and affinity was mentioned; in a few instances, an extensive kinship network had been mobilised to help. For example, in 1619 Margaret Ven was harboured for a time by her aunt, Marian Bevis, in Salisbury, but the girl's stepfather from Gloucestershire eventually took the matter in hand and arranged for her to go to live with another aunt in London.[27] Such cases illustrate how wider kinship ties, though not of prime importance in the structure of early modern English society, could be invoked in times of family crisis.[28]

Although harbouring cases were more numerous than other types of prosecution for aiding and abetting, it is evident that by no means all offenders were reported to the ecclesiastical authorities. Substantial numbers of women detected for bastard-bearing or illicit pregnancy never appeared in court to answer for their offence, and

[23] W.R.O., B/ABO 2, fol. 27.

[24] W.R.O., AW/ABO 4, 22/5/1610, *Office v. Frie*; cf. AW/ABO 5, 13/10/1618, *Office v. Elizabeth Compton*.

[25] W.R.O., AS/ABO 13, 20/3/1624, *Office v. Curtis*.

[26] W.R.O., B/ABO 8, 11/3/1617, *Office v. Gilbert*.

[27] W.R.O., B/ABO 9, 2/8/1619, *Office v. Bevis*.

[28] On kinship, see above, p. 127.

must have been lurking somewhere under the roofs of relatives or other householders, who, according to the strict letter of the law, should themselves have been detected for sheltering them. If this procedure had been consistently followed, the numbers of prosecutions for harbouring would have been substantially higher than was actually the case. In fact it seems unlikely that the principle implicit in court action, that householders were responsible for the moral conduct of those who lived within their doors, was ever fully recognised. Further, the prime source of parochial concern about harbouring – the fear that the woman and her child would burden the poor rates – could often be dispelled without reference to the church courts. Statutory and manorial regulations against the taking of 'inmates' (lodgers) provided an alternative means of action.[29] In addition, it was possible for parish officials to take bonds from anyone receiving a pregnant woman (or any other incomer, for that matter) to ensure that the parish would be 'saved harmless': that is, to guarantee that the newcomer would not become a charge on parochial relief. To judge by references in the Wiltshire church courts and elsewhere, the use of such bonds was becoming increasingly common in the early seventeenth century.[30] To be sure, some harbourers were reported to the ecclesiastical authorities even after they had given bond; but the likelihood is that in many cases, once such financial safeguards had been entered into, moral concerns alone proved insufficient to ensure presentment to the church courts.

In any case there was often little to be gained by presenting harbourers, save to register a sense of disapproval and to put the culprit to some trouble and expense. The courts usually ordered the individual concerned to produce the woman, but by the time the case was dealt with this was frequently impossible for the simple reason that she had fled. Defaulting or blatant offenders were sometimes ordered to perform penance (usually in one of its milder forms), or to make a payment in money or corn for the benefit of the local

[29] Taking inmates was forbidden by statute 31 Eliz. I c. 8. For an example of a manorial order against the receiving of bastard children from other parishes, see W.R.O., 288/1, court baron (Bulkington), 16 Apr. 11 Jac. I (1613).

[30] For references to the taking of bonds in Wiltshire cases, see W.R.O., B/ABO 9, 2/8/1619, *Office v. Bevis*; B/ABO 11, 25/5/1624, *Office v. William Godsell*; AW/ABO 6, 12/7/1632, *Office v. Thomas Pickering*. See also Philip Styles, 'The evolution of the law of settlement', *Univ. of Birmingham hist. jl*, 9 (1963–4), pp. 35–9.

poor; many were simply dismissed after they had revealed whatever they knew of the circumstances. In fine, even the church courts themselves did not treat harbouring cases very strictly, and in these circumstances consistently zealous presentment by local officers was hardly to be expected.

Ecclesiastical court prosecutions for aiding and abetting are best seen as but one element in a much more extensive network of sanctions directed against sexual offenders, above all against the bastard-bearers who were the bugbear of Elizabethan and early Stuart churchwardens and overseers of the poor. In numerical terms such prosecutions were clearly of subsidiary importance. Whereas actual fornicators and adulterers were cited in their scores or even in their hundreds, the number of prosecutions for harbouring and other forms of condonation could in an average-sized archdeaconry in an ordinary year be counted on the fingers of one or at most two hands. In the archdeaconry of Chichester in 1594, for example, there were four such detections; in the archdeaconry of Leicester in the legal year 1615–16 there were five.[31] In Wiltshire the episcopal visitation of 1585 uncovered only seven cases.[32] In this county prosecutions for aiding and abetting appear to have peaked around the end of Elizabeth's reign: the courts of the bishop of Salisbury and the archdeacons of Salisbury and North Wiltshire handled a combined total of 15 cases in 1602 and 11 in 1603. But as the system of taking bonds became more systematised, and (probably more crucially) as the actual incidence of bastardy declined sharply, the flow of cases gradually diminished. Thus the three main Wiltshire jurisdictions yielded a combined total of 40 cases in the period 1615–19, 35 in the next five years, and only 16 in the quinquennium 1625–9. By the 1630s prosecutions for harbouring pregnant women and for similar matters were, at least in numerical terms, of merely marginal significance to the church courts and to the local communities which furnished them with detections.[33]

[31] In Chichester archdeaconry in 1625 there were to be 3 cases, and in Leicester archdeaconry in 1586 there had been 8. These statistics are based on search of W.S.R.O. Ep. I/17/8, 21; L.M., 1 D 41/13/12, 40.

[32] Based on search of W.R.O., B/*Detecta* Bk 6.

[33] For further detail, see Ingram, 'Ecclesiastical justice in Wiltshire', p. 254 (Table 15).

10. *Sexual slander*

Suits alleging defamation of character, mostly concerning slanders of a sexual nature, formed one of the most prominent classes of litigation handled by the church courts in this period, in Wiltshire as in the rest of England. Such suits were part of a wider development: slander business was booming in the secular courts too, and the rush to take legal action to clear sullied reputations has been called 'a phenomenon of the age'.[1] Yet some previous historians of the church courts have been either puzzled by the abundance of defamation causes or dismissive of them. Brian Woodcock, writing of slander suits in the diocese of Canterbury in the fifteenth century, commented that 'in some cases it is not really clear why the plaintiff should have taken exception to such a degree as to bring a suit'; while Ronald Marchant, though emphasising that the church courts offered a legally more sophisticated remedy for slander than the secular tribunals, implies that many of the cases actually dealt with in the diocese of York in the late sixteenth and early seventeenth centuries were hardly worth the trouble of litigation.[2] But in terms of contemporary mentalities and social structures the phenomenon is, in fact, readily comprehensible. Slander suits in the church courts sprang from a society in which sexual reputation, 'credit' or 'honesty' was of considerable and probably growing practical importance and a major touchstone of respectability. Equally they reflected the small-scale tensions and rivalries characteristic of local communities in this period – tensions which were relieved if not resolved by legal action. Defamation causes were thus part of the very warp and weft of contemporary society. Already fairly popular at the start of this period, they became even more so in the late sixteenth and early seventeenth centuries, and were to flow back into

[1] Marchant, *Church under the law*, p. 61.
[2] Woodcock, *Medieval ecclesiastical courts*, p. 88; Marchant, *Church under the law*, pp. 61, 63, 244.

the courts in considerable numbers when the structure of ecclesiastical justice was revived after the Restoration.

Defamation suits between parties were not the only means available in the church courts to deal with slander, but they were by far the most effective. Sometimes the judges brought disciplinary prosecutions on the basis of presentments from churchwardens. But such cases were fairly rare in most areas in this period; generally they were directed against local busybodies or troublemakers who were molesting many people in a single parish, or more rarely concerned utterances which were not only defamatory but also offensive to religion. Thus John Riman was reported to the archdeacon of North Wiltshire in 1592 for declaring that 'there be but three honest women in the parish of Lea and Cleverton', while in 1603 two Urchfont men were in trouble for reciting

> Ave Maria, full of grace,
> Frye doth lie in Gilbert's place;
> Thy kingdom come, Thy will be done,
> Lie there Frye till Gilbert come.[3]

A recourse open to individual victims of slander was to use the procedure of compurgation – whereby neighbours of the defamed person appeared in court to swear to their belief in his or her innocence – sometimes supplemented or replaced by certificates of good fame and credit signed by 'honest neighbours'.[4] It was not necessary to await a summons from the courts before these procedures could be used: a steady trickle of people made *voluntary* appearances and offered to undergo compurgation to clear their names.[5] But compurgation was not cheap and inevitably placed the defamed person in jeopardy. Punishment was likely if for any reason the attempt to purge proved a failure, while even a successful performance was normally followed by an admonition to avoid cause for suspicion in the future – in other words, the shadow of discredit was not entirely lifted.[6]

A defamation cause reversed the roles, the accused becoming the accuser. In legal theory an action for defamation in the church

[3] W.R.O., AW/*Detecta* Bk, 1586–99, fol. 74; AS/ABO 8, fol. 145.

[4] For example, see W.R.O., AS/ABO 8, fol. 92v; AS/ABO 11, 23/3/1616, *Office v. Bryant*.

[5] For example, see W.R.O., B/ABO 8, 14/6/1617, *Office v. Greene*; B/ABO 8, 10/12/1617, *Office v. Howse*.

[6] Lyndwood, *Provinciale*, p. 347.

courts was a 'mixed' cause with both civil and criminal attributes.[7] In its civil aspects it was a means of gaining satisfaction from the slanderer. The church courts could not award cash damages, but the remedy they offered may have been equally if not more attractive to litigants from small-scale communities: the convicted defamer had to perform a penance which included asking forgiveness of the victim.[8] But the use of public penance signified also that defamation was conceived to be a public offence as well as a private injury; and in this sense the plaintiff in a slander suit assumed a position of moral advantage. The abject fate which awaited the convicted defendant is well illustrated by a case from Devizes in 1566; the court ordered that William Smithe

> shall...at the time of divine service come into the said parish church and there being shall have a white rod of an ell long in his right hand standing under the pulpit converting his face unto the people in the body of the church, being bareheaded, and so standing until divine service be ended shall immediately before the departure of the people then congregated together come to the pew or seat where the said [Helen] Broune shall sit, and kneeling upon his knees shall ask her forgiveness in that he hath slandered her, and also desire the people to forgive him for the offence committed unto them and desire them to take example by him to avoid and eschew the like.[9]

Further attractions of the church's law of defamation were its flexibility and the fact that matters of slander could be entertained under a variety of legal forms. Slandered ministers could sue for 'opprobrious words against the clergy'. (Some cases of this type have already been discussed, and unless they involved sexual matters will not be commented upon further here.)[10] There were also special remedies for verbal violence against laymen or clergy committed in church or churchyard, which could embrace utterances of a slanderous nature.[11] Of more general importance was a remedy against words of 'defamation or reproach'. Grounded in the principle of

[7] Clarke, *Praxis*, p. 160.
[8] R. H. Helmholz, 'Canonical defamation in medieval England', *American jl legal history*, 15 (1971), pp. 266–7.
[9] W.R.O., B/ABI 3, fol. 67.
[10] See above, p. 110.
[11] 5 Edw. VI c. 4. Prosecutions under this statute could be of either the 'mere office' or the 'promoted office' variety; the essence of the offence lay in words of quarrelling or brawling, but in practice such utterances were often defamatory.

maintaining harmony and charity within the Christian community, its scope extended beyond slander strictly defined to include insults or 'words of reproach' presumed to spring from malice.[12] The remedy could only be used, however, within one year of the alleged incident. An alternative not subject to this time limit was to bring an action under a provincial constitution of 1222 which specified that 'we excommunicate all them that for cause of lucre, hatred or favour, or for any other cause put upon any man maliciously any manner of crime by means whereby he is defamed'. The canonist William Lyndwood noted that the word 'crime' was here to be interpreted strictly, and actions under this constitution could not be used as a remedy for defamations imputing a condition (such as illness or bastardy) rather than a crime, or for words of reproach which were not of themselves defamatory. But Lyndwood stressed that in other respects the constitution was to be interpreted broadly: for example, it was not an adequate defence to say that the accusation was true or that the defamed person's reputation was already damaged.[13] Only when made as a formal accusation according to due legal processes could an imputation of crime be excused, an exception which the canons of 1604 reiterated by specifying that defamation suits could not be brought against churchwardens for making presentments.[14]

The most important limitations on the church courts' jurisdiction over slander were not inherent in ecclesiastical law but were imposed by other tribunals. The spiritual courts' competence in this sphere appeared to be safeguarded by a statute of 1286;[15] and indeed up to the end of the middle ages there was no serious challenge from the common law.[16] Thus in the fifteenth century, although sexual defamation cases were already prominent, many suits involved imputations of secular crimes like theft.[17] It was from around 1500 that the

[12] Ayliffe, *Parergon*, p. 212; Conset, *Practice*, pp. 335, 337. See also Marchant, *Church under the law*, pp. 71–4.

[13] Clarke, *Praxis*, pp. 160–5; Lyndwood, *Provinciale*, pp. 345–7. See also Marchant, *Church under the law*, pp. 71–2; Helmholz, 'Canonical defamation', pp. 256–61.

[14] Canon 115.

[15] 13 Edw. I (*Circumspecte agatis*).

[16] Pleas for slanderous words were, however, entertained by many manorial and borough courts, which in effect enjoyed a concurrent jurisdiction with the church courts: for example, see R. H. Hilton, 'Small town society in England before the black death', *Past and present*, no. 105 (Nov. 1984), pp. 71–2.

[17] Helmholz, 'Canonical defamation', pp. 257–8, 260; Woodcock, *Medieval ecclesiastical courts*, p. 88.

common law rapidly encroached on the church courts' slander jurisdiction, offering as a remedy an action on the case which made damage rather than the insult itself the gist of the action and provided for recompense in the form of pecuniary damages.[18] By 1583 it had been established that defamations could be tried in the church courts only if they were distinguished by three 'incidents'. First, they had to concern spiritual matters: that is, offences within the jurisdiction of the church courts, including many sexual offences but excluding slanders of theft and so on. Secondly, they should concern matters 'only' spiritual. Mixed defamations ('thief and whore', etc.) and slanders of crimes over which the spiritual and temporal courts had joint jurisdiction should, according to a strict interpretation of the law, go to the secular courts; on these grounds some commentators even tried to argue that to say that a woman had had a bastard was triable in the temporal courts, since that offence was in certain circumstances punishable by the justices of the peace. Finally, it was re-emphasised that slander suits in the church courts were merely 'for the soul's health': in no circumstances could cash damages be awarded. However, potential litigants were in some respects allowed a degree of leeway: for example, commentators allowed that if a woman was defamed of some spiritual crime such as fornication whereby she lost the chance of a marriage, she could sue either in the ecclesiastical courts for her reputation or in the temporal courts for the damage she had sustained.[19]

Having thus poached on the church courts' preserves in ways which even threatened ecclesiastical jurisdiction over some types of sexual slander, common law judges rapidly became appalled by the flood of defamation suits which they were called upon to hear. Some lawyers viewed the multiplication of actions as the symptom of a social disease, and it was claimed that many suits were merely vexatious.[20] More basically, perhaps, practitioners of the common law (trained in matters of property) were not wholly in tune with the issues raised by the concept of reputation. In any event, from the late sixteenth century the secular courts devised strict rules of law to limit the flow of suits. Action was denied in cases where the victim was

[18] Milsom, *Historical foundations of the common law*, pp. 332–44; Baker, *Introduction to English legal history*, pp. 364–8.

[19] John March, *Actions for slaunder* (1647); William Vaughan, *The spirit of detraction* (1611), pp. 161, 163–4; Ayliffe, *Parergon*, pp. 212–15.

[20] Baker, *Introduction to English legal history*, pp. 368–70; for a typical contemporary expression of these views, see March, *Actions for slaunder*, pp. 2–3.

simply called 'knave', 'villain', 'forsworn rogue', or the like, on the extremely dubious grounds that such terms of abuse were of uncertain meaning and commonly uttered in passion or choler without any real intention of harming a person's reputation.[21] In addition, the courts erected into a principle the traditional axiom that 'words are to be taken in the better sense'. Had this been applied only in cases where the words at issue were genuinely doubtful it would have served a valuable purpose. But to judge by some of the cases in contemporary law reports, alleged slanders came to be examined with the minuteness that was more properly applied to technical legal documents like writs, and the principle came near to developing into the doctrine that words should not be construed as defamatory if a non-defamatory sense could be twisted out of them. Such was the ingenuity employed, thought the legal historian William Holdsworth, that to bring an action for slander at the common law could be as hazardous as entering a lottery.[22]

These factors may have helped to limit common law encroachments on church court slander business, and in particular to preserve ecclesiastical jurisdiction over sexual defamation. The actual nature of common law actions for slander in the late sixteenth and early seventeenth centuries is indicated in Table 12, which analyses cases of defamation dealt with in sample periods at the twice-yearly sessions of pleas held by the justices of the liberty of Ely. (Although this franchise belonged to the bishop of Ely, its jurisdiction was temporal, and the proceedings of the courts were subject to the common and statute law; the cases heard were similar to those in the great common law courts at Westminister, from which the inhabitants of the Isle of Ely were debarred.)[23] Predictably, the cases overwhelmingly concerned slanders which could have made the victim liable to prosecution in the secular courts, accusations of theft being by far the most prominent. Unspecific slanders like 'rogue' and 'knave' were not uncommon in the late sixteenth century but became much rarer in the early seventeenth, presumably as a result of the legal developments already noted. Two striking features

[21] Vaughan, *Spirit of detraction*, pp. 167–8.

[22] W. S. Holdsworth, 'Defamation in the sixteenth and seventeenth centuries', *Law quarterly rev.*, 40 (1924), pp. 405–12; but cf. Baker, *Introduction to English legal history*, pp. 369–70.

[23] Edward Miller, 'The liberty of Ely', in *V.C.H. Cambridgeshire and the Isle of Ely*, vol. 4, pp. 9, 12–13, 20. Figures in Table 12 are based on analysis of C.U.L., Ely D.R., E/1/4/3–E/1/8/1; E/1/9/2–E/2/3/2.

Table 12 *Actions for slander at common law in the liberty of Ely*

	1571–95				1610–39			
No. of sessions for which records survive	38				34			
Slanders alleged	M	HW	F	T	M	HW	F	T
Treason	1	0	0	1	0	0	0	0
Homicide/attempted homicide/infanticide	2	0	0	2	1	1	0	2
Witchcraft	0	0	0	0	0	3	0	3
Rape/attempted rape	1	0	0	1	1	0	0	1
Theft/accessory to theft	26	3	1	30	18	4	4	26
Extortion/fraud/perjury	4	0	0	4	7	1	0	8
Making false record (court official)	1	0	0	1	0	0	0	0
Fathering bastard	0	0	0	0	1	0	0	1
Bankrupt	1	0	0	1	0	0	0	0
Knave/rogue/forsworn man, etc	7	1	0	8	2	0	0	2
Totals	*43*	*4*	*1*	*48*	*30*	*9*	*4*	*43*

M = Male plaintiff.
HW = Husband and wife joint plaintiff.
F = Female plaintiff.
T = Total plaintiffs.

which (as will be seen) contrast with the situation in the church courts were a heavy preponderance of male plaintiffs and the virtual absence of sexual matters apart from occasional slanders of rape. Only a case in which a man was defamed as being 'a runaway rogue...who might have stayed and fathered his bastard before he...went away' involved anything approaching a straightforward sexual slander.[24]

But party and party actions of defamation were not the only means of common law encroachment on ecclesiastical slander jurisdiction. The temporal courts were also developing in the late sixteenth and early seventeenth centuries a *criminal* jurisdiction over slander and libel, on the grounds that these could be seditious when they concerned magistrates or the ecclesiastical hierarchy and a breach of the peace when directed against private persons.[25] The

[24] C.U.L., Ely D.R., E/2/2/6, *Trove v. Jackson.*
[25] Holdsworth, 'Defamation', pp. 305–6.

records of the Wiltshire quarter sessions and of the star chamber reveal that sexual slanders were prominent among these cases of criminal defamation; some of them took the form of the elaborate derisive rhymes and songs which were discussed in Chapter 4. However the total numbers of cases in this period were inconsiderable and did not represent a major challenge to the business of the ecclesiastical courts.[26]

Indeed, despite common law encroachments, suits for defamation flourished in the church courts under Elizabeth and the early Stuarts. Already quite common in the early to mid-sixteenth century,[27] they increased in numbers in most areas after about 1560 to jostle with tithe suits as numerically the most important class of litigation in the decades preceding the civil war. In the consistory court of Chester, suits for defamation increased fourfold over the period 1544–94, while total business only doubled. In the consistory court of the huge diocese of York, slander causes nearly tripled from 60 in the legal year 1571–2 to 170 in 1591–2; in the early seventeenth century the annual number of suits in the consistory fluctuated between about 100 and 150, while substantial numbers of additional cases were by this time being heard in the archbishop's chancery court.[28] Totals from smaller dioceses are naturally more modest but reveal similar trends. In the consistory court of Ely there were 37 defamation causes in the legal year 1615–16, compared with only 8 in 1588–9.[29] In the archdeaconry of Chichester there were 14 causes in 1588, 20 in 1620 and 20 again in 1640.[30] The situation in Wiltshire again conformed broadly to the pattern found in other areas of England. In the Salisbury consistory court in 1566 some 22 Wiltshire defamation suits can be identified, while around 1615 the court was handling between 50 and 60 such suits each year. In the twelvemonth period from March 1640, a total of 51 defamation causes

[26] For examples, see P.R.O., STAC 8/98/20; STAC 8/164/18; STAC 8/172/12; W.R.O., QS/GR East. 1604/124; QS/GR Trin. 1613/120; QS/GR Mich. 1626/104.

[27] Houlbrooke, *Church courts and the people*, pp. 82–3, 87, 276–7.

[28] Christopher Haigh, 'Slander and the church courts in the sixteenth century', *Trans. Lancashire and Cheshire Antiquarian Soc.*, 78 (1975), p. 2; Marchant, *Church under the law*, pp. 62, 68.

[29] Based on analysis of Norfolk and Norwich R.O., ACT 21/24a (stray Ely act book, 1588–90, unfoliated); C.U.L., Ely D.R., D/2/33, fols. 1–151v.

[30] Based on analysis of W.S.R.O., Ep.I/10/16, fols. 104–79v; Ep.I/10/34, fols. 2–131v; Ep.I/10/45, fols. 116v–78.

were begun in the Salisbury consistory, of which 42 came from parishes in Wiltshire.[31]

Some of these defamation suits involved accusations of witchcraft or sorcery, drunkenness, the fact of being a bastard, and abusive 'words of reproach' which were insulting though not strictly defamatory. In 1586, to take a Wiltshire example, the wife of a former mayor of Salisbury was scandalised when a neighbour ranted 'Where is Mistress Stinks, Mistress Fart... Mistress Jakes, Mistress Tosspot and Mistress Drunkensoul?'; while in 1615 a woman sued a man for saying that 'looking forth I did see a candle and lanthorn and did also... see the turd that came from her arse and also her c— etc. [*sic*] and all that ever God made'.[32] Up to the end of the sixteenth century the courts also occasionally heard cases involving opprobrious terms like 'knave' and 'rogue', though these tended to disappear in most areas in the early seventeenth century as a result of common law rulings that such words were actionable in neither the spiritual nor the temporal courts.[33] But in all areas in Elizabeth's reign sexual slanders underlay the great majority of suits, and there are indications that their preponderance increased over time. In Wiltshire in the 1580s and the diocese of York in the 1590s, sexual slanders represented about 85 per cent of cases. In Wiltshire by the second and third decades of the seventeenth century the proportion had risen to about 95 per cent. Comparative data from York are not available for this period, but in the diocese of Ely in the early seventeenth century the proportion of sexual slanders was similarly well over 90 per cent. It was primarily as a defence of sexual reputation that church court defamation causes attracted litigants.[34]

Table 13 analyses the nature of the sexual slanders alleged in samples of cases drawn from Wiltshire, the diocese of York and the diocese of Ely in the late sixteenth and early seventeenth centuries.

[31] Figures for 1566 and 1640–1 based on analysis of W.R.O., B/ABI 3, fols. 31–72v; B/Citations 5/20–280, collated with B/ABI 54. The Salisbury act books for the reign of James I do not normally specify the nature of instance suits; the figures for the incidence of defamation causes around 1615 are estimates based on the collation of act book entries with surviving files of cause papers and with deposition books.

[32] W.R.O., B/DB 9, fol. 170v; B/DB 29, fol. 117.

[33] But cf. Sharpe, *Defamation and sexual slander*, pp. 10, 14.

[34] Figures for Wiltshire are based on analysis of W.R.O., B/DB 8–11, 29–43, collated with surviving files of cause papers and with act books; and for Ely on C.U.L., Ely D.R., K/5–6. Figures for York diocese are calculated from information in Sharpe, *Defamation and sexual slander*, p. 10.

Table 13 *Nature of sexual slanders before the church courts in late Elizabethan and early Stuart England*

	Wiltshire 1580s				York 1590s				Wiltshire 1615–29				Ely early 17th c.			
	Males		Females		Males		Females		Males		Females		Males		Females	
	N	%	N	%	N	%	N	%	N	%	N	%	N	%	N	%
Illicitly has/begets child	5	25	3	6	3	10	3	6	16	29	11	13	10	25	7	11
Adultery/fornication	7	35	13	28	7	23	14	27	19	35	26	30	14	35	20	31
Attempting chastity	0	0	0	0	0	0	0	0	9	16	0	0	4	10	0	0
Immodesty/suspicious circumstances	0	0	0	0	0	0	0	0	3	5	5	6	0	0	0	0
Venereal disease	1	5	1	2	4	13	4	8	1	2	4	5	0	0	1	2
Keeping bawdy house	0	0	0	0	0	0	0	0	1	2	1	1	0	0	1	2
Whoremaster, etc. (males only)	1	5	—	—	13	43	—	—	3	5	—	—	8	20	—	—
Cuckold (males only)	5	25	—	—	3	10	—	—	3	5	—	—	4	10	—	—
Whore/quean, etc. (females only)	—	—	30	64	—	—	30	59	—	—	40	46	—	—	35	55
Bigamy	1	5	0	0	0	0	0	0	0	0	0	0	0	0	0	0
Totals	*20*	*100*	*47*	*100*	*30*	*99*	*51*	*100*	*55*	*99*	*87*	*101*	*40*	*100*	*64*	*101*
Total plaintiffs			*67*				*81*				*142*				*104*	

Too much importance should not be attached to apparent minor differences between the various areas, since some of the totals are small and in any case a degree of random variation is to be expected. Far more striking are the major similarities. Sexual defamation cases were not the prerogative of either sex, but everywhere female plaintiffs outnumbered males: 60–70 per cent of cases were in fact brought by women, a large majority of whom (about 70 per cent) were married. To a far greater extent than the common law, the church courts catered for female victims of slander and for housewives in particular.

Of the male plaintiffs, most had been the victims of fairly specific slanders accusing them of fathering bastards, begetting children illicitly on married women, committing fornication or adultery, being found in highly compromising circumstances, or tempting women to commit sexual sins. Comparatively few cases brought by male plaintiffs involved slanders of venereal disease or derisive accusations of cuckoldry. In Wiltshire such generalities as 'whoremaster' and 'whoremonger' were also uncommon; they were slightly more prominent at Ely and in the diocese of York. Many female plaintiffs had likewise been the victims of specific accusations of bastard-bearing, adultery, and so on, and in some of the samples such cases were in absolute terms more numerous than those involving males. But the most striking feature of cases brought by women was the high proportion which involved very unspecific slanders. With variations from area to area and period to period, some 50–60 per cent of females were suing over utterances which, though often elaborately worded and embroidered with scandalous or derisive detail, really boiled down to such generalities as 'whore', 'jade' and 'quean'. (All these words signified a sexually immoral female, without necessarily implying prostitution.)

The predominance of female plaintiffs, and the high proportion of very unspecific slanders alleged by them, reflect the existence to some degree of a double standard of morality. Women were more sensitive, and probably more subject, to sexual slander for two main reasons. First, fornication and adultery were more seriously regarded in the female than in the male. Secondly, the fact that contemporaries conventionally assigned passive, dependent, home-based roles to women, in contrast to the active, extra-domestic functions of the male, meant that sexual reputation was more central to the female persona. The nature of slanders alleged by men in the common law courts, concerning probity in business dealings, social rank and status, and 'honesty' in its modern sense, were probably a fair reflection of the central issues around which male reputation revolved (Table 12). The pattern of cases in the church courts reflected the fact that for women the central issue was that of 'honesty' in its now obsolete sense of 'chastity' – was she an honest woman or a whore? However, it is clear that the notion of a double standard must not be pressed too far: it was in this period a matter of degree rather than an absolute dichotomy between the ways in which male and female reputations were regarded. Considerable numbers of men were evidently sensitive to sexual slanders, few of which were accusations of cuckoldry (the male counterpart of 'whore' according to the logic of the double standard). As will be seen, one reason for such sensitivity was fear of disciplinary proceedings by the church courts. More fundamentally, it would seem that the traditional moral teaching of the church, which insisted that both sexes were equally culpable in matters of fornication and adultery, had to some extent been absorbed into popular attitudes.[35]

These considerations explain the general ideological context in which sexual slander actions occurred. To penetrate more deeply into the social circumstances which underlay suits requires detailed examination of the evidence produced and cross-referencing where necessary to other kinds of record. The following analysis is based mainly on an intensive scrutiny of about 150 sexual slander cases, all relating to Wiltshire, from the bishop of Salisbury's consistory court in the period 1615–29. These represent about a quarter to a fifth of all the sexual defamation causes commenced in that court in those years: the sample is biased towards the better-documented cases, which are illustrated by deposition evidence. The discussion is supplemented by reference to other late sixteenth- and early seventeenth-century defamation suits; again these derive mainly from Wiltshire, but it is probable that the conclusions which follow are, at least in their main outlines, applicable to other areas of Elizabethan and early Stuart England.[36]

What sort of people were involved in slander cases? Over 80 per cent of suits were between people who lived in the same parish.

[35] For a broader discussion of some of the issues raised in these paragraphs, see Thomas, 'Double standard', *passim*.

[36] These conclusions are congruent with findings from the diocese of York reported in Sharpe, *Defamation and sexual slander*, *passim*.

Moreover, the evidence of depositions, and supplementary information gleaned from other sources, indicate that the litigants were often from the same hamlet or street, or members of the same manor; sometimes they were next-door neighbours. Close proximity was obviously a potent factor in the making of an action for slander.[37] The sex ratio among plaintiffs has already been discussed; as regards defendants, at Salisbury in the period 1615–29 males outnumbered females in a ratio of about 6:4, a rather higher proportion of men than Carol Wiener found in late Elizabethan Hertfordshire, but consistent with her observation that both sexes were well represented.[38] The records rarely contain formal indications of the social status of either plaintiffs or defendants, but the main patterns are none the less clear. Servants were occasionally involved, but the great majority of litigants were householders (in the case of females, this is evident from the predominance of wives over single women among both plaintiffs and defendants). A sprinkling of minor gentry were implicated; some of them were suing social inferiors for slanders which represented the impotent anger of the weak against the strong, as when the wife of a certain John Springford of Sutton Mandeville railed against their landlord in 1624 after he had given them notice to quit.[39] But most sexual defamation suits did not reflect such class tensions; rather they were fought out between people of more or less *equal* status, usually drawn from the middling ranks of yeomen, husbandmen and craftsmen. In sum, slander actions in the church courts were characteristically the product of tensions between neighbours of medium substance living cheek by jowl in the small-scale communities which made up the fabric of early modern English society.

The slanders at issue were uttered in a wide variety of circumstances, which in many cases can be only imperfectly recovered from the surviving evidence. However, there is enough information to identify a number of characteristic situations. A minority of suits involved what may be described as quasi-judicial accusations, virtually formal charges but not exempt from prosecution as slanders

[37] The surviving Salisbury episcopal records often fail to make clear the abode of both parties in a suit; supplementary information on this point has therefore been derived from records of the dean of Salisbury for the same period: W.R.O., D/Citations 8–12; D/Libels 6–9.

[38] Carol Z. Wiener, 'Sex roles and crime in late Elizabethan Hertfordshire', *Jl social history*, 8 (1974–5), pp. 45–7, 57 n. 49.

[39] W.R.O., B/Libels 3/1; for a rather similar case, see B/DB 37, fol. 100.

because they did not actually emanate from churchwardens making presentments in due legal form. Of these the most important were paternity nominations made by unmarried pregnant women, and various complaints and accusations relayed by parishioners to justices of the peace or local officials. Some of these latter were deliberately designed to hurt an enemy; others occurred without much malice aforethought – for example, when individuals heard that they were to be presented to the church courts for some offence or other and angrily responded by naming others whom they reckoned to be equally or more deserving of prosecution. Thus in 1620, when the churchwardens of Charlton confronted John Rymell with a fame of adultery with one Oram's wife, he retorted that 'others should then also be presented as well as he' and went on to accuse a certain John Cooper of incontinence with his maidservant.[40]

More common were slanderous tales and rumours. As was noted in Chapter 4, a feature of early modern English society was endemic gossip about sexual reputation, which served both as an informal means of social control and as an outlet for the prurience and spite of the bored and sexually repressed. Some of the alleged slanders were simply manifestations of this constant tittle-tattle. In 1581, for example, a group of male and female reapers sat at dinner in the fields of Collingbourne Ducis, and amid other conversation Robert Stake reported that 'William Jones...hath been in trouble in the bum court at Marlborough for a widow and a maid and now will marry neither of them'; while at Stanton St Quintin in 1623, Edmund Serjeant concluded his business at a wheelwright's shop with the words: 'I will tell you some news...The Sparrow hath begotten Mag Bird with child...She sits now at Hullavington and will hatch very shortly.'[41] More sinister than such idle gossip was malicious talebearing by local busybodies who clearly took delight in spreading scandal and would go to considerable lengths to nose it out; a perfect example was Cicily Goodwin of Draycot Cerne around 1626, who spied on her neighbours during the night, maliciously alerted cuckolded husbands and circulated spicy tales which show a real talent for vivid detail.[42] Even more insidious were people who deliberately spread slanders to harm others against whom they bore a grudge. Such a one was Mary Bowlter of Wroughton in 1619.

[40] W.R.O., B/DB 36, fols. 97v–8.
[41] W.R.O., B/DB 8, fol. 101; B/DB 39, fol. 101v.
[42] W.R.O., B/DB 41, fols. 24–30v.

Asked how she was by the company at dinner, she replied that 'she was the worse for...James Spackman and his bastards, and that he...had one bastard in Oxford and another in every corner, and that she cared not who did hear her say it'.[43]

In contrast to these covert or calculated accusations, the majority of slanders which led to court action were more or less spontaneous outbursts, usually uttered face to face and in hot blood. Sometimes the victims had done nothing to provoke the attack: thus in 1626 John Hodges of Salisbury, discontented because a man had bound his son apprentice with Thomas Jervis and his wife instead of with him, vented his frustration by abusing the Jervises across the open street.[44] More frequently, such slanderous outbursts occurred in reaction to some real or imagined injury which the defamed person was supposed to have committed against the defamer. Often they were uttered when both parties were chiding and brawling: occasionally, the result of this was that each of the disputants initiated almost simultaneous church court defamation suits against the other, or one of the parties appealed to the ecclesiastical judges while the other resorted to a slander action in the secular courts or complained to a justice of the peace.[45]

Such a background of quarrelling and mutual anger is in certain cases important in explaining why plaintiffs decided to resort to legal action. We shall return to this point later. Meanwhile, a more obvious approach to understanding the motives of suitors is to investigate in what ways and to what extent the slanders at issue entailed harmful social consequences for the victim. One such hazard was the possibility of being prosecuted for the crimes or sins specified by the defamer: the risk, for example, that a woman slandered as an adulteress would be detected as such at the next visitation. Christopher Haigh argues that such concerns were of major importance for suitors, and moreover suggests that the increase in defamation suits in the church courts in the late sixteenth century in part reflected a *growing* fear of disciplinary proceedings against sexual offenders and hence a greater determination to preserve sexual reputation intact. J. A. Sharpe is sceptical of these arguments,

[43] W.R.O., B/DB 34, fols. 93v–4.
[44] W.R.O., B/DB 41, fols. 6v–9v.
[45] For examples of cross-suits, see W.R.O., B/DB 30, fols. 10v, 42v; B/DB 30, fols. 35v, 39v; B/Libels 3/5, 17; B/DB 32, fol. 116v; B/ABI 43, 29/4/1617, *Comin v. Crew*; B/DB 34, fols. 128, 170; B/DB 41, fols. 2–3.

but in fact they are by no means as implausible as he suggests. As earlier chapters have emphasised, both the church courts and the justices of the peace were increasingly active in the pursuit of sexual offenders, and in these circumstances there was a growing hazard that public slanders might lead to prosecution. No doubt this was not the sole or even the main reason for the growing popularity of defamation causes, but it should not be discounted altogether.[46] In any event it can be shown that, at least by the early seventeenth century, many defamation suits were paralleled by disciplinary proceedings for the offence specified in the slander, or were commenced when such proceedings were under serious discussion. If the victim was lucky, bringing a defamation suit served to forestall the danger of prosecution, especially since churchwardens and other parish officers were usually reluctant to report doubtful charges. Otherwise the disciplinary prosecution and the defamation cause might proceed side by side. In 1616, for example, Elizabeth Mattock of Great Cheverell reported to the local officers that she had seen Thomas Barckley committing adultery with the wife of Hugh Hudden, but the churchwardens knew that she had a grudge against Barckley and were unwilling to take action. She threatened, however, that if they did not present the matter she would get them prosecuted for negligence. As a result the presentment went forward – and Barckley began a defamation suit against Mattock. Slander suits were also sometimes employed when initial disciplinary proceedings had gone badly for an accused individual. Henry Stratton of Brinkworth, charged in 1616 with being the father of Jane Barcksby's child, had denied culpability before the bishop's correction court, but the record of proceedings is incomplete and it is probable that he had been unable to find compurgators; his defamation suit was another attempt to clear his name.[47]

Straightforward prosecution for whatever sexual offence was alleged in a slander was the prime but not the only legal danger. Both the spiritual and the temporal courts attached importance to assessing the general character or 'credit' of those under examination, as well as ascertaining the facts specifically pertaining to the alleged offence; and knowledge of character was often of prime

46 Haigh, 'Slander and the church courts', pp. 5–9; Sharpe, *Defamation and sexual slander*, pp. 25–6.

47 W.R.O., B/DB 31, fols. 156v–7; B/DB 31, fols. 175v–81v; B/ABO 8, 11/6/1616, 18/7/1616, *Office v. Stratton*.

importance when disputes and lawsuits were referred to substantial parishioners for arbitration locally. Some plaintiffs in defamation suits were not actually in danger of prosecution for the matter with which they were slandered, but feared that such slanders would lower their credit and hence damage their chances in other court proceedings or arbitration settlements. In 1621, for example, John Bright of Codford St Peter took action against Elizabeth Randall because the latter tried to win advantage in a matter to be settled before a justice by claiming that Bright had 'sought' her some years before; in 1623, John Wilmote of Purton was sued because he incautiously discussed the prospects of a case with two arbitrators and blackened the character of one of the parties; while in 1628 Thomas Huet of Bremhill found himself the defendant in a defamation cause because he allegedly gave false evidence about a woman's character before a tribunal of senior yeomen who had met to arbitrate a lawsuit in which she was involved.[48]

It is not possible to determine exactly in what proportion of cases these legal and quasi-legal hazards were at issue. Parallel proceedings in the church courts (or, in some cases, the quarter sessions) can often be discovered by cross-referencing, but this method obviously breaks down when prosecution was a serious risk but was not actually put into effect. Knowledge of informal arbitration proceedings or out-of-court hearings by justices depends on incidental information in depositions. In view of these limitations on our evidence, it is striking that nearly 30 per cent of the sample of better-recorded cases in Wiltshire in the period 1615–29 can be shown to have been related to actual or seriously projected legal proceedings. Rather more men than women were involved, and virtually all the cases figured slanders of a specific nature – paternity charges or circumstantial accusations of fornication or adultery with named individuals. There was evidently little danger that simply to be called 'whore' or 'whoremaster', or to be vaguely accused of some sexual offence, would bring the victim into serious legal question.

Slanders of immorality could entail other more or less serious social consequences. Apparently the least common of these was an effect on economic relationships. A linkage between sexual 'credit' and probity in business dealings was implied in 1623 by the rector of Barford St Martin, when he testified in favour of his servant, Edward Page, who was implicated by a slander of immorality

[48] W.R.O., B/DB 39, fols. 71v–2; B/DB 39, fols. 111v–12; B/DB 43, fols. 20–1.

though not actually the plaintiff: 'for these seven years, the time of Page's continuance in this deponent's service, this deponent himself hath credited him with his whole estate, and other men with whom he hath negotiated...have commended him for a just dealer in his contracts and of his civil demeanour, without spot of infamy until this foul aspersion cast upon him'.[49] But definite instances of sexual ill-fame affecting employment or commercial dealings are rare (save that it was evidently common for servant-girls who were actually pregnant to be dismissed by their masters). In a case in 1605, a certain Agnes Sharpe claimed that she had been prevented from getting a new place by her former mistress: the latter sent her potential employer a message that 'she did marvel that she would entertain such a one as she...was' and that 'she was a whore' whom she had turned out of her own service 'for her loose and licentious life'. One rather similar case, but relating to a man, occurred in the sample period 1615–29: Asa Scandaver of North Newnton claimed that he had been dismissed from the earl of Hertford's service after three women had defamed him for having sex with a certain Bridget Humphrey.[50]

Another hazard of sexual slander was the disruption of marital relations. As a result of a malicious accusation of adultery at Minety in 1587, 'great strife arose betwixt...Noble and his wife'; and in 1628, when Walter Longe scoffed at William Burges of Semington with the words 'thou art a wittol and canst not pull on a hose of [i.e. over] thy head for the bigness...of thy horns', the result was to breed 'much evil will between the said Burges and his wife even almost to the parting of them one from the other'.[51] Wider family relations were also occasionally affected. In 1616 a witness deposed on behalf of Henry Stratton, who had been accused of fathering a bastard, that 'besides the discredit she thinketh the [accusation]...hath been and is a great grief to himself, his wife and friends [i.e. relatives]'; and in the case of *Knight v. Ambrose* (1616), the defendant had apparently spread rumours that his sister-in-law was committing adultery, to discredit her in the eyes of her mother and so get her disinherited.[52] However, it must be said that such family

[49] W.R.O., B/DB 39, fols. 79v–80.
[50] W.R.O., B/DB 23, fol. 40; B/DB 36, fols. 48v–9.
[51] W.R.O., B/DB 10, fol. 6; B/DB 42, fols. 111, 115v. For similar cases see B/DB 5, fol. 52; B/DB 11, fol. 3v.
[52] W.R.O., B/DB 31, fol. 176v; B/DB 32, fol. 5v.

tensions do not bulk large in defamation causes, a reflection no doubt of the relative weakness of kinship ties in early modern English society. Conversely, there is little evidence that family members in Elizabethan and early Stuart England, unlike those in some Mediterranean societies until the recent past, regarded a slight on the sexual reputation of one as dishonouring to all and formed a united front against the slanderer.[53] Indeed a few defamation causes were actually fought *between* close kin, as in Stapleford in 1581, when a man accused his own mother of being a whore, and at Keevil in 1599, when Moses Jones slandered his brother with adultery.[54]

Yet another hazard for slander victims was a threat to their marriage chances; though again the importance of this danger should not be exaggerated. Contemporary moralists conventionally cited sexual reputation, both of the man and of the woman, as a factor to take into account when choosing a marriage partner. In practice, however, it is unlikely that suspicion or even proof of immorality was in normal circumstances sufficient to blight an individual's marriage chances for life: indeed study of the sexual offenders in Wylye and Keevil reveals instances in which even women who had actually given birth to bastards were subsequently able to marry. Yet there are indications in some of these cases that the women's notoriety had at least had the effect of reducing the range of possible marriage partners. Thus Elizabeth Dalmer of Keevil, the daughter of a reasonably wealthy husbandman, bore a bastard in 1621; she did eventually get married, but not till 1640. Alice Silke, on the other hand, was able to get married only two years after the birth of her illegitimate child in 1621; but her bridegroom was a sexagenarian widower.[55] The Wylye and Keevil men-

[53] Cf. J. K. Campbell, *Honour, family and patronage: a study of institutions and moral values in a Greek mountain community* (Oxford, 1964), pp. 185–203; Abou A. M. Zeid, 'Honour and shame among the Bedouins of Egypt', in J. G. Peristiany (ed.), *Honour and shame: the values of Mediterranean society* (1965), pp. 245–59.

[54] W.R.O., B/DB 8, fols. 120–1; B/DB 16, fol. 171v.

[55] W.R.O., AS/ABO 13, 14/7/1621, *Office v. Dalmer*; cf. W.R.O., 653/1, baptism of Elizabeth Dalmer, 28/2/1602, marriage of George Ruddle and Elizabeth Dalmer, 20/4/1640; AS/ABO 13, 19/4/1621, *Office v. Silke*; cf. W.R.O., 653/1, baptism of John Lucas, 31/10/1563, marriage of John Lucas and Alice Silke, 14/6/1623. See also the case of Mary Clement: AS/ABO 12, 23/3/1616, *Office v. Clement*; cf. W.R.O., 653/1, marriage of James Palmer and Mary Clement, 19/11/1621. In addition see Alan Macfarlane, 'Illegitimacy and illegitimates in English history', in Laslett *et al.* (eds.), *Bastardy and its comparative history*, pp. 75–6.

folk accused of sexual immorality were certainly not thereby debarred from finding mates, and there is no clear indication that they were forced to settle for inferior brides; but it is none the less possible that individual women found them unacceptable on account of their earlier misdeeds. These various observations are consistent with the fact that the effect of sexual slander on the matrimonial prospects of both men and women was regularly, though not frequently, at issue in defamation suits. When Thomas Shermore was accused of fornication with Agnes Archard, two witnesses deposed that 'the speaking of the foresaid words...is a great blot and stain to him in the preferment of his marriage being a bachelor'; while when Susan Scott was told that George Leciter had 'used a woman's company' during his wife's last years, she 'did...think worse of him...than before and thereupon in some sort did withdraw her former liking and good opinion from him as any woman would in the like case...he...being at that time a suitor unto...[her] for marriage'. In another case, Jane Seymour was alleged to have been always 'reputed and taken to be a modest, civil and honest young woman' till Anthony Ryder claimed to have deflowered her, whereupon she was 'like to be put by of a good match which otherwise had proceeded'; while the importance of good reputation for women who lacked wealth was neatly expressed by the rector of Barford St Martin in 1623 when he spoke of a poor girl's 'innocency and credit, the only dowry she hath to work her preferment'.[56] Overall, in the sample period 1615–29, the effects of sexual defamation on the plaintiff's marriage prospects were specifically mentioned in five Wiltshire cases, of which three were brought by females and two by men; but a further five cases were prosecuted by women in circumstances which suggest that this issue was a prominent motive for action.[57]

A more general kind of social disability was the shame and humiliation which sexual slander could involve. Rebecca Atnoke's mother was said to 'fret' and 'grieve' when her daughter was defamed, while Mary Tucker 'took great grief and went her way crying' when her sexual honesty was impeached. In 1602 it was said that because a certain Robert Stone had slandered the wife and daughters of John

[56] W.R.O., B/DB 32, fols. 121–2; B/DB 18, fols. 73–4; B/DB 32, fol. 120v; B/DB 39, fol. 78.

[57] For example, the case of *Plympton v. Maton* (1619) was associated with a matrimonial cause: W.R.O., B/DB 36, fol. 58v; cf. B/ABI 45, fol. 131v.

Nicholas, claiming that William Adlam 'kept them at his command', 'neither she nor her daughters...[could] come in any company but they...[were] laughed and jested at'.[58] The fact that Richard Napier's case books report examples of people who had been seriously disturbed by village gossip is a confirmation of how powerful the feelings of insecurity and rejection induced by defamation could sometimes be.[59]

Defamers were well aware of the hurt they could cause, and often deliberately uttered their slanders in a taunting and challenging way to humiliate the victim as much as possible. Thomas Willier, for example, provoked Thomas Shermore with the challenge: '"Thou occupiedst Nassy Archard, and I will maintain it." And showing of some money said, "Gage it if thou durst".' Similarly John Blathat, accusing Oliver Stoneax of having caught the pox from a 'Winchester goose', demanded 'that the said Oliver should show unto him...his prick and he...would show him...his hand'; the bystanders picked up the challenge and urged that Stoneax 'should be searched to see whether he had been burnt or no'.[60] In some cases slanders were expressed so powerfully and so widely disseminated that they stimulated considerable local interest, leading to rigorous inquiries into the substance of the slander and to side-taking by neighbours and friends. Thus in 1616 Rebecca Atnoke of Alvediston was accused of having been discovered in bed with a widower in Shaftesbury and punished by the mayor, and a section of the inhabitants of her tiny home village came to the conclusion that the charge was true. Thomas Morris, a neighbour, was 'willed by half a dozen' to tell the girl's mother that this was so. John Toomer, on the other hand, took the side of the defamed woman and asserted that her accusers were 'rascals for that...[he] knew the contrary having enquired thereof of the mayor'; indeed he ventured to impeach the honesty of the original source of the accusation, Catherine Hitchcock, who promptly cited him in a defamation cause on her own behalf. Amid all this gossip and activity Rebecca Atnoke was plainly in a threatened and humiliating position.[61]

Even general terms of abuse like 'whore' and 'quean' could involve real humiliation. Such slanders were often framed to show

[58] W.R.O., B/DB 31, fol. 87v; B/DB 32, fols. 138–9; B/DB 21, fol. 22.
[59] MacDonald, *Mystical bedlam*, pp. 105–6.
[60] W.R.O., B/DB 32, fol. 118; B/DB 33, fols. 22–3v.
[61] W.R.O., B/DB 31, fols. 80v–9; B/DB 32, fols. 62v–141, *passim*.

the victim in a ridiculous light, or made more powerful by evoking the symbolism of filth, beastliness, disease and vagrancy. Typical slanders of this type were 'hedge whore, barn whore,... hollow tree whore'; 'whore, a rotten whore, and a bitchery whore'; 'a rascal jade, a scurvy rascal quean, a stinking gill, and thou carriest thy honesty in thy pocket and art able to shame a hundred honest women'.[62] Not only did such utterances themselves have power to wound; there is also evidence that a victim who failed to respond, either by direct or legal action, could thereby lose face. In 1618 Mary Crooke screamed before Anne Moxam's house in South Wraxall: 'bobtail whore and whore bitch, saying she was hot in the tail and had been and showed her arse before the king, and scratching at her... through the window said that if she had her forth she... would pull her... in pieces and scratch out her eyes'. Anne Moxam stayed indoors, only to be told by a neighbour the next day that 'she was a very coward that being overnight called so many whores she would not come forth of her house'.[63]

Victims of slander could thus suffer legal hazards, specific social consequences, humiliation and loss of face – or any combination of these ill effects. On this perspective church court defamation causes were important as a means of defending reputation, reflecting a society in which sexual 'credit' or 'honesty' were, especially for women, of considerable and probably growing importance (albeit not as vital as in some classic 'honour and shame' cultures, where an individual would normally be reluctant to suffer the humiliating publicity of slander litigation and instead would seek some privy means of revenge which might amount to the killing of the defamer).[64] However, these considerations are by no means always sufficient to explain why insulted or defamed individuals decided to go to the lengths of taking legal action, especially when the slander at issue was of a very general nature. Defamation causes can only be fully understood in the wider context of tensions and rivalries among the middling groups of local society, and enmities arising from such quarrels must often be taken into account in explaining the motives of suitors. Likewise the increasing popularity of defamation suits in the late sixteenth and early seventeenth centuries should at least in

[62] W.R.O., B/DB 34, fol. 170v; B/DB 36, fols. 31v, 77v.
[63] W.R.O., B/DB 34, fols. 104v–5.
[64] Julian Pitt-Rivers, 'Honour and social status', in Peristiany (ed.), *Honour and shame*, pp. 29–31.

part be viewed in these terms: as a reflection either of an increase in parochial tensions (consequent on the demographic and social structural shifts of the period), of a greater propensity to pursue the resulting quarrels through the medium of litigation, or of a combination of these factors.[65]

Like many other forms of lawsuit, actions for defamation were capable of being sued for malicious purposes; and a few cases represented no more than cynical attempts, under colour of clearing a sullied reputation, to vex an opponent. In 1621–2, for example, John Collett of South Wraxall sued William Kippin and Elizabeth Iles for saying that he had 'occupied' Kippin's wife. But the defendants' view of the matter was that Collett himself had originated the rumours in order to cause a breach between the Kippins, and had tried to do the same thing with Thomas and Elizabeth Iles. This version of the truth was probably the more reliable, since it is known from other sources that Collett was at enmity with a number of the inhabitants of South Wraxall, was repeatedly bound over to keep the peace or be of good behaviour, and was the subject of long and well-attested articles of complaint, addressed to the quarter sessions in 1621 and 1624, accusing him of a variety of unneighbourly offences. This context suggests strongly that his slander suits were vexatious.[66]

More commonly, the motives of suitors were consciously or unconsciously tinctured with malice in the sense that, even before slanders were uttered, potential plaintiffs already bore a good deal of ill-will towards defendants, which made them the more ready to resort to legal action. To put the matter another way, the degree to which slanders were resented depended in part on the nature of the relationship and state of feeling between defamer and victim; and when, as was frequently the case, slanders were uttered in the context of quarrels and brawls, it was inevitable that pre-existing anger and tension should often carry over and influence the decision to prosecute a defamation suit. An example will illustrate the complexities of motive and circumstance which were frequently involved. In 1616 Maud Spender of Coulston brought an action of defamation against her neighbour Alice Francklin on the grounds that the latter had called her 'a fine whore, a burnt tailed whore and a pocky whore',

[65] Cf. Haigh, 'Slander and the church courts', pp. 9–13.
[66] W.R.O., B/DB 37, fols. 87v–8; B/DB 39, fols. 9v–10; QS/GR Mich. 1621/164; QS/GR East. 1624/141.

adding that 'the pox had eaten thee out if my sister had not holpen thee of them'. But there is evidence that Spender had provoked this outburst by first railing against Francklin, and had been bound over to keep the peace towards her. In any case there was already bad blood between them. The dispute had arisen because Francklin had given hostile evidence before commissioners investigating a lawsuit in which Spender was involved, and it may be (as the latter obviously thought) that this action was itself essentially aggressive. Clearly her decision to commence a slander prosecution was not simply a response to Francklin's act of defamation but also articulated earlier grievances.[67]

In circumstances of this sort, acts of defamation and the slander suits which succeeded them may be seen as complementary forms of aggression, both the expression of underlying sources of tension. What generalisations may be made about these more basic quarrels? Depositions specify a wide variety of reasons why the litigants had 'fallen out', ranging from squabbles over card games to disputes over religion. However, most of these 'jars' resolve into a few basic categories of roughly equal importance numerically: tensions over lawsuits already in train; quarrels over money or bargains; personal jealousies, whether sexual or otherwise; and disputes over various minor trespasses such as damage done by pigs, shooting at dogs, or the beating of a neighbour's maidservant.[68] To modern eyes many of these small-scale disputes appear ludicrously trivial, but their capacity to generate anger and enmity must be understood in context. Between status-conscious neighbours dwelling in close proximity it was possible for irritating tensions and petty jealousies to grow and fester, erupting eventually into rancorous outbursts. Moreover, when cases are investigated beyond the evidence immediately available in depositions, it is sometimes found that the quarrels which precipitated acts of slander were only the most recent manifestations of extremely long and tangled histories of strained relations – the symptoms, in other words, of more profound tensions than appear at first sight. In the case of *Prudence Earth of Mildenhall v. Susan Goddin* (1628), for example, the immediate cause of strife was said to

[67] W.R.O., B/DB 30, fols. 130–1.

[68] For examples of these various forms of underlying tension, see W.R.O., B/DB 30, fol. 91 (cards); B/DB 32, fol. 97 (religion); B/DB 37, fol. 100 (lawsuit); B/DB 43, fol. 5 (bargains, etc.); B/DB 38, fols. 3v, 75, 89 (jealousies); B/DB 30, fol. 89v, B/DB 34, fol. 104, B/DB 36, fol. 10 (trespasses).

have been 'the gathering of a few green apples in the orchard'. But there is complementary evidence that the two households were in fact involved in a whole web of conflicts, and that there had been litigation between the families as long ago as 1620.[69] Even more strikingly, the two cases brought by Elizabeth Cowslade of Rodbourne Cheney against her neighbours Alice Adee and Robert Osborne in 1618 and 1619 turn out to have been merely a part of a frogspawn mass of litigation pursued not only in the Salisbury consistory court but also the king's bench, the Highworth court leet, the Wiltshire quarter sessions, the correction courts of both the bishop of Salisbury and the archdeacon of North Wiltshire, and the star chamber.[70] A case from the village of Keevil provides a further illustration: *Robert Blagden v. Moses Jones* (1607) emerges as an incident in a long-running feud between the families of Blagden and Jones which led to a multitude of lawsuits in a variety of courts in the first three decades of the seventeenth century. In this and similar cases, the issues really boiled down to local rivalry and struggles for prestige: when Robert Blagden brought a star chamber suit against the Joneses in 1619, one of the affronts of which he complained most bitterly was that he, a wealthy yeoman hovering on the brink of gentry status, had been indicted by his opponents for barratry under the demeaning title of 'husbandman'.[71]

In so far as defamation suits represented the pursuit of other quarrels via the church courts, their social utility might be questioned. In fact it is likely that even vexatious or semi-vexatious suits did serve a useful social function, if only in providing a non-violent means of expressing aggression. Violence can often be seen lurking in the obscure background of slander suits. Quarrels could easily lead to the disputants 'falling by the ears' and assaulting each other, and some slanders were deliberately uttered in the hope of provoking a fight.[72] Even something akin to duelling was not unknown among yeomen and husbandmen involved in the interpersonal disputes

[69] W.R.O., B/DB 42, fols. 4–12, 26–8, 53–4, 107–10; B/ABI 46, 7/3/1620, *Earth v. Godwin* (i.e. Goddin); QS/GR Mich. 1627/171.

[70] W.R.O., B/DB 34, fols. 132–57v, *passim*; B/DB 35, fols. 33v–4v; B/ABO 9, 23/6/1619, *Office v. Ade*, 8/7/1619, *Office v. Osborn*; AW/ABO 5, 16/4/1619, *Office v. Osberne*; QS/GR Hil. 1621/178, 180–1; P.R.O., STAC 8/110/3, STAC 8/226/2.

[71] W.R.O., B/DB 24, fols. 60–75v, *passim*; P.R.O., STAC 8/59/11.

[72] For examples, see W.R.O., B/DB 34, fols. 104–5; B/DB 37, fol. 121; B/DB 43, fol. 5v. Cf. P.R.O., STAC 8/89/13.

which so often underlay defamation causes. In a case in 1616, a certain Alexander Knight was said to have carried a petronel (a large pistol) around for a fortnight in the hope of meeting his opponent Richard Ambrose, and on one occasion the disputants came near to combat: 'the field was challenged and... Knight was in the field, but... Ambrose came not'.[73] It is noteworthy that in about a fifth of the better-recorded Wiltshire cases studied for the period 1615–29, one or both of the principals or their close relatives resorted to the peace-keeping apparatus of the quarter sessions. Clearly society was still violent enough to make quarrels between neighbours a danger to the peace, and resort to an action of defamation in expression of such quarrels must be seen as the lesser of two evils.[74]

It must be emphasised, in any case, that the popularity of church court defamation suits never got out of hand. The totals cited earlier were substantial, but from a very local perspective the incidence of suits was less remarkable. In Wiltshire, there was some clustering of cases in certain of the parishes in the north and north-west of the county, probably reflecting the prominence in the local social structure of the middling groups characteristically involved as litigants, but otherwise suits were drawn from all parts of the county. The average parish would experience an action for defamation perhaps once in every five years, and cases which proceeded as far as the calling of witnesses were rarer still. In Wylye in the period 1591–1630 there were three seriously prosecuted suits (1613, 1615, 1621), in Keevil four (1599, 1607, 1617, 1619).[75]

The arduous business of going to law, moreover, served to defuse tensions and to allow anger to cool. The surviving Salisbury consistory court act books for the period 1615–29 – which, on account of gaps and imperfections, in fact cover only about twelve years' worth of business – record a mere 82 final sentences in defamation causes, of which 18 were pronounced after a confession by the

[73] W.R.O., B/DB 30, fol. 150; B/DB 32, fol. 4.

[74] For divergent views on levels of violence in early modern English society, see Macfarlane, *Justice and the mare's ale*, *passim*; Lawrence Stone, 'Interpersonal violence in English society, 1300–1980', *Past and present*, no. 101 (Nov. 1983), pp. 22–33; J. A. Sharpe, 'The history of violence in England: some observations', *Past and present*, no. 108 (Aug. 1985), pp. 206–15, and Stone's 'Rejoinder', *ibid.*, pp. 216–24.

[75] W.R.O., B/Misc. Ct Papers 29/48, fols. 3–6v; B/DB 30, fols. 34v–5; B/DB 37, fols. 104v–7v; B/DB 16, fols. 171v–2; B/DB 24, fols. 60–75v, *passim*; B/DB 32, fols. 128v–33; B/DB 35, fols. 40v–4.

defendant rather than as the result of a fully contested action. Plainly the great majority of suits were simply not prosecuted as far as a final verdict. This was evidently not because judgements favourable to plaintiffs were in point of law difficult to obtain, for such verdicts easily predominated in completed causes: thus of the 64 sentences which did not depend on a confession, as many as 52 were adjudicatory and only 12 absolutory. Of the many discontinued suits, some were no doubt simply abandoned when rancour evaporated or the money ran out. Others were settled by mediation or arbitration. As was noted earlier, it was a basic principle of ecclesiastical law that litigants should be given every opportunity to achieve a reconciliation and out-of-court settlement, and the records yield occasional references to attempts by apparitors or other court officers to persuade the parties to submit to arbitration.[76] More commonly, it would seem, cases were referred for settlement to parish ministers, local gentry, or other substantial and well-trusted neighbours: acting with varying degrees of formality, such intermediaries would consider the matter at issue and the evidence relating to it, arrange for the settlement of court expenses and if appropriate persuade the defendant to make an apology. In all but the most obdurate cases, it was thus possible to reconcile the parties and restore peace between them, avoiding the bitterness and expense of fighting a suit to the finish. If in their origins defamation suits were often a means of covertly expressing aggression, once under way they could serve as avenues towards the re-establishment of amity.[77]

To sum up. Attacks on sexual reputation occasioned the great majority of defamation causes in the ecclesiastical courts, which were far and away the most important tribunals for dealing with sexual slander. It hardly needs emphasising that Elizabethan and early Stuart England was not a classic 'honour and shame' society. None the less, for both men and women (but more especially for the latter), sexual reputation or 'credit' was conventionally regarded as important; to an extent it was also of real significance in everyday life, quite apart from the fact that individuals were legally liable for

[76] For example, see W.R.O., B/DB 35, fol. 31. In the act books discontinued suits were often noted as being *sub spe concordiae*, *in tractatu pacis*, or *concordata*: all these annotations indicated that mediation or arbitration proceedings were in train and reflected the courts' readiness to accept such extra-judicial settlements.

[77] For examples and further discussion of out-of-court settlements, see Ingram, 'Communities and courts', pp. 125–7; Sharpe, '"Such disagreement betwyx neighbours"', pp. 173–8.

personal immorality. Fears of being prosecuted for suspected immorality and the desire to defend reputation do not, however, wholly account for the popularity of defamation causes: at least in part, such suits were often motivated by enmities which existed even before the alleged slander had been uttered. Characteristically such hostile feelings sprang from small-scale but often bitter disputes between neighbours, usually people of middling rank, who formed the majority of litigants. Some of these tensions were endemic, and certain suits can be shown to relate to long-standing struggles for status and prestige among wealthy yeoman and minor gentry families in particular parishes; but many of the conflicts were apparently transient, and peace could be relatively easily restored through well-established mechanisms of mediation and arbitration. In fine, in their close association with matters of reputation and standing, in reflecting the ambivalent relationships between neighbours in small towns and country villages, and in exemplifying the importance of law in mediating social relations, defamation causes emerge as peculiarly characteristic of early modern English society; their popularity and social significance are readily comprehensible.

Part 3

Church courts and society

11. *The effectiveness of ecclesiastical justice*

The church courts of late Elizabethan and early Stuart England have often been portrayed as purveyors of outmoded or unwanted values. This book has argued the contrary case: many of the courts' activities were either in line with the existing attitudes and expectations of honest householders in the parishes (as in the pursuit of notorious sexual offenders), or represented a realistic attempt, normally supported by at least a section of local opinion, to nudge the mass of the people towards improved standards of morality and religious observance. However, the most vehement criticisms of ecclesiastical justice have been concerned less with its *intentions* than with its effectiveness: in the last resort, it has often been maintained, the church courts' endeavours were vitiated by lack of teeth. Such arguments have already been subjected to implicit criticism: in a multitude of ways, it has been shown, the courts did contribute to or reinforce important social processes. This chapter draws together the threads of preceding discussions by focusing specifically on the coercive apparatus of ecclesiastical justice and re-evaluating its efficiency. Certainly the courts were never able to achieve anything like 100 per cent compliance, and it is hardly surprising that idealists – whether contemporary puritans or modern commentators – should have judged them harshly. Yet in view of the magnitude of the courts' tasks and of the social structures in which they had perforce to operate, and in comparison with the levels of performance achieved by other contemporary tribunals, it is arguable that the ecclesiastical courts did remarkably well; their effectiveness should not be underestimated.

The most convenient means of studying the coercive powers of the courts is to review the main stages whereby cases, especially disciplinary prosecutions, were initiated and processed. This boils down to assessing the presentment system; the process of compurgation; the deterrent effects of penance and of the other penalties which the courts were able to impose; and the effectiveness of excommunication to compel attendance and obedience to court orders.

Earlier chapters have repeatedly emphasised how heavily the disciplinary work of the church courts depended on the detection of offenders by churchwardens and sidesmen. Apparitors and court officials could themselves do something to identify culprits, but they could not be everywhere and often lacked detailed local knowledge; while ministers, though sometimes influential in galvanising churchwardens into action, generally made only sparing use of their discretionary powers of direct presentment, probably because they felt that their pastoral function would be prejudiced by unduly prominent involvement in the judicial process. It was open to individual parishioners to commence 'promoted' office cases against notorious offenders; but to do so involved considerable trouble, risk and possible expense, and it was hardly likely that promoters would come forward in any numbers. It was so much easier to leave matters to the duly constituted agents of detection.

Churchwardens and sidesmen were, as we have seen, usually drawn from the ranks of middling and substantial householders, normally elected by more or less formalised rotation systems.[1] They thus formed a virtually random cross-section of the upper half of parish society, and their individual zeal and competence naturally varied. However, the courts could rely on at least a basic level of co-operation. H. Gareth Owen's findings for late Elizabethan London diocese, that visitations were usually well attended by churchwardens and that there was generally little difficulty in eliciting from them bills of presentment, appear to be generally applicable in this period.[2] Thus in the Wiltshire deaneries of Cricklade and Malmesbury and a subdivision of the deanery of Avebury (87 parishes and chapelries), at the archidiaconal visitation of Michaelmas 1602, bills were lacking in only two cases. For the whole archdeaconry of North Wiltshire (123 parishes and chapelries), at Michaelmas 1621, only eight bills were not immediately forthcoming, and only eleven at Michaelmas 1640; some of these missing presentments probably came in later.[3] In the archdeaconry of Salisbury (135 parishes and

[1] See above, pp. 83, 116, 120.

[2] H. Gareth Owen, 'The episcopal visitation: its limits and limitations in Elizabethan London', *Jl ecclesiastical history*, 11 (1960), pp. 179–85.

[3] Based on search of W.R.O., AW/ABO 1, fols. 98v–9v, 104–8; AW/Visitation Bk, 1621–42 (unfoliated).

chapelries), in 1603, ten pairs of churchwardens were prosecuted for failing to exhibit bills of detection at one or other of the two visitations held that year; in 1615 the total was thirteen and in 1629 eleven. In over half these cases, however, the churchwardens did eventually conform.[4] Detailed analysis reveals that a tiny proportion of very small parishes or chapelries were comparatively frequent offenders in failing to produce bills; their few inhabitants probably had little to present and were understandably reluctant to undertake the expense of attending visitations.[5] Otherwise, apart from the merest hint of a concentration in the areas of recusant strength in the southernmost part of the county, the topographical distribution of Wiltshire cases of non-presentment was apparently random. Probably the most usual reason for failing to present was simply the negligence of individual churchwardens; outright refusal to make a report, as opposed to mere neglect, was very rare.

Admittedly the bills exhibited did not necessarily provide a full return of presentable matters. At the archdeacon of North Wiltshire's Easter visitation in 1621, for example, 18 out of 66 parishes for which copy presentments survive merely recorded *omnia bene* ('all is well'). In many of these cases it is hard to believe that absolutely nothing of a presentable nature had occurred since the previous Michaelmas. Of the bills which were not blank, many contained little matter, and again it is stretching credulity to accept that they were comprehensive.[6] Sometimes churchwardens were summoned to present more fully, but the courts could only take such action effectively when they had some alternative source of information or when (as occasionally happened) it was obvious from the form of the presentment itself that information was being withheld.[7]

The evident selectivity of presentments scandalised some contemporary observers, who viewed it as a symptom of mass perjury. 'How many oaths', wrote one commentator, 'are ministered daily to

[4] Based on search of W.R.O., AS/ABO 8, 11, 14.

[5] The most notable of these defaulting parishes/chapelries were Alton Barnes, Kellaways and Blunsdon St Andrew.

[6] Based on search of W.R.O., AW/Misc. Visitation Papers: Note-book, 1602–20 [*recte* 1602–22].

[7] For examples, see W.R.O., AS/ABO 11, 11/11/1615, *Office v. Hugh Bartlett, Richard Hopkins and Robert Fiveash*; *ibid.*, 11/11/1615, *Office v. Christopher Harris and Nicholas Morrell*. In the archdeaconry of Chichester it is clear that bills were carefully scrutinised, and churchwardens were routinely summoned to amplify their presentments and explain discrepancies: for examples, see Johnstone (ed.), *Churchwardens' presentments* (*17th century*), pt 1, pp. 30, 37, 47 and *passim*.

churchwardens [and other officers]...and no man regardeth them any more than the taking up of a straw.'[8] But moralistic judgements of this sort showed scant appreciation of the realities of life in Elizabethan and early Stuart communities and the very real difficulties and dilemmas which faced churchwardens – and, for that matter, other local officers such as constables and hundred jurors, since the phenomenon of under-presentment was by no means confined to the church courts.

Churchwardens were required to make their presentments on the basis of turgidly written and closely printed booklets of visitation articles, and these undoubtedly posed some problems of comprehension.[9] The difficulties were, however, reduced to the extent that over this period a growing proportion of the men responsible for making detections were literate, a function of the spread of reading and writing skills among middling social groups in general.[10] Of churchwardens and sidesmen who subscribed bills of detection in the Wiltshire parishes of the dean of Salisbury's jurisdiction in 1616, 40 per cent signed their names, while 60 per cent made marks; in 1634 the proportions were 53 and 47 per cent respectively. In both years, over 90 per cent of bills were subscribed by at least one person who could actually sign (a skill which implies reasonable fluency in reading).[11] Presumably the literates were prepared to share their knowledge with their fellows; and it may hence be inferred that, with the additional help of court officers and with accumulated parochial experience of what the authorities were interested in, it was possible for churchwardens and sidesmen in most parishes in the early seventeenth century to have a reasonable idea of what they were supposed to report. Comparison of the contents of signed and marked bills indicates that higher literacy rates would probably have improved the fullness of presentments to some extent, though not dramatically, since educational levels were by no means the only factor conditioning churchwardens' responses. Highly detailed bills invariably came from parishes where at least one and usually more competent literates were involved in presentment; however, such bills were

8 Quoted in Thomas, *Religion and the decline of magic*, p. 67.

9 Cf. Wrightson, 'Two concepts of order', pp. 27–8. Printed articles for Salisbury diocese are listed in the Bibliography under 'England, church of'.

10 See above, pp. 92, 115, 119.

11 Based on search and analysis of W.R.O., D/Pres. 1616, 1634. On the ability to sign as an indicator of literacy, see Cressy, *Literacy and the social order*, pp. 53–5.

always very much in a minority, and most signed presentments were not perceptibly more thorough than marked ones.

If churchwardens were reasonably cognisant of what was required of them, it cannot be assumed that in practice they were fully informed of offences committed in their parishes. The notion that this was a society in which everyone knew everyone else's business is surely a myth. Except in the tiniest of nucleated villages, even the most zealous churchwardens must have found it difficult to oversee the behaviour of the entire population (including mobile servants), and this would have been especially hard in sprawling urban centres and some regions of scattered settlement in a period of rapid demographic expansion. Some areas, including in Wiltshire certain forest districts and some ancient liberties, were not part of the parochial network at all, and precisely how (if at all) they fitted into the presentment system is not clear.[12] Then as now, many offenders must have escaped prosecution simply because they were never found out.

Undeniably, however, churchwardens often neglected to present offences of which they were well aware or which they could have discovered with relative ease. They faced, as E. R. C. Brinkworth has remarked, 'many temptations to turn the blind eye and the deaf ear'.[13] Not surprisingly, deference and caution often inhibited churchwardens from presenting offenders of gentry rank, except for routine, semi-administrative matters such as neglecting to pay rates or to maintain ecclesiastical buildings.[14] Lesser fry might also be passed over if they threatened reprisals, or contrariwise if they enjoyed ties of kinship, affinity, interest or close neighbourhood with churchwardens in office.[15] On occasion, considerations of humanity also prevailed over strict duty: in 1619, for example, the churchwardens of Fisherton Delamere confessed that they had omitted to detect a certain Richard Grumbold for incontinence 'for that the wife of the said Grumbold was very sick and like to die and [they] feared it would then have shortened her life'.[16] But even more

[12] For administrative problems posed by such extra-parochial areas, see *H.M.C., Various collections*, vol. 1, pp. 100–1.

[13] Brinkworth (ed.), *Archdeacon's court*, vol. 2, p. vi.

[14] For a contemporary local protest on this issue, see W.R.O., AS/ABO 15, 12/1/1639, *Office v. William Marshman*; cf. Hill, *Society and puritanism*, p. 312.

[15] W.R.O., AW/ABO 3, 15/2/1609, *Office v. Roger Malam*; AW/ABO 5, 22/6/1620, *Office v. Abraham Light*; AS/ABO 15, fol. 98v.

[16] W.R.O., AS/ABO 12, 6 Feb. [*sic*: *recte* Mar.] 1619, *Office v. Henry Dibble and John Levell.*

important than factors like these was simple indolence: it took time and effort to make the necessary inquiries and draw up a really detailed bill of presentment, and many churchwardens simply could not be bothered to do so.

As preceding chapters have emphasised, however, there were more positive sides to churchwardens' reticence. Their selective approach to making presentments was the result not simply of negligence but also of laudable discretion, and their deliberations before returning detections undoubtedly acted as a valuable filtering mechanism. If each and every delict had been reported the courts would have been totally swamped: as it was, churchwardens showed a robust regard for distinctions between the serious and the trivial. Even when faced with graver matters they exercised a sturdy commonsense, and some of their omissions (in cases of female adultery, for example), were based on the realistic appreciation that presentment could sometimes lead to futile conflict and bitterness rather than wholesome correction. Further, in accordance with the best principles of canon and civil law, churchwardens showed a responsible and realistic attitude to rules of evidence. Of course there were exceptions, and some detections were made on poor evidence or even false information; but undoubtedly the norm was to resort to prosecution only when there were strong grounds for doing so. This applied even to cases – many of them concerning sexual immorality – based on 'common fame'. Contrary to what some historians have supposed, this concept should not be equated with mere rumour or gossip. A witness in 1608 was typical in holding that 'the report and speech of six sufficient men in a parish maketh a public fame': in other words, it was a public verdict of some solidity, usually based on a build-up of suspicious circumstances and other forms of evidence, to be contrasted with mere 'flying fames', 'idle speeches' or the unsupported opinions of individuals.[17] Such caution, wholly characteristic of this intensely legalistic society, obviously resulted in some offenders escaping prosecution; the countervailing advantage was that charges which went forward were generally well grounded and there was little cause for complaint of vexatious proceedings.

It would in any case be wrong to exaggerate the degree of under-presentment. In spite both of negligence and of caution on the part

[17] W.R.O., B/DB 26, fol. 7; see also B/DB 38, fol. 74; C.U.L., MS Dd 12.20–21, fol. 136v (I owe this reference to Keith Thomas); cf. Hill, *Society and puritanism*, p. 310.

of churchwardens, the total numbers of detections were by the early seventeenth century very impressive. Blatant sexual offenders, especially bastard-bearers, were extremely liable to be reported, while the less heinous sin of bridal pregnancy was also becoming a matter of regular presentment in some regions.[18] As regards other areas of ecclesiastical discipline, there was a fair, though admittedly far from complete, response to the authorities' demands for information about decayed church buildings and defects in furnishings and liturgical requirements;[19] while negligence in paying church rates and similar dues – an offence which naturally annoyed the prompt payers – was fairly consistently reported. Obstinate recusants were presented with sufficient regularity to fulfil the church and state authorities' aim of identifying and isolating the catholic minority. Other persistent absentees from church were also likely sooner or later to be detected, while householders who failed to turn up for communion on Easter day were simply asking for trouble. Overall, it may be fairly said that during the reigns of James I and Charles I churchwardens were consistently complying with the letter of the canons of 1604 in presenting *notorious* crimes and scandals; and the ecclesiastical authorities, for their part, were able to oversee parochial life more thoroughly than had hitherto been possible.[20]

The *ex officio* oath imposed on accused persons, to ascertain the truth of charges made against them and establish the names of accomplices and other relevant circumstances, was viewed by contemporaries as an important element in the coercive battery of the church courts. Bitterly attacked by certain puritan writers and by common lawyers, on the grounds that it compelled self-incrimination, it was as strenuously defended by the advocates of ecclesiastical discipline.[21] Just how effective was it, and how important for the administration of justice? Defendants accused of relatively minor offences, such as neglect of church attendance or failure to pay rates, were often excused the oath but none the less confessed the charge.

[18] See above, Chapters 7–9.

[19] In some dioceses the churchwardens' presentments of defects in church buildings, etc., were occasionally supplemented by more thorough 'church inspections'; inevitably these revealed many matters which had been passed over in presentments: see Fletcher, *County community in peace and war*, pp. 85–7.

[20] Canon 109.

[21] The debate is surveyed in Hill, *Society and puritanism*, pp. 382–408. See also Maguire, 'Attack of the common lawyers on the oath *ex officio*', *passim*.

Moreover, many of the confessions in more serious cases were forthcoming simply because denial was pointless rather than because the defendants were compelled by oath. Charges of antenuptial fornication, for example, were usually admitted because the woman was manifestly pregnant at marriage; likewise bastard-bearers could hardly deny that they had committed fornication, and usually had little to gain by concealing the circumstances in which they had offended or hiding the name of their partner. Defendants who were not manifestly guilty of sexual immorality – males, married women, and single women who had not conceived – were far less likely to confess, and it must be surmised that many were willing to forswear themselves. On the other hand, the *ex officio* oath probably did induce some defendants to make confessions which they would otherwise have avoided, and there are indications in some cases of fears of supernatural penalties for perjury. The case of Anne Nightingale of Barford St Martin in 1635 was particularly striking. Her master, having got her with child, had offered her ten pounds to nominate her fellow-servant as the father. She succumbed to the temptation, but afterwards repented: 'she confesseth to have done him great wrong and doth desire God's great mercy to forgive her...and she likewise confesseth that God is a just and a righteous God unto her and that he hath justly punished her for her foul and false accusation by taking from her the use of her limbs'.[22]

On the whole, however, it seems doubtful whether the *ex officio* oath was a very effective inquisitorial instrument in dealing with the common run of moral offenders; and, in the context of puritan and common law attacks, it may almost have been more trouble than it was worth. In some jurisdictions, for example the archdeaconry of Chichester, the judges in the late sixteenth and early seventeenth centuries made very sparing use of the oath, tendering it in disciplinary cases only when there was some particular reason to do so. Apparently this did not undermine efficiency, and it probably represented the wisest policy in the circumstances. Certainly it obviated an unfortunate development which occurred in the Wiltshire courts, where the *ex officio* oath was routinely employed except in the very simplest cases: that is, a slight but increasing tendency for defendants to refuse flatly to be sworn. Such defiance was very rare in the late sixteenth century and the early years of the seventeenth. In the

[22] W.R.O., QS/GR East. 1635, examinations, etc., contemporary no. 15. See also QS/GR East. 1605/178; AW/ABO 5, 16/2/1620, *Office v. Thomasine Cale*.

archdeaconry of Salisbury from 1623, however, no year for which records survive elapsed without at least one defendant refusing the oath. There were four such cases in 1637 and five in 1639, and in these years, when the total number of people attending the court was comparatively small, the non-jurors formed a significant proportion of all defendants. Just what was at issue in these cases? They related to a variety of different ecclesiastical offences, and, apart from a knot of recalcitrants from the south Wiltshire parish of Tilshead in the 1620s, the defaulters came from widely scattered localities.[23] When George Forde of Durrington refused an oath in 1637 on the grounds that he had 'done too much already', it may have been simply that he had imagined that an unsworn confession would suffice and was reflecting that oath, articles and examination were together going to cost him over five shillings. The motives of William Marshman of Teffont Evias in 1639 were more complex: on being excommunicated for refusing to take the oath, he told the judge that 'that was the worst that he could do and...that he never knew any rich man cited to this court though they go to plough or commit any other offences'.[24]

It is intriguing that these defendants were willing to come to court only to be excommunicated for refusing to be sworn, when they could have stayed comfortably at home and been excommunicated for simple contumacy. Probably they were people in whose minds the impulses to obedience and disobedience were fairly evenly matched: in the 1620s, though less commonly in the next decade, some of the non-jurors eventually decided to submit. It would appear that news of the controversy about the *ex officio* oath had filtered down into the parishes and suggested to some individuals an issue of principle on which the church courts could be challenged.

Defendants who denied serious disciplinary charges usually had to undergo a further test which depended, at least in theory, on the power of oaths. This was the process of compurgation, whereby neighbours of the accused appeared in court to swear to their belief in his or her innocence. Some historians have argued that the persistence of compurgation in the church courts was a glaring an-

[23] For the Tilshead offenders, see W.R.O., AS/ABO 14, 13/11/1624, *Office v. the wife of William Humphry* (cf. AS/ABO 13, 2/6/1621, *Office v. William Humphry*; *ibid.*, 19/7/1623, *Office v. William Humfry*); AS/ABO 14, 23/5/1627, *Office v. Joan Pinckney*; *ibid.*, 23/1/1628, *Office v. John Hill alias Elliot.*

[24] W.R.O., AS/ABO 15, 28/1/1637, *Office v. Forde*; *ibid.*, 12/1/1639, *Office v. Marshman.*

achronism at a time when common lawyers had largely eliminated trial by the analogous secular procedure of wager of law; but the comparison is a misleading one.[25] The use of compurgation in the church courts was largely confined to cases of suspected immorality, where there was usually no clear-cut evidence and no individual victim whose interests had to be safeguarded. In these circumstances it made sense to establish a presumption of guilt or innocence by testing local opinion. It should be noted, on the other hand, that although as a formal process wager of law was virtually obsolete, some secular courts such as quarter sessions continued to use something analogous to compurgation in the form of certificates of innocence or creditworthiness subscribed by local inhabitants on behalf of accused persons; and, more generally, concepts of good and bad 'fame' (reputation) were influential even in cases of trial by jury.[26] On occasion, justices who were perplexed by the circumstances of bastardy cases actually referred the matter to compurgation in the church courts or took the results of compurgation into account as evidence.[27]

As we have seen in earlier chapters, the number of compurgators required (including the accused's own 'hand') varied from three to nine depending on the gravity of the offence, the weight of evidence, the economic and known moral status of the defendant and the discretion of individual judges. In the Wiltshire courts in the early seventeenth century monitions to purge with four or with five hands were about equally numerous, and occurred in approximately three-quarters of all compurgation cases; monitions to purge with six or with seven hands were also about equal in number and together accounted for another fifth of cases. However, in Wiltshire and elsewhere the judges were occasionally willing to accept one compurgator less than the number originally demanded. They also showed some flexibility with regard to the date set for compurgation proceedings, sometimes deferring the matter to allow the defendant more time to make the necessary arrangements. Judges were especially sympathetic to the difficulties faced by poor defendants, oc-

[25] Hill, *Society and puritanism*, p. 310.

[26] Thomas, *Religion and the decline of magic*, p. 528 and the references there cited; Ingram, 'Communities and courts', pp. 125–34; Sharpe, *Crime in seventeenth-century England*, ch. 10; Cynthia B. Herrup, 'Law and morality in seventeenth-century England', *Past and present*, no. 106 (Feb. 1985), pp. 102–23.

[27] For examples, see W.R.O., QS/GR Hil. 1603/272; QS/GR Hil. 1607/129; QS/GR Hil. 1621/198. See also Marchant, *Church under the law*, p. 225.

casionally permitting paupers to make their purgation locally or even to dispense altogether with the formal procedure and to clear themselves by their own oath.[28] Such concessions reflected the fact that compurgation was a very real test. The compurgators were actual people, not legal fictions, while there is absolutely no evidence that they could be picked up for hire at the doors of the church courts. Local studies indicate, moreover, that for the most part compurgators were, as required by ecclesiastical law, neighbours of the accused with actual knowledge of his or her character and of approximately equal social status.[29]

Compurgation proceedings could be blocked by objectors willing to prove that the defendant was guilty or that the compurgators were unworthy of credit or otherwise failed to fulfil canonical requirements. Admittedly these objections were entered in only a small minority of cases; and such objectors as appeared, far from being disinterested individuals who felt a public duty to bring home to offenders the penalties of sin, were normally persons with a very close interest in the case – usually pregnant or bastard-bearing women (or their relatives and friends) who were trying to establish paternity, occasionally people with a grudge against the accused.[30] The rarity of formal objections does not necessarily imply, however, that the defendant's fellow-parishioners were normally indifferent to the outcome. Probably the circumstances were debated locally before the day fixed for compurgation proceedings, and if the adverse evidence was strong the accused person simply found it impossible to secure compurgators.

The results of compurgation proceedings confirm that the ordeal was by no means a formality. Of the act books of the Wiltshire jurisdictions, those of the archdeaconry of Salisbury provide the fullest and most reliable record of attempted purgations. Table 14 summarises the results of 223 cases occurring in the period 1615–29. In 12 cases the judge had second thoughts and revoked the purgation

28 For examples, see W.R.O., AS/ABO 2, fols. 32v, 39, 46, 85v; AS/ABO 3, fols. 70, 102, 105v, 123v; L.M., 1 D 41/13/40, fol. 51v. See also Marchant, *Church under the law*, pp. 228–9.

29 Based on detailed investigation of Wylye and Keevil offenders and their compurgators. On the qualities required of compurgators, see Ayliffe, *Parergon*, pp. 450–1.

30 For examples, see W.R.O., AS/ABO 1b, fols. 27v, 30; AS/ABO 3, fols. 39v, 41v, 47, 109v, 112, 118; AS/ABO 12, 24/2/1616, 9/3/1616, *Office v. Jeremy Gybbins*; AW/ABO 1, fols. 90v, 101v.

Table 14 *Compurgation proceedings in the archdeaconry of Salisbury, 1615–29*

	Men	Women	Total
Purgation revoked	9	3	12
Passed	77	14	91
Probably passed	1	2	3
Failed	67	13	80
Probably failed	11	3	14
Outcome unknown	11	11	22
Inhibition entered	0	1	1
Total	*176*	*47*	*223*

order, usually dismissing the defendant; in a further 23 the outcome is unknown, in one instance because the matter was removed to a higher court. In half the remaining cases the purgation was successful. But approaching 100 defendants were unable to produce compurgators; and it is interesting to note that men, despite the existence to some degree of a double standard of morality in society at large, apparently found it no easier than women to clear their names.[31] This rate of failure is rather higher than that found by Houlbrooke in the mid-sixteenth-century church courts and by Helmholz for the medieval period, and perhaps reflects increasingly rigorous local attitudes to sexual offenders.[32] Just how many people who successfully passed their purgation were actually guilty, and how many of those convicted were really innocent, of course can never be known; but the overall impression is that compurgation provided a reasonable test which was not too heavily weighted either for or against the defendant.

The puritan *Admonition to the parliament* of 1572 accused the church courts of punishing 'whoredoms and adulteries with toyish censures', and the idea that ecclesiastical penalties were far too mild has sometimes been uncritically accepted by modern historians.[33] It

[31] The existence of the double standard is discussed above, pp. 154, 262, 269, 285, 302–3.

[32] Houlbrooke, *Church courts and the people*, pp. 45–6; R. H. Helmholz, 'Crime, compurgation and the courts of the medieval church', *Law and history rev.*, 1 (1983), p. 19.

[33] Frere and Douglas (eds.), *Puritan manifestoes*, p. 34; cf. Hill, *Society and puritanism*, pp. 312–13.

must be appreciated, however, that most contemporary critics had in mind as alternatives the death penalty or other harsh physical sanctions. Unmindful or unaware that excessively rigorous legal penalties often prove counter-productive, resulting in a general unwillingness to prosecute offenders at all, they innocently assumed that sexual misbehaviour was best dealt with by 'sharp' measures.[34] Yet, as we have seen, the introduction of the death penalty for incest and adultery during the Commonwealth was to prove largely a dead letter, partly because of intractable problems of proof, but more fundamentally because few cared to hang their neighbours for such crimes. Even the penalty of three months' imprisonment (with death for a second offence) which the 1650 act laid down for fornication, irrespective of the circumstances or of the social status of the culprits, was probably perceived as excessive by the majority of people, and prosecutions were not numerous. Thus in the Wiltshire quarter sessions in 1653, the year of most intense activity under the 1650 act in that court, only nine people were indicted. It was much the same in other areas, and J. A. Sharpe's comment on the situation in Essex provides a suitable epitaph on the working of the adultery act: 'a total of only twenty five people were tried in ten years under the 1650 legislation, as many as might have been presented for the offences covered by this act at any one sitting of the archdeacon's court'.[35]

If hanging and imprisonment were too harsh, were ecclesiastical punishments really too light, to expiate such sins as adultery and fornication? For one thing it must be recalled that the penalties of the church courts were often supplemented by a substantial burden of fees, and some contemporaries spoke as if such cash payments in themselves constituted a significant deterrent. In 1607, for example, two Wiltshire justices reported to the sessions that they could not satisfactorily resolve a paternity case; but they took comfort from the fact that 'both the reputed fathers are called into the spiritual court...and are there likely to smart by the purse for their in-

[34] Johannes Andenaes, *Punishment and deterrence* (Ann Arbor, Mich., 1974), p. 24 and *passim*. On the background to calls for stiffer penalties against sexual offenders, see Thomas, 'Puritans and adultery', pp. 259–78.

[35] W.R.O., QS/Minute Bk 10 (unfoliated), indictments, 1653; Sharpe, *Crime in seventeenth-century England*, p. 61. But cf. Stephen K. Roberts, *Recovery and restoration in an English county*: *Devon local administration, 1646–1670* (Exeter, 1985), pp. 198–208, suggesting a rather more vigorous pattern of enforcement in Devonshire, at least with regard to fornication/bastardy.

continency'.[36] As regards penance as such, its impact depended partly on the status and general standing of the culprit. The study of slander litigation in Chapter 10 revealed how much middling and substantial householders and their wives valued their 'credit' and were jealous of their reputation and standing among their neighbours. In such social milieux, the humiliation of formal penance in church – with the culprit dressed in a white sheet and carrying a white rod – could undoubtedly bite hard. In a case from Doddington (Ely diocese) in 1618, a local minister petitioned that a man should be excused from the full rigour of penance for fornication on account of 'such extremities as it is plainly like that his natural mother will fall into upon his public shame, who swooned almost irrecoverably when she first heard him convicted of the crime'.[37] In Wiltshire in 1594, Richard Woodrofe of Malmesbury described how the performance of penance on two successive Sundays some time before had been 'no small grief and shame unto him until this day'. To judge by the allegations of certain defendants, moreover, the discredit of penance could have tangible economic and social consequences. In 1600 John Goslinge of Charlton, who had fathered a bastard, made a voluntary court appearance and confession in the hope of receiving a reduced form of penance, because, as was said, his 'whole estate...dependeth upon his credit and service only' and would be jeopardised by public exposure; while in 1639 Henry Norris of Bishopstone craved favour on the grounds that he was a bachelor and the performance of penance would prejudice his chances of finding a wife.[38] One would, of course, expect individual culprits to engage in some special pleading, but such allegations do have the ring of truth; and some defendants were actually supported by groups of neighbours who begged the judge not to impose the full rigour of public penance.[39]

It was because formal penance could involve undue hardship in particular cases, and because in a deferential and hierarchical society it was not necessarily in the interests of public order to expose leading citizens to shame and humiliation, that the ecclesiastical authorities ignored puritan objections and insisted on retaining the right to

[36] W.R.O., QS/GR Hil. 1607/118; cf. B/DB 30, fol. 149.
[37] C.U.L., Ely D.R., B/2/35, fol. 57v (note pinned to page).
[38] W.R.O., B/ABO 2, fol. 38; AS/ABO 7, fol. 100; D/AB 39, fol. 32v.
[39] For examples, see W.R.O., AS/ABO 4, fols. 178v, 199, 247; B/ABI 19a, fol. 28.

commute penances into money payments devoted to poor relief and other pious objects.[40] There was no set rate for composition, the precise sum levied depending on the judge's discretion, the nature of the offence, and the financial standing of the defendant. But culprits were sometimes willing to pay quite substantial sums either to avoid penance altogether or to perform it in one of its less public and humiliating forms. Thus in early seventeenth-century Wiltshire, mulcts of £3 or more were by no means unusual, though admittedly much smaller sums of a few shillings or so were recorded in some cases.[41] The impression is that the demand for commutations exceeded the supply: in Wiltshire and elsewhere in this period the judges generally used their discretionary powers very sparingly and, contrary to the impression given by some contemporary critics, only a tiny proportion of penances were in fact remitted for cash.[42]

Penance was most feared by those with a reputation to lose. It was probably a less powerful sanction – though still an unpleasant experience to be avoided if possible – among people whose poverty entitled them to little social regard, among the mobile population of young servants who were not firmly located in a neighbourhood status network, even perhaps among young people of middling families whose sins could be written off as wild oats. Some references even suggest that penance was lightly regarded by some people of threadbare credit. In 1618, for example, Florence Bayly of Erlestoke, who confessed sexual relations with three men and who had been in trouble in the church courts before, told how one of her lovers had promised to 'free her from all trouble saving the wearing of a white sheet' if she did not reveal his name.[43] In 1636 the churchwardens of Fittlesworth (West Sussex) presented a widow 'who hath had already two bastards and is ready to lie down with the third, and we think she will have many more if the court enjoin her no other penance than standing in a white sheet'. The judge responded positively to this parochial complaint, ordering the woman to perform an especially severe triple penance including an appearance at the

[40] Cf. Hill, *Society and puritanism*, pp. 311–12 and the references there cited.

[41] For examples, see W.R.O., AS/ABO 13, 8/6/1621, *Office v. George Passion* (5s. for reduction from formal to mild penance); AW/ABO 5, 31/7/1619, *Office v. Thomas Bradfield* (20s. for mild instead of formal penance); AW/ABO 7, 17/3/1635, *Office v. James Baynard and Joan Fisher* (£5 in full commutation of penance); D/AB 28, 7/2/1627, *Office v. William Keat, gent.* (£8 in full commutation).

[42] Cf. Marchant, *Church under the law*, pp. 138–9.

[43] W.R.O., AS/ABO 12, 20/6/1618, *Office v. Bayly.*

'old cross' in the neighbouring town of Petworth.[44] Market-place penances were likewise used occasionally in Wiltshire and elsewhere, while in certain jurisdictions, such as the archdeaconry of Leicester, they were quite regularly employed against notorious offenders.[45]

But probably such efforts to maximise the effects of the penalty did not wholly suffice; and no doubt the secular justices of the peace, who commanded statutory powers to punish the fathers and mothers of bastard children likely to burden the poor rates, were seen as providing a welcome supplement to ecclesiastical discipline.[46] However, the scale on which their powers were invoked should not be exaggerated. To be sure, the justices' involvement in bastardy proceedings became increasingly common after the passage of the enabling act of 1576, and by the 1620s was facilitated in some areas by the emergence of a regular system of referring cases from the localities to petty sessional meetings.[47] Yet for most of the period the justices handled only a small fraction of the cases dealt with by the church courts. Many of the cases they did see were primarily concerned with maintenance rather than punishment and were handled relatively informally: the reputed father was bound over to the quarter sessions and discharged when he had given bond to 'save the parish harmless'. Formal bastardy orders were generally made only when the parties were trying to evade maintenance, when there was a dispute over paternity, or occasionally to make an example. In Wiltshire as elsewhere, such orders were never very numerous in this period (Table 15). It should be emphasised, moreover, that not even formal bastardy orders necessarily involved physical punishment for the culprits: only a minority of the men were whipped or stocked, and at least up to the later years of James I a fair proportion of the women also escaped any corporal penalty. It is really only in the 1620s and 1630s that the secular punishment of bastard-bearers can be said to have had a very significant impact. By this time formal bastardy orders usually despatched the mother to the house of correction for one year, in accordance with the act of 1610; a higher

[44] W.S.R.O., Ep. I/17/26. fols. 254, 255v, 260.

[45] For Wiltshire examples, see W.R.O., AS/ABO 1a, fols. 9, 10v; AS/ABO 2, fol. 63; AS/ABO 3, fol. 72v; B/ABO 5, fol. 16. For Leicestershire examples, see L.M., 1 D 41/13/40, fols. 3v, 25v, 52.

[46] 18 Eliz. I c. 3; 7 Jac. I c. 4. For the background to the passage of these acts, see above, pp. 151–2.

[47] For indications of this development in Wiltshire, see W.R.O., QS/GR Hil. 1627/95 (minutes of petty sessions, Salisbury division); cf. QS/GR Mich. 1627/202, 224.

Table 15 *Bastardy orders filed on the Wiltshire quarter sessions rolls in sample years, 1603–38*

1603	3	1615	3	1627	7	1636	6
1604	8	1616	5	1628	[8]*	1637	5
1605	13	1617	5	1629	12	1638	10

* Record imperfect.

proportion of men than hitherto were being whipped; while the falling incidence of illegitimacy meant that the justices, without actually increasing their activities to any great extent, were now dealing with a sizeable *proportion* of all bastardy cases.[48]

The villages of Wylye and Keevil, though slightly atypical in witnessing an above-average number of bastardy orders, may be used to illustrate the increasing involvement of the justices in cases of illegitimacy, while at the same time driving home the point that in absolute terms the impact was limited; their experience also raises doubts whether the deterrent value of corporal punishment was in reality much greater than that of penance. In 1609 a Keevil carpenter was brought before the justices by the churchwardens and overseers of another parish and ordered to pay maintenance for an illegitimate child; he was not, however, whipped.[49] Apart from this case, there were no bastardy orders made against offenders in either of these villages between 1600 (the effective commencement of the main series of Wiltshire quarter sessions records) and the end of 1617. In the period 1618–40, in contrast, there were several cases in each parish. But the Keevil orders were occasioned by highly complex and unusual circumstances;[50] while in Wylye the justices' powers of

[48] Based on search of all the relevant Wiltshire QS records, 1600–40. For evidence from Somerset, revealing a somewhat different pattern in certain respects, but likewise stressing the limits of J.P.s' involvement in the punishment of bastardy, see Quaife, *Wanton wenches and wayward wives*, ch. 9.

[49] W.R.O., QS/GR East. 1609/49; QS/GR Trin. 1609/99; AS/ABO 10, 14/1/1609, 28/1/1609, *Office v. John Vynce*; *ibid.*, 26/4/1610, *Office v. John Vennye* (the same man) and *Office v. Joan Hancock*. The bastardy order described Hancock as being of Keevil, but she was in fact of Steeple Ashton.

[50] James Cratchley, the subject of a bastardy order in 1620, vehemently denied the paternity charge. He was evidently unpopular for other reasons, and the action against him may have been partly malicious. Later he was to claim that the inhabitants of Keevil had kept him in prison for seven years for refusing to

punishment were almost exclusively deployed against the two notorious multiple bastard-bearers in the village. In 1618 Elizabeth Long was whipped, together with her partner, when she produced her second bastard; but this did not stop her having another illegitimate child in 1620. In 1627 Susan Baker was sent to the house of correction while her husbandman lover was merely ordered to contribute to the maintenance of his bastard son; but she produced another illegitimate child in 1632, and yet another in 1634, when the exasperated justices again despatched her to Bridewell.[51]

In sum, the significance of the secular punishment of bastard-bearers and bastard-begetters should not be overestimated. Even during the years of maximum impact in the 1620s and 1630s, such punishment was very selectively applied; and, while the occasional whipping or incarceration of notorious strumpets and whoremongers was no doubt viewed with satisfaction by churchwardens and overseers of the poor, it did not always deter offenders. It seems unlikely that the use of secular penalties was directly responsible for the decline in illegitimacy in the early seventeenth century: bastardy rates began to fall *before* the activities of the justices can have had much effect. On the other hand, it would also be wrong to make excessive claims for the impact of ecclesiastical penalties; precisely what role (if any) they played in reducing immorality remains obscure.[52] But it can at least be said that public penance – only occasionally commuted, though often reinforced by a substantial burden of court fees – was by no means a negligible penalty, at least for offenders from the middling and upper ranks of village and small town society.

Whatever the deterrent value of penance, it was dependent on the church courts' ability to secure the appearance of culprits in the first instance and to ensure their obedience to court orders; and this in turn depended in large measure on the efficacy of excommunication. It is an historical commonplace that herein lay the most serious and

perform the terms of the order, and that some of them had prosecuted him in the star chamber: see W.R.O., QS/GR East. 1620/51, 231–2; QS/GR Trin. 1620/190–3; QS/GR Hil. 1627/138. The other two cases also present unusual features: see W.R.O., QS/GR East. 1629/137–8; QS/GR Mich. 1629/123; QS/Minute Bk 6 (unfoliated), East. 1631, order *re* Ann Lyne; cf. QS/GR East. 1631/12.

51 W.R.O., QS/GR Hil. 1618/190; QS/GR Mich. 1626/144; QS/GR Hil. 1627/135; QS/GR Trin. 1627/124; QS/GR Hil. 1635/26; QS/GR Trin. 1635/162.

52 On the decline of illegitimacy, see above, pp. 166, 276–7.

intractable of the weaknesses of ecclesiastical justice. The extensive use of excommunication in cases of contumacy, apparently futile in many instances, was bitterly attacked by contemporary puritan critics of the church courts, who urged that the sanction should be restored to the role it had played in the early centuries of the Christian church as a solemn penalty employed in only the most serious cases. Advocates of ecclesiastical discipline, such as archbishops Whitgift and Bancroft, were also concerned. Hence various schemes were mooted to remedy the situation, in terms both of reducing contumacy and of providing an alternative to excommunication as the front line sanction against non-appearance or disobedience to court orders; but all these proposed reforms involved formidable legal and administrative problems, and in the event nothing was done.[53] Modern historians have re-emphasised the issues. In one of the most influential articles ever written on the post-Reformation church courts, F. D. Price drew attention to lamentable levels of contumacy and the apparent ineffectiveness of excommunication in the diocese of Gloucester in the reign of Elizabeth; and, though subsequent writers have recognised that this was an extreme case, in part explicable in terms of lax administration and atypically blatant corruption, a good deal of evidence has been adduced to show that substantial rates of contumacy were a normal feature of ecclesiastical justice in Elizabethan and early Stuart England. According to the calculations of Ronald Marchant, excommunicates comprised as many as 5 per cent of the population of the dioceses of York, Chester and Norwich in the early seventeenth century; and on the assumption that the families of these people were almost equally recalcitrant, a further 10 per cent may be said to have belonged to the 'excommunicate classes'.[54]

Such data have proved extremely influential in shaping adverse historical views of post-Reformation ecclesiastical discipline. They lend themselves to the idea that at best the church courts rested on very shaky foundations and at worst faced obsolescence; and they have been taken to imply a massive degree of popular indifference to, or even defiance of, not only the church courts but also religion

[53] Hill, *Society and puritanism*, pp. 360–70; Houlbrooke, 'Decline of ecclesiastical jurisdiction', pp. 251–2; Houlbrooke, *Church courts and the people*, pp. 49–50, 267–9.

[54] Price, 'Abuses of excommunication', *passim*; Marchant, *Church under the law*, p. 227. See also Collinson, *Elizabethan puritan movement*, pp. 40–1.

and morality. Thus Price argues that the censures of the church had 'lost their spiritual terrors' by the late sixteenth century; while Marchant suggests that 'the large numbers of the contumacious formed a group of what can only be termed ethical dissenters. Rather than conform to the church's standards of morality, men and women of all classes preferred to accept the disabilities of excommunication as a permanent state of life.'[55] But there are manifest perils in concentrating unduly on the limitations of any legal system, without paying sufficient attention to the administrative and social constraints which inevitably circumscribe court action; and there are more subtle dangers in inferring religious and moral attitudes from conventionalised judicial processes. In the following pages, it is argued that the significance of contumacy levels in the church courts has been exaggerated and in important respects misunderstood.

At the outset it is necessary to establish the nature of excommunication and how it was supposed to work. The legal and social disabilities associated with the penalty were detailed in Chapter 1 and may be briefly recalled.[56] Lesser excommunication, or suspension, merely barred the culprit from the church. Greater excommunication, the form most often employed in this period, was in addition supposed to ostracise the offender from the company of other Christians and to entail specific legal disabilities. In principle, excommunication also consigned the culprit into the hands of Satan; however, this idea was extensively qualified in canonical thinking, and it would be naive to imagine that judges supposed, when they pronounced sentence, that they were thereby condemning the culprit to perdition. On the contrary, the primary aim of excommunication was medicinal rather than retributive, intended to secure the compliance of the offender for the good of his or her soul. Even if such submission was not forthcoming, it did not necessarily follow that the sinner was damned. In brief, even in theory excommunication was a more pragmatic form of penalty than is often assumed, and relied for its effect primarily on its immediate social and legal implications rather than on 'spiritual terrors' such as the possibility of punishment in the world to come.[57]

[55] Price, 'Abuses of excommunication', p. 114; Marchant, *Church under the law*, p. 243. [56] See above, pp. 52–3.

[57] For a penetrating discussion of the theoretical basis of excommunication, see R. H. Helmholz, 'Excommunication as a legal sanction: the attitudes of the medieval canonists', *Zeitschrift der Savigny-Stiftung für Rechtsgeschichte: kanonistische Abteilung*, 99/68 (1982), pp. 202–18.

In order to have any practical effect, moreover, it was dependent on a train of administrative acts whereby a sentence of excommunication was translated into social reality. After the sentence had been formally pronounced, the defendant's name was entered, normally along with others, in a 'schedule' of excommunication which was promulgated in open court by the judge (if he were in orders) or by a clerical deputy. The next stage was to send out 'letters of excommunication' instructing the minister of the offender's parish to 'denounce' the sentence in church; the schedules, or the individual names in them, were usually marked with the word *emanavit* ('sent out') or some other annotation to indicate that the letters had been duly despatched. Finally, the parish minister was supposed to certify the denunciation by signing the back of the instrument and returning it to the registry; it was also his duty to denounce excommunicates afresh every six months, in the hope of ensuring sustained enforcement.

In the light of these remarks, let us consider the scale of contumacy faced by the church courts and on this basis discuss the role and effectiveness of excommunication as it operated in practice. Marchant's study of the diocese of York revealed that the courts there experienced comparatively little difficulty in securing attendance in instance (party and party) and promoted office suits, and the same appears true for other areas.[58] In the bishop of Salisbury's court in 1615, when over 150 cases were begun, only 22 defendants (about 15 per cent) were decreed excommunicate for failing to appear and answer, and it would moreover appear that not all of these decrees were promulgated and notified to the parishes. (This does not imply inefficiency on the part of the court: in instance suits the judge proceeded to each stage of the case only at the express petition of the plaintiff.) A further 12 per cent of defendants failed to enter an appearance but were not excommunicated: these cases were simply dropped, presumably because the plaintiff had had second thoughts about the wisdom of prosecuting or had secured an early settlement with the defendant. The bulk of defendants (about 73 per cent) duly appeared, either personally or by proxy, to answer the case against them. The efficacy of court action after such an initial appearance

[58] Marchant, *Church under the law*, p. 204. The figures cited by Jean Potter suggest to me a similar conclusion for Canterbury diocese in the early seventeenth century, though her own interpretation is somewhat more pessimistic: see Potter, 'Ecclesiastical courts in the diocese of Canterbury', pp. 75–7, 82–3.

depended largely on how diligently plaintiffs or promoters pressed their case. As we have seen, it was extremely common to settle suits out of court or simply to abandon them, even at the point of final sentence. These practices far more frequently brought cases to a halt than contumacy. A few defendants did prove recalcitrant at a late stage in suits, but persistent plaintiffs could usually bring them to heel eventually, especially if they were willing to incur the expense of a writ *de excommunicato capiendo* to have them arrested.[59] Overall the courts seem to have provided a reasonably effective service in party and party litigation, probably comparable with that offered by secular tribunals; certainly there is no sign of any great dissatisfaction among suitors.

In disciplinary or 'mere office' proceedings the church courts were faced with contumacy on a much greater scale. In itself this is hardly surprising, and it does not necessarily imply that the structures of ecclesiastical justice were exceptionally weak. As some historians have long recognised, secular courts performing analogous roles likewise found it difficult to get offenders into court and to enforce the penalties imposed on convicted defendants.[60] The appropriate comparison is *not* with proceedings on indictment: most people tried thus had already been arrested and were either in prison or on bail, so problems of securing their appearance in court simply did not arise. A fairer comparison is with assize and quarter sessions proceedings based on the presentments of high constables, petty constables and hundred jurors; the accused individuals were normally at liberty at the time of presentment, and their appearance before the judges, like that of people detected to the church courts, had to be achieved by remote control. Initial process was generally by writ of *venire facias*, and the ultimate sanction at the disposal of the courts was outlawry, the secular equivalent of excommunication.[61] The problems of securing attendance using these methods are well illustrated by proceedings in the Wiltshire quarter sessions in the middle years of James I's reign – a telling example, since the court was at that time administered, and its records maintained with meticulous care, by an exceptionally able and efficient clerk of the peace.[62] In

[59] Suits for 1615 are registered in W.R.O., B/ABI 41–2. On the writ *de excommunicato capiendo*, see above, p. 53.

[60] Hill, *Society and puritanism*, p. 371.

[61] J. P. M. Fowle (ed.), *Wiltshire quarter sessions and assizes, 1736*, Wilts. Archaeol. and Natural History Soc.: Records Branch, 11 (Devizes, 1955), pp. xxiv–xxv.

[62] *Ibid.*, pp. ix–x, xlii–xliv.

1615 process went out against 117 individuals presented for a variety of offences, but by the end of 1618 only 67 (57 per cent) had entered an appearance.[63]

How did the church courts compare? The most widely quoted figures are those calculated by Marchant for courts in the province of York. He found that in the diocese of Chester in 1595 barely 30 per cent of defendants in disciplinary cases both appeared to answer charges and were subsequently obedient to court orders, while the corresponding figure in the diocese of York in 1623 was 33 per cent.[64] However, these data can hardly be regarded as representative of normal levels of performance by the ecclesiastical courts. The dioceses of York and Chester, especially the latter, posed exceptionally severe pastoral and administrative problems.[65] Further, these low figures (and a somewhat higher one of 43 per cent cited for the diocese of Norwich in 1627) relate to episcopal and provincial visitations conducted over huge areas, at comparatively infrequent intervals, and yielding thousands of detections: the visitors and the courts which subsequently processed cases were faced with an administrative task which was, given contemporary resources, of quite spectacular proportions. Dr Johnson's dictum surely applies: the thing was not well done but the wonder was to see it done at all. Marchant himself recognises that the archdeaconry courts (and episcopal courts in small dioceses), which could concentrate their energies on fewer cases and exert a more persistent influence through frequent visitations, were often much more effective. The fragmentary materials which Marchant had at his disposal indicated obedience levels in some archdeaconry courts well in excess of 50 per cent, reaching nearly 80 per cent in the archdeaconry of Cleveland in 1634.[66]

These more favourable results are supported by data available for the Wiltshire courts and for the archdeaconries of Leicester and Chichester and the diocese of Ely, at least as regards the initial appearance of defendants to answer charges. (The issue of compliance with court orders imposed on convicted defendants presents some complexities and will be discussed separately later.) The Wilt-

[63] Based on search of W.R.O., QS/Minute Bks. 3–4.

[64] Marchant, *Church under the law*, pp. 203–12.

[65] Ronald A. Marchant, *The puritans and the church courts in the diocese of York, 1560–1642* (1960), p. 15 and *passim*; Haigh, *Reformation and resistance*, *passim*.

[66] Marchant, *Church under the law*, pp. 208, 231, 233–4.

shire materials will be considered first and in greatest detail. Regrettably many of the act books of the church courts operating in this county in the period 1570–1640 cannot be used to compute accurate appearance/contumacy figures, since they do not provide a full record of proceedings. Thus the activities of the archdeaconry court of North Wiltshire in the late sixteenth century are represented mainly by a *detecta* book, or register of presentments, which includes only spasmodic and partial notes on how the offenders were dealt with; while many of the early seventeenth-century records of both the Wiltshire archdeaconries, together with the entire series of disciplinary act books for the court of the bishop of Salisbury, are essentially appearance books, which do not consistently register cases in which the defendant was contumacious.[67] The data presented in Table 16 are based on a selection of act books and related materials (visitation presentments, schedules of excommunication, etc.) which *are* sufficiently complete to provide an accurate picture. They relate to the archdeaconry of Salisbury in 1573, 1587 and 1602; the archdeaconry of North Wiltshire in 1602 and part of the same area in 1621; and the Wiltshire parishes subject to the dean of Salisbury in 1634 (the visitation held that year was nominally a metropolitical one, conducted under the auspices of archbishop Laud, but was actually carried out in the usual fashion by the normal decanal officers).[68]

The construction and content of Table 16 require some words of explanation. Basically the figures refer to *individuals* subject to court action, rather than to 'cases': thus, for example, the male and female involved in a typical case of fornication or adultery have been counted separately. Following court practice, however, pairs of churchwardens, married couples and (occasionally) larger family groups who were detected together for the same offence have generally been counted as one party; only when the courts themselves treated them separately have they been individually itemised.[69] The category 'no action' comprises parties named in bills of presentment

[67] For further details, see Ingram, 'Ecclesiastical justice in Wiltshire', pp. 54–6.

[68] The figures are based on detailed analysis/collation of material in W.R.O., AS/ABO la, 2–3, 7–8; AS/Excommunications Bk, 1572–82; AW/ABO 1, 5; AW/Misc. Visitation Papers: Note-book, 1602–20 [*recte* 1602–22]; D/Pres. 1634; D/Citations 13.

[69] Cf. Marchant, *Church under the law*, p. 234. In the diocese of Ely and the archdeaconries of Chichester and Leicester, husband and wife were generally treated as separate defendants.

Table 16 *Attendance levels in the Wiltshire church courts in sample years and visitations*

	AS 1573	AS 1587	AS 1602	AW 1602	AW 1621*	D 1634
No action	—	—	—	—	2	22
Appeared on citation	129	165	138	137	95	69
Appeared after excommunication	24	22	46	88	9	13
Total appeared	*153*	*187*	*184*	*225*	*104*	*82*
Never appeared	58	108	86	145	43	39
Less: Recusants	—	3	18	6	3	4
Process discontinued	30	51	12	18	2	9
Dead/in prison	0	0	1	2	0	0
Contumacious: adjusted total	*28*	*54*	*55*	*119*	*38*	*26*
GRAND TOTAL PROSECUTED	211	295	270	370	147	121
Crude appearance rate	73%	63%	68%	61%	71%	68%
Adjusted appearance rate	85%	78%	77%	65%	73%	76%

* 66 parishes/chapelries only.
AS = Archdeaconry of Salisbury.
AW = Archdeaconry of North Wiltshire.
D = Dean of Salisbury's jurisdiction.

but apparently not prosecuted (mostly for very good reasons which implied neither negligence nor corruption on the part of court officers);[70] such cases only come to light when the formal registers of proceedings can be compared with the original visitation returns, and they have been ignored in calculating the total number of parties prosecuted. The category 'appeared on citation' includes defendants

[70] Reasons for inaction included the following. (1) Churchwardens presented some matters as uncertain, for example whether wills had been proved or curates licensed; the registry staff presumably investigated such cases in their own records and weeded out those which did not require attention. (2) Minor matters concerning church repairs, etc., were sometimes ignored in the case of very small parishes/chapelries. (3) A few minor delicts, such as a minister's failure to go on perambulation, were probably ignored because the registry staff knew of excusatory circumstances. (4) Presentments against aristocrats or ecclesiastical dignitaries were sometimes reserved for out-of-court treatment. (5) Very occasionally, offences were probably ignored through oversight or favour. For example, in 1634 the presentment of Margery Lymington of West Harnham for fighting in church was probably missed because it came into the registry in the form of a small slip separate from the main bill of presentment; on the other hand, the presentment of Mrs Weanman of Gt Bedwyn for not attending church may conceivably have been ignored through favour: W.R.O., D/Pres. 1634/14, 93.

who obeyed the courts' initial summonses;[71] 'appeared after excommunication' refers to parties who were at first contumacious and suffered the usual penalty for this, but did eventually come to court to seek absolution and/or to answer the charges against them.[72] The total number of parties who sooner or later entered an appearance, expressed as a percentage of all defendants, yields the 'crude appearance rate'.

As Marchant recognised, such a simple ratio between attenders and non-attenders gives an unduly pessimistic impression of the courts' ability to secure compliance and of the impact of excommunication. Adjustments are required. However, the precise nature of such modifications is debatable, and it should be noted that the procedures followed here in calculating an 'adjusted appearance rate' differ in some respects from those used by Marchant. The latter discounted individuals presented for 'standing excommunicate' – that is, remaining in a state of excommunication for forty days or more – on the principle that by definition such people had previously proved unamenable to discipline and their inclusion alongside fresh offenders would bias the figures; he found that very few culprits of this type did in fact attend court.[73] This example has *not* been followed here, since in Wiltshire as in certain other areas a reasonable proportion of people presented for remaining excommunicate did come to court to seek absolution. Thus in Table 16, excommunicates presented as such have simply been treated as if they were new offenders.

On the other hand, in calculating the adjusted appearance rate I have ignored defendants in 'discontinued' prosecutions: that is, cases in which citations were sent out but which were subsequently 'reserved' from session to session, and ultimately dropped, without the culprits being excommunicated.[74] In most cases the cessation of proceedings was evidently the result of deliberate policy on the part

[71] They did not necessarily turn up immediately, however; cases were often 'reserved' for several sessions to allow time for compliance.

[72] The time between excommunication and eventual appearance varied from days to months; in a few cases it was a year or more.

[73] Marchant, *Church under the law*, pp. 204, 206, 227.

[74] Marchant assumed that the majority of defendants in cases where the record was incomplete were in fact excommunicated (Marchant, *Church under the law*, pp. 205–6). This may well be correct for the records he was dealing with. As regards the Wiltshire materials, however, collation of act book entries with extant schedules of excommunication indicates that most incomplete entries represented genuinely 'discontinued' cases.

of court officials, not of inefficiency or corruption, and on these grounds it seems reasonable to distinguish non-appearers favoured in this way from the hard core of recalcitrants. It will be noted that discontinued cases were relatively numerous in the archdeaconry of Salisbury in the 1570s and 1580s; this apparently reflects a tendency on the part of judges around that time to be as moderate and flexible as possible, especially with regard to less serious delicts.[75] By the early seventeenth century proceedings in this archdeaconry were rather more formal, and discontinued cases were fewer in number. Of those which occurred, most involved ministers and churchwardens summoned to answer for semi-administrative matters like church repairs or the provision of liturgical equipment. Evidently in cases like this the courts thought in terms of a gradual remedial campaign, extending if necessary over several visitations; they were loath to victimise individual churchwardens, or to deprive a parish of the services of its minister, by over-hasty excommunication.

Other adjustments conform with Marchant's procedures. People who died while their cases were being processed, or who were imprisoned by other courts, should obviously be discounted. Obstinate recusants are likewise best ignored in calculating an adjusted appearance rate. By definition they denied the authority of the courts of the established church, which had virtually no expectation of securing their appearance. The government regarded the secular courts and the high commission as the chief means of inflicting tangible penalties on catholics and other sectaries; the role of the ordinary church courts was simply to keep them in a constant state of excommunication and to maintain, on the basis of churchwardens' presentments, a recusant register.[76]

The tedious calculations described in preceding paragraphs yield interesting results which demonstrate just how much the church courts managed to achieve. The lowest level of attendance revealed in Table 16 was in the archdeaconry of North Wiltshire in 1602. This area was populous and in parts difficult of access, while its remoteness from the administrative centre of the diocese made necessary a system of peripatetic courts; further, in the recent past the arch-

[75] People who benefited had characteristically been presented for absence from church or non-payment of rates; sexual offenders and the like were very rarely favoured. In 1587 some cases were discontinued because the work of the archdeaconry court was about to be temporarily suspended by the episcopal visitation of 1588.

[76] Marchant, *Church under the law*, p. 204.

deaconry had been maladministered by a corrupt official, William Watkins.[77] None the less, the adjusted appearance rate emerges as a respectable 65 per cent; while the figures for 1621 suggest that by then rather better results were being achieved in this area. At the other extreme, an adjusted rate of 85 per cent was attained in the archdeaconry of Salisbury in 1573; however, this partly depended on a relatively high incidence of discontinued cases and on the fact that the court's efforts to enforce church attendance and other religious observances were less consistent than they were to become later.[78] Most of the records sampled yield appearance rates hovering around 75 per cent, and this figure may be taken as fairly representative of normal performance levels in the Wiltshire courts in this period.

Year by year and month by month scrutiny of the records indicates, however, that all the Salisbury courts were liable to experience brief periods when the attendance rate was much lower than usual. These lapses serve to prove the rule of normal efficiency, since it can often be shown that they were the result of special circumstances over which the courts had no control. Thus in 1603 the rate of attendance in the court of the archdeaconry of North Wiltshire was some 15 per cent lower than in the previous year, with much of the absenteeism concentrated in the autumn sessions. At first blush it might appear that the cause lay in administrative slackness, since collation of the surviving schedules of excommunication with the act book entries reveals that many sentences were never transmitted to the parishes. The reality of the situation was that the county was suffering from a plague epidemic. Orders imposed by the Wiltshire justices at the Michaelmas quarter sessions imposed severe restrictions on movement, and it was evidently very difficult either for culprits to attend court or even for the apparitors to enter the parishes to serve processes.[79]

The Wiltshire data may be fruitfully compared with attendance figures for other southern English dioceses, of which a more or less random selection is presented in summary form in Table 17.[80] Attendance levels in the archdeaconry of Leicester were roughly

77 See above, pp. 66, 212. 78 Cf. above, pp. 107–8.

79 *H.M.C.*, *Various collections*, vol. 1, p. 74. For further details on contumacy levels in 1603, see Ingram, 'Ecclesiastical justice in Wiltshire', pp. 341–2, but note that the interpretation offered there is superseded by the present discussion.

80 Figures are based on analysis/collation of material in W.S.R.O., Ep. I/17/8; Ep. I/17/25; Ep.I/13/2; C.U.L., Ely D.R., B/2/11; B/2/37; L.M., 1 D 41/13/12, 40.

Table 17 *Attendance levels in various church court jurisdictions in sample periods*

	N	CAR	AAR
Archdeaconry of Chichester			
Jan.–June 1594	331	74%	83%
Jan.–Mar. 1636	158	87%	94%
Diocese of Ely			
Nov.–Apr. 1590–1	367	86%	93%
Episcopal visitation 1619	185	67%	83%
Archdeaconry of Leicester			
Annunciation visitation 1586	133	56%	69%
Michaelmas visitation 1615	591	63%	73%

N = Total number of defendants.
CAR = Crude appearance rate.
AAR = Adjusted appearance rate.

similar to those found in Wiltshire: the adjusted appearance rate was some 69 per cent in 1586 and 73 per cent in 1615. Given that the jurisdiction covered a fairly large and populous county which had perforce to be served by mobile courts, these results represent no mean achievement. Attendance levels were even better in the fairly small and compact archdeaconry of Chichester: in the period January–March 1636 even the crude appearance rate was 87 per cent, while the adjusted rate reached 94 per cent. The similarly high levels achieved in the diocese of Ely raise some points of special interest. The Ely courts in this period were still using the lesser form of excommunication, or suspension, as the front-line sanction in cases of contumacy, in contrast to most ecclesiastical courts, which had, in the difficult days of the mid-sixteenth century, switched to the use of full excommunication and never subsequently reverted.[81] The peculiarity of the Ely procedure was, however, more apparent than real. In most areas in the late sixteenth and early seventeenth centuries the church courts did not try to enforce the complete social ostracism of excommunicates, as is shown by the extreme paucity of prosecutions for illegally consorting with people under the major ban.[82] Thus in practice there was little to choose between excommunication and suspension, the main effect in each case being to

[81] Houlbrooke, *Church courts and the people*, p. 49.
[82] This is true of all the jurisdictions on which the present study is based and was evidently also true in the diocese of York: see Marchant, *Church under the law*, pp. 221–2.

exclude the culprit from church and sacraments.[83] According to Marchant, the Ely courts were also unusual in another respect, one which supposedly explains their high level of efficiency: as custodian of the liberty of Ely the bishop enjoyed secular as well as spiritual powers, so that offenders had a simple choice of frying-pan or fire.[84] This idea is based on a misconception. In reality the bishop's temporal authority extended only over the parishes of the Isle of Ely, not over the Cambridgeshire portion of the diocese, and in any case was probably of little importance in affecting attendance levels in the diocesan courts. The effectiveness of ecclesiastical justice in the see of Ely was due not to extraneous factors but to the compact size of the diocese and the very close supervision, based on a system of quarterly presentments supplemented by 'informations' from apparitors and ministers, which the bishop's officers were able to exercise.[85]

The achievements and limitations of church discipline may be further illuminated by study of spatial variations in the courts' impact *within* particular dioceses or archdeaconries. Some of the general factors conditioning such variations have already been discussed by Marchant, and his findings may be briefly reviewed in the light of the new evidence from Wiltshire and elsewhere in southern England. Marchant found that the church courts were often unable to make much impact in areas of marked recusant strength in the dioceses of York and Chester.[86] In contrast, the concentration of catholic recusants in parts of the archdeaconry of Chichester does not seem to have undermined the courts there to any significant degree. In Wiltshire, recusancy existed in strength in only a few parishes in the south, and even in these it apparently had little effect on the processes of ecclesiastical justice: thus in Stourton, the most catholic parish in the county, contumacy among the non-recusant population was not noticeably higher than elsewhere in the archdeaconry of Salisbury. Marchant's generalisation that urban centres were often exceptionally contumacious is supported to the extent that the Wiltshire courts always experienced difficulties in securing

[83] Probably it was only when the culprit encountered the *legal* disabilities of being under the major ban (inability to act as a plaintiff, for example) that the additional burdens of greater excommunication weighed heavily.
[84] Marchant, *Church under the law*, p. 226.
[85] Miller, 'Liberty of Ely', pp. 1–27; Owen, *Ely records*, pp. 7, 20.
[86] Marchant, *Church under the law*, p. 208.

the attendance of offenders from places like Malmesbury, Westport and Bradford.[87] However, evidence from other counties indicates that some boroughs posed no such special problems: in the town of Leicester in 1615, for example, contumacy was no greater than the average for the archdeaconry as a whole. Probably it was not towns as such that were associated with exceptionally low attendance levels, but more specifically sprawling urban areas, often based on industry, with a high proportion of poor people living in crowded suburbs;[88] *rural* parishes with a rather similar social and economic structure could likewise exhibit relatively high contumacy rates.[89] In contrast, as might be expected, the church courts' easiest task generally lay in compact country villages. Yet too much should not be made of such spatial variations. A few blackspots apart, contumacy tended to be a ubiquitous but therefore locally unspectacular phenomenon.

More striking is that contumacy was associated with certain offences much more than others. Analysis of court proceedings from Wiltshire, the diocese of Ely and the archdeaconries of Leicester and Chichester reveals a common pattern which is in turn similar to that reported in studies of other areas. Contumacy was most pronounced among defendants charged with major sexual offences. The precise levels varied from area to area, but very commonly well over 50 per cent of individuals detected for adultery, fornication or bastard-bearing never appeared in court and were excommunicated. Most other classes of offenders, including people brought in question for bridal pregnancy, were far more likely to be obedient.[90] Part of the reason for this pattern, as Houlbrooke has observed, was simply that people accused of major sexual sins had more to lose by attending court. Whereas culprits guilty of lesser offences like failure to pay parochial rates or irregular attendance at church could expect to be discharged with an admonition and a modest burden of fees, fornicators and adulterers faced the humiliation of public penance or, at least, the considerable trouble and expense required to clear their names by compurgation.[91] It may also be true that people guilty of

[87] *Ibid.*, pp. 207–8. Regrettably, the disciplinary records relating to the city of Salisbury and adjacent parishes (under the jurisdiction of the subdean of Salisbury) have largely perished.

[88] Marchant, *Church under the law*, p. 208; cf. Houlbrooke, *English family*, p. 23.

[89] For example, see Collinson, 'Cranbrook and the Fletchers', pp. 174–5, 183–4.

[90] Ingram, 'Ecclesiastical justice in Wiltshire', pp. 344–6; Marchant, *Church under the law*, p. 217; Collinson, 'Cranbrook and the Fletchers', pp. 183–4.

[91] Houlbrooke, *Church courts and the people*, p. 86.

blatant immorality were more likely than other offenders to be 'ethical dissenters' in Marchant's sense, indifferent to religion or to the censures of the church: an example of such a type was William Nicholas of Calne, the reputed father of a bastard child, who openly declared around 1619 that 'he careth not for the spiritual court nor what it can do to him'.[92] However, these considerations by no means wholly account for the tendency towards contumacy among sexual offenders. Important also were the cultural and social characteristics of the groups most likely to be involved in immorality: young, unmarried people, including many servants.

As previous chapters have demonstrated, many such fornicators and bastard-bearers were unthinking and foolish rather than egregiously immoral or self-consciously defiant, and in terms of behaviour there was often little to choose between a pregnant bride and an unmarried mother.[93] If such sexual offenders were 'irreligious' it was in the sense that young people generally were *de facto* allowed a measure of irresponsibility before they took on the serious duties of householders and assumed full membership of church and commonwealth. Their games and dances were mostly tolerated, their attendance at church and even participation in the communion were slackly enforced; indeed it is hardly too much to say that there existed an adolescent culture, associated above all with servants, one of the features of which was a degree of liberty.[94] The fact that many sexual offenders were thus at the stage in the life-cycle when official religion had least impact inevitably posed problems for the church courts. But probably of equal or even greater importance was another feature of adolescent culture: spatial mobility. The ease and frequency with which young people migrated created special difficulties in the administration of excommunication, and it is hardly surprising that the records yield many references to the disappearance of culprits. The hostile social pressures which drove some pregnant women from their homes have already been described.[95] Male sexual offenders lacking strong local ties or responsibilities were also likely to migrate and faced fewer obstacles in doing so. Some would no doubt have moved on in any case; others were galvanised into

[92] W.R.O., D/Pres. 1619 (unnumbered), loose slip included in bundle of presentments.
[93] See above, Chapters 7–8.
[94] Cf. Collinson, *Religion of protestants*, pp. 219–20, 227–30.
[95] See above, pp. 286–7.

movement by fears of the trouble and expense of appearing before the church courts, of having a bastardy order enforced upon them or of pressures to marry the woman they had seduced. Such fugitives could only too easily pass the diocesan or archidiaconal boundary, or at least disappear beyond the ken of the community where their offence was committed. In 1624, for example, a man questioned by the justices in Wiltshire described how he had come from Hampshire some months previously 'for that he was charged with a bastard, by reason whereof he was constrained to travel to seek harvest work'; while in 1631 the churchwardens of Great Bedwyn presented that John Bryant had been accused of begetting a child upon a certain Joan Hart, 'upon which they are both fled and now live out of the parish, where we know not'. The abundance and stereotyped nature of such statements indicate that flight was a commonplace.[96]

Sexual offenders were particularly prone to migration, but a smaller proportion of other kinds of culprit likewise slipped away. Overall, removal was a significant cause of contumacy. To contemporaries in local society the flight of offenders may often have been seen as a satisfactory outcome of legal action against them; the excommunication they incurred aptly symbolised their riddance from the parish. In any event, the migration of culprits was obviously a problem which the ecclesiastical authorities could do little or nothing to remedy, and should be treated as a mitigating circumstance in retrospectively assessing the church courts' performance. Moreover it helps to explain a feature of ecclesiastical justice which has often excited comment and criticism, the fact that writs *de excommunicato capiendo* were rarely used to try to secure the appearance of recalcitrants in disciplinary cases. The judges' reluctance to invoke the secular arm was not simply because such writs were expensive and administratively cumbersome; they were also a complete waste of time if the culprit had left the parish, since there was little chance that he or she would be apprehended by the sheriff's officers.[97]

[96] W.R.O., QS/GR Mich. 1624/171; D/Pres. 1631/3.

[97] Cf. Price, 'Abuses of excommunication', pp. 112–13; Marchant, *Church under the law*, p. 222; Houlbrooke, *Church courts and the people*, p. 50. However, the secular arm was occasionally invoked to make an example of particular individuals who *could* be apprehended, especially when they were the cause of major scandal in the parish. William Prior of Keevil, who had begotten several illegitimate children on his maidservant, was eventually brought to heel by this means: see above, pp. 273–4.

If the footloose young were least amenable to ecclesiastical discipline, the converse was true of the settled householder. Not only were householders and their wives more subject to a variety of external pressures to religious and social conformity, but these were in addition powerfully reinforced by internalised values. As we have seen, participation in the communion, and attendance at church at least 'as often as the neighbours', were strongly associated with status and reputation and with the myriad neighbourhood rivalries whose monument lies in the records of pew disputes and defamation causes.[98] No doubt there were variations at different social levels and from individual to individual: we know that for the very poor the state of marriage and householder status could themselves be very fragile, while inevitably some people were indifferent to the attractions of respectability. But among householders and their wives (even down to the level of poor cottager or labourer) the divide between the 'honest' and the 'lewd' was sharper than among adolescents, and either greater discretion or more self-conscious defiance was required of those who desired not to conform. It would appear that, at least in the villages, the great majority chose to appear respectable. Hence it is readily understandable that, among sexual offenders prosecuted in the church courts, newly married couples guilty of prenuptial fornication were most likely to appear and answer: their compliance signified that they were on the threshold of new responsibilities and patterns of self-assessment, about to assume a full adult role in the commonwealth. Such a life-cyclical shift in attitudes also accounts for some cases in which culprits guilty of more serious offences sought absolution after a lapse of time. Roger Jorden of Keevil, for example, was excommunicated in 1603 for fathering a bastard, and went away to Hampshire. Two years later he returned to submit himself to the court, asserting that he had since married an 'honest woman' and was repentant for his earlier misdeeds. He settled down in Keevil and was never subsequently in serious trouble.[99]

The burden of the foregoing discussion has been that the problem of contumacy was not as serious, or at least does not reflect as badly on the church courts, as has sometimes been suggested. This is true in another sense too. As was noted earlier, some historians have

[98] See above, pp. 111–12, 118, 123.
[99] W.R.O., AS/ABO 8, 9/11/1603 and 22/4/1605, *Office v. Jorden.*

assumed that unabsolved excommunicates remained in a permanent state of defiance of or indifference to official religion, 'ethical dissenters' cut off till their dying day from the services of the church.[100] No doubt this was the case with some; but there are grounds for thinking that certainly a significant and perhaps a large proportion of excommunicates slipped back into normal life without securing a formal absolution. Migration was one factor which facilitated this process. Of those who removed, some were genuinely unaware of their legal position. Thus the curate of Donhead St Mary wrote on behalf of a certain Hester Jacins that 'when she was presented or to be presented [she] knew not of it being in Dorsetshire'.[101] More commonly, no doubt, fugitives were well aware that they would most likely be excommunicated in their absence but lacked certain knowledge. In any event, it was probably fairly easy for absconders to fit into a community ignorant of their past and so escape the penalties of excommunication, especially if they settled down and left their wild oats behind them. The existence of a complex web of ecclesiastical jurisdictions was in their favour. Thus Henry Tayler, minister of Great Bedwyn, wrote revealingly to the dean of Salisbury's registrar in 1620 that

> the bearer hereof hath been a poor servant of mine these twelve months and more, but before he came to me he had a wench with child in Kessom parish [?Chesham in Buckinghamshire] and since that, the court there hath excommunicated him for coming away and not answering for his fact; he is now determined to marry with the same party and cannot be married except he be absolved. I pray you tell him in whose jurisdiction it is, for I know it not, and to whom he may go for absolution... Till he was fully asked with us [i.e. until his banns had been thrice published] I knew it not.[102]

An alternative to making a new life elsewhere was to return eventually to the original parish of departure. As in the case of Roger Jorden already quoted, such people sometimes had to secure a formal absolution; but there are signs that others found that the excommunication had in their absence fallen into oblivion. William Coller of Sutton Benger, accused in 1601 of fathering a bastard, fled to Gloucestershire and was surprised to find on his return two years

[100] Marchant, *Church under the law*, pp. 220–1, 227, 235, 243.
[101] W.R.O., AS/Excommunications: miscellaneous bundle marked 'Excommunications, various dates', no. 1.
[102] W.R.O., D/Pres. 1620 (unnumbered).

later that the matter had not been forgotten; while Coller failed in his ruse, it may be surmised that others succeeded.[103]

The eventual lapsing of sentences without formal absolution occurred even in cases where the culprit did not resort to flight. In common with other courts in this period, the tribunals of the church found it hard (and probably did not realistically expect) to secure indefinite enforcement of their edicts. Because of practical difficulties – the rapid turnover of curates in some parishes, for example – it is unlikely that the regular six-monthly denunciation of excommunicates in church envisaged by the 1604 canons was at all widely observed, while certainly only a small proportion of people theoretically excluded from the church were regularly presented for 'standing excommunicate' as the letter of the law required.[104] Inevitably churchwardens, especially in larger communities, became hazy about which members of the parish were excommunicate. Thus in 1601 the presenting officers of Calne reported somewhat testily that 'all these foresaid women we present for having bastards by those foresaid persons named with them. Some of them stand already (by the information of the apparitors) in your courts excommunicated, but who they are we perfectly know not; you shall find them in your records and registers.' Likewise the churchwardens of Mere reported uncertainly in 1600 that 'Mary Pascall now the wife of Thomas Hopkyns standeth excommunicate as we think, notwithstanding she cometh to the church unreformed of the same as we think'.[105] Especially when the original offence was comparatively trivial, it was eventually possible for excommunications to recede into oblivion.

This and some of the other important features of the way excommunication worked in practice as opposed to theory may be illustrated from the parishes of Wylye and Keevil. In Wylye, in the three decades 1600–29, 19 people failed to appear in court to answer charges against them and apparently remained unabsolved excommunicates.[106] In two of these cases, both concerning probate, it is probable that the sentences were of merely formal significance and

[103] W.R.O., AW/ABO 1, 27/6/1603, *Office v. Coller*.

[104] Marchant, *Church under the law*, p. 227; Ingram, 'Ecclesiastical justice in Wiltshire', pp. 350–1.

[105] W.R.O., D/Pres. 1600-2, Calne, Jan. 1601, Mere, Aug. 1600.

[106] In two cases there is no positive evidence that the culprits were excommunicated for their contumacy.

were never actually notified to the parish.[107] In about a third of the remaining cases there are signs that the sentences, mostly for less serious matters, were allowed to fall into oblivion. Thus two members of the wealthy Potticarie family were excommunicated in 1604, probably for absence from church; but since both subsequently appeared to answer other charges in the church courts and were not treated as excommunicates, while it is in any case clear that at least one of these men was continuing to play a full and active part in parochial life, it would seem that these sentences were rapidly forgotten.[108] Another lapsed sentence was that passed on Guy Potticarie in 1627 for selling meat on the sabbath; he was in office as churchwarden by 1629 and it is most unlikely that by then the excommunication was still being enforced against him.[109] A sentence against Elizabeth Baker alias Cheate, widow, decreed in 1604 following a presentment for incontinence, was apparently allowed to lapse after her alleged lover passed his purgation; she was not treated as an excommunicate when she appeared to answer another presentment in 1619.[110] Even the two multiple bastard-bearers in the parish benefited to a certain extent from a flexible attitude to excommunication. Susan Baker failed to appear to answer for her fornication in 1627 and 1634. On both occasions she was, in fact, in Bridewell, and whether sentences of excommunication were inflicted on her is unclear. In any event she was duly excommunicated in 1632, when she failed to attend court to answer for another of her illegitimate children. Yet she was married by January 1640, as far as can be seen without having first procured a formal absolution.[111] Elizabeth Long, likewise presented several times for fornication and bastard-bearing, sometimes made an appearance and sometimes not; but she was finally excommunicated, and notification thereof sent to her village, in the summer of 1626. By the end of 1627, however, she too was married; probably she left the village soon afterwards with her new husband, a semi-itinerant labourer who was ejected from

[107] W.R.O., AS/Excommunications, 1607–33/63 (Nicholas Potticarie and Susan Bower).

[108] W.R.O., AS/ABO 8, fol. 163v; cf. AS/ABO 12, 18/7/1618, *Office v. Richard Potticary*; B/ABO 6, fol. 124; Hadow (ed.), *Wylye registers*, pp. 15, 40–2, 48.

[109] W.R.O., AS/Citations *quorum nomina*, 1626/73; Hadow (ed.), *Wylye registers*, pp. 7, 29.

[110] W.R.O., AS/ABO 8, fol. 285; cf. AS/ABO 12, 27/11/1619, *Office v. Elizabeth Baker*.

[111] W.R.O., AS/Citations *quorum nomina*, 1630–6/16, 20; AS/Excommunications, 1607–33/27; AS/ABO 15, fol. 144v.

Wylye in 1627.[112] Apart from this woman, six of the other unabsolved excommunicates almost certainly left the parish either before or immediately after they incurred the sentence; most of them were transients rather than members of established families. George Hellier, for example, accused of being the father of a bastard child born in March 1611, was a servant who by May of the same year was said to be living in Dorset.[113] There remain only four cases in which there is any likelihood that the culprits continued to live in Wylye as lifelong sufferers of the penalty of excommunication, and even these are not certain. In any case, they were many times outnumbered by the inhabitants of Wylye who duly appeared, in some cases repeatedly, before the episcopal and archdeaconry courts to answer charges.

In Keevil in the same three decades, 21 people remained unabsolved after incurring excommunication for non-appearance in disciplinary cases. Joan Harris, excommunicated in 1603 for an unknown offence, was dead within the year.[114] Two sentences pronounced in the archdeacon's court in 1628 against women who had neglected a probate almost certainly lapsed (if indeed they had ever taken full effect) when the will was proved in the bishop's court later in the same year; but there is no note of formal absolution.[115] Most established residents of the parish sooner or later submitted when they found themselves in trouble with the church courts, and some of the apparent exceptions can be explained by migration. Elinor Deverell, the mother of a bastard child, was 'conveyed away' and apparently managed to procure a marriage.[116] Mary Polehampton, wife of a cottager, was excommunicated for an unspecified offence (possibly non-attendance at church or failure to receive the communion) in 1621, the 'letters of excommunication' being despatched to the parish in November. She had been named as one of the 'honest neighbours' who had assisted the midwife at a bastard birth in 1620,

[112] W.R.O., B/ABO 8, 28/2/1617, *Office v. Longynowe*; AS/Excommunications, 1607–33/13, 41, 95; AS/ABO 13, 12/5/1621, *Office v. Long*; B/ABO 11, 12/6/1628, *Office v. William Denmead*; QS/GR Trin. 1627/117; Hadow (ed.), *Wylye registers*, pp. 27–8.

[113] W.R.O., B/ABO 6, fol. 85v, *Office v. Susan Dew*.

[114] W.R.O., AS/ABO 8, 9/7/1603, *Office v. Harris*; cf. W.R.O., 653/1, burial of Joan Harris, 28/4/1604.

[115] W.R.O., AS/ABO 14, 23/1/1628, *Office v. Edith and Mary Russell*; cf. Episcopal consistory of Salisbury probate records, will of John Russell, 11/10/1628.

[116] W.R.O., AS/ABO 14, 22/6/1627, *Office v. Deverell*; QS/GR East. 1629/137–8.

and her contumacy seems surprising. The explanation, as manorial records reveal, is that she and her husband had left the parish, certainly by 1624 and probably by December 1621.[117] Walter Passion was with his wife and daughter excommunicated in 1601 for failing to receive the communion; Susan, the wife, was again not forthcoming when named in an accusation of adultery against Robert Blagden in 1609. Yet the Passions had been amenable to church court discipline in the 1590s. The fact is that their association with Keevil was somewhat tenuous. Walter, much indebted, was often away (including spells at sea and in Ireland), while on one occasion Susan was said to be of the parish of Steeple Ashton. In the early years of the new century the couple severed their ties with Keevil forever; they are later found living in the town of Trowbridge.[118]

Of the other recalcitrants, most were either servants and other transients or people who, though born in Keevil, are known to have been living away from the village in service or in some other capacity around the time of their excommunication. These people left no traces of subsequent habitation in the parish among the various forms of surviving record, and it may be fairly assumed that they had gone for good. As in Wylye, only a handful of people could have remained in the village as permanent excommunicates, and certain of these are highly doubtful instances. Take, for example, the case of Charles Fricker. Probably a fairly poor individual, he was excommunicated in 1609 for an unspecified offence and there is no evidence of absolution. Since he had been amenable to discipline in 1593 – he did penance for a bastard child and married the woman after her delivery – his later contumacy is perhaps a little surprising. Probably the truth is that, like the Polehamptons and the Passions, he migrated from the village, though in his case positive evidence is lacking.[119]

The preceding discussion of contumacy and excommunication has been concerned only with the courts' efforts to secure the appearance of suspects in the first instance to answer charges against them. But the threat of excommunication was also used to compel culprits to

[117] W.R.O., AS/Excommunications, 1607–33/79; QS/GR East. 1620/231; 288/1, courts baron, 18 Dec. 19 Jac. I (1621), 17 Oct. 20 Jac I (1622), 31 Mar. 22 Jac. I (1624).

[118] W.R.O., AS/ABO 7, fols. 175v, 184v, 204v; cf. AS/ABO 4, fol. 36; AS/ABO 5, fol. 48; B/ABO 2, fol. 22v; QS/GR East. 1617/152.

[119] W.R.O., AS/ABO 10, 17/6/1609, *Office v. Fricker*; cf. AS/ABO 4, fols. 130v, 137, 140, 164v.

obey court orders after their cases had had a first hearing. The commonest of such orders were to remedy some fault or omission (such as failure to receive the communion), to perform penance, to reappear after adjournments, or to pay court fees, and normally offenders were required to certify that they had duly performed them. Unfortunately it is often impossible to determine how efficient the courts were in enforcing their orders, since the scribes were often lax in registering certificates and other post-trial information. The records of peripatetic courts, such as those of the archdeacons of Leicester and North Wiltshire and the visitation courts of the bishop of Salisbury, are for obvious reasons particularly unreliable in this respect. In jurisdictions which did maintain a consistent record, however, it is generally found that the enforcement of orders was reasonably efficient. Marchant's extensive sampling indicated that the great majority of offenders were obedient once they had appeared to answer charges,[120] and the records of Ely diocese and the archdeaconry of Chichester in this period support a similar conclusion.

In the archdeaconry of Salisbury – the only major Wiltshire jurisdiction where certificates and so forth were regularly registered – it was much the same story up to the early years of the seventeenth century. Thus of 184 attenders in this court in 1602, only 17 subsequently disobeyed a court order and were excommunicated. By the 1620s and 1630s, however, the position was far less satisfactory: of some 190 individuals who appeared in court in 1622, no fewer than 80 were subsequently decreed excommunicate for failing to certify penance or otherwise obey the mandates of the court. Underlying this situation appears to have been a good deal of administrative irregularity. Comparison between act book sentences and surviving schedules of excommunication reveals that only about half the scheduled names were annotated to indicate that 'letters of excommunication' had been despatched to the parishes, and in some cases it is possible that people decreed excommunicate had not even had their names entered on schedules for the sentence to be formally pronounced.[121] In brief, it would appear that efforts to enforce court orders had become very slack and haphazard, and it is hardly

[120] Marchant, *Church under the law*, pp. 205–6, 214. There were, however, areas and periods where this was not true, especially in the late sixteenth century: see *ibid.*, p. 209.

[121] Based on analysis of entries in W.R.O., AS/ABO 13, collated with AS/Excommunications, 1607–33. For further details, see Ingram, 'Ecclesiastical justice in Wiltshire', pp. 360–2.

surprising that obedience levels suffered – a reminder that, whatever the intrinsic strengths of the procedures of ecclesiastical justice, inefficient administration could render them nugatory.

The immediate cause for this slackness was probably a tendency on the part of the staff of the archdeacon of Salisbury's registry to neglect less profitable activities. To the administrators who ran the courts, the initial appearances of defendants were particularly important, since these offered the best opportunity of collecting fees; most effort, it would seem, was hence concentrated on the early stages of each case. Matters such as the enforcement of penance were generally of little financial interest to the registry staff, and it is perhaps not entirely surprising that they showed less concern about these later aspects of the disciplinary process. More generally, these problems of enforcing court orders may be seen as part of the administrative malaise which, as was suggested in Chapter 1, seems to have infected the church court establishment in Wiltshire in the twenty years or so immediately preceding the civil war, and which can be attributed to complacency, ageing personnel and poor leadership. It will be obvious from the central chapters of this book that these problems by no means totally eroded the viability of the Wiltshire church courts; on the contrary, they continued to do good business and to perform important social roles. However, such slackness must have undermined them to some extent, and no doubt gave ammunition to the enemies and critics of the spiritual jurisdiction. Indeed it is tempting to link failings of the church court establishment like those visible at Salisbury with the destruction of ecclesiastical justice in the 1640s. But it is well to keep the matter in perspective. In truth the fate of the church courts was largely determined by factors other than episodes of slackness or inefficiency in particular dioceses. The more central reasons for what happened to the spiritual jurisdiction after 1640 will be briefly reviewed in the final chapter.

12. *Church courts and society in 1640: retrospect and prospect*

Traditionally the church courts of late Elizabethan and early Stuart England have been condemned as corrupt, inefficient and unpopular. This view, rooted in the partisan judgements of contemporary puritan and common law critics, has in recent decades been undermined by a series of detailed studies of the administration of ecclesiastical justice; yet the myth still lives on. Thus Margaret Stieg, on the basis of a limited and superficial survey of the work of the church courts in the diocese of Bath and Wells in the period 1600–40, confidently reiterates the old clichés. In their relations with the laity, she asserts, the ecclesiastical courts were 'almost totally ineffectual', and what little they did achieve was 'at the expense of great unpopularity'. They were 'expensive', 'venal', 'partial', and hence 'contemptible', their activities 'almost completely pointless'. In brief, she concludes, 'by the seventeenth century the diocesan courts were anachronisms...dependent upon abandoned premises'.[1]

The aim of this book has been to show conclusively just how misleading such judgements are. None of the derogatory labels conventionally applied to ecclesiastical justice can be accepted without major qualification. Of course the courts had weaknesses, but many of the defects were characteristic of early modern justice in general rather than of the church courts in particular, while the remainder were less acute than has often been supposed. Ecclesiastical justice was neither exceptionally expensive nor unusually dilatory; while evidence of egregious corruption or abnormal partiality is slight. Rather more common were episodes of administrative slackness, sometimes accompanied by a certain amount of low-level venality, as in the Wiltshire portion of the diocese of Salisbury in the 1620s and 1630s. Yet at Salisbury as elsewhere such periods of torpor were offset by more dynamic phases (much depended on the

[1] Margaret Stieg, *Laud's laboratory: the diocese of Bath and Wells in the early seventeenth century* (Lewisburg, Pa, 1982), pp. 279–80.

personnel of the courts at particular times); while even in the worst periods the credibility of the courts was by no means totally eroded.

Admittedly the church courts faced a persistent problem of contumacy; but historians have been inclined to magnify its scale and, in failing to recognise the complexity of the problem, have exaggerated how far it discredited the structures of ecclesiastical justice. The threat of excommunication was usually sufficient to secure the appearance before the courts of settled householders: their compliance reflected the fact that, for such people, participation in the communion, attendance at church and involvement in other aspects of parochial life were (irrespective of their purely religious significance) important touchstones of social respectability and local 'credit'. Servants and other youngsters – always prominent among sexual offenders – were inevitably less amenable to discipline, not least because their characteristic mobility easily put them beyond the range of the courts' summonses and sanctions. This was simply a fact of life, an inescapable feature of the social environment in which the courts operated. It should not be assumed, however, that the defaulters who failed to respond to the citations of the ecclesiastical courts and were thus excommunicated were utterly lost to the church. Probably a sizeable proportion of the young people involved eventually experienced the usual life-cyclical shift in attitudes associated with the assumption of marital and household responsibilities, left their wild oats or unfortunate histories behind them and conformed to the normal standards of respectable behaviour among 'honest householders'. For this and other reasons there was not in most areas the massive build-up of perpetual excommunicates that some historians have supposed: the notion of a thick stratum of 'ethical dissenters' is a myth. In assessing the significance of contumacy, moreover, it must always be borne in mind that the problem was by no means confined to the church courts: secular tribunals such as quarter sessions faced similar difficulties, rooted in intractable social circumstances and the persistent administrative rigidities which were so characteristic of early modern England. In view of the problems which faced them, the church courts did remarkably well.

Irrespective of contumacy, the church courts were far more effective than has often been supposed – though it would of course be unrealistic to expect too much from *any* Tudor or Stuart legal institution, or for that matter even from a modern one. The penalties imposed by ecclesiastical court judges, especially the more rigorous forms of penance backed up by a substantial burden of fees, were far from derisory; in particular they seem to have been much feared by substantial householders who valued their local reputation. Yet the courts' impact did not depend wholly or even principally on the effects of discipline on individual offenders. Rather, their success was a function of the *persistent pressure* exerted by the ecclesiastical tribunals, the routine pursuit in visitation after visitation, generation after generation, of a variety of sins of omission and commission. Notoriously such a pattern of discipline failed to satisfy the more extreme puritan activists, hot for reformation grounded in zealous evangelism backed up by sharp measures to curb the unregenerate; yet in retrospect it is plain that immorality and impiety *were* combated in an undramatic but by no means ineffectual war of attrition. Over the period 1570–1640 the church courts played a significant part in improving clerical standards. They also helped to marginalise catholic recusants and to nudge the mass of the population towards more rigorous standards of religious devotion and observance. In the spheres of marital and sexual behaviour, the courts consistently upheld the immorality of incest, adultery and fornication and facilitated the decline in the incidence of illegitimacy which occurred in the early seventeenth century. Further, the expansion in many areas after about 1590 of church court prosecutions for antenuptial fornication re-emphasised the ideal of premarital chastity, and may even have helped to stimulate the actual fall in bridal pregnancy rates discernible in some parishes by the reign of Charles I. Implicitly such prosecutions also underlined the importance of the church wedding as the only acceptable mode of entry into the married state; and the same principle was evident in the way the church courts adjudicated disputes over extra-ecclesiastical marriage contracts or spousals. The reluctance of the judges to pronounce in favour of disputed contracts both reflected and reinforced the decline of spousals as a significant feature of social life; the small number of marriage contract suits coming before the courts by the 1620s and 1630s was a sign that the church's centuries-long struggle to secure popular acceptance of the need for marriage in church had at last been won.[2] Prosecutions for taking part in clandestine wedding ceremonies served to consolidate this tightening of ecclesiastical control

[2] Note, however, that there are signs of a resurgence of consensual unions in the later seventeenth century: see Ingram, 'Reform of popular culture?', p. 143.

over marriage, while other aspects of the church courts' work – including sexual slander cases, prosecutions for aiding and abetting sexual offences and a variety of actions and prosecutions relating to marital breakdown – all helped to a greater or lesser extent to reinforce the ideals of personal chastity, communal responsibility for sexual behaviour and stable matrimony.

To describe the ecclesiastical courts as 'unpopular' is highly misleading. Indeed, given the wide range and complexity of their social and administrative roles, this word is far too crude to carry any real meaning; at the least a more discriminating approach is required, capable of distinguishing between such utterly diverse aspects of the church courts' work as the routine granting of probates and administrations on the one hand, and the pursuit of witches and sorcerers on the other. Preceding chapters have focused primarily on the sex and marriage business of the courts and, to a lesser extent, on prosecutions designed to enforce or encourage basic religious observances. These activities, occurring in a context in which a good deal of legal regulation of social life was taken for granted, can hardly be described as inimical to the population at large. Indeed the contrary is true. Presentments for not attending church or receiving the communion, prosecutions for bastard-bearing and other notorious forms of sexual immorality, lawsuits over sexual slander – all these meshed to a greater or lesser degree with pressing local concerns, and it can be safely assumed that court action on such issues largely met with the approval of substantial sections of society. The maintenance of a reasonable working relationship between the courts and the communities they dealt with was encouraged by the fact that ecclesiastical justice depended so heavily on local co-operation for the detection and prosecution of offenders, with the result that within limits it was often possible for communities to construct their own disciplinary agendas. In framing bills of presentment, parish officers naturally concentrated on matters which most nearly approximated to local concerns; unless the diocesan or archidiaconal authorities were especially insistent, matters which were perceived to be irrelevant or inimical to local interests tended to go by default.

Why then were the church courts to be swept away in the early 1640s, amid a barrage of criticism at Westminster against ecclesiastical justice in particular and episcopal government in general? Much the same sort of question might be asked about the monarchy itself: this appeared to be functioning perfectly adequately at least until the late 1630s, yet by 1640 the king was at odds with the bulk of the political nation and by 1642 at war with a section of it; while Charles I's execution in 1649 was to inaugurate a period of republican government which few could even have dreamed of a decade earlier. In explaining these developments, including the problems both of the king and of the bishops, recent studies have emphasised the importance of short-term factors and interactions – the personalities of the leading political actors, the royal policies of the 1630s, the play of events during the crucial months of 1640–2, the fog of misperception and mutual suspicion which militated against compromise and settlement.[3] Certainly these considerations are relevant to the fate of the church courts. It now seems plain that the 'root and branch' movement against episcopal government which developed in 1640–1 was primarily a reaction against the innovations of archbishop Laud and his associates and was, broadly speaking, strongest in those areas which had 'received the firmest imprint of Arminianism'. Anthony Fletcher has vividly described the blend of bafflement and irritation with which Laudian innovations were received in parishes in the diocese of Chichester; similarly in Ely diocese, the root and branch petitioners specifically complained of the Arminian policies of bishop Matthew Wren, enshrined in a 'book of visitatory articles to the number of one hundred forty and seven'.[4] In important senses, it should be noted, the campaign against episcopal government was less radical than it may at first sight appear; and, while it envisaged a remodelling of the existing structure of ecclesiastical jurisdiction, it did not necessarily imply an end to public discipline over religious behaviour and personal morality. Thus plans debated in parliament in the summer of 1641 proposed that, pending the creation of a new system of church government, the erstwhile spiritual jurisdiction would be exercised by lay and clerical commissioners. Despite these safeguards for the continuance of public discipline – still widely regarded as essential to the well-being of the commonwealth – the 'root and branch' programme proved far too radical for the majority of members of parliament and for the country at large: eventually it stimulated a

[3] See especially Anthony Fletcher, *The outbreak of the English civil war* (1981), *passim*.

[4] Fletcher, *Outbreak*, p. 95; Fletcher, *County community in peace and war*, ch. 4; Palmer (ed.), *Episcopal visitation returns*, p. 73.

powerful conservative reaction which protested at the dangerous experiment of tampering with a liturgy and system of church government which had for so long provided a satisfactory framework for religious and social stability. These conservative sentiments found a voice in many counties (including Wiltshire) in a series of petitions in defence of episcopacy and of the prayer book which were circulated in the months from autumn 1641 to spring 1642. Among the concerns of the petitioners was the actual collapse of much of the machinery of ecclesiastical justice – following the destruction of the courts' coercive powers by the act of 17 Car. I c. 11 against the high commission – without an adequate alternative being established. It should be emphasised that a collapse of this nature was hardly willed: it happened by default, a symptom of the stalemate which by autumn 1641 existed among the conflicting interests which were eventually to drift into civil war.[5]

Thus the church courts' downfall in the early 1640s should not be seen as an inevitable result of long-standing weaknesses and of accumulated grievances against them; its prime causes must rather be sought in the personalities and policies of the years immediately preceding the calling of the Long Parliament, and in the play of events and opinion at Westminster and in the localities in the period 1640–2. But of course this was not the whole story: the church courts were vulnerable in certain respects, and though these weaknesses would in normal circumstances not have been sufficient to shake the edifice of ecclesiastical justice, arguably they did *facilitate* the courts' destruction in the overturning days which succeeded the breakdown of Charles I's personal rule. In the first place, the tradition of puritan and common law abuse of the church courts provided a ready-made vocabulary of denigration and a stereotyped analysis of what was wrong with them; in their time of trouble, the courts found themselves in the invidious position of a dog with a bad name or (to change the animal metaphor) as excellent candidates for the role of scapegoat. No matter how zealously and efficiently the church courts and their personnel operated, they could not wholly dispel the effects of puritan smears; and the stock criticisms were especially mordant when they had at least some demonstrable basis in fact. That by the end of Elizabeth's reign and on into the early seventeenth century the catalogue of complaints had been absorbed into the

[5] Fletcher, *Outbreak*, chs. 3, 9.

consciousness of all levels of society is evident from the outbursts of criticism and contempt to which church court officials, in Wiltshire as elsewhere in England, were occasionally subjected. In 1592 a certain Walter Kingman protested that 'the fees which were taken were taken by extortion', while John Stokes of Bishopstrow observed bitterly in 1621 that 'so the court had monies it was no matter'. In 1609 Henry White of Wanborough concluded other criticisms with the comprehensive statement that 'this might be called a wrong court'. Such utterances from disgruntled defendants could plausibly be dismissed as insignificant (secular court judges also suffered abuse); but they did betoken an undercurrent of hostility which was evidently activated in 1640–1.[6] More obviously damaging, in 1641 the minister of Stockton wrote to the recently appointed diocesan chancellor to complain of the immorality of certain women, adding urgently:

> I pray for example sake do something...Here we have had many...without any or very small exemplary punishment...The last most impudent drab, to the great scandal of your court, was in my absence dismissed by Giles Thornborough with a slight confession...She was able to have afforded some profit, but the world saith ye of spiritual courts care not for punishment of sin for example and discipline in beggars who are able to pay no fees.

These strictures, made at the end of a period when (as we have seen) the administration of the Salisbury courts had grown rather slack, were not without cogency. To be sure, the minister admitted that the new chancellor had begun to reform matters: 'I hear that you have well begun doing many worthy and commendable acts'; none the less he went on to describe the bishop's consistory as 'your despised court' – ominous words when the house of commons was debating root and branch.[7]

Arguably a second factor which facilitated the attack on ecclesiastical justice in 1640–2 was a certain weakening, in the decade or so before the cataclysm, of the favourable symbiosis between church courts and society which had prevailed for most of our period, and whose nature was sketched earlier in this chapter. Although many aspects of the courts' work attracted popular support, it was above

[6] W.R.O., B/ABO 2, fol. 25v; AS/ABO 13, 22/10/1621, *Office v. John Stokes and Robert Graunt*; AW/ABO 3, 30/5/1609, *Office v. White.*

[7] W.R.O., B/Citations 5/9.

all their pursuit of notorious sexual offenders, especially bastard-bearers, which made ecclesiastical discipline seem of relevance to parochial interests and concerns. In the decades around 1600 the courts could indeed be plausibly seen as an essential bulwark against a rising tide of illegitimacy: the Paul's Cross preacher who opined around 1584 that but for punishment more than half the children in a parish would be bastards was but voicing a common phobia.[8] But the incidence of illegitimacy declined markedly after about 1620 and was at a relatively low level by the 1630s; moreover by this time an increasing role in the punishment of bastard-bearers was being taken by the secular justices of the peace. Inevitably a greater proportion of the courts' time was now spent on matters which aroused less heartfelt support in the parishes. In dioceses under Laudian control this incipient shift in balance was reinforced by the authorities' efforts to implement the new programme of liturgical and related reforms. In Wiltshire, which under the staunchly Calvinist bishop Davenant escaped rigorous enforcement of Laudian innovations, developments in the late 1620s and the 1630s took a slightly different but also potentially provocative form. As cases of sexual immorality decreased in number, the officers of the Salisbury courts appear to have stepped up prosecutions for Sunday and holiday work – matters which had traditionally been marginal to parochial interests. Thus in the court of the archdeacon of North Wiltshire in 1637, more people were brought to court to answer charges of working on Sundays or holidays than had appeared for these offences in any year throughout the period 1615–29. In the court of the archdeaconry of Salisbury in the years 1615–20, when prosecutions for sexual immorality were still running at a high level, an average of fewer than 10 people per annum appeared to answer charges of labouring on Sundays or holidays. But already in 1627, when bastardy cases were becoming noticeably fewer, as many as 39 Sunday or holiday workers were compelled to attend court; significantly, at least some of these had not been detected by churchwardens but were the victims of apparitorial inquiries. In 1637, 26 individuals were compelled to answer for unlawful work, and again it is probable that many of them had not been presented by churchwardens. In fact some defendants were 'pumped' in court to reveal the identity of other offenders; further, it is noticeable that many were

[8] Brinkworth (ed.), *Archdeacon's court*, vol. 2, pp. xxiii, 227.

charged a hefty burden of fees.[9] It would seem that the staff of the courts were trying to recoup on business lost through the decline of bastardy, fornication and adultery cases by bringing people into court for offences which had previously been passed over. The result was probably to put some strain on the relationship between the courts and the communities with which they had to deal, and hence perhaps to make them more vulnerable to attack in the years 1640–2. In this limited sense, there may be said to be a grain of truth in Christopher Hill's notion of the obsolescence of the ecclesiastical courts before the civil war.[10]

How the spiritual jurisdiction, and the relationship between the courts and the wider society, would have developed if the breakdown between king and parliament had been averted can only be conjectured. In the wake of the restoration of Charles II the church courts were rapidly and in some ways effectively re-established, with their pre-civil war powers virtually intact.[11] There is no doubt, however, that the role and standing of the ecclesiastical tribunals had been profoundly affected by what had happened between 1641 and 1660, and they were to be further altered by a variety of later developments. It would appear, indeed, that it was in the later seventeenth century that many aspects of the church courts' work began to suffer a decisive decline. A good deal of further research is required to establish the processes involved and to illuminate regional variations, but some of the most important general factors were probably as follows.[12] Illegitimacy levels continued to be relatively low in the period 1660–1700, and in these conditions the problem of sexual immorality must have appeared less acute than it had earlier. Some studies indicate, moreover, that in the Restoration period discipline over personal morality was increasingly exercised

[9] Based on search of W.R.O., AW/ABO 5–7; AS/ABO 12–15. For indications of apparitorial inquiries, see AS/Citations *quorum nomina*, 1636/73 (showing the names of four offenders from Wylye added, almost certainly by an apparitor, to a citation schedule bearing the names of people presented in the usual way). For examples of 'pumping', see AS/ABO 15, 15/6/1639, *Office v. Christopher Bollen* and accompanying notes; *ibid.*, 23/11/1638, *Office v. Stephen Bradden* and accompanying notes.

[10] Cf. Hill, *Society and puritanism*, pp. 309–15.

[11] Anne Whiteman, 'The re-establishment of the church of England, 1660–1663', *Trans. Roy. Hist. Soc.*, 5th ser., 5 (1955), pp. 111–31; I. M. Green, *The re-establishment of the church of England, 1660–1663* (Oxford, 1978), ch. 6; Jones, 'Ecclesiastical courts before and after the civil war', *passim*.

[12] For discussion of the wider context, see Lenman, 'Limits of godly discipline', pp. 140–2; Sharpe, *Crime in early modern England*, pp. 178–9.

through the institutions and personal relationships of the parish.[13] In such circumstances, ecclesiastical penalties for immorality were perhaps perceived to be less vital. Another relevant factor, so far little studied, was a shift in legal philosophy and practice which militated against uncertainty or imprecision in legal processes. Increasingly the accent was on specific, readily definable offences and on means of prosecution which depended on individual, ascertainable accusers and prosecutors. One of the results of this trend was to encourage the decline of the system of presentments made by local officers, which were prone to lack the required precision and specificity; and, although this applied to presentments in quarter sessions and assizes as well as in the church courts, the change naturally affected the spiritual jurisdiction more profoundly, since this relied so heavily on the system of parochial delation.[14] More crucial to the fate of the ecclesiastical tribunals were religious changes. The growth of presbyterian and sectarian congregations during the civil war and interregnum, and the relatively narrow basis on which the Anglican church was re-established in 1660–3, ensured the existence of protestant nonconformity on a significant scale in Restoration England. The prosecution of dissenters and catholic recusants in fact represented the major task of the revived church courts, certainly in Wiltshire, where (according to Anne Whiteman) 'the presentment of nonconformity engrossed increasingly more of the churchwardens' attentions, to the exclusion of other topics'.[15] Unfortunately the church courts – heavily dependent as they were on spiritual sanctions – were as ill-adapted to eliminate protestant dissent as they were to eradicate catholic recusancy. Further, the breakdown of protestant consensus which the phenomenon of dissent represented could not but undermine other aspects of the church courts' disciplinary functions, especially in areas where nonconformity was strong: a system of moral discipline exercised by a church which significant sections of the population repudiated inevitably declined in credibility. The vagaries of royal policy under Charles II and James II made the role of the spiritual jurisdiction even more difficult. Ultimately the declaration of indulgence of 1687 and the toleration act of 1689 were to prove well-nigh mortal blows for the disciplinary work of the church

[13] Wrightson and Levine, *Poverty and piety*, pp. 182–3.
[14] For other symptoms of the shift suggested here, see Sharpe, *Crime in early modern England*, pp. 178–9.
[15] Whiteman, 'Re-establishment', p. 125.

courts. Presentments of dissenters rapidly ceased, and more and more bills of detection reported that 'all is well'.[16] The instance side of ecclesiastical court business was still reasonably active, and of course the church continued to provide a highly important service in proving wills and granting administrations. But, taken as a whole, by 1700 the spiritual jurisdiction was only a shadow of what it had been a few generations earlier. By the nineteenth century the church courts, once so prominent in English social life as agents of ecclesiastical and communal discipline over immorality and irreligion, were in full decay, and the records of their earlier and more vital period of existence were relegated to that obscurity from which they have only recently been rescued.

[16] G. V. Bennett, *The tory crisis in church and state, 1688–1730: the career of Francis Atterbury, bishop of Rochester* (Oxford, 1975), pp. 9, 14–15; Whiteman, 'Re-establishment', p. 125.

Bibliography

Note Items marked with an asterisk were used for the detailed studies of Keevil and Wylye.

MANUSCRIPT SOURCES

BRITISH LIBRARY

Abstracts of returns of preachers, etc.	Harley MS 280
Diocese of Exeter: Consistory Court Register, 1637–8	Egerton MS 2631

CAMBRIDGE, CORPUS CHRISTI COLLEGE

*Parker certificates, 1561	MS 97

CAMBRIDGE UNIVERSITY LIBRARY

Ely diocesan records

For a detailed description, see Dorothy M. Owen, *Ely records: a handlist of the records of the bishop and archdeacon of Ely* (Cambridge, 1971). The following items are cited in the Notes and/or were subjected to detailed study.

Visitation Book, 1619	B/2/37
Consistory of Ely: Instance Act Books, 1580–1640	D/2/12, 22, 24, 27, 30–31a, 33, 36–8, 40, 42–5, 47, 49–50
Consistory of Ely: Office Act Books, 1614–18	B/2/34–6
Consistory of Ely: court papers, various dates	K/2, K/5–6
Temporal Jurisdiction: records of courts of pleas and gaol delivery for the liberty of Ely, 1571–95, 1610–39	E/1/4/3–E/1/8/1; E/1/9/2–E/2/3/2
Metropolitical Visitation Book, 1590–2	B/2/11
Metropolitical Instance Act Books, 1585–8, 1615–21	D/2/18a, D/2/34
Metropolitical Office Act Book, 1588–92	D/2/18

LEICESTER MUSEUMS AND ART GALLERY, DEPARTMENT OF ARCHIVES

Leicester archdeaconry records

For a detailed description, see A. M. Woodcock, *Handlist of records of Leicester archdeaconry* (Leicester, 1954). The following items are cited in the Notes and/or were subjected to detailed study.

Instance Court Act Books, 1587–9, 1630–4	1 D 41/11/21, 65
Correction Court Act Books, 1585–8, 1615–16, 1636–8	1 D 41/13/12, 40, 64

NORFOLK AND NORWICH RECORD OFFICE, NORWICH

Norwich diocesan records

Stray Ely Instance Act Book, 1588–90	ACT 21/24a

PUBLIC RECORD OFFICE, LONDON

Court of High Commission Act Books, 1634–6, 1639–40	SP 16/261, 324, 434
*Court of Requests Proceedings, Elizabeth I	REQ 2
*Court of Star Chamber Proceedings, James I	STAC 8
*Lay Subsidy Rolls, various dates	E 179
*Prerogative Court of Canterbury Wills	PROB 11
*Significations of Excommunication, Salisbury diocese, 1578–99	C 85/151–2

WEST SUSSEX RECORD OFFICE, CHICHESTER

Records of the diocese and archdeaconry of Chichester

For a detailed description, see Francis W. Steer and Isabel M. Kirby, *Diocese of Chichester: a catalogue of the records of the bishop, archdeacons and former exempt jurisdictions* (Chichester, 1966). The following items are cited in the Notes and/or were subjected to detailed study.

Instance Books, 1582–9, 1600–3, 1616–22, 1630–3, 1638–42	Ep. I/10/15–16, 21, 33–4, 39, 45
Detection Books, 1586–9, 1592–6, 1606–9, 1624–6, 1633–7, 1635–6	Ep. I/17/6, 8, 12, 21, 25, 26
Excommunications, 1631–65	Ep. I/13/2

WILTSHIRE RECORD OFFICE, TROWBRIDGE

Salisbury diocesan records

For a detailed description, see Pamela Stewart, *Diocese of Salisbury: guide to the records of the bishop, the archdeacons of Salisbury and Wiltshire, and other archidiaconal and peculiar jurisdictions*, Wiltshire County Council, Guide to the Record Offices, 4 (Devizes, 1973).

1. Bishop of Salisbury:	
*Act Books (Instance), 1565–1642	B/ABI 3–54
*Act Books (Office), 1584–1635	B/ABO 1–12
*Deposition Books, 1565–1641	B/DB 5–57
Libels, etc., 1615–34	B/Libels 1–4
Citations, 1631–41	B/Citations 1–5
**Detecta* Books, 1584–5	B/*Detecta* Bks. 5–6
Miscellaneous Court Papers, selected items:	
Depositions, 1586–7	B/Misc. Ct Papers 29/47
Depositions, 1604–5	B/Misc. Ct Papers 29/46
*Depositions, 1612	B/Misc. Ct Papers 29/48
Fragment of Salisbury High Commission Act Book, 1583–4	B/Misc. Ct Papers 29/54
*Exhibit Book, 1613	—
*Miscellaneous papers and books:	
Agreement concerning seating in the church of Wylye, 1664	—
2. Archdeacon of Salisbury:	
*Act Books (Office), 1572–1642	AS/ABO 1a–16
*Citations *quorum nomina*, 1604–40	—
*Excommunications Book, 1572–82	—
*Schedules of Excommunication, 1607–33	AS/Excommunications, 1607–33
Excommunications, various dates	—
3. Archdeacon of North Wiltshire:	
Act Books (Office), 1601–42	AW/ABO 1–7
Detecta Book, 1586–99	—
Visitation Book, 1621–42	—
Miscellaneous visitation papers:	
Note-book, 1602–20 [*recte* 1622]	—
4. Dean of Salisbury:	
Act Books, 1564–1645	D/AB 2–41
(*Note*: *D/AB 21 includes draft acts for the court of the archdeacon of Salisbury, 1609–10.)	
Deposition Books, 1577–1641	D/DB 1–14
Libels, etc., 1585–1641	D/Libels 1–14
Citations, 1588–1641	D/Citations 2–16
Churchwardens' Presentments, 1583–1641	D/Pres.

5. Peculiar of the Precentor:

Churchwardens' Presentments, 1614–40	Precentor/Pres.

Wiltshire Quarter Sessions Records

*Great Rolls, 1603–50	QS/GR Hil. 1603–QS/GR Mich. 1650
*Minute Books, 1598–1653	QS/Minute Bks. 2–10

Wiltshire Probate Records

*Episcopal Consistory of Salisbury Probate Records, 1560–1680
*Archdeaconry Court of Salisbury Probate Records, 1560–1680

Manorial Records

*Keevil cum Bulkington Court Books, 1602–25, 1644–64	W.R.O., 288/1–2

Parish Registers

Alvediston	W.R.O., 1052/1
Bromham	W.R.O., 518/1
Fisherton Delamere	W.R.O., 522/1
Idmiston	W.R.O., 1098/1
*Keevil	W.R.O., 653/1–2
Kington St Michael	W.R.O., 1187/1–2
Latton	W.R.O., 633/11
Steeple Ashton	W.R.O., 730/1–2
Stockton	W.R.O., 203/1

Other Parochial Records

Lacock Churchwardens' Book, 1583–1821	W.R.O., 173/1

PRINTED PRIMARY SOURCES

Ayliffe, John. *Parergon juris canonici anglicani* (1726).
Babington, Gervase. *The workes of Gervase Babington* (1615).
Bacon, Matthew. *A new abridgment of the law*, 4th edn, 5 vols. (1778).
Becon, Thomas. *The worckes of Thomas Becon*, 3 vols. (1560–4).
Bridges, John. *A defence of the government established in the church of Englande for ecclesiastical matters* (1587).
Brinkworth, E. R. C. (ed.). *The archdeacon's court: liber actorum, 1584*, Oxfordshire Record Soc., 23–4 (Oxford, 1942–6).
Brinsley, John, Sr. *The true watch and rule of life*, 5th edn (1611).

Bunny, Edmund. *Of divorce for adulterie, and marrying againe* (Oxford, 1610).

Cardwell, Edward (ed.). *The reformation of the ecclesiastical laws* (Oxford, 1850).

Synodalia: a collection of articles of religion, canons, and proceedings of convocations, 2 vols. (Oxford, 1842).

Clarke, Francis. *Praxis in curiis ecclesiasticis* (Dublin, 1666).

Coke, Sir Edward. *The first part of the institutes of the lawes of England* (1628).

The second part of the institutes of the laws of England, 3rd edn (1669).

The third part of the institutes of the laws of England (1644).

Conset, Henry. *The practice of the spiritual or ecclesiastical courts* (1685).

Cosin, Richard. *An apologie of and for sundrie proceedings by iurisdiction ecclesiastical* (1591).

Cunnington, B. H. (ed.). *Records of the county of Wilts.* (Devizes, 1932).

Dent, Arthur. *The plaine mans path-way to heaven* (1601).

Dod, John, and Cleaver, Robert. *A godly forme of houshold government* (1630 edn).

Downame, John. *Foure treatises tending to diswade all Christians from swearing* (1609).

Elton, G. R. (ed.). *The Tudor constitution*, 2nd edn (Cambridge, 1982).

England, church of. Visitation articles: Salisbury diocese:

1581	John Piers	*S.T.C.*	10327
1599	Henry Cotton	*S.T.C.*	10327.5
1614	Henry Cotton	*S.T.C.*	10328
1616	Robert Abbot	*S.T.C.*	10329
1619	Martin Fotherby	*S.T.C.*	10329.3
1620	Robert Townson	*S.T.C.*	10329.7
1622	John Davenant	*S.T.C.*	10330
1628	John Davenant	*S.T.C.*	10331
1631	John Davenant	*S.T.C.*	10331.5
1635	John Davenant	*S.T.C.*	10332

Fowle, J. P. M. (ed.). *Wiltshire quarter sessions and assizes, 1736*, Wilts. Archaeol. and Natural History Soc.: Records Branch, 11 (Devizes, 1955).

Frere, W. H., and Douglas, C. E. (eds.). *Puritan manifestoes* (1954).

Furnivall, Frederick J. (ed.). *Child-marriages, divorces, and ratifications, etc. in the diocese of Chester, A.D. 1561–6*, Early English Text Soc., original ser., 108 (1897).

Gardiner, Samuel Rawson (ed.). *The constitutional documents of the puritan revolution, 1625–1660*, 3rd edn (Oxford, 1906).

Gibson, Edmund. *Codex juris ecclesiastici anglicani*, 2nd edn, 2 vols. (Oxford, 1761).

Godolphin, John. *Repertorium canonicum: or, an abridgement of the ecclesiastical laws of this realm* (1678).

Gouge, William. *Of domesticall duties* (1622).

Gough, Richard. *The history of Myddle*, ed. David Hey (Harmondsworth, 1981).
Griffith, Matthew. *Bethel: or, a forme for families* (1633).
*Hadow, G. R. (ed.). *The registers of the parish of Wylye in the county of Wilts*. (Devizes, 1913).
Hale, W. H. *A series of precedents and proceedings in criminal causes from 1475 to 1640* (1847).
Herbert, George. *The works of George Herbert*, ed. F. E. Hutchinson (Oxford, 1941).
H.M.C., *Calendar of the manuscripts of the Most Hon. the Marquis of Salisbury*, 24 vols. (1883–1976).
H.M.C., *Fourth Report* (1874).
H.M.C., *Report on manuscripts in various collections*, 8 vols. (1901–14).
Hooker, Richard. *Of the laws of ecclesiastical polity*, Everyman edn, 2 vols. (1954).
Jenkins, C. (ed.). *The act book of the archdeacon of Taunton*, Somerset Record Soc., 43 (1928).
Johnson, Francis. *An inquirie and answer of Thomas White his discoverie of Brownisme* ([Amsterdam], 1606).
*Johnson, H. C. (ed.). *Wiltshire county records: minutes of proceedings in sessions, 1563 and 1574 to 1592*, Wilts. Archaeol. and Natural History Soc.: Records Branch, 4 (Devizes, 1949).
Johnstone, Hilda (ed.). *Churchwardens' presentments (17th century)*, 2 pts., Sussex Record Soc., 49–50 (Lewes, 1949–50).
*Kerridge, Eric (ed.). *Surveys of the manors of Philip, first earl of Pembroke and Montgomery, 1631–2*, Wilts. Archaeol. and Natural History Soc.: Records Branch, 9 (Devizes, 1953).
Lyndwood, William. *Provinciale (seu constitutiones angliae)* (Oxford, 1679).
March, John. *Actions for slaunder* (1647).
Marshall, G. W. (ed.). *The visitation of Wiltshire, 1623* (1882).
Moore, C. G. (ed.). *The registers of Broad Chalke, Co. Wilts.* (1881).
Nevill, Edmund. 'Marriage licences of Salisbury', *Genealogist*, new ser., 24–38 (1908–22), *passim*.
Palmer, W. M. (ed.). *Episcopal visitation returns for Cambridgeshire: Matthew Wren, bishop of Ely, 1638–1665* (Cambridge, 1930).
Parry, J. H. (ed.) *The registers of Allcannings and Etchilhampton* (Devizes, 1905).
Perkins, William. *The works of William Perkins*, 3 vols. (Cambridge, 1616–18).
Petti, Anthony G. (ed.). *Recusant documents from the Ellesmere manuscripts*, Catholic Record Soc., 60 (1968).
Phillipps, Sir Thomas. *Institutiones clericorum in comitatu Wiltoniae*, 2 vols. (Salisbury and Middle Hill, 1821–5).
Pound, John F. (ed.). *The Norwich census of the poor, 1570*, Norfolk Record Soc., 40 (Norwich, 1971).
Raine, J. (ed.). *Depositions and other ecclesiastical proceedings from the*

courts of Durham, extending from 1311 to the reign of Elizabeth, Surtees Soc., 21 (1845).

Robinson, Hastings (ed.). *The Zurich letters*, Parker Soc. (Cambridge, 1842).

Rogers, Daniel. *Matrimoniall honour* (1642).

Rye, W. B. (ed.). *England as seen by foreigners in the days of Elizabeth and James I* (1865).

Sandys, Edwin. *The sermons of Edwin Sandys*, ed. John Ayre, Parker Soc. (Cambridge, 1842).

Schroeder, H. J. (ed.). *Canons and decrees of the council of Trent* (St Louis, Mo., 1960).

Scudder, Henry. *The Christians daily walke in holy securitie and peace*, 7th edn (1637).

Sermons or homilies appointed to be read in churches in the time of queen Elizabeth (Liverpool, 1799 edn).

Sheils, William J. (ed.). *Archbishop Grindal's visitation, 1575: comperta and detecta book*, Borthwick texts and calendars: records of the northern province, 4 (York, 1977).

Slack, Paul (ed.). *Poverty in early Stuart Salisbury*, Wilts. Record Soc., 31 (Devizes, 1975).

Stubbes, Phillip. *Phillip Stubbes's anatomy of the abuses in England in Shakspere's youth, A.D. 1583*, ed. Frederick J. Furnivall, 2 vols. in 3, New Shakspere Soc., 6th ser., 4, 6, 12 (1877–82).

Swinburne, Henry. *A briefe treatise of testaments and last willes* (1590–1).

A treatise of spousals or matrimonial contracts (1686).

Tawney, R. H., and Power, Eileen (eds.). *Tudor economic documents*, 3 vols. (1924).

Vaughan, William. *The spirit of detraction* (1611).

Vives, Juan Luis. *A very frutefull and pleasant boke called the instruction of a christen woman, turned out of Laten into Englysshe by R. Hyrd* (?1529).

Whately, William. *A bride-bush: or, a direction for married persons* (1623 edn).

Williams, Barrie (ed.). *The subscription book of bishops Tounson and Davenant, 1620–40*, Wilts. Record Soc., 32 (Devizes, 1977).

Williams, C. H. (ed.). *English historical documents, 1485–1558* (1967).

PRINTED SECONDARY WORKS

Andenaes, Johannes. *Punishment and deterrence* (Ann Arbor, Mich., 1974).

Appleby, Andrew B. *Famine in Tudor and Stuart England* (Liverpool, 1978).

Baker, J. H. *An introduction to English legal history*, 2nd edn (1979).

Barnes, Thomas G. 'County politics and a puritan cause célèbre: Somerset churchales, 1633', *Trans. Roy. Hist. Soc.*, 5th ser., 9 (1959), pp. 103–22.

'Star chamber litigants and their counsel, 1596–1641', in J. H. Baker (ed.), *Legal records and the historian* (1978), pp. 7–28.
Beier, A. L. *The problem of the poor in Tudor and early Stuart England* (1983).
'Vagrants and the social order in Elizabethan England', *Past and present*, no. 64 (Aug. 1974), pp. 3–29.
Bennett, G. V. *The tory crisis in church and state, 1688–1730: the career of Francis Atterbury, bishop of Rochester* (Oxford, 1975).
Biggs, J. M. *The concept of matrimonial cruelty* (1962).
Bossy, John. 'The counter-reformation and the people of catholic Europe', *Past and present*, no. 47 (May 1970), pp. 51–70.
The English catholic community, 1570–1850 (1975).
Bradby, Edward. *Seend: a Wiltshire village past and present* (Gloucester, 1981).
Brinkworth, E. R. C. 'The Laudian church in Buckinghamshire', *Univ. of Birmingham hist. jl*, 5 (1955–6), pp. 31–59.
Shakespeare and the bawdy court of Stratford (London and Chichester, 1972).
'The study and use of archdeacons' court records, illustrated from the Oxford records, 1566–1759', *Trans. Roy. Hist. Soc.*, 4th ser., 25 (1943), pp. 93–119.
Brooks, C. W. 'Litigants and attorneys in the king's bench and common pleas, 1560–1640', in J. H. Baker (ed.), *Legal records and the historian* (1978), pp. 41–59.
Brown, E. H. Phelps, and Hopkins, S. V. 'Seven centuries of the prices of consumables, compared with builders' wage-rates', *Economica*, new ser., 23 (1956), pp. 296–314.
Brown, Roger Lee. 'The rise and fall of the Fleet marriages', in R. B. Outhwaite (ed.), *Marriage and society: studies in the social history of marriage* (1981), pp. 117–36.
Burke, Peter. *Popular culture in early modern Europe* (1978).
Campbell, J. K. *Honour, family and patronage: a study of institutions and moral values in a Greek mountain community* (Oxford, 1964).
Canon law of the church of England, being the report of the archbishops' commission on canon law (1947).
Churchill, Irene J. *Canterbury administration*, 2 vols. (1933).
Cioni, Maria L. 'The Elizabethan chancery and women's rights', in DeLloyd J. Guth and John W. McKenna (eds.), *Tudor rule and revolution* (Cambridge, 1982), pp. 159–82.
Clark, Peter. 'The ecclesiastical commission at Canterbury, 1572–1603', *Archaeologia cantiana*, 89 (1974), pp. 183–97.
The English alehouse: a social history, 1200–1830 (1983).
English provincial society from the Reformation to the revolution: religion, politics and society in Kent, 1500–1640 (Hassocks, 1977).
'The migrant in Kentish towns, 1580–1640', in Peter Clark and Paul Slack (eds.), *Crisis and order in English towns, 1500–1700* (1972), pp. 117–63.

Clarkson, L. A. *The pre-industrial economy in England, 1500–1750* (1971).

Coleman, D. C. *The economy of England, 1450–1750* (Oxford, 1977).

Industry in Tudor and Stuart England (1975).

'Labour in the English economy of the seventeenth century', *Econ. hist. rev.*, 2nd ser., 8 (1955–6), pp. 280–95.

Collinson, Patrick. 'Cranbrook and the Fletchers: popular and unpopular religion in the Kentish Weald', in Peter Newman Brooks (ed.), *Reformation principle and practice* (1980), pp. 171–202.

The Elizabethan puritan movement (1967).

The religion of protestants: the church in English society, 1559–1625 (Oxford, 1982).

Cressy, David. *Literacy and the social order: reading and writing in Tudor and Stuart England* (Cambridge, 1980).

Davies, Kathleen M. 'Continuity and change in literary advice on marriage', in R. B. Outhwaite (ed.), *Marriage and society: studies in the social history of marriage* (1981), pp. 58–80.

Davies, M. F. *Life in an English village* (1909).

Derrett, J. Duncan M. *Henry Swinburne (?1551–1624): civil lawyer of York*, Borthwick papers, 44 (York, 1973).

Dibden, Sir Lewis, and Healey, Sir Charles Chadwyck. *English church law and divorce* (1912).

Donahue, Charles, Jr. 'The canon law on the formation of marriage and social practice in the later middle ages', *Jl family history*, 8 (1983), pp. 144–58.

Duncan, G. I. O. *The high court of delegates* (Cambridge, 1971).

Elliott, Vivien Brodsky. 'Single women in the London marriage market: age, status and mobility, 1598–1619', in R. B. Outhwaite (ed.), *Marriage and society: studies in the social history of marriage* (1981), pp. 81–100.

Elton, G. R. *Reform and renewal: Thomas Cromwell and the common weal* (Cambridge, 1973).

Emmison, Frederick G. 'Tithes, perambulations and sabbath-breach in Elizabethan Essex', in Frederick G. Emmison and Roy Stephens (eds.), *Tribute to an antiquary: essays presented to Marc Fitch by some of his friends* (1976), pp. 177–215.

Ewen, C. L'Estrange. *Witchcraft and demonianism* (1933).

Fincham, K. C. 'Ramifications of the Hampton Court conference in the dioceses, 1603–1609', *Jl ecclesiastical history*, 36 (1985), pp. 208–27.

Flaherty, D. H. *Privacy in colonial New England* (Charlottesville, Va, 1972).

Fletcher, Anthony. *A county community in peace and war: Sussex, 1600–1660* (1975).

The outbreak of the English civil war (1981).

Foster, Joseph. *Alumni Oxonienses: the members of the university of Oxford, 1500–1714*, 4 vols. (Oxford, 1891–2).

Fox, Robin. *Kinship and marriage* (Harmondsworth, 1967).

Gillis, John R. 'Conjugal settlements: resort to clandestine and common law marriage in England and Wales, 1650–1850', in John Bossy (ed.),

Disputes and settlements: law and human relations in the west (Cambridge, 1983), pp. 261–86.

Goody, Jack. *The development of the family and marriage in Europe* (Cambridge, 1983).

Goring, Jeremy. *Godly exercises or the devil's dance? Puritanism and popular culture in pre-civil war England*, Friends of Dr Williams's Library lecture, 37 (1983).

Greaves, Richard L. *Society and religion in Elizabethan England* (Minneapolis, 1981).

Green, I. M. *The re-establishment of the church of England, 1660–1663* (Oxford, 1978).

Habakkuk, Sir John. 'The rise and fall of English landed families, 1600–1800: III. Did the gentry rise?', *Trans. Roy. Hist. Soc.*, 5th ser., 31 (1981), pp. 195–217.

Haigh, Christopher. 'The continuity of catholicism in the English Reformation', *Past and present*, no. 93 (Nov. 1981), pp. 37–69.

'From monopoly to minority: catholicism in early modern England', *Trans. Roy. Hist. Soc.*, 5th ser., 31 (1981), pp. 129–47.

'Puritan evangelism in the reign of Elizabeth I', *Eng. hist. rev.*, 92 (1977), pp. 30–58.

Reformation and resistance in Tudor Lancashire (Cambridge, 1975).

'Slander and the church courts in the sixteenth century', *Trans. Lancashire and Cheshire Antiquarian Soc.*, 78 (1975), pp. 1–13.

Hair, Philip E. H. 'Bridal pregnancy in rural England in earlier centuries', *Population studies*, 20 (1966), pp. 233–43.

'Bridal pregnancy in earlier rural England further examined', *Population studies*, 24 (1970), pp. 59–70.

Hajnal, John. 'European marriage patterns in perspective', in D. V. Glass and D. E. C. Eversley (eds.), *Population in history* (1965), pp. 101–43.

Hall, Hubert. 'Some Elizabethan penances in the diocese of Ely', *Trans. Roy. Hist. Soc.*, 3rd ser., 1 (1907), pp. 263–77.

Helmholz, R. H. 'Canonical defamation in medieval England', *American jl legal history*, 15 (1971), pp. 255–68.

'Crime, compurgation and the courts of the medieval church', *Law and history rev.*, 1 (1983), pp. 1–26.

'Excommunication as a legal sanction: the attitudes of the medieval canonists', *Zeitschrift der Savigny-Stiftung für Rechtsgeschichte: kanonistische Abteilung*, 99/68 (1982), pp. 202–18.

Marriage litigation in medieval England (Cambridge, 1974).

Herrup, Cynthia B. 'Law and morality in seventeenth-century England', *Past and present*, no. 106 (Feb. 1985), pp. 102–23.

Hill, Christopher. 'Irreligion in the "puritan" revolution', in J. F. McGregor and B. Reay (eds.), *Radical religion in the English revolution* (Oxford, 1984), pp. 191–211.

Society and puritanism in pre-revolutionary England (1964).

The world turned upside down: radical ideas during the English revolution (1972).

Hilton, R. H. 'Small town society in England before the black death', *Past and present*, no. 105 (Nov. 1984), pp. 53–78.

Hockaday, F. S. 'The consistory court of the diocese of Gloucester', *Trans. Bristol and Gloucestershire Archaeol. Soc.*, 46 (1924), pp. 195–287.

Hoffer, Peter C., and Hull, N. E. H., *Murdering mothers: infanticide in England and New England, 1558–1803* (New York, 1981).

Holdsworth, W. S. 'Defamation in the sixteenth and seventeenth centuries', *Law quarterly rev.*, 40 (1924), pp. 302–15, 397–412.

Houlbrooke, Ralph. *Church courts and the people during the English Reformation, 1520–1570* (Oxford, 1979).

'The decline of ecclesiastical jurisdiction under the Tudors', in Rosemary O'Day and Felicity Heal (eds.), *Continuity and change: personnel and administration of the church in England, 1500–1642* (Leicester, 1976), pp. 239–57.

The English family, 1450–1700 (1984).

'The making of marriage in mid-Tudor England: evidence from the records of matrimonial contract litigation', *Jl family history*, 10 (1985), pp. 339–52.

'The protestant episcopate, 1547–1603: the pastoral contribution', in Felicity Heal and Rosemary O'Day (eds.), *Church and society in England: Henry VIII to James I* (1977), pp. 78–98.

Hunt, William. *The puritan moment: the coming of revolution in an English county* (Cambridge, Mass., 1983).

Hunter, Michael. 'The problem of "atheism" in early modern England', *Trans. Roy. Hist. Soc.*, 5th ser., 35 (1985), pp. 135–57.

Hurstfield, Joel. 'County government, c. 1530–c. 1660', in *V.C.H. Wilts.*, vol. 5, pp. 80–110.

The queen's wards: wardship and marriage under Elizabeth I (1958).

Ingram, Martin. 'Communities and courts: law and disorder in early seventeenth-century Wiltshire', in J. S. Cockburn (ed.), *Crime in England, 1550–1800* (1977), pp. 110–34.

'The reform of popular culture? Sex and marriage in early modern England', in B. Reay (ed.), *Popular culture in seventeenth-century England* (1985), pp. 129–65.

'Religion, communities and moral discipline in late sixteenth- and early seventeenth-century England: case studies', in Kaspar von Greyerz (ed.), *Religion and society in early modern Europe, 1500–1800* (1984), pp. 177–93.

'Ridings, rough music and mocking rhymes in early modern England', in B. Reay (ed.), *Popular culture in seventeenth-century England* (1985), pp. 166–97.

'Ridings, rough music and the "reform of popular culture" in early modern England', *Past and present*, no. 105 (Nov. 1984), pp. 79–113.

'Spousals litigation in the English ecclesiastical courts, c. 1350–c. 1640', in R. B. Outhwaite (ed.), *Marriage and society: studies in the social history of marriage* (1981), pp. 35–57.

Jones, W. J. *The Elizabethan court of chancery* (Oxford, 1967).

Jordan, W. K. *Edward VI: the threshold of power* (1970).

Justice, Blair, and Justice, Rita. *The broken taboo: sex in the family* (1980).

Kelly, Henry Ansgar. 'Clandestine marriage and Chaucer's "Troilus"', *Viator*, 4 (1973), pp. 435–57.

Kent, Joan. 'Attitudes of members of the house of commons to the regulation of "personal conduct" in late Elizabethan and early Stuart England', *Bull. Inst. Hist. Res.*, 46 (1973), pp. 41–71.

Kerridge, Eric. 'Agriculture, c. 1500–c. 1793', in *V.C.H. Wilts.*, vol. 4, pp. 43–64.

King, Walter J. 'Leet jurors and the search for law and order in seventeenth-century England: "galling persecution" or reasonable justice?', *Histoire sociale: social history*, 13 (1980), 305–23.

Kitching, Christopher. 'The prerogative court of Canterbury from Warham to Whitgift', in Rosemary O'Day and Felicity Heal (eds.), *Continuity and change: personnel and administration of the church in England, 1500–1642* (Leicester, 1976), pp. 191–214.

Knafla, Louis A. '"Sin of all sorts swarmeth": criminal litigation in an English county in the early seventeenth century', in E. W. Ives and A. H. Manchester (eds.), *Law, litigants and the legal profession* (1983), pp. 50–67.

Kussmaul, Ann. *Servants in husbandry in early modern England* (Cambridge, 1981).

Lander, Stephen. 'Church courts and the Reformation in the diocese of Chichester, 1500–58', in Rosemary O'Day and Felicity Heal (eds.), *Continuity and change: personnel and administration of the church in England, 1500–1642* (Leicester, 1976), pp. 215–37.

Laslett, Peter. *Family life and illicit love in earlier generations* (Cambridge, 1977).

'Introduction: comparing illegitimacy over time and between cultures', in Peter Laslett, Karla Oosterveen and Richard M. Smith (eds.), *Bastardy and its comparative history* (1980), pp. 1–70.

The world we have lost, 2nd edn (1971).

The world we have lost further explored (1983).

Laslett, Peter, Oosterveen, Karla and Smith, Richard M. (eds.), *Bastardy and its comparative history* (1980).

Lenman, Bruce. 'The limits of godly discipline in the early modern period with particular reference to England and Scotland', in Kaspar von Greyerz (ed.), *Religion and society in early modern Europe, 1500–1800* (1984), pp. 124–45.

Levack, Brian P. *The civil lawyers in England, 1603–1641* (Oxford, 1973).

Levine, David, and Wrightson, Keith. 'The social context of illegitimacy in early modern England', in Peter Laslett, Karla Oosterveen and Richard M. Smith (eds.), *Bastardy and its comparative history* (1980), pp. 158–75.

Luxton, Imogen. 'The Reformation and popular culture', in Felicity Heal and Rosemary O'Day (eds.), *Church and society in England: Henry VIII to James I* (1977), pp. 57–77.

MacDonald, Michael. *Mystical bedlam: madness, anxiety and healing in seventeenth-century England* (Cambridge, 1981).

Macfarlane, Alan. *The family life of Ralph Josselin: a seventeenth-century clergyman* (Cambridge, 1970).

'Illegitimacy and illegitimates in English history', in Peter Laslett, Karla Oosterveen and Richard M. Smith (eds.), *Bastardy and its comparative history* (1980), pp. 71–85.

Marriage and love in England: modes of reproduction, 1300–1840 (Oxford, 1986).

'Modes of reproduction', *Jl development studies*, 14, no. 4 (July 1978), pp. 100–20.

The origins of English individualism: the family, property and social transition (Oxford, 1978).

Review of Stone, *Family, sex and marriage*, in *History and theory*, 18 (1979), pp. 103–26.

Witchcraft in Tudor and Stuart England (1970).

Macfarlane, Alan, and Harrison, Sarah. *The justice and the mare's ale: law and disorder in seventeenth-century England* (Oxford, 1981).

McGrath, Patrick. 'Elizabethan catholicism: a reconsideration', *Jl ecclesiastical history*, 35 (1984), pp. 414–28.

McGregor, J. F., and Reay, B. (eds.) *Radical religion in the English revolution* (Oxford, 1984).

Maguire, Mary H. 'Attack of the common lawyers on the oath *ex officio* as administered in the ecclesiastical courts in England', in *Essays in history and political theory in honour of Charles Howard McIlwain* (Cambridge, Mass., 1936), pp. 199–229.

Maisch, Herbert. *Incest*, trans. Colin Bearne (1973).

Manning, Roger B. 'The crisis of episcopal authority during the reign of Elizabeth I', *Jl British studies*, 11 (1971–2), pp. 1–25.

Religion and society in Elizabethan Sussex (Leicester, 1969).

Marchant, Ronald A. *The church under the law: justice, administration and discipline in the diocese of York, 1560–1640* (Cambridge, 1969).

The puritans and the church courts in the diocese of York, 1560–1642 (1960).

Marsh, A. E. W. *A history of the borough and town of Calne* (Calne, 1903).

Menefee, Samuel Pyeatt. *Wives for sale: an ethnographic study of British popular divorce* (Oxford, 1981).

Miller, Edward. 'The liberty of Ely', in *V.C.H. Cambridgeshire and the Isle of Ely*, vol. 4, pp. 1–27.

Milsom, S. F. C. *Historical foundations of the common law* (1969).

Moore, A. Percival. 'Marriage contracts or espousals in the reign of queen Elizabeth', *Reports and papers of associated architectural socs.*, 30 (1909), pp. 261–98.

Morris, Colin. 'The commissary of the bishop in the diocese of Lincoln', *Jl ecclesiastical history*, 10 (1959), pp. 50–65.

Noonan, John T., Jr. 'Power to choose', *Viator*, 4 (1973), pp. 419–34.

Nuttall, Geoffrey F. *Visible saints: the congregational way, 1640–1660* (Oxford, 1957).

O'Day, Rosemary. *The English clergy: the emergence and consolidation of a profession, 1558–1642* (Leicester, 1979).

'The role of the registrar in diocesan administration', in Rosemary O'Day and Felicity Heal (eds.), *Continuity and change: personnel and administration of the church in England, 1500–1642* (Leicester, 1976), pp. 77–94.

Outhwaite, R. B. 'Age at marriage in England from the late seventeenth to the nineteenth century', *Trans. Roy. Hist. Soc.*, 5th ser., 23 (1973), pp. 55–70.

Inflation in Tudor and early Stuart England, 2nd edn (1982).

Owen, Dorothy. 'Ecclesiastical jurisdiction in England, 1300–1550: the records and their interpretation', in Derek Baker (ed.), *The materials, sources and methods of ecclesiastical history*, Studies in church history, 11 (Oxford, 1975), pp. 199–221.

'An episcopal audience court', in J. H. Baker (ed.), *Legal records and the historian* (1978), pp. 140–9.

The records of the established church in England excluding parochial records, British Records Association, archives and the user, 1 (1970).

Owen, H. Gareth. 'The episcopal visitation: its limits and limitations in Elizabethan London', *Jl ecclesiastical history*, 11 (1960), pp. 179–85.

Ozment, Steven. *The age of reform, 1250–1550* (New Haven, Conn., 1980).

When fathers ruled: family life in Reformation Europe (Cambridge, Mass., 1983).

Palliser, D. M. *The age of Elizabeth: England under the later Tudors, 1547–1603* (1983).

Peters, Robert. *Oculus episcopi: administration in the archdeaconry of St Albans, 1580–1625* (Manchester, 1963).

Phythian-Adams, Charles. 'Ceremony and the citizen: the communal year at Coventry, 1450–1550', in Peter Clark and Paul Slack (eds.), *Crisis and order in English towns, 1500–1700* (1972), pp. 57–85.

Pilgrim Trust survey of diocesan archives, 4 vols. (1952).

Pitt-Rivers, Julian. 'Honour and social status', in J. G. Peristiany (ed.), *Honour and shame: the values of Mediterranean society* (1965), pp. 19–77.

Pollock, Sir Frederick, and Maitland, Frederic William, *The history of English law before the time of Edward I*, 2nd edn, 2 vols. (Cambridge, 1898).

Pound, John F. *Poverty and vagrancy in Tudor England* (1971).

Powell, Chilton Latham. *English domestic relations, 1487–1653* (New York, 1917).

Powell, W. R., and Crittall, Elizabeth. 'Bromham', in *V.C.H. Wilts.*, vol. 7, pp. 179–86.

Price, F. D. 'The abuses of excommunication and the decline of ecclesiastical discipline under queen Elizabeth', *Eng. hist. rev.*, 57 (1942), pp. 106–15.

'Bishop Bullingham and chancellor Blackleech: a diocese divided', *Trans. Bristol and Gloucestershire Archaeol. Soc.*, 91 (1972), pp. 175–98.
'The commission for ecclesiastical causes for the dioceses of Bristol and Gloucester, 1574', *Trans. Bristol and Gloucestershire Archaeol. Soc.*, 59 (1937), pp. 61–184.
'Elizabethan apparitors in the diocese of Gloucester', *Church quarterly rev.*, 134 (1942), pp. 37–55.
'An Elizabethan church official – Thomas Powell, chancellor of Gloucester diocese', *Church quarterly rev.*, 128 (1939), pp. 94–112.
'Gloucester diocese under bishop Hooper, 1551–3', *Trans. Bristol and Gloucestershire Archaeol. Soc.*, 60 (1938), pp. 51–151.
Purvis, J. S. *An introduction to ecclesiastical records* (1953).
Quaife, G. R. *Wanton wenches and wayward wives: peasants and illicit sex in early seventeenth-century England* (1979).
Rabb, Theodore K., and Hirst, Derek. 'Revisionism revised: two perspectives on early Stuart parliamentary history', *Past and present*, no. 92 (Aug. 1981), pp. 55–99.
Ramsay, G. D. *The Wiltshire woollen industry in the sixteenth and seventeenth centuries*, 2nd edn (1965).
Reardon, Bernard M. G. *Religious thought in the Reformation* (1981).
Reeves, Marjorie E. 'Protestant nonconformity', in *V.C.H. Wilts.*, vol. 3, pp. 99–149.
Ritchie, Carson I. A. *The ecclesiastical courts of York* (Arbroath, 1956).
Roberts, Stephen K. *Recovery and restoration in an English county: Devon local administration, 1646–1670* (Exeter, 1985).
*Rogers, K. H. 'Keevil', in *V.C.H. Wilts.*, vol. 8, pp. 250–63.
Rushton, Peter. 'Women, witchcraft and slander in early modern England: cases from the church courts of Durham, 1560–1675', *Northern history*, 18 (1982), pp. 116–32.
Russell, Conrad. 'Parliamentary history in perspective, 1604–29', *History*, 61 (1976), pp. 1–27.
Parliaments and English politics, 1621–1629 (Oxford, 1979).
Sharp, Buchanan. *In contempt of all authority: rural artisans and riot in the west of England, 1586–1660* (Berkeley, 1980).
Sharpe, J. A. *Crime in early modern England*, 1550–1750 (1984).
Crime in seventeenth-century England: a county study (Cambridge, 1983).
Defamation and sexual slander in early modern England: the church courts at York, Borthwick papers, 58 (York, 1980).
'Enforcing the law in the seventeenth-century English village', in V. A. C. Gatrell, Bruce Lenman and Geoffrey Parker (eds.), *Crime and the law: the social history of crime in western Europe since 1500* (1980), pp. 97–119.
'The history of violence in England: some observations', *Past and present*, no. 108 (Aug. 1985), pp. 206–15.
'"Such disagreement betwyx neighbours": litigation and human relations in early modern England', in John Bossy (ed.), *Disputes and*

settlements: law and human relations in the west (Cambridge, 1983), pp. 167–87.

Sharpe, Kevin (ed.). *Faction and parliament: essays on early Stuart history* (Oxford, 1978).

Sheehan, Michael M. 'The formation and stability of marriage in fourteenth-century England: evidence of an Ely register', *Mediaeval studies*, 33 (1971), pp. 228–63.

Sheils, William J. 'Some problems of government in a new diocese: the bishop and the puritans in the diocese of Peterborough, 1560–1630', in Rosemary O'Day and Felicity Heal (eds.), *Continuity and change: personnel and administration of the church in England, 1500–1642* (Leicester, 1976), pp. 167–87.

Slack, Paul. 'Books of orders: the making of English social policy, 1577–1631', *Trans. Roy. Hist. Soc.*, 5th ser., 30 (1980), pp. 1–22.

'Poverty and politics in Salisbury, 1597–1666', in Peter Clark and Paul Slack (eds.), *Crisis and order in English towns, 1500–1700* (1972), pp. 164–203.

'Vagrants and vagrancy in England, 1598–1664', *Econ. hist. rev.*, 2nd ser., 27 (1974), pp. 360–79.

Slater, Miriam. *Family life in the seventeenth century: the Verneys of Claydon House* (1984).

Slatter, M. Doreen. 'The records of the court of arches', *Jl ecclesiastical history*, 4 (1953), pp. 139–53.

Smith, A. Hassell. *County and court: government and politics in Norfolk, 1558–1603* (Oxford, 1974).

Spufford, Margaret. *Contrasting communities: English villagers in the sixteenth and seventeenth centuries* (Cambridge, 1974).

Small books and pleasant histories: popular fiction and its readership in seventeenth-century England (1981).

Squibb, G. D. *Doctors' Commons: a history of the College of Advocates and Doctors of Law* (Oxford, 1977).

Stieg, Margaret. *Laud's laboratory: the diocese of Bath and Wells in the early seventeenth century* (Lewisburg, Pa, 1982).

Stone, Lawrence. *The crisis of the aristocracy, 1558–1641* (Oxford, 1965).

The family, sex and marriage in England, 1500–1800 (1977).

'The history of violence in England: a rejoinder', *Past and present*, no. 108 (Aug. 1985), pp. 216–24.

'Interpersonal violence in English society, 1300–1980', *Past and present*, no. 101 (Nov. 1983), pp. 22–33.

Storey, R. L. *Diocesan administration in fifteenth-century England*, 2nd edn, Borthwick papers, 16 (York, 1972).

Strype, John. *The life and acts of John Whitgift*, 3 vols. (Oxford, 1822 edn).

Styles, Philip. 'The evolution of the law of settlement', *Univ. of Birmingham hist. jl*, 9 (1963–4), pp. 33–63.

Supple, B. E. *Commercial crisis and change in England, 1600–1642* (Cambridge, 1959).

Symonds, W. 'Winterslow church reckonings, 1542–1661', *Wilts. archaeol. magazine*, 36 (1909–10), pp. 27–49.

Taylor, C. C. 'Population studies in seventeenth- and eighteenth-century Wiltshire', *Wilts. archaeol. magazine*, 60 (1965), pp. 100–8.

Tentler, Thomas N. *Sin and confession on the eve of the Reformation* (Princeton, 1977).

Thirsk, Joan (ed.). *The agrarian history of England and Wales: IV. 1500–1640* (Cambridge, 1967).

'Seventeenth-century agriculture and social change', *Agric. hist. rev.*, 18, supplement (1970), pp. 148–77.

Thomas, Keith. 'Age and authority in early modern England', *Proc. Brit. Acad.*, 62 (1976), pp. 1–46.

'The double standard', *Jl history of ideas*, 20 (1959), pp. 195–216.

The perception of the past in early modern England, University of London, Creighton Trust lecture (1983).

'The puritans and adultery: the act of 1650 reconsidered', in Donald Pennington and Keith Thomas (eds.), *Puritans and revolutionaries: essays in seventeenth-century history presented to Christopher Hill* (Oxford, 1978), pp. 257–82.

Religion and the decline of magic: studies in popular beliefs in sixteenth- and seventeenth-century England (1971).

'Women and the civil war sects', *Past and present*, no. 13 (Apr. 1958), pp. 42–62.

Tyacke, Nicholas. 'Puritanism, Arminianism and counter-revolution', in Conrad Russell (ed.), *The origins of the English civil war* (1973), pp. 119–43.

Tyler, Philip. 'The church courts at York and witchcraft prosecutions, 1567–1640', *Northern history*, 4 (1969), pp. 84–109.

'The significance of the ecclesiastical commission at York', *Northern history*, 2 (1967), pp. 27–44.

Underdown, David. 'The chalk and the cheese: contrasts among the English clubmen', *Past and present*, no. 85 (Nov. 1979), pp. 25–48.

'The problem of popular allegiance in the English civil war', *Trans. Roy. Hist. Soc.* 5th ser., 31 (1981), pp. 69–94.

Revel, riot and rebellion: popular politics and culture in England, 1603–1660 (Oxford, 1985).

Usher, Roland G. *The rise and fall of the high commission*, 2nd edn, with introduction by Philip Tyler (Oxford, 1968).

Vage, J. A. 'Ecclesiastical discipline in the early seventeenth century: some findings and some problems from the archdeaconry of Cornwall', *Jl Soc. Archivists*, 7 (1982), pp. 85–105.

Victoria history of the county of Cambridge and the Isle of Ely, 8 vols., in progress (1938–).

Victoria history of Wiltshire, 12 vols., in progress (1953–).

Wall, Alison. 'Faction in local politics, 1580–1620: struggles for supremacy in Wiltshire', *Wilts. archaeol. magazine*, 72/73 (1980), pp. 119–33.

Whitaker, Wilfred B. *Sunday in Tudor and Stuart times* (1933).

White, Stephen D. *Sir Edward Coke and the grievances of the commonwealth* (Manchester, 1979).

Whiteman, Anne. 'The church of England, 1542–1837', in *V.C.H. Wilts.*, vol. 3, pp. 28–56.

'The re-establishment of the church of England, 1660–1663', *Trans. Roy. Hist. Soc.*, 5th ser., 5 (1955), pp. 111–31.

Wiener, Carol Z. 'Sex roles and crime in late Elizabethan Hertfordshire', *Jl social history*, 8 (1974–5), pp. 38–60.

Williams, Penry. *The Tudor regime* (Oxford, 1979).

Woodcock, Brian L. *Medieval ecclesiastical courts in the diocese of Canterbury* (1952).

Woodward, Donald. 'Wage rates and living standards in pre-industrial England', *Past and present*, no. 91 (May 1981), pp. 28–46.

Wrightson, Keith. 'Alehouses, order and reformation in rural England, 1590–1660', in Eileen Yeo and Stephen Yeo (eds.), *Popular culture and class conflict, 1590–1914* (Brighton, 1981), pp. 1–27.

English society, 1580–1680 (1982).

'Infanticide in earlier seventeenth-century England', *Local population studies*, 15 (1975), pp. 10–22.

'Infanticide in European history', *Criminal justice history*, 3 (1982), pp. 1–20.

'Two concepts of order: justices, constables and jurymen in seventeenth-century England', in John Brewer and John Styles (eds.), *An ungovernable people: the English and their law in the seventeenth and eighteenth centuries* (1980), pp. 21–46.

Wrightson, Keith, and Levine, David. *Poverty and piety in an English village: Terling, 1525–1700* (New York, 1979).

Wrigley, E. A. *Population and history* (1969).

Wrigley, E. A., and Schofield, R. S. *The population history of England, 1541–1871: a reconstruction* (1981).

Youngs, Frederic A., Jr. 'Towards petty sessions: Tudor JPs and divisions of counties', in DeLloyd J. Guth and John W. McKenna (eds.), *Tudor rule and revolution* (Cambridge, 1982), pp. 201–16.

Zeid, Abou A. M. 'Honour and shame among the Bedouins of Egypt', in J. G. Peristiany (ed.), *Honour and shame: the values of Mediterranean society* (1965), pp. 243–59.

UNPUBLISHED THESES

Anglin, J. P. 'The court of the archdeacon of Essex, 1571–1609' (University of California Ph.D. thesis, 1965).

Ingram, Martin. 'Ecclesiastical justice in Wiltshire, 1600–1640, with special reference to cases concerning sex and marriage' (University of Oxford D.Phil. thesis, 1976).

Jones, Martin D. W. 'The ecclesiastical courts before and after the civil war: the office jurisdiction in the dioceses of Oxford and Peterborough, 1630–1675' (University of Oxford B. Litt. thesis, 1977).

Potter, J. M. 'The ecclesiastical courts in the diocese of Canterbury, 1603–1665' (University of London M. Phil. thesis, 1973).

Index

Note. With the exception of a few well-known locations and the names of some ecclesiastical jurisdictions, all place-names mentioned in the Index refer to Wiltshire unless otherwise indicated.

Past and Present Publications

General Editor: PAUL SLACK, *Exeter College, Oxford*

Family and Inheritance: Rural Society in Western Europe 1200–1800, edited by Jack Goody, Joan Thirsk and E. P. Thompson*
French Society and the Revolution, edited by Douglas Johnson
Peasants, Knights and Heretics: Studies in Medieval English Social History, edited by R. H. Hilton*
Towns in Societies: Essays in Economic History and Historical Sociology, edited by Philip Abrams and E. A. Wrigley*
Desolation of a City: Coventry and the Urban Crisis of the Late Middle Ages, Charles Phythian-Adams
Puritanism and Theatre: Thomas Middleton and Opposition Drama under the Early Stuarts, Margot Heinemann*
Lords and Peasants in a Changing Society: The Estates of the Bishopric of Worcester 680–1540, Christopher Dyer
Life, Marriage and Death in a Medieval Parish: Economy, Society and Demography in Halesowen 1270–1500, Zvi Razi
Biology, Medicine and Society 1840–1940, edited by Charles Webster
The Invention of Tradition, edited by Eric Hobsbawm and Terence Ranger*
Industrialization before Industrialization: Rural Industry and the Genesis of Capitalism, Peter Kriedte, Hans Medick and Jürgen Schlumbohm†*
The Republic in the Village: The People of the Var from the French Revolution to the Second Republic, Maurice Agulhon†
Social Relations and Ideas: Essays in Honour of R. H. Hilton, edited by T. H. Aston, P. R. Coss, Christopher Dyer and Joan Thirsk
A Medieval Society: The West Midlands at the End of the Thirteenth Century, R. H. Hilton
Winstanley: 'The Law of Freedom' and Other Writings, edited by Christopher Hill
Crime in Seventeenth-Century England: A County Study, J. A. Sharpe†
The Crisis of Feudalism: Economy and Society in Eastern Normandy c. 1300–1500, Guy Bois†
The Development of the Family and Marriage in Europe, Jack Goody
Disputes and Settlements: Law and Human Relations in the West, edited by John Bossy
Rebellion, Popular Protest and the Social Order in Early Modern England, edited by Paul Slack
Studies on Byzantine Literature of the Eleventh and Twelfth Centuries, Alexander Kazhdan in collaboration with Simon Franklin†

Past and Present Publications

The English Rising of 1381, edited by R. H. Hilton and T. H. Aston*
Praise and Paradox: Merchants and Craftsmen in Elizabethan Popular Literature, Laura Caroline Stevenson
The Brenner Debate: Agrarian Class Structure and Economic Development in Pre-Industrial Europe, edited by T. H. Aston and C. H. E. Philpin*
Eternal Victory: Triumphal Rulership in Late Antiquity, Byzantium, and the Early Medieval West, Michael McCormick†
East-Central Europe in Transition: From the Fourteenth to the Seventeenth Century, edited by Antoni Mączak, Henryk Samsonowicz and Peter Burke†
Small Books and Pleasant Histories: Popular Fiction and its Readership in Seventeenth-Century England, Margaret Spufford**
Society, Politics and Culture: Studies in Early Modern England, Mervyn James*
Horses, Oxen and Technological Innovation: The Use of Draught Animals in English Farming 1066–1500, John Langdon
Nationalism and Popular Protest in Ireland, edited by C. H. E. Philpin
Rituals of Royalty: Power and Ceremonial in Traditional Societies, edited by David Cannadine and Simon Price
The Margins of Society in Late Medieval Paris, Bronisław Geremek†
Landlords, Peasants and Politics in Medieval England, edited by T. H. Aston
Geography, Technology, and War: Studies in the Maritime History of the Mediterranean, 649–1571, John H. Pryor
Church Courts, Sex and Marriage in England, 1570–1640, Martin Ingram*
Searches for an Imaginary Kingdom: The Legend of the Kingdom of Prester John, L. N. Gumilev
Crowds and History: Mass Phenomena in English Towns, 1780–1835, Mark Harrison
Concepts of Cleanliness: Changing Attitudes in France since the Middle Ages, Georges Vigarello†
The First Modern Society: Essays in English History in Honour of Lawrence Stone, edited by A. L. Beier, David Cannadine and James M. Rosenheim
The Europe of the Devout: The Catholic Reformation and the Formation of a New Society, Louis Châtellier†

* Published also as a paperback
** Published only as a paperback
† Co-published with the Maison des Sciences de l'Homme, Paris